T0300317

ROUTLEDGE LIBRARY EDITIONS:
WORK & SOCIETY

Volume 5

BRITISH LABOUR MANAGEMENT & INDUSTRIAL WELFARE

BRITISH LABOUR MANAGEMENT & INDUSTRIAL WELFARE

1846–1939

ROBERT FITZGERALD

Routledge
Taylor & Francis Group

LONDON AND NEW YORK

First published in 1988 by Croom Helm Ltd.

This edition first published in 2024
by Routledge
4 Park Square, Milton Park, Abingdon, Oxon OX14 4RN

and by Routledge
605 Third Avenue, New York, NY 10158

Routledge is an imprint of the Taylor & Francis Group, an informa business

© 1988 Robert Fitzgerald

All rights reserved. No part of this book may be reprinted or reproduced or utilised in any form or by any electronic, mechanical, or other means, now known or hereafter invented, including photocopying and recording, or in any information storage or retrieval system, without permission in writing from the publishers.

Trademark notice: Product or corporate names may be trademarks or registered trademarks, and are used only for identification and explanation without intent to infringe.

British Library Cataloguing in Publication Data
A catalogue record for this book is available from the British Library

ISBN: 978-1-032-80236-7 (Set)
ISBN: 978-1-032-81291-5 (Volume 5) (hbk)
ISBN: 978-1-032-81293-9 (Volume 5) (pbk)
ISBN: 978-1-003-49910-7 (Volume 5) (ebk)

DOI: 10.4324/9781003499107

Publisher's Note
The publisher has gone to great lengths to ensure the quality of this reprint but points out that some imperfections in the original copies may be apparent.

Disclaimer
The publisher has made every effort to trace copyright holders and would welcome correspondence from those they have been unable to trace.

BRITISH LABOUR MANAGEMENT & INDUSTRIAL WELFARE
1846-1939

ROBERT FITZGERALD

CROOM HELM
London • New York • Sydney

© 1988 Robert Fitzgerald
Croom Helm Ltd, Provident House, Burrell Row,
Beckenham, Kent, BR3 1AT
Croom Helm Australia, 44-50 Waterloo Road,
North Ryde, 2113, New South Wales

Published in the USA by
Croom Helm
in association with Methuen, Inc.
29 West 35th Street
New York, NY 10001

British Library Cataloguing in Publication Data

Fitzgerald, Robert
    British labour management and industrial welfare
    1846-1939.
    1. Welfare work in industry — Great
    Britain — History
    I. Title
    658.3'8'0941   HD7261
    ISBN 0-7099-4928-6

Library of Congress Cataloging-in-Publication Data

ISBN 0-7099-4928-6

CONTENTS

Contents

Contents

TABLES

PREFACE

I am thankful to a number of institutions which allowed me to research their archives and which freely offered their time and help. These are: the British Steel Corporation's Record Offices, Unilever PLC, Imperial Chemicals Industries PLC, the Brewers' Society, the Industrial Participation Association, and the Industrial Society. I am, of course, also indebted to public institutions, like the Public Record Office, the Greater London Record Office, the Westminister Record Office, the British Library, the University of London Library, the British Library of Political and Economic Science, and the Modern Records Centre, Warwick University. The renamed Economic and Social Research Council should be acknowledged for its role as a financer of research, and, in particular, for enabling me to undertake the doctoral thesis which forms the basis of this book.

I am grateful to Professor Keith Burgess of the Roehampton Institute of Higher Education and to Dr David Jeremy of the Business History Unit, London School of Economics for their useful comments. I must also mention Dr Geoffrey Alderman of Royal Holloway and Bedford New College, who had a hand in bringing this work to publication. Lastly and above all, I must express my gratitude for the unstinting help and knowledgeable advice I received from Dr John Turner, also of Royal Holloway and Bedford New College.

Bob Fitzgerald,
Royal Holloway and Bedford New College, London University.

Chapter One

INDUSTRIAL RELATIONS, THE COMPANY, AND WELFARE

(i) INTRODUCTION: INDUSTRIAL RELATIONS AND WELFARE CAPITALISM

This book assesses the place of industrial welfare in British labour management from 1846-1939. It concentrates on the role of the company and its internal organisation rather than upon the growth of trades unionism, collective bargaining, and battles over wages and hours. Businessmen used many techniques to restrain industrial conflict, from supervisory control, the deskilling of work, and collective bargaining, to reliance on slack in the labour market. Although there have been studies into specific welfare schemes, the importance of welfare in industrial relations has more often been overlooked.(1) This book, however, is intended to present a monographic study of industrial welfare over nearly one hundred years before the Second World War.

There are few works about the development of British management practice, and the existence of industrial welfare poses questions about the nature of firms and their labour policies. The behaviour of companies and employers cannot be understood with reference only to the market theories of neo-classical economists, which depict employers and workers as "rational" agents seeking maximum reward for minimum effort.(2) According to such theories, employers and workers bargained with each other as equals in the market-place to determine the division between profits and wages. Employers were merely profit-maximisers, refusing to produce beyond the point where factor costs became greater than the revenue from each subsequent article produced. Competition forced employers to hire and fire workers as the fluctuations in market forces dictated. It is no coincidence that the theories of neo-classical economics were evolved during the 19th Century, when the British economy was characterised by small competitive firms and notorious trade cycles.

Men, of course, were never simply materialistic rationalists, and competition between companies rarely reflected the explanatory models of economic text-books.

1

Because businessmen had greater resources and owned the capital, the bargaining relationship was in reality an unequal one. Industrial relations, therefore, were often a matter of power and class-conflict and a cause of social divisions, rather than some objective mechanism between employers and workers to secure economic efficiency. As human institutions, companies required pragmatic solutions to cope with the "social" context of industrial production.

In addition, the "economic" context of highly competitive markets, which had so influenced industrial relations, altered. From the 1890s, mergers between companies created a growing number of large and oligopolistic concerns.(3) A.D.Chandler has outlined the growth patterns of the "modern" corporation. He argues that employers had strategies other than profit-maximisation through the market mechanism. Large companies run by managerial bureaucracies aimed to replace markets with the planning of production from the raw material to the distribution stage. Such a company structure was designed to secure supplies or product-markets, and to improve the speed and cost of processing and selling goods.(4) The implications of these developments for micro-economic theory have been more fully worked out by O.E.Williamson and other economists. Their work undermines neo-classical assumptions about profit-maximisation as the single motive of companies. Managers, having different interests to shareholders, might put sales-maximisation before profits.(5)

H.F.Gospel, C.R.Littler and others have pointed out that larger company structures had implications for labour management. They link developments in business organisation with deskilling and the growth of internal labour markets. By replacing manual skills, machinery and production-line technology cheapened labour, made it more easily replaceable, and allowed managers to assume the actual organisation and planning of work. Such policies were made famous by the "scientific management" theories of F.W.Taylor.(6) Furthermore, oligipolistic companies which enjoyed greater market stability were in a position to undertake long-term planning. Labour could, therefore, be employed on an equally long-term basis, and a core of permanently-employed workers could be offered job-security and a career and benefits structure within the company. Workers could also be employed directly. While employers had traditionally left labour management to foremen or sub-contractors, managers began to assume responsibility for hiring, firing, work-organisation, and industrial discipline. The sub-contracting of work to a leading-hand had been common in steel manufacture and coal-mining, although it had never had a place in an industry like the railways with their large managerial bureaucracies. Sub-contracting remained prominent in British industry until the Second World War.(7)

As company structures so influenced industrial relations,

an examination of the connection between commercial considerations, business organisation, and industrial welfare is a central part of this book. It recognises that the form and purpose of welfare schemes were influenced by many factors like traditions of early paternalism, the siting of companies and their labour-supply problems, the type of labour employed, the demands of work-discipline, union organisation, and the extent of capitalisation and internal labour markets. The greatest influence, however, was the nature of a company or an industry's market. The history of industrial welfare in natural monopolies like railways is markedly different from that of competitive trades like iron and steel production. But the increasing control of competitive markets through corporate structures enabled those companies engaged in them to adopt to some degree the internal labour markets and welfare practices of railways.

This work seeks to establish industrial welfare as an important aspect of the employment relationship for the larger part of the British workforce. Salaried staff, who enjoyed job-security and formed the earliest internal labour markets, undoubtedly received more extensive sick pay and pension benefits. Their loyalty was essential to the running of the firm, and, with the creation of large managerial bureaucracies from the turn of the century, companies needed to increase their investment in their staff. But the experiences of salaried workers were not typical of employees generally, and their particular circumstances make the extensive welfare services provided for them worthy of a separate study.(8) This book is principally concerned with the more recalcitrant problems involved in the management of labour.

The book does not cover every aspect of industrial relations during this period. Nor does it assume that its subject matter can be considered as more important than questions of collective bargaining or deskilling. It is a history of the industrial relations of welfare capitalism. The term welfare capitalism is not meant to imply freedom from economic exploitation. Unregulated markets and unemployment were widespread enough and income levels were low enough to cause misery and poverty, but many employers, at least in practice, recognised that the wage-contract or the labour market transaction of popular economic theory were inadequate means of managing, organising or fully utilising a workforce. Workers in sickness, infirmity, and old age required income-maintenance. This factor was, before the establishment of a Welfare State, an overriding consideration of the real labour market. Because companies were human institutions, many companies realised the value of meeting the needs of their workforces, upon which efficient production depended. Industrial welfare was clearly more a question of business organisation than one of philanthropy or social justice.

* * * * *

3

Industrial Relations, the Company, and Welfare

Before detailing the history of industrial welfare from 1846 to 1939, it will be necessary, in section (ii), to discuss industrial relations in general, including the influence of scientific management and collective bargaining. Section (ii) will also explain the origins of company welfare provision, how developments in managerial strategies and structures influenced its nature and organisation, and the underlying purpose of welfare as an employers' labour strategy. The last section will outline the framework of the book.

(ii) LABOUR STRATEGIES AND THE COMPANY

(a) Introduction
Employers were able to adopt a number of labour strategies, including, in addition to welfare, collective bargaining and scientific management.(9) Yet, collective barg- aining was generally limited to the questions of wages and hours, while the extent and importance of scientific management techniques have been questioned. It was welfare which could provide solutions for particular problems of company organisation and labour management.

(b) Collective Bargaining and Scientific Management
For employers, collective bargaining was often preferable to conflict. Furthermore, the economy in this period was largely dependent upon the skills and labour of its workers rather than upon machinery and technology. Craftsmen exercised a degree of unilateral self-regulation in the organisation of work, sometimes through the system of sub-contracting. The scope for autonomous work-regulation and its influence on industrial relations has been exaggerated,(10) but employers did make collective bargaining agreements in order to increase their control over the pace, price and organisation of work.(11) Union leaders could sometimes ensure the acceptance of joint agreements despite rank and file objections, and, for employers, industrial discipline was, consequently, easier to enforce. Unions, in return, won the advantage of official recognition, and secured some say in the determination of pay and conditions.(12)

Employers' associations and collective bargaining dealt in most cases with the primary questions of wages and hours, but these two issues were only a part of the vexed problem of employment relations. National and regional bargains before 1939 in iron and steel, cotton-spinning, and coalmining were basically sliding-scale arrangements in which wages fluctuated with the market price of the product. Collective bargaining merely made the market determination of wages and hours more acceptable to workers.(13) The 1898 Terms of Settlement in the engineering industry, on the other hand, accepted the right of management to determine the manning and operation of machinery. It also sought to remove any limitation on the numbers of apprentices in the hope of cheapening the supply of skilled labour.(14) But Jonathan Zeitlin has pointed out that even the powerful Engineering Employers Federation failed at the factory-floor to gain the full exercise of managerial prerogative for its members. The importance of labour skills to production could not be replaced by signed agreement. Such a transition required investment in new machinery, and the small firms of the engineering industry did not have the resources to undertake large-scale mass production. Competitive rivalries, moreover, would have made such investment unprofitable. It was company and industrial structures and not collective bargaining which limited the possibilities for internal management.(15) The 1898 Settlement, in any case, allowed individual companies the flexibility of workplace bargaining over wage-rates, piecework, and overtime.(16)

Where employers' associations existed, the independence and sovereignty of the company were not necessarily undermined. The British iron and steel, textile, coalmining, shipbuilding, engineering, and motor car industries were examples of failures of cooperation amongst employers.(17) This situation was reflected in the chemicals trade before 1914. Iron and steel was particularly notable for its regional collective bargaining machinery from the 1860s onwards. But steel companies often undermined their regional associations by bidding up the wages fixed by agreement, if it was in their short-term interests.(18) Furthermore, companies like the railways required a complex set of rules governing the relations between workers, supervisors, and managers just to operate. The devolving of labour matters to joint negotiating machinery was opposed as a hindrance to the smooth running of their large enterprises. The company-level conciliation boards established in 1907 were forced upon the railways by the Liberal government.(19)

It is hard to discern a trend towards national collective bargaining before the Great War. The Whitley Report of 1916-17 recognised the deficiencies of the pre-War industrial relations system.(20) Employers' associations were often poorly supported, limited in their aims, and split by the divergent interests within them. War-time interest in joint negotiation waned with the power of the trades union movement during the 1920s, and the patchy framework of collective bargaining continued. It was within companies that important developments in labour matters took place.(21)

* * * * *

Henry Braverman has outlined the restructuring of work in the 20th Century as an explanation of the way employers determined the nature of industrial relations within companies. Manual skills were replaced with the furthest

5

division of labour, and broken up into many repetitive processes. Workers became unskilled and easily replaceable. These trends in production were aided by developments in mass-production technology, and managerial supervision replaced labour´s control over the organisation of work. Braverman´s study begins with an analysis of F.W.Taylor, who published his Principles of Scientific Management in 1913.(22)

Taylor argued that scientific management required the manager´s organisational skills to be coupled with the brute-force of the worker and preferably one with the "mentality of an ox". Inefficient, "rule-of-thumb" techniques could be replaced by scientific ones, and labour had to be shown how high wages depended upon low labour costs and increased output. The manager could analyse any task, and calculate the most economical methods of work. Then, the "unit efficiency", equal to what the "best" man could produce in a given time, could be calculated. Bonuses would be paid for output over the stipulated amount. The scientific measurement of unit output would ensure that the task was within human capacity, and measured rest-periods would enable output to be sustained over a long period. The manager was responsible for ensuring coordination between the segmented operations of each worker. Faster work could only be achieved through the "enforced standardisation of methods" and even, paradoxically, "enforced cooperation". Taylor assumed that high wages would make managerial authoritarianism acceptable, and provide a solution to class conflict and industrial relations problems.(23)

Braverman´s study, however, is not a detailed historical analysis of Taylorism.(24) There were several reasons why Taylor´s principles could not be applied in British industry. In 1913, Edward Cadbury, a leading partner in the famous Quaker chocolate firm, replied to Taylor´s book. He acknowledged that any employer was concerned about the scientific organisation of labour and machinery. But he criticised Taylor for ignoring the human costs of production. Cadbury argued that trades unions would resist any system which speeded up work and that individual men could not be reduced to living tools. Industrial disputes, moreover, were not merely a fight for higher wages and shorter hours, but stemmed also from "an increasing knowledge on the part of the workman of his lack of control of the conditions of his own life". In practice, workers had to be consulted by management and feel that their personalities and labour were of worth. Full efficiency required the workers´ cooperation and loyalty, and, therefore, demonstrable proof of their mutual interests with employers. Housing, sick pay, and pensions provided the basis of a just employment policy at Cadburys.(25) Yet, Taylor had been a manager and did not deprecate "semi-philanthropic and paternal aids", because they made "more intelligent and better workmen" and promoted "kindly feeling among the men for their employers".(26) At other times, Taylor ridiculed welfare work.(27)

But, just as the engineering industry's capital structure and segmented markets prevented the introduction of Taylorism,(28) even British motor car producers rejected the techniques supposedly popularised by Henry Ford in Detroit. They relied instead upon a mixture of industrial welfare and bonuses.(29) Like Cadburys, they sought cooperation rather than authoritarianism. Indeed, Fords itself introduced profitsharing in 1914 and began organising clubs and social events after the Great War. One contemporary commentator linked the development of the American corporation with the introduction of welfare schemes. General Motors, quoted by Chandler as the principal founder of corporate management techniques, was an enthusiastic supporter of industrial welfare, and had introduced by 1929 stock ownership, sickness and accident insurance, a savings plan, and sports and recreational facilities for their employees.(30) J.D.Mooney, Vice-President of General Motors, in 1937 argued that the problems of human relations and cooperation in industry were more urgent than those of efficiency in production. The dilemma between the individual worker and the group or the company was solvable by guarantees of social security for workers. Continuity of employment, however, was dependent upon the more stable markets which the large, corporate company could provide. Mooney was critical of state social security because, unlike industrial welfare, it did not enable workers to identify with their place of work.(31) If Fords' welfare schemes were ungenerous, this was a product of its lack of internal managerial development rather than the success of Taylorism. The personal and autocratic style of Henry Ford contributed to the rapid decline of his firm's profits and market share during the Inter-War years.(32)

Littler has demonstrated that the influence of Taylorism in Britain was significantly diminished by trades union resistance, and the continuation of traditional management.(33) Employers adjusted theory to the practicalities of industrial life, and Taylorism emerged as only one of many strands of scientific management. Another of these, "human factor" psychology, was prominent in Britain because manpower shortages during the Great War interested government in the problems of industrial fatigue. Long working hours had brought diminishing productivity and resulted in greater absenteeism, bad time-keeping and reduced effort. The Health of Munitions Workers Committee of 1915-17 was appointed to investigate the problem. Improvements in workshop conditions were introduced in controlled establishments and armaments factories with the object of increasing productivity.(34) The growth in the size of munitions works caused "the numerous problems of labour efficiency and the personal welfare of the employees". One large employer submitted evidence to the Committee acknowledging he was involved in "duties beyond those realised through the medium of the wage office....." His firm had adopted "an organised system of what is called social or welfare work". It aimed to humanize shop-floor conditions and "keep alive those right relationships which are the basis of a well-ordered and harmonious community". Another employer told the Committee that welfare work was not extraneous to ordinary factory management but was a vital and integral part. The economic results of welfare expenditure were seen as justifying the original outlay.(35) The Committee believed that the best could be obtained from the "human machine" by the application of an "industrial scientific management" which accounted for the health and contentment of workers.(36)

The Industrial Fatigue Research Board was founded in 1918 as a direct successor to the Health of Munitions Workers Committee. It formed links with the National Institute of Industrial Psychology, established in 1921, which in the Inter-War period came under the direction and influence of the management theorist C.S.Myers. His writings and name became associated with "human factor" industrial psychology, which gradually came to concentrate on boredom and work-disaffection rather than on physical fatigue. Myerism, like the welfare movement of the First World War, sought to increase unit output with a more empirical and broader approach than Taylor's single method. Yet, it is hard to discern the practical benefits of "human factor" research.(37) Although it encouraged interest in shop-floor conditions or in what was termed "internal" industrial welfare, the working environment of most British workers remained poor. Factories established by "new" industries in the Midlands and South, and which, on their building, incorporated welfare amenities into their structure were not typical.(38) Questions of "external" industrial welfare, like pensions, sick-pay, or even sports and social clubs, were outside the National Institute's remit. Yet, it was "external" welfare which formed the basis of company provision.(39)

The influence of the "Hawthorne experiment" and the works of Elton Mayo, although widely discussed in management literature, seem even less significant in practice than "human factor" psychology. The Western Electric Company of Chicago undertook from 1924-1936 the investigation of industrial behaviour at its Hawthorne Works. Its main conclusion was that individual output could be improved by transferring workers between jobs and thereby relieving the monotomy of work. Workers also protected their interests as a group by preventing the speeding up of production. Mayo argued that management had to adapt these social instincts by integrating them with loyalty to the company as a whole. Carey has shown how the Hawthorne experiments produced few results or conclusions of worth.(40) Employers did not reorganise work-systems and plant-layout to account for "social sentiments" and individual requirements.(41) "External" industrial welfare was a useful alternative because it did not need to interfere with the process of production itself.

* * * * *

Collective bargaining and scientific management were important aspects of industrial relations during this period. Emphasis upon collective bargaining, however, ignores the role of the company in determining the nature of labour markets and the employment relationship, while scientific management´s focus upon the "labour process" separated production from the social context within which industry operated. Managers recognised Taylorism´s solutions to industrial strife as simplistic, and unions resisted the "speeding up" of work. Companies had to cope with the "human factor" in industry, and labour skills generally remained crucial to production. Welfare was a means of fulfilling those human needs not met by the cash nexus. Furthermore, the growth in the size of firms enabled employers to exercise some control over the movements of the market, and increased the possibilities for labour management. The next two sections, consequently, will analyse the origins and purpose of industrial welfare, and its relation to the role and structure of the company.

(c) Paternalism and Industrial Welfare

Welfare services existed from the very founding of British industry in the cotton mills of Lancashire. Within the typically small factory of the 18th and 19th Centuries, the role of a single employer or family was crucial in all aspects of the business. Company provision, consequently, was notably paternalistic. By 1830, the cotton industry had many notable examples of paternalism.(42) In part, such paternalism had its roots in the traditions of landed society, and in the relations between aristocrats and gentry with their labourers and tenants.(43) Industrialists assumed the role of another propertied estate. Employer and landowner, as local dignitaries, gained respect and standing by holding entertainments and displaying generosity.(44) But, from the outset, industrial paternalism met the particular demands of factory-production. Greater firm size, mechanisation, and the sub-division of labour necessitated the imposition of industrial discipline, but also increased the need for rest-periods and maintaining the health and reliability of workers. Nonconformist employers, in particular, attempted to instill the utilitarian values of hard work, temperance, and self-enlightenment. They sought to undermine the social values of landed-society and the Tory "old regime". The paternalism of the "socialist" Robert Owen at the New Lanark cotton mill merely typified an autocratic management which linked greater efficiency with the good treatment of workers.(45)

Patrick Joyce has described the nature of industrial

relations in the Lancashire cotton industry principally after 1850. He outlines the close relationship between industry, society, culture, and politics. Within the factory village or local community, the patronage of an employer and his family was extensive and pervaded social and religious life. As the heads of their community, they had to demonstrate its cohesiveness. Their influence extended to the voting behaviour of their employees. Deference was both an economic necessity of life for workers and a cultural phenomenon. Paternalism and patriarchialism were evident in family-life, in society at large, and in religious teaching. Within the factory itself, men became spinners while women undertook less skilled tasks.(46) The employment-relationship, of course, produced class-conflict as well as deference, but the success of factory-production depended upon an unwritten agreement of cooperation between employers and workers. Yet, whatever its cultural or social perspectives, paternalism in practical and material terms dealt with the provision of housing, social amenities, old age pensions, and sick pay.

Although the ideology of self-help and individualism in the 19th and early 20th Centuries might have been a factor militating against the actual provision of industrial welfare, in practice the employers' need to meet the requirements of his labour force was probably a greater influence. Employers, in any case, generally recognised the value of welfare services which promoted independence. Contributory shop clubs were a tribute to notions of self-help and providence. Employers often began to support such societies after they had been spontaneously formed and funded by the men because company support made these clubs financially viable. Employers were keen to involve workers in their running as compensation for their lack of control over investment and production matters. It was a more effective strategy for colliery owners to provide financial assistance to miners' mutual provident societies than to organise the collection and payment of benefits themselves.(47)

Paternalism was symptomatic of a direct and personal relationship between employer and employee, and was unsuited to large companies and professionalised management. Joyce, therefore, contends that in Lancashire the personal relationship between cotton employer and worker was superseded by the large combines of the 1890s.(48) But, although the sociological and cultural aspects of paternalism may have declined with the small communities in which it thrived, welfare continued, and, indeed, expanded under the new joint stock companies.(49) The Quaker chocolate employer, B.Seebohm Rowntree was still convinced that in 1905 "Probably much more beneficial influence upon the character of the working classes may be exercised through the medium of their places of employment than is at present exercised by the churches'". The usefulness of industrial welfare to employers remained.(50)

Yet, even paternalism was common in many industries until the early 1900s, and continued throughout the 20th Century in trades like brewing, wool and worsted, pottery, and footwear whose production continued to be small scale.(51)

Ex gratia benefits were the only means available to most 19th Century employers for the provision of welfare. H.I.Dutton and J.E.King have questioned the commitment of the Lancashire cotton magnates to paternalism. They doubt their ability to pay and sustain benefits when trade cycles restricted the availability of profits for welfare spending.(52) The very structure of small firms, often over-competing for limited markets, did damage profitability and employment levels. Strong international competition, in particular, exacerbated the harshness of the wage-contract. These circumstances were also true of other staples like coalmining, engineering, shipbuilding, and iron and steel production. But ex gratia benefits, though useful in the management of labour, did not commit an employer to expensive, long-term outlays, and payments could be adjusted according to revenue. Paternalism had an important influence on 19th Century industrial relations, even if its extent was constrained by market considerations. A welfare policy with set contributions and guaranteed benefits required the managerial and organisational resources which most Victorian family firms did not possess.

A central theme of this book, however, is to show that monopolies like the railways, which did not face competition and enjoyed more constant revenues, had well-developed welfare policies throughout this period. Railway companies required a large managerial bureaucracy in order to administer their complex operations and large workforces. They needed an extensive internal labour market, and a high labour turnover was an expensive problem. Welfare services protected their investment in the training and disciplining of their workforce. Railways, therefore, had both the means and the need to systemise welfare provision by removing the ex gratia element. The administration of their contributory mutual provident societies did not rely upon the ad hoc discretion of employers and managers.(53)

Moreover, the fact that the corporate structures of the railways were imitated by other industries is another subject crucial to the book. Cooperation and mergers rationalised competition and made extreme fluctuations in supply and demand less likely, and the managers of large companies could then plan production from the raw material to the distribution stage.(54) The operations of company bureaucracies gradually replaced the market mechanism as a means of economic exchange, and the corporate company, consequently, required an industrial relations strategy in addition to the wage-relationship.(55)

From the outset of a merger, considerable investment was

required to ensure that management resources were adequate for their increased role.(56) The loyalty of salaried workers was assured by perquisites, stable wages, benefits, and job-security. Industrial welfare for staff was undoubtedly extensive, and foremen, often responsible for employing, organising, and sacking workers, could be equally protected. Yet, obtaining the co-operation of the workforce in the process of rationalisation from 1900 has been overlooked despite the contributory and systematic welfare schemes which were founded as a consequence. A reorganisation of management brought reforms in the administration of welfare. Developments in company provision were linked, therefore, to changes in managerial structure. The Federation of British Industry in 1935 noted the benefits of coordinated production and marketing, and their potential for maintaining fair conditions of employment.(57)

The growth of professional management was linked to arguments favouring a more ethical form of business organisation. Oliver Sheldon, who worked as a manager at Rowntrees, in 1923 stated that the replacement of employers by managers would be mirrored by the supersession of the profit-motive as the principal business incentive. Men would become more service and community-minded, and the factory was, consequently, capable of replacing class as the basis of association. Such "social ethics" would require, not just the payment of wages, but guarantees of minimum living standards and adequate social security. Human relations and the search for industrial peace were moral questions, and could not be reduced to scientific calculation.(58) Industrial conflict, therefore, was seen as resulting from arbitrary management and was an abnormality rather than being an integral element of the employment-relationship. By the Inter-War period, Scientific Management did not imply the harsh practices of Taylorism, but the establishment of mutually-agreed goals in the interest of successful and efficient production.(59) Rationalisation and scientific management were seen as complementing each other, and were answers to socialism. In 1927, Industrial Peace stated that rationalisation, "in its widest significance, is identical with scientific management". Rationalisation dealt with the relationship between producers, while scientific management stood "for a particular method of organising the productive processes in an establishment, and particularly a method of dealing with the human factor in production".(60) Sheldon believed that the addition of rationalisation to the "first" industrial revolution and the adding of the "human element" to the "mechanical revolution" would together produce unconceived levels of wealth.(61)

(d) Welfare as a Labour Strategy

Labour is a commodity which is bought and sold, and, in that sense, the employment-relationship is a market transact-

12

ion. Because the division between profits and wages inevitably produces conflict between employers and workers, industrial relations are predominately a power-relationship. Although market factors like the demand for labour affected the bargaining power which either side could exercise, trades unions relied upon solidarity and organisation to protect the living standards of their members. Employers also had an extensive influence over the form and nature of industrial relations, and the industrial discipline they exercised was dependent upon a conscious system of internal management and supervision. But cooperation was as essential as discipline in overcoming the workers´ resistance to managerial direction.

While competition between companies was approved by neo-classical micro-economics, competition between employers and workers within the firm was illegitimate because industrial production required cooperation. Employers needed to emphasise the "unitary" ideal of the company. They attempted to win the loyalty of those they employed by offering certain wage or welfare benefits. The insecurity caused by the threat of old age and sickness was an important cause of strikes and work-disaffection. Benefits provided income beyond that of the market transaction which exchanged labour for cash. Profitsharing, pensions and sick pay mollified and justified an employment relationship in which the place of the worker was subordinate. They imbued a degree of loyalty to the firm. Moreover, company provision directly improved labour efficiency by increasing the labour supply and retaining the skills and experience of workers.

Oligopoly increased the stability of markets and enabled companies to exercise greater "discretionary behaviour" in the administration and organisation of their companies. Company objectives could be decided more by internal bargaining within the firm instead of leaving events to the verdict of the market. Corporate companies, therefore, had greater scope for planning in labour management. But the balance of personal, administrative, or group pressures placed limits upon management´s "discretionary behaviour", and such pressures included the workers´ ability to hinder production or to strike. Employers were in a position to minimise class conflict and had to limit the effects of work-disaffection. The presentation of the rising managerial class as a neutral and adjudicating factor in the battle between capital and labour, however, was belied by the consequences of "human factor" and industrial welfare policies. Company provision helped mould a labour force more suited to the requirements of production. Welfare coped with the "human relations" aspects of business as well as the objectives of "economic man" and income-maintenance. While the cost and worth of wages could be quantified, the value of welfare to the employee was not so easily assessed. The effects of the goodwill engendered by welfare on efficiency and production were an immeasurable quantity.(62)

A major objective of welfare policy was to remove workers´ "fears" about sickness, injury, old age, and unemployment.(63) Employers realised that their workers´ perception of their company influenced industrial relations. Sir William Lever of Lever Brothers acknowledged that the deficiencies of the wage-contract were often the root of working-class grievances: "I feel that three great ghosts are haunting each one of us. It is astonishing how each of us lives in fear, in fear of unemployment, the fear of sickness, and the fear of death, and the way it will leave our widows and dependants". Lever also provided for his workers´ old age. Despite the existence of state social security, he considered labour´s "fears" as the proper object of an employer´s concern.(64)

The administration and funding of sick pay and pensions were, in addition, an avenue for employer-employee cooperation. Managers and employers legitimised their control over questions of production and investment by granting the labour force some say in welfare provision. Workers, as human beings, sought at their place of work intangible objects, like companionship, a sense of purpose, and a voice in the managerial hierarchy above them. The innate expressions of human psychology did not cease to exist in an industrial context, required the administrative means to cope with them, and could not be countered by faith in the rationale of marginal labour economics alone. As Industrial Peace put it in 1917: "The first thing is to find a means of giving effect to the demand of Labour for some share in the control of Industry. That does not necessarily mean control of the high politics of manufacture, but it does emphatically mean some control of the conditions of workshop life".(65) A Federation of British Industries memorandum in 1919 recognised industry to be "an autocratic system". Unions, consequently, demanded either the nationalisation of industry or workers´ control. The first was condemned by the F.B.I. as giving power only to bureaucrats. The second demand was dismissed if it meant self-governing work-shops. The Federation argued that they suffered from a lack of discipline and business expertise. Participation "in the control of working conditions", however, was acceptable.(66) Works councils provided labour with a forum for voicing grievances, and often undertook the administration of welfare schemes. C.H.Northcott, another writer on management from the Rowntree factory, in 1933 said that welfare matters were the "definite limits" of joint decision-making "in the experience of many firms in the country".(67)

Elections to positions of responsibility in industrial provident societies encouraged the participation of their members, and helped reduce feelings of a deferential relationship.(68) Profitsharing, by giving workers a stake in

14

their firms, similarly improved the "status" of an employee, and the committees which ran such schemes were often a means of consultation and cooperation between employers and employees. Copartnership, or the election of worker-directors by profitsharers, further embodied the promotion of joint interests and at the highest level in a company. Many employers recognised that the dividends from profitsharing and copartnership schemes were an insufficient means of winning the loyalty of their workers since they formed only a minor part of their incomes. The sharing of profits was generally only one element of a company's benefit system. Profitsharing committees often assumed the role of works councils and likewise undertook the administration of many forms of company provision.(69)

Labour policies had administrative consequences which had to be determined within the firm. Works councils could be established to give workers a say in the running of their companies. Alternatively, when sickness became a constant problem and men were slow to return to work, sick benefit clubs could be founded. The solutions adopted depended on the sophistication of managerial planning and operation. An internal labour market, in particular, was an example of the exercise of "discretionary behaviour" in labour management, because it was segregated from the workings of the labour market as a whole.(70) The internal labour market was the minimum number of workers required by a company to sustain a level of output which would meet the demands of its more secure markets. Oligopolistic companies, therefore, could maintain large "core" workforces. Moreover, differing plant-layouts, combinations of machinery, and products made many labour requirements firm-specific. Trained and experienced in these firm-specific skills and often in machine-specific skills, "core" workers were differentiated by management from the "pool" of residual, non-permanent workers and treated accordingly. They were a lost or devalued investment if labour-turnover or work-disaffection were at high levels. Machinery could possess unique idiosyncracies which could only be understood through operating experience, and could be adapted by individual workers to suit particular factory requirements. Disruptions to production were particularly expensive for more capital-intensive companies. They were more likely to retain workers in even unprofitable production so long as the interest and charges on capital could be redeemed. Large, corporate companies pledging themselves to massive capital investment sought to safeguard expected rates of return by planning the numbers and stability of their workforces on whose cooperation the full and efficient use of new plant could depend.

Like the job-security and "status" bestowed by internal labour markets, systematic welfare schemes provided workers with rights, namely to benefits. Indeed, the economic security offered by benefits was often contingent upon being accepted as a permanent employee. The less extensive welfare services typical of the small firm or unsystematic management, on the other hand, were usually favours, not rights, and could be withdrawn at any time. They were a minor investment in sporting and social clubs, unsystematic sick clubs in receipt of a voluntary subvention, or ex gratia pensions. Company sports and social clubs burgeoned in the years just after the Great War. They were seen as expressing and encouraging a team spirit, and instilled the mutual purpose essential to coordinated production.(71) The impact of introducing sports and social facilities would undoubtedly have been greater in a time of lower wages, fewer leisure facilities, and the beginnings of cinema, radio, and television.(72) Many industries, like steel and coalmining, were also more geographically isolated than others and required social amenities.

Yet, ex gratia welfare contained no commitment to any individual employee, the cost of a football club, for example, being general. The use of sports facilities would be open to any of the men who happened to be employed at the works. Profitsharing, and contributory old-age pensions and sick pay, however, dealt with personal requirements, contributions, and benefits. Foremen were often the first to be offered the opportunity to contribute to pension schemes, because of their important supervisory role and the security of their employment. Standing-men were then considered, and the extension of internal labour markets led to schemes incorporating a major part of a more settled workforce. The scale of the administrative task this necessitated, as well as the need to account for large sums of money, required the systemisation of company welfare policies. Bureaucratic rules and guidelines normally implied per capita contributory schemes and set benefits, although some companies, whose markets were less stable or whose management was less developed, favoured non-contributory schemes funded by company trusts and with set and limited subventions from employers or company stock. They, nevertheless, paid guaranteed benefits. Pension provision, in particular, was improved by such systemisation. A large number of contributors was needed in order to pool the actuarial risks involved. The very cost of pensions encouraged contributory schemes, as stability and confidence were essential to such a long-term investment.

In addition to proving the "unitary" ideal of the company and to providing some measure of "workers' democracy", welfare schemes often had specific aims. Increasing the labour supply and protecting the health of the worker were common objectives. Pensions especially were connected with the reduction of labour turnover. The head of Ford's in 1913 reckoned that every new worker cost $38 to train and that the teaching of the required manual skills amounted to $2 million

a year.(73) Steel companies which in the 1930s invested in
flow-process technology sought to protect the skills of the
men which operated the new plant. Reliable and trusted workers
became of greater value.(74) Any worker, considering leaving a
firm, had to decide whether the loss of benefits and
particularly pension rights was greater than the gains from
new employment.

Furthermore, the value of company welfare before 1939
would have had a psychological effect that is hard for a
generation accustomed to state-provision guaranteeing freedom
from the worst poverty to appreciate. (The worth of the
benefits stated throughout the book can be gauged from the
wages table on the following page.) Workers since 1945 have,
moreover, gained a spending power that leaves them less
reliant on the perceived munificence of their employers.
Littler, however, has argued that industrial welfare schemes
in Britain were stunted by social legislation.(75) Yet,
governments before the Beveridge Report of 1942 did not seek
to establish a universal social safety-net, nor even to
provide sustenance. They wanted to encourage private thrift,
and state and industrial schemes were seen as viable
alternatives. Employers had the reason and the resources to
provide income maintenance during infirmity, adequate housing,
and social amenities. They were, consequently, given the
opportunity to organise basic or supplementary industrial
provident societies within the terms of statutory schemes.
Employers influenced the passing of social legislation, and,
through their commitment to company provision, found state
schemes more acceptable. A significant reason for the growing
support for welfare in this period can be attributed to
changes in the structure of companies and the economy.(76)

Although industrial welfare has been depicted, at least
during the 1890s and early 1900s, as the particular
accomplishment of Quaker businessmen like Seebohm
Rowntree,(77) their policies were not markedly different to
those adopted by many other employers. Self-managed provident
societies were seen by Rowntree as combatting "ca´canny",
establishing mutual confidence, and enabling the easy
"introduction of labour-saving machinery and improved
administration". Rowntree believed that workers were in
reality unconcerned with industry´s major problems, but wanted
joint control over welfare matters as "something more
intimately associated with their daily lives". Even this most
limited area of workers´ participation at Rowntrees was
restricted by managerial veto. He was also convinced that
works committees enabled "fair-minded and thoughtful workers"
to realise that someone had to be "in supreme control".(78)
Quaker employers believed they had a Christian duty towards
their workers, although their views were shared by other
Nonconformist businessmen, especially Congregationalists and
Unitarians. But managerial and business considerations were

17

Table I: Average Weekly Wages of Manual Workers on an
Industry by Industry basis, 1886-1931
(figures in shillings and pence)

Industry	Wages		Industry	Wages	
	Men	Women		Men	Women
1886			**1931**		
Cotton manufacture	25/3	15/3	Cotton	45/3	27/3
Woollen manufacture	23/2	13/3	Woollen &		
Worsted & stuff	23/4	11/11	worsted	49/4	27/7
Linen	19/9	8/11	Linen	36/5	20/8
Silk	22/3	10/1	Silk & rayon	60/0	26/7
Coal,iron ore &			Coalmining	41/11	
iron-stone mines	22/11	8/2	Gas supply	62/11	
Gasworks	27/2		Pig iron	54/5	
Pig iron	24/0		Iron & steel	54/11	
Engineering &			Engineering	51/8	
machinery	25/8		Shipbuilding &		
Shipbuilding (iron			repairing	51/9	
& steel)	28/8		Sheet metal		
Tinplate works	33/5	10/4	working	51/9	26/0
Boot & shoe			Boot & shoe		
(factory)	24/3	12/6	(ready-made)	52/10	31/3
Breweries	24/3		Brewing, malting		
			& bottling	57/6	24/11
			Cocoa, chocolate,		
1906			confectionary	61/5	27/0
Cotton	29/6	18/8	Tobacco	58/10	36/9
Woollen & worsted	26/10	13/10	Chemicals	59/2	27/0
Linen	22/4	10/9	Railways	56/4	
Silk	25/8	11/2	Preserved food,		
Gas supply	32/6		jam & sauce	56/4	25/9
Pig iron	34/4				
Iron & steel	39/1				
Engineering &					
boilermaking	32/5	13/1			
Tinplate	42/0	14/9			
Boot & shoe					
(ready-made)	28/8	13/1			
Malting & brewing	26/3	9/4			
Cocoa, chocolate &					
sugar confectionary	30/9	11/9			
Tobacco, cigar,					
cigarette, snuff	30/6	12/0			
Chemical					
manufacture	29/1				
Railway service	26/9				

Source: Department of Employment British Labour Statistics:
Historical Abstract (HMSO 1971), pp.92-97.

normally more crucial, and markets and company structures determined the opportunities employers had for company welfare provision.(79)

*   *   *   *   *

As labour was resistant to industrial requirements, welfare services were provided where the wage-contract had failed to achieve employers' objectives. Company provision was not a peripheral labour strategy and its importance in Britain has been underestimated. Paternal and systematic welfare had the same objectives, and differences in the market, managerial, or capital structure merely moulded the levels of company provision which were desirable or possible. Firstly, industrial welfare attempted to mollify the class-conflict inherent in the employment-relationship. A tangible demonstration of the "unitary" ideal of the firm was a prophylactic against strikes, work-disaffection, and resistance to managerial direction. Secondly, many employers believed that a large part of industrial unrest originated from a lack of economic security. They were, therefore, willing to organise or finance pensions, sick pay, and accident compensation. Thirdly, the existence of company provision enabled employers to cooperate with workers in one area of industrial life, while leaving managerial prerogative over production matters intact. The wish of employees to extend their freedom of choice at work was canalised into works and profitsharing committees, the election of co-partnership directors, and balloting for the appointment of organisers of provident funds and sports clubs. Labour was, therefore, given a participatory role. Fourthly, industrial welfare augmented a policy of internal labour markets. Systematic or contributory welfare, as opposed to ex gratia benefits, bestowed rights through membership of a pre-determined scheme, and reduced the high costs of retraining due to labour turnover.

The most important unit in an industrial economy is the company itself. Industrial welfare was a strategy organised on a company basis and its extent and potential were dependent on general developments in managerial structure. It was the timing and influence of managerial reorganisation - rather than simply increases in company size - which largely influenced changes in the comprehensiveness and organisation of company provision. Indeed, it would be surprising if changes in the structure of industry and management had not affected internal labour management.

(iii) MARKETS AND CASE-STUDIES

The following chapters rely on a wide range of new evidence, largely collected from company records, to challenge the assumption that examples of industrial welfare for British

19

workers were exceptional. Moreover, few works have yet assessed the role of internal labour markets in British industry, and the influence of company organisation and skill requirements on labour management and industrial welfare is fully examined.

Industrial welfare policies changed over time and varied from industry to industry. But these variations are explicable, and were principally the result of different market and industrial structures. While strong competition exacerbated the harshness of the wage contract, monopolies like the public utilities were able to provide stability of employment.

Chapter 2 concentrates on the railway industry. Railways were the first corporate companies, whose operations required an extensive internal labour market supported by a sophisticated system of welfare benefits. Chapter 3 further investigates the purpose of industrial welfare in another natural monopoly, the gas industry.

Chapter 4 is concerned with the "old" staple industry of iron and steel. Company provision was important to its labour management, and the large companies established in the Inter-War period, especially in the expanding tinplate and tube sectors, were able to systemise their welfare provision. Chapter 5 looks at a competitive trade which expanded in the 20th Century. The chemical industry reached a high degree of company rationalisation, and its welfare provision was, consequently, extensive. While major developments in management and welfare occurred in the monopolistic railway and gas industries during the 19th Century, crucial developments in steel and chemicals happened in the 1920s and 1930s.

Chapter 6 analyses brewing, an industry which remained composed of small-scale family firms. Its welfare continued to be notably paternalistic. Chapter 7 further extends the themes of the previous chapters by looking at other industries, although in less detail. It also compares the welfare provision of different trades.

Chapter 8 investigates the purpose and achievements of organisations which specialised in the promotion of welfare schemes. Chapter 9 looks at the links between state and industrial welfare. It explains the involvement of employers in the drawing up of social legislation, and raises questions about its objectives.

Chapters 2 and 4 on the railway and steel industries are central to this book, and they contain much theoretical material illustrating the connection between company size, managerial structure, and industrial welfare. The subject-matter presented in other chapters depends upon arguments developed in them. The concluding section of Chapter 7 should be consulted for the comparisons it makes between industries. Chapter 9 should be read for its assessment of the

Industrial Relations, the Company, and Welfare

political implications of company provision.

NOTES

1. Joseph Melling and Patrick Joyce are notable exceptions - cf. Bibliography.
2. Cf. W.S.Jevons The Theory of Political Economy (1871); A.Marshall Principles of Economics (1890). Cf. also P.L. Williams The Emergence of the Theory of the Firm: from Adam Smith to Alfred Marshall (1978).
3. L.Hannah The Rise of the Corporate Economy (1979).
4. Cf. A.D.Chandler Strategy and Structure (1973); The Visible Hand (1977).
5. Cf. O.E.Williamson Markets and Hierarchies (1980).
6. Cf. s.(ii)(a) & (b) below.
7. H.F.Gospel & C.R.Littler Managerial Strategies and Industrial Relations (1983), esp. pp.1-24,171-196.
8. Staff schemes, where relevant, are mentioned throughout the text. Cf. also L.Hannah Inventing Retirement: the Development of Occupational Pensions in Britain (1986), chs. 1-2. On the extent of industrial welfare in general, cf. comments in C.R.Littler The Development of the Labour Process in Capitalist Societies (1982), pp.90-2,198-9; & Gospel and Littler (1983), pp.16-17.
9. Cf. J.Turner "Man and Braverman: British Industrial Relations", History (1985), pp.236-242, which is a useful review article on historical industrial relations literature.
10. Cf. R.Price Masters, Unions, and Men (1980).
11. Cf. K.Burgess The Origins of British Industrial Relations: the 19th Century Experience (1975).
12. A.Flanders "Collective Bargaining: A Theoretical Analysis", British Jl. of Industrial Relations (1968), pp.1-26.
13. Cf. R.Currie Industrial Politics (1979).
14. Cf. E.L.Wigham The Power to Manage (1973), pp. 54-73.
15. J.Zeitlin "The Labour Strategies of British Engineering Employers, 1890-1922" in Gospel & Littler (1983), pp.25-54.
16. Wigham (1973), p.59.
17. Cf. Ch.4, & Ch.7, ss.(ii)-(v),(vii).
18. J.C.Carr & W.Taplin History of the British Steel Industry (1962), pp.73-4,145-6,149-150.
19. Cf. Ch.2, ss.(i),(ii),(iii),(iv)(d).
20. Cf. Ch.9, s.(iv).
21. Cf. Hannah (1979), pp.27-40,90-122; & W.R.Garside "Management and Men: Aspects of British Industrial Relations in the Inter-War Period" in B.Supple Essays in Business History (1977), pp.244-270.
22. H.Braverman Labor and Monopoly Capital (1974).
23. F.W.Taylor The Principles of Scientific Management

21

(1913), pp.9-12,26,32-9,83,92,143.

24. Cf. S.Wood (ed.) The Degradation of Work: Skill, Deskilling, and the Labour Process (1982); Littler (1982).

25. E.Cadbury "Scientific Management in Industry: the Case against Scientific Management" (1913), pp.1-3,5-7 in A.D.Chandler Management Thought in Britain (1979). The Guild Socialist, G.D.H.Cole, however, doubted if the minima of control given to workers at Cadburys would assuage labour demands (pp.36-7). Cf. Ch.7, s.(viii).

26. F.W.Taylor Shop Management (1911), pp.58,118-19,199-120.

27. D.Nelson & S.Campbell "Taylorism versus Welfare Work in American Industry: H.L.Gantt and the Bancrofts", Am.H.R. (1972), p.5. Taylor's remarks are quoted by his biographer, F.B.Copley, in 1915.

28. Cf. above.

29. W.Lewchuck "Fordism and British Motor Car Employers 1896-1932" in Gospel and Littler (1983), pp.82-110.

30. R.W.Dunn Labor and Automobiles (1929), pp.148-9, 151-6,158-9.

31. J.D.Mooney "The Principles of Organisation" (1937) in L.H.Gulick & L.P.Urwick Papers on the Science of Administration (1969, 1st edn. 1937), pp.93-8. Cf. Ch.9, esp. s.(i).

32. Chandler (1973), pp.114-161,372-3. Cf. Ch.7, s.(vii).

33. Littler (1982), pp.80-96. This criticism applies also to the system introduced by the Bedaux company in the 1930s. As management consultants, they sought to determine a "fair" unit of work within a set time, and to pay workers by results. The Bedaux system had only limited success in "new", expanding industries like food processing, chemicals, and electrical engineering, and was resisted by management and unions (pp.99-140).

34. Cf. N.Whiteside "Industrial Welfare and Labour Regulation in Britain at the Time of the First World War", I.R.S.H. (1980) pp.307-331.

35. PP 1914-16 (C.8151) xl 985. Report on Industrial Canteens, Memo. no.8.

36. Cf. PP 1914-16 (C.8133) xix 289; PP 1916 (C.8213) xxxiii 449, Memos. no.7 & 10; Ministry of Munitions History of Ministry of Munitions, Vol.V (1919), pp.44-56.

37. M.Rose Industrial Behaviour: Theoretical Development since Taylor (1982), pp.65-100. Cf. C.S.Myers Industrial Psychology in Great Britain (1924) in particular.

38. H.Jones "Employers' Welfare Schemes and Industrial Relations in Inter-War Britain", Bus.Hist. (1983), pp.61-75.

39. Cf. C.S.Myers Business Rationalisation (1932), p.52. Cf. Ch.8, s.(iv).

40. A.Carey "The Hawthorne Studies: A Radical Criticism", American Sociological Review (1967), pp.403-16.

41. Rose (1982), pp.103-124,168-172. Cf. also E.Mayo Human

Problems of Industrial Civilisation (1936); L.F.Urwick The Life and Work of Elton Mayo (n.d.).
42. A.J.Robertson "Robert Owen, Cotton Spinner: New Lanark, 1800-1825" in S.Pollard & J.Salt (eds) Robert Owen, prophet of the poor (1971), pp.149-53.
43. Cf. F.D.Roberts The Paternalism of Early Victorian Britain (1979); & esp. G.Mee Aristocratic Enterprise: the Fitzwilliam Industrial Undertakings, 1795-1857 (1975).
44. S.Pollard "The Factory Village in the Industrial Revolution", E.H.R. (1964), pp.513-531.
45. Robertson in Pollard & Salt (1971), pp.145-165; E.P.Thompson The Making of the English Working Class (1968), pp.857-886. Cf. also N.McKendrick "Joseph Wedgwood and Factory Discipline", H.J. (1961), pp.30-55; S.Pollard The Genesis of Modern Management (1965), pp.213-225; E.P.Thompson "Time, Work Discipline and Industrial Capitalism", Past & Present (1967), pp.56-97. N.Abercombie & S.Hill "Paternalism and patronage", Brit. Jl. of Sociology (1977), pp.413-429 is a useful discussion of a difference between paternalism and patronage.
46. P.Joyce Work, Society and Politics (1983), passim.
47. Cf. Ch.7, s.(iii).
48. Joyce (1980), pp.331-44.
49. Cf. Ch.4, esp. s.(iii); Ch.5; Ch.7, ss.(i)-(v), (viii).
50. B.Meakin Model Factories and Villages: Ideal Conditions of Labour and Housing (1905), p.33.
51. Cf. Ch.6; Ch.7, ss.(i),(ii).
52. H.I.Dutton & J.E.King "The limits of paternalism: the cotton tyrants of North Lancashire, 1836-54", Soc.Hist. (1982), pp.59-74.
53. Cf. Ch.2, especially ss.(i),(ii),(iii).
54. Hannah (1979), passim. By 1907, the largest 100 firms in Great Britain controlled 15% of manufacturing net output; by 1939, 23% (p.180).
55. Cf. Ch.2, ss.(i),(ii),(iii); & Ch.4, ss.(i),(ii) for a further discussion of this point.
56. Cf. E.T.Penrose The Theory of the Firm (1972), passim.
57. FBI Report of the Committee on the Organisation of Industry (1935).
58. O.Sheldon The Philosophy of Management (1965, 1st edn. 1923), pp.13,20,27-28,78-9,150-151,166-7,178,196.
59. Industrial Welfare, Oct 1925, pp.336-8. Industrial Welfare was published by the Industrial Welfare Society. Cf. Ch.8, s.(iii).
60. Industrial Peace, July 1927, pp.133-6. Industrial Peace was published by the British Commonwealth Union. Cf. J.Turner "The British Commonwealth Union and the General Election of 1918", E.H.R. (1978), pp.528-551; & Businessmen and Politics (1984), pp.15-6,45-8.
61. Industrial Welfare, June 1923, pp.149-151.

62. G.L.Reid & D.J.Robertson Fringe Benefits, Labour Costs and Social Security (1965) analyses company surveys which assessed the extent and purpose of industrial welfare provision in the 20 years or so after the Second World War. Expenditure not directly related to the needs of production was seen as "an investment in the labour force", and the principal aim was to reduce labour-turnover. Occupational pensions induced a sense of security, facilitated the retirement of the old and the inefficient, and boosted morale and productivity. Medical treatment and sick pay helped men to return to health and, therefore, minimised the disruption to output. (Cf. pp.15-16,18,20-25,39-45.)

63. L.Urwick Personnel Management in Relation to Factory Organisation (1943), pp.8-9,15-6,25-6.

64. W.Lever Copartnership: Laying the Three Ghosts: Unemployment, Sickness, Death (1922).

65. Industrial Peace, November 1917, p.20.

66. FBI Archive, MSS/200/F/1/2/2, The Control of Industry, Memo. to all members of "Nationalisation" Committee, 30 June 1919.

67. C.H.Northcott "Principles and Practices of Industrial Relations" in Factory Organisation (1933), pp.112-150.

68. Given the involvement of workers in the administration of benefits, the small number of welfare workers employed in British industry throughout this period cannot be taken as indicative of the interest of employers in company provision (Cf. Littler (1982), p.199).

69. Cf. passim, esp. Ch.8, ss.(i),(ii).

70. Cf. P.Doeringer and M.J.Piore Internal Labour Markets and Manpower Analysis (1971), which is the classic text on internal labour markets.

71. Works Management, Dec 1919, pp.103-4. Cf. also Sheldon (1925), p.196.

72. A.G.P.Elliot "Company Welfare Benefits" in Reid and Robertson (1965), pp.300-309.

73. Gospel & Littler (1983), p.177.

74. Cf. Ch.4, esp. ss.(i),(ii).

75. Gospel & Littler (1983), p.185.

76. Cf. Ch.9.

77. Cf. Littler (1982), pp.90-1; J.Child British Management Thought: A Critical Analysis (1969), pp.35-7; M.M.Niven Personnel Management, 1913-63 (1967), pp.18-36.

78. B.S.Rowntree Industrial Unrest: a Way Out (1922), pp.3-13,15-17,22-6,30-5,37-9,56-60. Cf. also PRO BT55/2, Memo. on views of B.S.Rowntree to Balfour Committee.

79. I.C.Bradley Enlightened Entrepreneurs (1987), for example, is a hagiographic account of the philanthropy of ten prominent Victorian entrepreneurs, and overlooks the motive of managerial considerations behind the provision of welfare.

Chapter 2

THE RAILWAYS, MONOPOLY, AND LABOUR MANAGEMENT

(i) INTRODUCTION

By having to tackle the problems of large-scale organisation from their founding, railway companies had developed by 1850 the corporate management structures which few other industries had adopted even by 1900. While the family firm or partnership remained the norm in other sectors, special Acts of Parliament permitted joint-stock railway companies to be formed, because the scale of their initial investment was beyond the financial means of individuals. By 1875, the capital raised by railway companies amounted to £630 million, a sum which greatly outstripped investment in other industries, and the industry employed 275,000 people or 3% of the male labour force. By 1913, fixed capital exceeded £1330 million and employees numbered 643,000. In 1847, fifteen companies controlled 61% of the industry's capital, and, by 1870, the figure was 80%. After 1921, the whole network was owned by four giant concerns.(1)

In addition to granting the right to found joint stock companies, Parliament needed to regulate the compulsory purchase of land and the laying of track. Regulation was a barrier to free enterprise, but competition was also hindered by the capital costs of building permanent way and constructing rolling-stock. Intense commercial rivalry prevented an adequate return on investment. Moreover, monopoly increased after construction. The efficient working and scheduling of railways and the routing of "through" traffic necessitated inter-company cooperation and alliances.

As monopolies in control of large numbers of men and materials, railways found contemporary business practices inadequate. The industry, therefore, had an important role in the development of corporate administration, labour management and industrial welfare. Quaker employers, like Cadburys and Rowntrees, are normally viewed as innovators in systematic labour policies and industrial welfare,(2) while, in fact, the railways were the first practitioners of corporate labour

25

management. The railway amalgamations of the Victorian era were the model for the combinations formed in other industries during the late 1890s and the Inter-War period, and the managerial practices adopted by railways were also learnt by others. The organisation of an efficent flow of traffic over a geographically-dispersed enterprise like a railway was impossible without a systematic managerial structure, while few other businesses in the 19th Century needed full-time managers or a well-defined administration.(3) The market circumstances of monopoly, therefore, determined the organisation, planning and coordination of railway traffic. Monopoly guaranteed rates of return and the fullest utilisation of expensive capital. Lack of competition provided secure employment and established large internal labour markets. Railways funded industrial welfare in order to gain the loyalty of this permanent workforce.

Labour management in the industry depended upon a rigorous system of discipline. Safe and orderly working relied upon workers fulfilling the duties allotted to them. As employees in a public service, railwaymen were seen by their employers as company "servants" rather than as "workers". Yet, railway managers were aware that efficient service was as dependent upon incentives as on discipline. Paternalistic benefits given on a personal, ex gratia basis were unsuited to companies the size of railways. The systemisation of railway management was coupled with the adoption of conscious, company-wide labour policies. The industry became notable for its friendly societies with their benefits and contributions set according to predetermined rules.

* * * * *

Section (ii) of this chapter analyses the development of railway management, and section (iii) explores its connections with internal labour markets and welfare. Section (iv) outlines the history of company provision from 1846-1914, and section (v) explores the effects of rationalisation during the Inter-War period upon industrial welfare in railway concerns.

(ii) THE RAILWAYS AND CORPORATE MANAGEMENT

Parliament had to authorise compulsory land-purchase for the construction of railways, and, by preventing the random laying of permanent way, it limited the number of possible competitors. Before the reform of company law in the late 1860s, the formation of joint-stock concerns was sanctioned by private Acts of Parliament. The state, moreover, had to draw up and enforce railway safety standards. Yet, even the operational requirements of railways tended towards monopoly. Companies cooperated over "through" traffic because of the diseconomies of unloading passenger and freight trains on to different lines. In 1842, the Railway Clearing House was established to plan "through" routes, and it divided revenues amongst companies according to its own standard classification of goods and rates.(4) But it was the securing of sufficient returns from railway investment which made competition damaging and profitless. After the speculative investment of 1830-60, over-capitalisation increasingly became the object of criticism within companies and the subject of public debate. The pooling of traffic between railways replaced policies of competitive pricing and services.

Despite gradual rationalisation throughout the 19th Century, notable examples of rivalry did continue. The significance of such "disatrous" railway construction in relation to total investment has been disputed.(5) But monopoly was strong enough to be responsible for the industry's relative disregard of cost-control. Companies remained over-capitalised and pricing was not related to operating expenses. A sharp rise in costs in the early 1870s drove the industry's operating ratio (working costs as a proportion of gross revenue) up to fifty. The ratio stabilised from 1873-1890, but, during the 1890s, the aggregate figure was sixty.(6) Aldcroft, by using admittedly "crude" calculations of total railway traffic divided by the numbers employed, estimates that over the period 1860-61 to 1879-80 labour productivity rose by about 1.59% per annum, but declined from 1880-81 to 1909-10 to a virtual standstill yearly average of 0.17%.(7) Aldcroft attributes these failings to managerial shortcomings, while Irving favours the view that Parliamentary hostility to monopoly before 1914 hindered the pruning of uneconomic lines. Gourvish, on the other hand, challenges the view of managerial failure. He quotes the London and North Western and the North Eastern Railways as exemplars of advanced management, although neither collected information for assessing unit costs and labour productivity.(8) Changes in the organisation of railways were undoubtedly important managerial developments and had a direct influence upon industrial welfare policies.

In the railway industry, large amounts of men, money, and materials were concentrated into a single business unit. Problems of geography and distance had to be solved, and activities as diverse as work-shops, terminals, stations, warehouses, office buildings, telegraph lines, and signals had to be coordinated. Unlike canal traffic, the speed of rail travel, the maintenance of schedules, and the enforcement of safety-procedures necessitated direct control over rolling-stock. Managers, furthermore, had to respond daily to changes in the demand and type of traffic. Depreciation had to be financed and construction undertaken according to estimates determined by the collection and collating of regular data. Rates, costs, and wages had to be set at levels which provided reasonable returns.

The first railways of thirty to fifty miles employed as

few as fifty workers, and were administered by a superintendant who had a manager for each of the major functional tasks like transport or the maintenance of rolling-stock. But the scale of operations continued to increase, and the complexities of running a railway came to require a well-defined administrative structure. The lines of authority amongst the large numbers of full-time managers which railways employed had to be pre-determined. Responsibilty had to be allocated between the central office, departmental headquarters, and field units. Two innovations were central to the development of railway management. Firstly, because the general superintendant was unable to exercise operational control over a railway several hundred miles long, British companies began in the 1850s to divide up lines into regions under the control of an autonomous divisional superintendant who managed and coordinated the movement of trains, and hired and fired line personnel. The very delegation of authority under this "divisional system" made hourly, daily and monthly statements essential. Hourly operational reports could inform managers of the position of trains and reasons for their delay. Daily reports were given by conductors, station agents, and engineers, and they could be consolidated into monthly assessments of the costs and profits from each locomotive, department, or division. Such information enabled the central office to set rates on a rational basis. Handicaps to "through" traffic could be located and "dead weight" on return trips reduced. Secondly, the "line-and-staff" system, by which divisional superintendants assumed direct authority over specialist managers like engineers or freight agents as well as line staff, was adopted by certain companies in the 1900s. Difficulties had arisen over the role of functional officers in the divisions, because they had been responsible only to headquarters managers like the chief engineer. Divisional superintendants, therefore, had had little control over constructional work on the permanent way. Local passenger and freight agents had, within head office guidelines, independently adjusted rates, and organised the loading of trains. Coordination and communication between line or traffic operations with their support departments were, consequently, greatly hindered. The "line-and-staff" system placed line or operational officers and staff or functional officers under a unified hierarchy of command. Functional managers continued to set the standards and working practices in their specialised areas, but became answerable to the local superintendent.(9)

The London and North Western Railway, formed under Act of Parliament in 1846 by the amalgamation of the London and Birmingham, Grand Junction, and Manchester and Birmingham Railways, was the first to tackle the problems of large-scale management. The new grouping owned 500 miles of track, and, with £29m in capital, it was Britain's largest company. In

1846-47, it controlled 23% of the industry's passenger receipts and 25% of the freight revenues. The new company was statutorily committed to continue operating for five years as three separate units, but plans to deal with pending managerial problems were laid. In 1848, ad hoc sub-committees were established to cope with the increasing work-load. Three of these individually ran each of the amalgamated companies, and they reported to other sub-committees of the main Board like the Audit or Finance Committee.(10) An investigative committee was also appointed "to produce a more simple, economical and efficient system of Management".(11) Reports dealing with the rationalisation of staff duties, reductions in the number of depots, the use of company land, permanent way maintenance, locomotive power, foremen's wages, and coke supplies were issued.(12) The First Report argued for more central control through the appointment of chief officers answerable directly to the directors.(13) The Second Report called for an estimate of the type and numbers of managerial staff required, and, as part of a programme for building up a loyal and stable management, a staff superannuation fund was established and its solvency guaranteed.(14) The role of professional management, therefore, in the operation of railways was clearly acknowledged. A Third Report dealt with the welfare of all men below the rank of clerk.(15)

It was the London and North Western's adoption by 1848 of the district system for controlling the flow of traffic which was its most marked development. The appointment of chief officers disguised the fact that the regional administration of traffic became increasingly autonomous. The area sub-committees, which had been served by distinct managerial units, were replaced in 1851 by district supervisors with full authority to control the movement of trains. Specialist functions, however, continued to be supervised from the centre. Other ₁companies began adopting the L.N.W.R.'s divisional structure in the 1850s.(16) Moreover, organisation and the increasing size of railway central offices replaced the more personal control of managers like Huish of the L.N.W.R.(17) By the 1880s, every one of the L.N.W.R.'s ten divisional superintendants had an assistant and several travelling inspectors to control the scheduling of traffic in his section. In the six larger regions, there were separate divisional goods managers whose authority was parallel with the division's superintendants. Responsibilities for traffic and ancillary services were also divided at large stations.(18)

In 1902, the North Eastern Railway was the first to unite the operating and commercial sides of the business. Under the new system, the Line Superintendant became the General Superintendant with extended authority over the loading and unloading of trains, and over the maintenance of stock. Divisional Superintendants were also given full managerial authority within their sections. The North Eastern's example was soon followed by the Great Northern Railway.(19) The Lancashire and Yorkshire, and the Midland had adopted the "line-and-staff" system by the First World War.(20)

Only the London and North Eastern Railway of the four "Great" companies of the Inter-War period operated under a "line-and-staff" management. Local knowledge was seen as crucial to the company's responding flexibly to changing markets. The Great Western Railway continued with its divisional system because, being so predominately based on the infrastructure of the old G.W.R., it was little affected by amalgamation.(21) The London, Midland, and Scottish, however, soon found its centralised structure too rigid, and spent the period 1921-31 considering its organisation.(22) In 1927, the General Manager was replaced by an Executive Committee with a President, and four Vice-Presidents in charge of either the traffic, engineering, commercial or financial departments.(23) There was also a chief officer for labour and establishment. In 1931, Scotland, with its particular commercial and organisational needs, was the only section of the L.M.S. to be given full operational autonomy. By the 1930s, the L.M.S. and the Southern Railway had placed control over the maintenance of track, rolling-stock, and the marketing of traffic fully into the hands of divisional specialist officers, but they were responsible to the head-office and not to divisional superintendents.(24) Theirs was a hybrid system which combined the attributes of the divisional and line-and-staff structures.(25)

* * * * *

Most companies introduced a divisional system during the 19th Century. In the dozen years before the Great War, several British companies established a "line-and-staff" structure. The managerial organisation of one of these, the N.E.R., was adopted by the London and North Eastern at the time of the industry's rationalisation in 1921. Developments in management - at the L.N.W.R. in the 1840s, at the N.E.R. in the early 1900s, and at the L.N.E.R. in the 1920s - had a direct influence upon labour and industrial welfare policies in these companies. Consideration of management in general led to a detailed examination of labour requirements.

(iii) INTERNAL LABOUR MARKETS AND INDUSTRIAL WELFARE

P.W.Kingsford in his review of railway labour in the years 1835-1875 notes that the London and Birmingham Railway, in providing churches and schools at local stations and depots, drew upon the experiences of the Lancashire cotton industry. When building company houses at Wolverton, it followed the precedents of textile villages dominated by paternalistic employers. Railway directors were " like ordinary millowners bound to do for their population that which the millowners did ".(26) At first, therefore, railway welfare was ex gratia. Local shop clubs offered mutual protection to its members and might occasionally receive donations from the company. Faithful servants could be granted pensions by the Board on the personal recommendation of station or depot managers. It was a cumbersome, inefficient system with no financial control or planning.(27)

Welfare which was reliant upon the personal, discretionary largesse of an employer was as inappropriate for the growing size of railway operations as other forms of contemporary management. Moreover, the nature of railway employment, as well as the scale of operations, encouraged the systemisation of welfare. Monopolistic and capital-intensive companies required large "core" workforces, and railwaymen could look forward to a life-time's employment with their company. A secure market demand encouraged the establishment of a stable labour force, and gave companies the opportunity to introduce systematic, contributory welfare schemes with guaranteed rights. The reliabilty of railway workers added considerably to the operational efficiency of an industry dependent upon the detailed coordination of traffic and support services. Conscientious workers were an asset to an industry responsible for the safe carriage of passengers. As a public service, railways were particularly vulnerable to the effects of strikes, and, as highly capital-intensive enterprises, the financial costs of industrial action were equally daunting. Finally, the skills of footplatemen, guards, and signalmen took many years to acquire at a company's expense. For all these reasons, the men who worked on the permanent way were beneficiaries of railway welfare policy. While strong competitors, fluctuating trade, and the absence of a corporate structure limited the extent of industrial welfare in other industries, railways had the administrative means and the need to establish systematic company provision.

During its investigation into management in 1848, the London and North Western drew up a third report discussing labour policy. Adjustments in the methods of providing benefits were made because company-wide provident societies gave railways the ability to standardise benefits and to exercise a central control over welfare expenditure. Those below the rank of clerk were required to join superannuation funds. Those employed in the engineering workshops, where labour tended to be more mobile, could join voluntarily.(28) The crucial difference was that engineers acquired their skills after a seven-year apprenticeship system which was controlled by the workers themselves. Labourers employed for constructional work were casual workers dismissed as soon as particular projects were completed. Railwaymen, however, were a "core" workforce.

Sir George Findlay, General Manager of the London and

North Western Railway, in 1889 stressed the importance of internal labour markets to the organisation of labour in the industry: "The Company are very far from being unmindful of the material welfare of the men they employ, and indeed it is their constant study to maintain the most friendly and cordial relations with them, and to make them feel that their employers have a sincere interest in them and in their well-being at all times, apart from the mere buying and selling of their labour....." Mutual empathy was the "proper relation between master and man". Workers who were given managerial responsibilities, such as inspectors and station-masters, were chosen from the lower ranks, and the "most scrupulous attention is paid to the training of signal men". The training-period varied according to the importance of the signal-post they were to occupy. The guards of passenger trains had responsibility for passengers´ safety and needed training. "All these men are subjected to a rigid examination before being appointed, and due regard is had, not only to their knowledge and experience, but to their general intelligence, capacity, and character." Even those employed in unskilled jobs like those of porter and shunter were offered security of employment because they were the labour reserve for guards and signalmen.(29) Enginemen and firemen, on the other hand, had an autonomous apprenticeship system, but the knowledge of engine drivers, guards, and signalmen was "both specialised and localised". The work-experiences of complicated signal systems upon different branch lines were varied. Men accustomed to the Westinghouse brake could not use ordinary hand-brakes. The specific, practical knowledge of railwaymen, therefore, was of great value to the company, and its loss an expense.(30)

The particular skills of workers on the permanent way were recognised by Felix Pole, General Manager of the Great Western Railway, in 1923: "In no walk of civil life is discipline of more importance than in railway service, and there is no more valuable asset a railway company can possess than a loyal, contented and well-disciplined staff". Management had to instill high morale as well as discipline: "Loyalty and efficiency go hand-in-hand, and, to secure these excellent attributes in any service, it is impossible to give too much consideration".(31) Stern discipline by itself could cause resentment, and "resentment is never conducive to good work". Suspending men for breaches of discipline was avoided because experienced workers could not be easily replaced.(32)

The special circumstances of monopoly created an employment-relationship in the railway industry for which management had to develop an effective and positive labour policy. Railwaymen who worked on the permanent way formed a large internal labour market, and the advantages of a stable and experienced workforce compelled a large investment in industrial welfare. Changes in managerial structure occurred

in order to cope not only with commercial and operational
demands but with labour requirements.

(iv) THE RAILWAYS AND INDUSTRIAL WELFARE, 1846-1914

(a) Introduction

As a result of financial malpractices during the 1830s,
Parliament required railway Acts defining a company's articles
of association to provide for adequate public accountability.
The uses to which investors' money could be put were
restricted, and the proper accounting of revenue was
enforced.(33) The right of a company, therefore, to donate to
a welfare fund had to be sanctioned by legislation, and
railway friendly societies had to be properly constituted,
with set contributions and rights to benefit. Yet, these
societies tended in general to be technically insolvent and
dependent upon company grants. Railways simply met their
deficits. Faced, however, with an increasing financial burden,
particularly from the cost of paying pensions, companies were
to attempt subjecting their provident associations to
actuarial considerations.

(b) Origins

The London and Birmingham Railway's General Benefit
Society was established in 1839 to provide sick pay, death
assurance, and pensions.(34) Just as traffic operations could
not be wholly united at the L.N.W.R. at its founding in 1846,
the welfare practices of the constituent companies were
continued. Although a company-wide society was established
under the ultimate control of a sub-committee of the Board,
each operational district, corresponding to the old companies,
had a separate committee in charge of administering the
benefits. The L.N.W.R.'s Third Report on management in 1848
referred to the working of the friendly society. It was
recognised that the harsh discipline, personally supervised by
the chief officer, Huish, had drawbacks. Too many skilled or
semi-skilled men were leaving the company's employ, and they
were not easily replaced. Extensive bonuses and gratuities, it
was believed, would encourage loyalty, but the policy of
guaranteeing a railwayman 12s sick pay per week was seen as
too costly. An annual grant to its friendly society, according
to its financial situation, would be made instead. The scale
of sickness and pension allowances was revised, and membership
was made a condition of employment in the new company. Money
for the victims of accidents was allotted to departments.
Huish was an intuitive rather than a systematic manager, and
the Benefit Society was likewise an unsystematic if
contributory club. No attempt was made to balance revenue and
benefits. The L.N.W.R. also provided housing, because it aided
the transfer of labour throughout the company, and bettered

Founded

1833 Stockton and Darlington Mutual Provident Society
1839 London and Birmingham Provident Society
1841 Birmingham and Gloucester Railway Friendly Institution
1842 London, Brighton, and South Coast Railway
     Provident Society
1846 London and North Western General Benefit Society
1847 Great Western Railway Mutual Accident Society
1850 Great Northern Railway Locomotive Sick Society
1851 Great Eastern Railway Provident Society
1852 North British Railway Provident Society
1853 Great Northern Railway Sick and Funeral Allowance Fund
1857 *L. & B.R. Savings Bank
1859 *Lancashire and Yorkshire Railway Insurance Society,
     Midland Railway Friendly Society,
1861 Manchester, Sheffield, and Lincolnshire Savings Bank
1865 G.W.R. Enginemen and Footplatemen Mutual Accident,
     Sick and Superannuation Society
1866 Great Central Railway and Joint Lines Friendly Society
1868 South Eastern Railways Savings Bank
1871 L.N.W.R. Insurance Society
1874 G.C.R. and Joint Lines Accident and Pension Society,
     L.N.W.R. Provident Society
1875 G.N.R. Provident Society
1877 L.N.W.R. Servants Hospital Fund
1878 G.E.R. Accident Allowance Fund
1879 G.W.R. Provident Society
1880 G.W.R. Pension Society
1882 North Eastern Railway Benevolent Fund
1883 L.N.W.R. Pension Society
1885 G.W.R. Savings Bank, N.B.R. Provident Fund
1889 L.N.W.R. Provident and Pension Society
1890 G.E.R. Pension Fund
1893 *South Western Railway Widows and Orphans Benefit
     Society, N.E.R. Pension Society
1895 L.N.W.R. Savings Bank, G.E.R. Supplementary Pension
     Society, Taff Vale Railway Savings Bank
1897 G.N.R. Savings Bank
1898 G.C.R. Provident and Accident Society
1899 L.B.S.C.R. Pension Society
1903 G.C.R. Pension Society, G.W.R. Pension Society
1904 G.W.R. Mutual Accident Society
1907 N.E.R. Servants Pension Society, L. & Y.R. Pension
     Friendly Society
1908 Metropolitan Railway Pension Society
1914 N.E.R. Servants' Death and Endowment Society
1919 N.E.R. Cottage Homes and Benefit Fund
1923 London, Midland, Scottish Savings Bank
1930 L.M.S. Hospital Fund, Southern Railway Pension Society

* Indicates earliest date that institution cited.

industrial relations which were "seen as a vital factor in the maintenance of operational efficiency".(35)

Welfare policy was further systemised at the L.N.W.R. in the 1870s. The London and North Western Insurance Society was founded in 1871. It paid members death benefits and awards for permanent and temporary disablement. In return for compulsory membership, the company agreed to pay "from time to time" a sum equalling five-sixths of total premiums. In 1874, the railway donated £500 to establish the L.N.W. Provident and Pension Society. This scheme was a condition of employment for all new workers, and cost the majority of members 2d a week in subscriptions. The company agreed to apply for statutory powers to donate £1,000 per annum, and changes in the Society's rules had to be confirmed by the Board. The scheme provided disablement pensions, additional death benefits, medical expenses, and sick pay at a rate of 6s per week for those normally earning 12s. An old age Pension Fund was begun in 1883 and guaranteed retirement at 65 years for the healthy and at 60 for the ill. 1d a week won the right to a 7s pension and 2d a week a 10s pension, while the company paid about £6,000 per annum. All three societies were managed by the same committee of three managerial appointees and twelve members elected from each of the managerial districts. To avoid the expensive and time-consuming process of gaining individual statutory permission to donate to each welfare scheme, the company decided to obtain the 1882 L.N.W.R. Act. This stipulated that, with the permission of three-fifths of shareholders, the directors could contribute to any cause which enhanced the welfare of employees. The old age Pension and Provident Funds were amalgamated in 1889, but the Insurance Society continued as a separate organisation catering for the specific requirements of the 1880 Employers Liability Act.(36)

The Great Western Railway founded a Medical Fund Society in 1847 to pay donations to some twenty hospitals which treated their servants. By the 1890s, swimming and Turkish baths, and free surgical appliances were available to members. By 1901, the company provided dental services, and a treatment centre for consumptives.(37) The Provident Society, established in 1880, covered sick pay and funeral allowances.(38) A Pension Society, founded in the same year, paid pensions of between 10s and 14s according to the length of service.(39) Modelling itself upon the coffee-houses promoted by the L.N.W.R. at Crewe,(40) a Temperance Union was begun in 1883 and the G.W.R. Coffee Tavern Company was established as a subsidiary of the railway. The Union encouraged "healthy" activities like choir singing and sports as alternatives to drinking, and interested itself in the "promotion of good will in all relations of the Staff and the Company".(41) Social and sporting clubs in the railway industry promoted "esprit de corps", and railwaymen's institutes providing board and meals were essential for workers forced to travel many miles from home.

By the 1860s, the Great Northern Railway was concerned about the high labour-turnover due to the lack of housing near places of work, and the company began constructing houses at a cost of £120 each.(42) In 1875, the Board hoped to minimise wage-increases on the grounds that company cottages would induce men to stay with the railway. But 200 new homes were required in the Traffic Department alone, and other rented accommodation costing in London 6/6d per week, was often beyond a railwayman's means. In 1892, the company won the necessary Parliamentary authority to advance house-buying loans at 4%.(43)

As chairman of the South Eastern and the Manchester, Sheffield, and Lincolnshire Railways, Sir Edward Watkin made himself directly responsible for their industrial welfare. He founded a savings bank at the S.E.R. in 1869 which sought to encourage personal thrift. As the Bank's guest-speaker in 1881, the Bishop of London outlined Watkin's attitude to industrial relations as being "very wisely, in his own interests and in the care of the concerns which he represents and administers so effectively, to regard the well-being of those whom he employs".(44) The M.S.L.R. established a Sick and Burial Fund in 1870. Membership of the Mutual Provident and Accident Society, on its founding in 1874, was compulsory.(45) The right to benefit was restricted by the stern rules typical of 19th Century company friendly societies. Members of the fund at each place of work were delegated to visit the recipients of benefits every week and to report cases of fraud.(46)

(c) Employers Liability and Actuarial Valuation

The 1880 Employers' Liability Act bestowed on workers the right to sue employers whose negligence was the cause of their accidents. But, through its "contracting out" provisions, workers could renounce their legal right to go to court in return for mutual insurance cover with their employers. Consequently, railway companies had to decide whether to continue with their accident schemes or disband them in favour of workers resorting to litigation.

The G.E.R.'s Accident Allowance Fund altered its constitution in 1880 to accord with the Act, and it enticed its men to join by offering supplementary benefits.(47) The G.N.R. reviewed its allowances in 1888 from the "commercial aspect", and noted that the L.N.W.R., Midland and G.E.R. all had accident societies to which they had contributed £23,236, £9,000, and £4,472 respectively in the previous year. The Great Northern did not contribute to accident or sick funds but the company's practice was to pay the difference between full pay and benefits received from the workers' independent friendly society. It paid £1,379 in provident benefits and

£2,543 in retirement payments in 1887. The G.N.R. estimated that establishing a fund would be more costly than its present system.(48) The L.N.W.R. contracted out of the Act by founding a compulsory scheme. Unlike Employers Liability, payment did not depend on proving the responsibility of the employer. Litigation between employer and worker was seen by the company as potentially too detrimental to industrial relations.(49)

Employers formed contracting-out societies for two principal reasons. They disliked the prospects of litigation, and they wanted the levels of compensation to be limited by mutual agreement. The 1880 Act, therefore, encouraged company provision, but the 1897 Workmen's Compensation Act, by setting out a pre-determined scale of automatic benefits for accidents at work, removed the employers' two reasons for contracting out.(50) Nevertheless, the Great Central Railway, previously the Manchester, Sheffield, and Lincolnshire, noted, firstly, that Workmen's Compensation did not cover the loss of earnings in the first two weeks of convalescence. Secondly, pensions would not be available for bereaved widows and orphans. The directors decided, therefore, to continue both payments during the first weeks of recuperation and widows' pensions. The company agreed to match 10% of all its benefit society's funds, if provident contributions rose by 1d to 8d a week, and if members paid 1d extra for accident insurance.(51) The G.E.R. also founded a friendly society under the 1897 Act.(52) Although the N.E.R. decided that it would simply pay compensation claims made under the legislation, it concluded that a fund should be established specifically to cover the two weeks remitted by the law.(53) The North British Railway held that the additional costs of the Act demanded an increase in members' contributions, but instead agreed to giving a 10% donation because "this concession would have a very salutory and far reaching effect with the men, and be highly appreciated".(54) The L.N.W. Insurance Society was wound up, although a voluntary fund without company support was established by the men themselves. Special provision was made, however, by the railway for the early weeks of lost earnings.

The revision of welfare schemes was not instigated by the passing of social legislation only. The M.S.L.R. had contributed to its Mutual Provident and Accident Associations £1,300 every year since 1882. It was acknowledged by the company that the Associations' credibility in the eyes of the men depended on the company guaranteeing its liabilities. Action was needed, because a report in 1894 showed the societies to have a deficit of £29,538. The company, therefore, felt obliged to underwrite all sickness allowances for men over 70, and to carry the societies' pension burden "as a matter of good feeling". In return, a 1d increase in contributions was sought, but this condition was abandoned because it introduced "a disturbing element in the ranks".(55)

Changes to schemes were also halted by the opposition of

the Amalgamated Society of Railway Servants, which believed that company societies threatened their own welfare funds and discouraged strikes. The North Eastern Railway first drew up plans for a contributory pension scheme in 1884, and agreed to give 3d per week for each employee to provide a maximum pension of 10s. But, because the union was well organised on the N.E.R., the company was unable to establish such a contributory fund for more than twenty years.(56) Although the N.E.R. obtained the right under its 1889 Act to compel membership of a scheme, protests organised by the union ensured the clause was never effected. The men preferred non-contributory pensions even if they were financially inadequate.(57)

The North Eastern re-investigated its various funds in 1893, upon which it spent nearly £5,000 a year.(58) The directors wished to avoid resentment which changes in benefit levels might cause, and the scope for action was consequently limited. It was impossible to cease pension allowances altogether, for it was in the nature of railway work that the older and least efficient men were retired. Workers had to be reliable and fit, and good eyesight was a particular requirement. The singular advantage of discretionary grants, the right to alter or end payments at will, had been whittled away by increasing costs and the fact that benefits were paid to all workers as a matter of course. Moreover, discretionary pensions, being below sustenance, did not secure the employment of a "superior" class of workmen. A contributory scheme providing payments of 5s at 65 years was the only "proper solution of the pension question". By contributing themselves, the interest of workers in a friendly society was enhanced, and self-management and committee elections encouraged participation. The N.E.R.'s housing policy was also circumscribed by the need to maintain good industrial relations. By 1902, the N.E.R. had built 4,606 cottages, and, although the return on rents did not equal the interest due on the original investment, it was decided that increases "would create much discontent, and probably the effect in creating dissatisfaction amongst the men would do harm out of all proportion to the extra revenue available".(59)

Detailed memoranda on welfare were drawn up at the N.E.R. in the early 1900s, at a time when the company was considering all aspects of management. In 1903, it was reported that a large number of employees wanted to found a pension fund, but first wished to ascertain the prospects of financial support from the company. Delegates elected at fifty-six mass meetings were asked to formulate an appropriate scheme. The N.E.R. realised that the fund's success depended on its backing. It believed that, in terms of labour management, the influence of discretionary grants upon the men was "very much lessened by the fact that they are not assured" despite being awarded to all. The N.E.R. insisted that any scheme would have to be approved by the company, and no alterations in its rules which affected its financial basis could be made without the directors´ consent. A regular lump sum to a fund every year would, it was estimated, cost less than directly paying discretionary grants. A new scheme, therefore, was devised after fresh Parliamentary powers had been obtained in 1905. In order to avert threatened opposition, it was agreed to register the fund under the Friendly Societies Act 1896 which forbade compulsory membership.(60)

Sir Charles Dilke, the Radical-Liberal M.P., spoke against the involvement of railways like the Great Eastern in the personal affairs of its workers. In 1897, the company wanted to establish a Savings Bank.(61) Railway News disagreed with Dilke: "....a certain amount of philanthropy is quite compatible with the soundest principles of business. To encourage thrift, to give the rank and file of the staff a stake in the concern, to attach them permanently and devotedly to their service, are objects for the sake of which hard-headed directors and managers have found it worth while to sacrifice a few thousands a year in net revenue".(62) In support of such aims, the London, Brighton and South Coast Railway in 1899 successfully obtained an Act to revise its Pension Society´s rules. It transferred the members of the old scheme, without consulting them, to a new fund, and imposed tight financial control upon it.(63)

Despite the reorganisation and revaluation of friendly societies by many companies, a Board of Trade Report on Railway Superannuation Funds in 1910 concluded that most societies continued to produce a yearly deficit. The governing bodies of these funds had "apparently failed in the earlier stages properly to appreciate what the liability undertaken in respect of pensions would likely to amount to". The Report, in addition, concluded that even the membership of voluntary schemes tended to be universal because of the special inducements they offered. The General Secretary of the A.S.R.S., Richard Bell, was aware of the importance of company friendly societies to railwaymen, when he admitted he came "into touch with them more or less every day in some case or other".(64)

(d) Collective Bargaining and National Insurance
To avoid the prospect of a country-wide railway strike in 1907, Lloyd George threatened to enforce a system of conciliation boards unless they were appointed voluntarily by the companies. He also held out the "carrot" of rates revision. The 1894 Railway and Canal Traffic Act, which had frozen rates in an effort to curb monopolistic pricing, had encouraged companies to squeeze wages, with the effect that membership of the A.S.R.S. had grown dramatically. A hierarchy of conciliation boards at local, sectional, and central level was established in all companies, but agreement was reached

only after an assurance that unions would remain unrecognised
and that their officials would not sit on the boards.(65) The
industry had conceded three points. The privilege of
railwaymen to petition directors about their grievances became
a right. Official rather than ad hoc procedures for complaint
were established, and, where Sectional and Central Boards
failed to find agreement, outside arbitrators could be called
in. The scheme lasted till the outbreak of war in 1914, during
which time dissatisfaction with its working led to a national
strike in 1911. Rates were not revised until 1913.(66)

In negotiations on the conciliation boards, the companies
argued that the scale of welfare provision was reason enough
for low wage increases. The leverage given by the boards to a
more strident labour force worried the Great Eastern. In 1908,
the company issued a circular on the conciliation scheme to
its servants stating that it gave £28,500 to provident
societies every year. The railway additionally granted
allowances to those retired men who had been too old to join
pension societies when hired. The General Manager,
J.F.S.Gooday, set wages against free travel passes, paid
holidays, savings banks, cheap cottages, free uniforms, "and
other privileges". He asked the men "to seriously consider
whether you will break off the friendly relations which have
hitherto existed between the staff and the Board, and
introduce conditions which prevail where masters and men each
consider only their own interests, and under which directly a
man is incapable of performing his full amount of work he is
turned adrift without any consideration for his length of
service, and without any provision for his old age".(67)
During conciliation procedures at the L.N.W.R. in 1908, stress
on the advantages of the Pension and Provident Fund helped
reduce the level of the wages award.(68) Richard Bell argued
that his members contributed a substantial part of their
income to welfare funds. His central point, however, was that
it was in the nature of railway employment that the unfit had
to be retired and that pensions, therefore, had to be
provided. Employers were only fulfilling their responsibilities and in their own interests.(69)

While collective bargaining over wages and hours did not
directly concern railway welfare policy, social legislation
had the potential to affect its provision crucially. Yet, the
passing of the Old Age Pensions Act 1908 left the operations
of company pension funds untouched. Railway News criticised
the legislation on the basis that railway companies had drawn
heavily on their own resources "to largely solve the old age
pension problem many long years before the present
Administration...."(70) A G.C.R. memorandum in 1908 did
conclude that it was impossible to pay for state and company
pensions. But the railway continued to pay for those between
65 and 70 years who were not covered by the Act. Moreover,
because a man needed a weekly income of 12/1d before the state

pension of 5s was incrementally reduced, the G.C.R. ensured that its employees received from both sources a net sum of between 5s and 15s. Such sums matched its previous scale of benefits, and "the Company have no doubt that this action on their part has been much appreciated".(71)

The railways had reason, however, to be troubled by the implications of the National Insurance Bill in 1911.(72) The Railway Companies Association advised its members to establish Approved Societies under the Act, if for no other reason than to forestall the Amalgamated Society of Railway Servants forming their own. The G.C.R. doubted the worth of the voluntary Approved Societies, because the absence of compulsion was considered to lessen membership and to limit its influence over workers. But the G.C.R. concluded that through an Approved Society the Board would "be able to exercise a useful pressure from time to time". They were certain that "The Company will control it...."(73) The London, Brighton and South Coast Railway agreed to a voluntary fund but would "strive to maintain the house which is our own..." from the interference of the state.(74)

Railway provident schemes had to be reconstituted to suit the requirements laid down by the Insurance Commissioners. The G.N.R. withdrew its annual donation to its Sick and Funeral Allowance Fund, because, under the Act, it had to pay weekly contributions for every member instead. But the company agreed to administer the Society free of charge, and members' subscriptions were taken directly from wage-packets. Incentives, additions to the minimum benefits laid down by the Act, encouraged the men to join the company's Statutory Fund.(75) The N.E.R. paid benefits to workers under 16 years and above 70, who were not legally required to join the Health Insurance scheme.(76) The Great Central also revised the rules of its sickness fund on the advice of an actuary and offered supplementary benefits.(77) The L.N.W.R. enquired into the efficacy of its welfare policies and the costs of the new legislation. Its pension fund already showed a large deficit, a liability the company had accepted while their scheme was compulsory. It questioned its commitment, however, on the grounds that the loyalty engendered by the Provident and Pension Association had failed to prevent a strike in 1911. Before the provident section could become an Approved Society, the Association's deficit had to recovered by either increased contributions or reduced benefits. The first measure was seen as beyond members' means, the second as unfair to long-standing members. The L.N.W.R., therefore, agreed to donate an extra £93,000, £82,000 of which was allotted to providing pensions. The remaining £11,000 allowed higher sick benefits to be paid, death allowances for husbands and wives, and retirement gratuities. These sums were additional to the £50,000 to be paid every year in employers' contributions to the Approved Society. The chairman of the Company did not doubt that members of the Society would be "agreeably satisfied" with the new arrangements.(78)

(e) Summary

Friendly societies were an integral part of railway labour management during the years 1846-1914, and they were notable for being regularised and administered according to predetermined rules. Each company had to involve its sizeable workers in the membership of provident funds, in order to establish a cooperative, stable, and disciplined labour force. Indeed, many schemes were a condition of service. Extensive internal labour markets made the retention of skills through pension schemes and good conditions a useful instrument of employment policy. Although many of the original friendly societies were not ex gratia in the sense of effectively providing benefits for all, they were unsystematic and non-contributory and income was rarely related to expenditure. From 1846 to 1914, the costs of welfare and especially pensions continued to grow, and railway friendly societies increasingly became contributory. They generally remained, however, technically insolvent, and reliant upon the regular funds that railways as large, monopolistic companies could provide.

(v) RATIONALISATION AND INDUSTRIAL WELFARE, 1914-1939

Extensive changes occurred in the structure and management of the industry as a consequence of the Great War and the 1921 Railways Act. The demands of a war-time economy converted Parliament and businessmen in general to the advantages of combination. Greater efficiency was achieved by the Railway Executive Committee´s central direction of the industry. "Through" traffic was streamlined, and goods-wagons were pooled and more fully filled.(79)

The unions´ bargaining-power was increased by labour shortage during the War, and the industry´s wage-bill of £47m in 1913 had expanded to £173m by 1921. Companies, moreover, continued to provide welfare benefits for men temporarily called to the colours. The Railway Executive Committee in 1914 decided that companies should supplement official payments to soldiers´ dependants, and guarantee families a minimum of four-fifths of their customary income. This donation amounted to 7s plus 1s for each of the first three children. The men called up in August 1914 were members of the Territorial railway regiments, and they were technically still company employees. By the end of 1914, the families of employees joining the regular army received similar benefits, the aim being to encourage ex-railwaymen to rejoin their companies when demobilised.(80) The Great Central assisted all those whose husband or father was on active service and even

42

continued to pay his contributions to company friendly societies. These concessions cost the G.C.R. £3,033 in 1917. The N.E.R., therefore, appreciated the National Health Insurance Act 1916 because it was "designed mainly to strengthen the financial position of Societies, and to simplify their administration".(81) Railway News recognised the good work of the Ministry of Munitions in promoting industrial welfare. The Boys Welfare Association was commended for its work with the 1,000 boys employed on the Midland Railway. It was a policy "conducing to better work contentment and loyalty, facilitating discipline without friction, and assisting favourable relations between employers and employees, during the most impressionable years of a boy's life". Welfare work developed "a spirit of esprit de firm......"(82)

With the state controlling the railways, the government had to decide upon the future structure of the industry. But the Coalition Government procrastinated in the face of union opposition to the industry returning to private hands. Railway News conceded in 1919 that the unions would have to be given a say in management.(83) But the position of the unions was weakened by the Post-War Slump of the early 1920s, and they accepted, instead of nationalisation, the conciliation machinery established by the 1921 Railways Act. The employers still viewed the participation of workers in management as an expropriation of their rights as managers.(84) Yet, the Railway Companies Association was satisfied that all their recommendations for the rationalisation of the industry were incorporated into the 1921 Act. Four regional, privately-owned groupings were established and unnecessary competition was to be avoided. The new concerns were left to reach their own decisions about the practicalities of internal amalgamation, with the exception of the Great Western which was based on the old company of the same name.(85)

Managerial reconstruction required a review of labour management policies, and the London and North Eastern Railway investigated its welfare provision in 1924. The 1921 Act had left it in charge of the provident associations of its constituent companies, which all varied in methods of funding and in the payment of benefits. The contractual obligations of each of these societies were regarded by railwaymen as part of their conditions of employment. Their benefit rights were, in addition, protected by the law laid down in numerous railway Acts. Reconstituting the friendly societies without inflicting losses of benefits on some portion of the workforce was impossible. The Railways Act, moreover, stated that customary practices were inviolate unless changed by mutual agreement. The systemising of welfare provision during the 1920s, consequently, proved a complex process.

Mainly because of its parlous financial situation, the L.N.E.R. paid greatest attention to management and company structure in the hope of reducing costs. The railway adopted the working practices of its most efficient unit, the North Eastern.(86) A detailed report on the welfare work carried out in its constituent companies was commissioned in 1924. It concluded that provision could not be continued in an ad hoc manner. Twelve branches of welfare work were selected as being of primary importance: railway institutes, reading rooms, and social clubs; lectures and debating societies; improvement classes; mess rooms and canteens; athletic clubs; rifle clubs; musical societies and brass bands; the Old Comrades Association; allotments; the friendly societies, including official company schemes and "unofficial" ones founded by the men themselves; savings banks; and the North East Cottage Homes and Benefit Fund.(87) The investigating committee reported the existence of 993 organisations, of which 42 received direct company support and 139 the free use of land or buildings.

In May 1923, the Board placed all the different savings banks into one amalgamated fund, and agreed to collect all friendly society payments directly from wages.(88) By June 1924, the L.N.E.R. decided to retain all the railwaymen's institutes, although their free rent was ended. Athletic clubs continued to receive assistance but began to be charged for the use of grounds. Official company organisations were encouraged to coordinate sporting activities throughout the company. The Board, however, decided that "Consideration of new Welfare Work should be postponed until the Company is in calmer waters, and that the practice of the constituent companies would be normally continued....."(89) But the advantages of pooling actuarial risks in a large pension fund were too financially attractive to be overlooked. The N.E.R., G.N.R., and G.E.R. all had retirement funds, while the G.C.R., the Hull and Barnsley, and the Great North of Scotland granted ex gratia allowances. The aggregate cost in 1922 amounted to £207,180. Men were encouraged but could not be compelled to join associations organised on the basis of the N.E.R.'s fund. It was self-managed and contributory, gave refunds at a generous rate, and the company held its assets at a fixed rate of interest.(90)

The L.N.E.R's report in 1924 revealed its welfare philosophy. Firstly, it was in the employer's interests to have a "healthy, thrifty, contented, self-respecting and efficient staff", and labour as well as capital was an investment. Secondly, efficient workmen required adequate opportunities for education and recreation, healthy work-conditions, and decent housing. Thirdly, "many of these facilities are difficult for the staff to obtain by themselves, but can be readily provided by co-operation between the men, whose energy will carry out the schemes, and the employer, who is able to provide the necessary financial and technical assistance". Fourthly, welfare mollified class hatred. Fifthly, "this spirit of cooperation or esprit de corps will make it easier as time goes on to interest the staff in improving industrial efficiency..." The L.N.E.R. recognised the distinction between "external" and "internal" welfare. Because internal welfare dealt with the physical conditions of work in factories, railways were committed to providing institutes, savings banks, and friendly societies - or external welfare. Such provision was a channel for shop-floor grievances: "It is important that the men should feel, especially in matters of external welfare, that the initiative is with them, and that the Company are not trying in any way to force schemes upon them". Welfare administration was democratic but "subject to (the) necessary financial safeguards". External provision also tied even trade union activists to the company: "There is a growing desire among the men to avail themselves of any help from the Company in carrying out the welfare schemes in which they are interested, and there is no doubt that an active share in the management of such concerns give the men's representatives, most of whom are leading men in the Trades Unions, a more direct interest in the Company as an organic whole". Although the N.U.R.'s Railway Review described welfare as "capitalistic dope and industrial soothing syrup", the L.N.E.R. believed it promoted "a co-operative sense" and loyalty which was "impossible to value in money".(91) The Report suggested that a full-time welfare officer be appointed to maximise the advantages of company provision. He could establish uniformity in the paying of benefits, and concentrate his efforts on teenage recruits, who required pastoral guidance.(92)

When the L.N.E.R. considered ending financial support for the N.E.R.'s Cottage Homes and Benefit Fund in 1926, the Fund pointed out its importance to the daily lives of workers. One member recounted how his local relief committee was applauded at an N.U.R. branch meeting for assisting a widow. Moreover, "The contributions by the Company have to a very large extent been one of the dynamoes by which the men have been able to carry their increased membership amongst the rank and file; the fact that the company were backing us up financially". Company concern for the "human factor" induced the interest of the men in their work. The railway's conciliation boards supported the Fund's case.(93)

The London, Midland, Scottish attempted to rationalise management by adopting the practices of the L.N.W.R., but the inter-company rivalries which resulted proved obstructive.(94) The L.N.W.R. Hospital Fund was allocated in 1922 an additional £1,000. In 1923, its benefits were extended to the whole L.M.S. after the company had promised to match 50% of the amount contributed by the men. By 1930, there were 946 branches of the Fund, covering 240,000 members or 88% of the workforce. Between 1923-29, the Fund paid £565,590 to hospitals as well as donating to the costs of doctors' consultation fees and surgical and dental treatment.(95) The L.M.S. established a welfare department in 1923, and divisional welfare officers were appointed under the direction of the Chief Officer for Labour and Establishment. The department built new recreational facilities like the Headstone Lane sports ground in 1924 for the use of wages staff at Euston. It organised annual company-wide sporting competitions, and suggestion and housing schemes.(96) Through its company magazine, the L.M.S. was keen to point out the large sums it gave to friendly societies, orphanages, hospital treatment, convalescent homes, dental and optical assistance, lectures and continuation classes, canteens, mess-rooms, railwaymen's institutes, libraries, and social and sports facilities.(97)

The L.M.S. claimed not to believe that industrial disputes were a result of the worker's greed for wages, but due to "the absence of a proper understanding between the parties concerned, those in a position of authority in the industrial world frequently lacking either the opportunity or the inclination to exercise personal sympathy and interest in their helpers or co-workers...." The point was to give railwaymen an appreciation of the difficulties of managing a large company.(98) As W.J.Blake of the L.M.S. stated: ".....the necessary link between the men who find wages and those who depend on those wages for their existence was to be found in the right conception and application of the principles and practice of industrial welfare..."(99)

The Great Western Railway was from its founding in 1922 a unified company,(100) and the company's friendly society continued to function as before the War.(101) Public Utility Societies were founded in the early 1920s,(102) as a result of the 1919 Housing Act. They provided subsidies for the construction of industrial housing, because, with the rationalisation of lines, labour had to be transferred.(103) The Southern Railway by 1922 was likewise able to adopt a unitary corporate structure.(104) In 1930, the company obtained Parliamentary authority to amalgamate pension provision. Section 6 of the L.B.S.C.R. (Pensions) Act 1899 had firstly to be repealed, and the Southern had to guarantee the solvency of the new fund.(105)

Although the difficulties of rationalisation both necessitated and hindered the streamlining of welfare benefits, action had to be taken to comply with the 1925 Widows, Orphans, and Old Age Pensions Act. The G.W.R., for example, supplemented from 1904 the benefits paid by its Pension Fund. In fact, the company calculated it paid 60% of the total cost of its workers' pensions. But the G.W.R. were confident that the 1925 Act would not substantially alter the details of their pension provision. Those who joined the fund in 1926 would when retired receive company allowances worth 25% less than those who had joined prior to the legislation.

The cut, however, was only equal to the Great Western's contributions to the new state scheme. Although the Widows and Orphans' Benevolent Fund was wound up, the company promised to pay any benefits due to present members. Any widows unable to obtain state allowances after 1925 were also promised financial help.(106) Because the L.N.E.R. was to contribute some £125,000 per annum under the legislation, donations to voluntary pension funds were proportionately reduced. Ex gratia allowances, paid on certain constituent parts of the railway, were continued. The objective, as before the 1925 Act, was to guarantee a pension income from both the state and the company of between 5s and 15s. The railway had, in any case, reduced allowances when their recipients reached 70 years of age and became eligible to the 5s a week paid under the 1908 Pensions Act. Mortality had ensured that payments to over-70s amounted to only £8,500 per annum. As the 1925 Act introduced pensions at 65, the company believed that, with the majority of its pensioners in their sixties, it could save large sums. The company sought revisions to its funds in the hope of cutting costs by £63,000 per annum. Moreover, lump-sum gratuities to widows and orphans, which cost the company £5,300 a year, were ended.(107) The fact, however, that higher state pensions of 10s became payable at 65 was not justification under the 1921 Railways Act for altering customary benefits, and the L.N.E.R.'s friendly societies invoked its protection in 1926. The company believed it could win its case in court but preferred an amicable solution. It was mutually agreed to continue supplementing pensions by 50% for seven years after retirement.(108)

* * * * *

As a result of the Railways Act 1921, companies were required to maintain the levels of welfare benefits, and were not successful in streamlining company provision. Many of the friendly societies established by the pre-1921 companies survived even the nationalisation of the industry in 1947.

(vi) CONCLUSION

Railway companies, as the first businesses to tackle the managerial complexities of large-scale organisation, were equally innovators in labour managment and industrial welfare. The better managed railways, moreover, were undoubtedly the more systematic in the provision of welfare. The London and North Western introduced extensive company provision as an element of company re-organisation after 1846. The North Eastern Railway in the early 1900s established a line-and-staff management and restructured its welfare organisation. The L.N.E.R. during the Inter-War period was the most systematic in corporate and labour management.

The scale of the railways' investment in welfare was

possible because of secure profits and was necessitated by the creation of large internal labour markets. Yet, some trades continued throughout this period to rely on casual, unskilled labour,(109) while others only more gradually founded more capital-intensive concerns and the corporate structures they required. By the 20th Century, other industries began to adopt the scale and type of provision originally utilised by railways.(110) Such a commitment was indicative of the value placed by the railways upon the semi-skilled workforce employed on the permanent way. This made the industry active as an employers´ group in the drawing up of social legislation, and the Parliamentary experience it gained in negotiations over railway legislation proved invaluable in protecting company provision from encroachment by the state.(111)

NOTES

1. T.R.Gourvish Railways and the British Economy 1830-1914 (1980), p.9.
2. Cf. Ch.1, s.(ii)(d), esp. p.17; Ch.7, s.(viii).
3. Chandler (1973), pp.15-16.
4. Cf. P.S.Bagwell The Railway Clearing House in the British Economy, 1842-1922 (1968).
5. T.R.Gourvish "The Performance of British Railway Management after 1860: the Railways of Watkins and Forbes", Bus.Hist (1978), pp.186-200.
6. R.J.Irving "The Profitability and Performance of British Railways, 1870-1914", Econ.H.R. (1978), pp.186-200.
7. D.H.Aldcroft "The Efficiency and Enterprise of British Railways, 1870-1914" (1st pub. 1968), in Studies in British Transport History, 1870-1970 (1974). Aldcroft´s views on "entrepeneurial failure" in late Victorian Britain have, however, altered: cf. D.N.McCloskey Essays on a Mature Economy: Britain After 1840 (1971), passim.
8. Gourvish (1978), pp.186-200.
9. Chandler (1977), pp.79-97,102-4. Cf. also "The Railroads: Pioneers in Modern Corporate Management", Bus.H.R. (1965), pp.16-40. There is room for confusion in the terminology used to explain managerial structures (cf. Chandler, for example). The "district" or "divisional" system on the railways more closely corresponds to the "departmental" system adopted by large corporations in other industries, in which middle managers were answerable for their specialised functions only to a central headquarters. The railway´s "line-and-staff system" resembles the creation of fully autonomous units under the "divisional system" in other trades.
10. T.R.Gourvish Mark Huish and the LNWR: a study of management (1972), pp.109-11; "A British Business Elite: the

Chief Executives of the Railway Industry, 1850-1922", Bus.H.R. (1973), pp.289-316.
11. Rail 1008/93, 1st Report of LNWR Committee of Inquiry, 13 May 1848.
12. Gourvish (1972), p.153.
13. Rail 1008/93, 1st Report, 13 May 1848.
14. Ibid, 2nd Report, 10 June 1848. A formal pension scheme for LNWR staff was established in 1853 (cf. Rail 1086/2).
15. Ibid, 3rd Report, 15 July 1848. Cf. s.(iii) below.
16. Gourvish (1972), pp.106,108-9,116,164-5,167,170; M.R. Bonavia The Organisation of British Railways (1971), pp.13-15,18; Chandler (1977), p.107.
17. J.L.MacLean The British Railway System: a Description of the Work Performed in the Principal Departments (1883), pp.15,22,30,41,48-49,56,58.
18. Sir G.Findlay The Working and Management of an English Railway (1889), p.69.
19. Bonavia (1971), pp.21-23,26.
20. D.R.Lamb Modern Railway Management (1941), pp.4, 15-16.
21. Ibid.
22. Lamb (1941), pp.8,12-13,31.
23. Bonavia (1971), pp.28-29,31.
24. Lamb (1941), pp.2-4,5-6,13-14.
25. Bonavia (1971), pp.29-30.
26. P.W.Kingsford "Labour Relations on the Railways, 1835-1875", Jl. of T.H. (1953-54), pp.65-81. Cf. Ch.7, s.(ii) on textiles.
27. Rail 1008/93, LNWR, 3rd Report, 15 June 1848.
28. Ibid. Cf. Ch.7, s.(v).
29. Findlay (1889), pp.72-75,82-83.
30. J.Mavor The Scottish Railway Strike 1891: A History and a Criticism (1891), pp.49-50.
31. F.Pole, Preface to K.J.Norman Browne The Browne and other Systems of Railway Discipline (1923).
32. Browne (1923), pp.1,25.
33. Cf. M.C.Reed Investment in Railways in Britain, 1820-1844 (1975).
34. Rail 1008/10, L&BR, Board Minutes, 10 Oct 1839; Letter, 11 July 1860.
35. Rail 1008/93, LNWR, 3rd Report, 15 June 1848; Gourvish (1972), pp.61,95-7,113-4,153,155,174,264.
36. Findlay (1899), pp.77-81; Rail 1007/629.
37. Rail 1115/17, GWR Medical Fund Society, Half-Yearly Report for 31 Dec 1883 & 31 Dec 1895; Yearly Report for 1901.
38. Rail 1115/27, Report of GWR Provident Society, 1904.
39. Rail 250/751.
40. On Crewe and paternalism, cf. W.H.Chaloner The Social and Economic Development of Crewe, 1780-1923 (1950), pp.xix,45-51,146; & forthcoming Ph.D. thesis by D.Drummond of

Royal Holloway & Bedford New College. Such provision, however, was especially designed to attract skilled engineering labour to the workshops - cf. s.(iii). Swindon too was developed by the G.W.R. in the 1850s as a model village with a Mechanics Institute and Medical Centre. Cf. also the Calendonian Railways' Springburn and St Rollox works, and the North British Railway which also had works at Springburn, in J.Melling "British Employers and the Development of Industrial Welfare, c.1880-1920: an Industrial and Regional Comparison" (Glasgow Ph.D., 1980), pp.206-216.

41. Rail 1115/30, GWR Temperance Union, Annual Report 1912. By the 1920s, the Union was renamed the Social and Educational Union. Cf. ibid, 1922. As late as 1950, as B.R.'s Western Region Staff Association, it was considered "an integral part of the social life" of the men. Cf. ibid, 1950.

42. Rail 236/286, GNR, Memos, 13 May 1861, & 6 Sept 1861. On the destruction of urban working-class housing by railway building, cf. G.S.Jones Outcast London (1984), pp.161-4; H.J.Dyos "Railways and Housing in Victorian London", Jl. of T.H. (1955), pp.11-21,90-100, & "Some Social Costs of Railway Building in London", Jl. of T.H. (1957-8), pp.23-31; J.R. Kellett Railways and Victorian Cities (1979), pp.324-336.

43. Rail 236/317, No.18, GNR, Memos, 17 July, 15 Nov 1875; 11 May, 15 & 18 Nov, 14 Dec 1892.

44. Rail 1115/47, SER Provident Savings Bank, Annual Report for 1881,1886,1890.

45. Rail 226/526, GCR Memo., 1908.

46. Rail 226/372, Rules of GCR Mutual Provident and Accident Society, 1898.

47. Rail 390/338, GER Accident Fund, Memo., 16 March 1923.

48. Rail 236/362, Letter, 9 April 1888.

49. Findlay (1889), pp.77-80.

50. Cf. Ch.9, s.(ii).

51. Rail 226/372, GCR, Circular to members of Mutual Provident and Accident Society.

52. Rail 390/338, GER Accident Fund Scheme, Memo., 16 March 1923.

53. Herapath's Railway Journal, 3 June 1898.

54. Rail 226/372, GCR Memorandum, 21 Sept 1898.

55. Rail 226/372, Memo. on deficiency of Mutual Provident Society, 14 April 1894.

56. Rail 527/230, Memo., 10 Aug 1906. On the A.S.R.S. and the N.E.R., cf. P.S.Gupta "Railway Trade Unionism in Great Britain, c.1880-1900", Econ.H.R. (1966), pp.124-153.

57. Rail 527/1161, Letter to Secretary of NER, 8 March 1889; Letter, 11 March 1889.

58. In 1893, the NER's gross revenue was £7,183,463; net revenue £3,071,976: cf. R.J.Irving The North Eastern Railway Company, 1870-1914: an economic history (1976), p.285.

59. Rail 527/31, NER, Memo. for Board, 4 Dec 1902.

60. Rail 527/230, Board Memo. on Proposed Servants´ Pension Fund, 29 Jan 1903; Memo., 10 Aug 1906.
61. Railway News, 27 Feb 1897, p.365.
62. Ibid, 6 March 1897, p.389.
63. PP 1899 (C.9203) xxxiii 871. Report to the Home Department on Shop Clubs, Qs.3629-30.
64. PP 1910 (C.5349) lvii 35, pp.30,32; PP 1911 (C.5484) xxix-Pt.I 687, Qs.3548,3593.
65. Cf. P.J.Cain "Railway Combination and Government 1900-1914", Econ.H.R. (1972), pp.623-41.
66. Cf. G.Alderman "The Railway Companies and the Growth of Trades Unionism in the Late Nineteenth and Early Twentieth Century", H.J. (1971), pp.129-51; P.S.Bagwell The Railwaymen: a History of the N.U.R (1963), pp.275-7,284-5.
67. Railway News, 23 May 1908, p.912.
68. Rail 1007/629, LNWR Pension and Provident Society and the N.I. Act, April 1912, Appendix to a Memo.
69. Rail 1025/21, GWR Wages and Hours Arbitration, 10 May 1909, pp.19,32-4,72-3.
70. Railway News, 8 Aug 1908, p.278.
71. Rail 226/531, GCR, Memo., 1908.
72. Cf. Ch.9, s.(iii).
73. Rail 226/530, GCR Board, subject no.28, NI Act, 26 April 1912.
74. Rail 1115/43, LBSCR, Report of Provident Society, 1913.
75. Rail 1115/4, GNR Sick and Funeral Allowance Fund, Accounts, 31 Dec 1912.
76. Rail 527/1098, NER, Conditions of Service in the Traffic Department, 1912.
77. Rail 226/526, GCR and Joint Lines Friendly Societies, Statement of Accounts, 31 Dec 1911.
78. Rail 1007/629, LNWR Pension and Provident Society, Minutes of Meeting, 7 May 1912.
79. Cf. Aldcroft in Aldcroft (ed.) (1974), pp.42-3.
80. Rail 226/596, Circular from REC, 19 Aug 1914.
81. Ibid, GCR, Letter from S.Fay, 26 Aug 1914; Rail 1115/4, Report of NER Sick and Funeral Allowance Fund, 31 Dec 1917.
82. Railway News, 30 May 1919, pp.895,899. Cf. Chapter 8, s.(iii).
83. Ibid, 24 Oct 1919, pp.510,528; 31 Oct 1919, p.566.
84. Bagwell (1963), pp.377-379,382-3,397-8,404-11; Railway News, 24 Oct 1911, p.531.
85. H.Ellis British Railway History, Vol.II (1959), ch.iii. Cf. also Cain (1972), pp.623-641.
86. M.R.Bonavia Railway Policies between the Wars (1981), p.9. Cf. s.(ii).
87. Rail 390/439, Memo. by Organisation Committee on Welfare Work.
88. Ibid, LNER, Report on Welfare Work, Feb 1924.

89. Ibid, Memo. to Directors, 20 June 1924.
90. Rail 390/311, LNER, Pension Arrangements, 1924 Report.
91. Rail 390/439, LNER, Report on Welfare Work, Feb 1924.
92. Ibid, Welfare Committee Meeting, 30 July 1924.
93. Ibid, LNER, Transcript of meeting of N.E. Area Board and Cottage Homes and Benefit Fund, 22 April 1926.
94. Bonavia (1981), p.9.
95. Rail 1007/555, LNWR Hospital Fund, Memo., 19 May 1930.
96. LMS The LMS Centenary (1938), pp.156-9.
97. Rail 1115/49, Leaflet on LMS Hospital Fund, 1930; Rail 1007/555, Memo., LMS, 19 May 1930; LMS Railway Magazine, Dec 1923, pp.43-4,68; Jan 1924, pp.100-1,107-9; May 1924, pp.232,275-6,429-30; Oct 1924, pp.429-30; Nov 1924, pp.466-7; Dec 1924, pp.74-5,108,110-1,135,482,498-500.
98. LMS Railway Magazine, March 1925, p.108.
99. Unity, Dec 1925, p.119.
100. Bonavia (1981), p.9.
101. Rail 1115/23, cf. accounts for 1925.
102. Rail 250/244 & 1115/14.
103. Rail 425/4, LMS, G.P.Committee, 26 Oct 1923; memo., 5 Dec 1923.
104. Bonavia (1981), p.9.
105. Rail 1115/64, SR, Memo., 1930.
106. Rail 250/751, GWR, Pension Society.
107. Rail 390/546, Memos, Dec 1925, 5 & 8 Jan 1926.
108. Rail 390/439.
109. Cf. Ch.7, s.(i).
110. Cf. esp. Ch.4; also, Ch.6.
111. Cf. Ch.9.

Chapter 3

LABOUR IN THE METROPOLITAN GAS INDUSTRY

(i) INTRODUCTION

Both the railways and the gas industry were capital-intensive, naturally-monopolistic, joint-stock utilities. They were, therefore, increasingly subjected to government regulation throughout the 19th Century. London, due to its size and importance, was the object of the bulk of gas legislation. Being so little researched, the gas industry deserves investigation, and articles on the subject have so far focused on the development of regulatory legislation and its political implications.(1) But controlling legislation had a direct influence upon the profitability, management and commercial strategy of the companies. In the late 1860s, the Metropolitan gas concerns embarked upon a policy of amalgamation, rationalisation, and new investment. Returns to scale could be secured only by efficiently planning the distribution network over a large enough area. Avoiding the duplication of services reduced high capital costs.

The passing of controls over monopolistic pricing induced gas employers to refuse increases in labour costs, which could no longer just be passed on to the consumer. Gas legislation was similar in effect, therefore, to the Railway and Canal Traffic Act of 1894 because both helped provoke industrial strife. The complexity of managing gas companies was not as great as railway operations which had to be closely coordinated according to a pre-determined schedule and carried out despite the communication problems on a national, rather than a local or city-wide, scale. Yet, gas companies were too large to be administered by one man and were too capital-intensive to be owned by one family.

Gas employers imposed an autocratic regime. Managerial authority was exercised strictly in the industry because of the workers' ability to halt an essential supply. The necessity for work-discipline was also increased by the cost of capitalisation and machinery, and the need to keep it continually operative and productive. Gas employers failed,

53

however, to establish a large internal labour market because trade was affected by the seasonal demand for light which fluctuated throughout the year. It was necessary, nonetheless, to build up a "core" workforce, consisting principally of stokers who formed the majority of gas workers. Despite the scale of investment required in retorts, gas-holders, and mains, the industry depended upon the physical effort of men to stoke the coal from which the gas was extracted. Consequently, ex gratia paternalism was an inappropriate means of maintaining their loyalty, although much welfare provision in London did remain discretionary. Gas employers responded inadequately to the establishment of larger works and firms during the 1870s. Their general attitude continued to be that workers were servants who should simply have respect for the social status held by employers. Welfare in the gas industry was only gradually systemised as a response to serious labour strife in 1889, and copartnership was instrumental in the process of systemisation.

* * * * *

Section (ii) in this chapter outlines the development of gas legislation and its influence upon rationalisation and investment in new, larger works. Section (iii) analyses the effect of these changes upon labour relations and industrial welfare in the years before the First World War, when the basis of gas company labour policies was largely determined. Section (iv) looks at welfare provision in the years 1914 to 1939.

(ii) MUNICIPAL REGULATION AND RATIONALISATION

The Gas Light and Coke Company was the first enterprise to manufacture gas at a central works and to distribute it through pipes. Requiring a large capital-outlay, the company successfully applied to Parliament in 1810 to be incorporated as a joint-stock enterprise. In 1812, the G.L.C.C. was granted a statutory charter bestowing the right to lay underground pipes within the City of London, Westminister, and Southwark. The company could operate, consequently, without the consent of local authorities. It became known as the Chartered, although other companies in subsequent years were designated trading areas.(2) Competition, however, was possible, as non-statutory companies could operate with the permission of local authorities. Moreover, the trading-areas of statutory companies often overlapped.(3) Private gas companies, rather than municipal concerns, flourished in London, partly because no local authority was large enough to own a gas company until the founding of the Metropolitan Board of Works in 1855.

The necessary civic regulation of road-works and high capital-entry limited competition and increased monopolistic tendencies. Companies avoided the duplication of mains to secure greater returns on their investment.(4) Over-capitalised companies facing low returns restricted trading to mutually-agreed districts. Collusion encouraged the government regulation of prices and dividends, which by the 1840s were recognised as exorbitant.(5) Competition finally ended south of the Thames by 1853 and in north London by 1857.(6) The London vestries attributed high prices, low illuminating power, and weak gas-pressure to the policy of "districting". The Metropolis's 1861 Sale of Gas Act sanctioned the principle of monopolisitic trading areas,(7) "in order to economise Capital and avoid the too frequent opening of the public streets". But inspectors were appointed to investigate company accounts every three years to ensure that any dividends paid were justifiable, and maximum prices were set for particular qualities of gas.(8) Yet, the Honorary Secretary to London's "united vestries" believed the Bill had been emasculated. Municipalities were the only bulwark "against the giant joint-stock interest which is gradually absorbing all other interests in the House of Commons....." A clause seeking to link dividends with prices along a sliding-scale had been abandoned.(9)

The price of London's gas remained high, and its quality was said to be poor. The Corporation of London, therefore, published a Bill in 1866 seeking to municipalise the gas interests within its boundaries.(10) The G.L.C.C. and the Imperial Company, in parlous financial circumstances, responded by introducing Bills proposing their purchase by the Metropolitan Board of Works, but Parliament would not countenance the municipalisation of established companies.(11) Instead, the City of London's Gas Act 1868 appointed commissioners to judge whether dividends were a result of "due care and management". A Board of Gas Referees would decide on the maximum impurities to be allowed in gas supplies.(12) Moreover, the G.L.C.C., City, and Great Central companies had to submit within a year proposals for amalgamation which would reduce expenditure and reposition gas-works in less populous areas. Otherwise, three "impartial persons" would rule on the issue.(13) In the meantime, gas companies on the South Bank met the President of the Board of Trade and voluntarily agreed to amalgamations.(14) The provisions of the City of London Gas Act were extended to the G.L.C.C.'s trading area outside the City by another Act in 1868, and to the South Metropolitan and Imperial in 1869. London gas companies had to accept the rationalisation of London's gas supplies, and they preferred agreement to compulsion. The G.L.C.C. absorbed the two other City companies in 1870, and an Act in 1871 conferred upon the company powers to amalgamate with adjacent concerns if the terms of the 1868 Act were extended to them also. This Act and similar legislation for the South Metropolitan in 1876 was eventually to place the supply of London's gas in the hands of two companies.(15) They would gradually achieve uniformity in the price, illuminating power, and purity of supply on either side of the Thames.(16) Between 1879-1885, the S.M.G.C. amalgamated with three companies,(17) while, in the years 1870-76, the G.L.C.C. effected seven amalgamations, and four more were achieved by 1914.(18)

The G.L.C.C.'s acceptance of amalgamations derived from the new commercial strategy of its secretary, J.O. Phillips.(19) The Gas Light and Coke Company Act of 1868 provided for the erection of the world's largest gasworks at Barking, where the company could construct port facilities on the bank of the Thames. It was intended to supply a new and bigger concern, and the G.L.C.C., moreover, could reduce its costs by not having to tranport coal inland.(20) An efficient, well-located works supplying a larger trading area increased the ratio between sales and capital-expenditure. Moreover, demand was exceeding the potential of the company's three old works.(21) The G.L.C.C.'s financial position was saved by these developments. The company realised that by building Beckton it would be well placed to take over those companies with which it had to amalgamate.(22) Construction work at Beckton began in 1868, and gas was first produced there in 1870,(23) while an Act in 1870 specifically gave the G.L.C.C. the opportunity to supply adjacent companies in bulk.(24) As part of its expansionist policy, the South Metropolitan built new works at East Greenwich. The dual policy of centralised manufacture and amalgamations in London reduced leakages, and by 1875 had made the buying of coal cheaper by 4s a ton.(25)

The Metropolitan Board of Works, however, argued that price rises always followed amalgamations to pay for investments like Beckton.(26) In 1873, the Board complained that it was impossible for gas commissioners to assess the vague and immeasurable criterion of "due care and management". Though unable by law to pay shareholders above a 10% dividend, companies had just resorted to issuing new stock to existing shareholders.(27) In 1876, a bill for the amalgamation of the G.L.C.C. with the Imperial and Independent was accepted on condition that the new company agreed to the public auction of new shares and the automatic adjustment of prices with dividends along a sliding scale. Similar arrangements were introduced into the S.M.G.C. Act 1876.(28)

Rationalisation required companies to adjust internal management structures. The gas companies were too large to be run by a single man or family, and capital demands were so large that directors were appointed to represent shareholders. Courts of Directors met regularly to discuss operational matters, but they relied heavily upon the advice of station engineers and chief administrators. Head-offices collected revenue, purchased raw materials, and took responsibility for the processing and sale of by-products. Station engineers were in day-to-day charge of works, manufacture, mains, pipe-laying, distribution, and labour matters. The 19th

Century gas industry, with production and distribution matters separated from commercial decisions, had a basic departmental structure.(29)

The growth of gas outlets increased the size of operations. Home-lighting expanded in the 1880s with the introduction of the Welsbach mantle. Pre-payment meters for working-class homes were installed in the 1890s, and cooking, water and space heating appliances began to be sold. District offices were abandoned for showrooms in shopping centres, and this advancement in sales administration required greater managerial and financial resources.(30) At the S.M.G.C., there was an increase in the number of chief officers at head office before and during the Great War. While operational management remained mainly under the control of station-engineers, the methods of working in specialist functions were determined by others.(31)

Milne-Watson, who became Governor of the Chartered in 1918, believed in large-scale organisation. He was determined, moreover, to preserve labour relations during any transformation in the scale of industrial organisation by extending welfare schemes. In the 1920s, the G.L.C.C.´s area grew from 134 to 265 square miles, which Milne-Watson saw as a practical organisational limit. In 1934, A.E.Sylvester was employed to oversee financial policy and to increase the number of appliances and outlets for gas. Sylvester added a Budget Audit Department to the Rental, Gas Sales, Stores, Stove and Meter Departments. He saw "departmentalism" as inappropriate to the new size of the business. The concept of "territorial" as opposed to "departmental" organisation was adopted. All the company´s activities at the new divisional level were put under the charge of a single management officer, who had the help of a number of technical officers. Each divisional headquarters controlled the sub-offices and showrooms. The delivery work of the Stove and Meter department and the despatch of fitters became divisional responsibilities. This decision brought the better coordination of customer services. Trunk mains continued to be overseen by the chief Distributing Engineer, but local mains were laid and repaired by the divisions. The G.L.C.C. became a decentralised, divisional company during the 1930s, although the new structure was not completely established till 1941.(32)

* * * * *

The gas legislation of the 1860s was a compromise of benefit to the companies as well as to consumers in the Metropolis. Controls avoided the need for municipalisation, while amalgamations encouraged the formation of private monopolies. Regulation directly affected the scale and management of gas production, but the commercial strategies of the companies overlooked labour requirements. Without a labour and welfare policy suited to the changes which took place, industrial relations worsened. It was the industrial disputes of 1889 which convinced gas companies of the need to undertake the systemisation of welfare.

(iii) WORK-DISCIPLINE AND INDUSTRIAL WELFARE, 1860-1914

Despite extensive capital commitments, gas companies introduced few mechanised techniques in the 19th Century. Loading the retorts depended upon physical effort and the necessary cooperation of the stokers. A labour policy of work-discipline and industrial welfare aimed to maintain security of supply in an essential public service. But companies responded to the regulating of prices and dividends by increasing work-loads, and the centralisation of production increased the workers´ ability to combine. The threat of strikes in 1889 forced employers to concede an eight-hour day. As a tactic for regaining managerial control over the retort-house, the employers introduced systematic welfare schemes to replace ex gratia benefits. Moreover, the expansion of outlets during the 1890s helped reduce seasonal fluctuations in demand, and internal labour markets were expanded.(33)

Fully-fledged gas-stokers were semi-skilled workers enjoying permanent employment and high wages, and they, consequently, led disputes in the industry. Other hands were generally hired as casual workers in the Winter. Permanent stokers that were not required in the Summer were given alternative employment on repair or building work. They were offered "allowances, sick payment, and superannuation, and in some places holidays with full pay". Stokers learnt their trade in approximately a month, but becoming a "fully-fledged stoker" was marked by a celebration at the works.(34) New men were "Unused for the most part, to work in organised gangs, in which every unit depends upon the other". They were "unaccustomed to the clockwork regularity essential to good stoking" which "required incessant supervision, accentuated by the elimination of hopeless wasters". Then, to complete training, ".....all that is required is to gradually ´speed up´ the gangs....."(35) One of the reasons for paying benefits was to encourage trained work-teams broken up for the Summer to return in Winter. Even experienced temporary workers in London were sometimes found employment in trades with seasonally high demands in the Summer - as local bricklayers´ mates or dockers - and asked to return to the gas-works in the Winter. But the continuance of casual and temporary labour hindered the systemisation of company provision in the industry.(36)

Until 1830, the G.L.C.C.´s Court of Directors personally dealt with workmen as an "old-fashioned landowner" treated his servants. Four weeks´ sick-pay and allowances during the whole period of convalescence from industrial accidents were paid. Widows' grants of £5 or £10, according to the deceased's status or length of service, were awarded, and annual beanfeasts were held. As the company had increased in size, the Court dispensed with ex gratia sick-pay in 1830, and established a provident fund to which the company donated £20 per annum and money for the services of a surgeon. Weekly contributions of 4d or 6d secured benefits of 10s or 12s a week for six months. Old age and widows' pensions remained at the discretion of the Court's Pension and Allowance Committee, but in practice they accepted the advice of the station engineers who actually managed the men. A workers' pension scheme was suggested but turned down in 1843.(37) Pensions, however, were accepted as essential and expected in an industry where only the fittest could be retained in employment.(38) Discretionary payments allowed the company to exercise sanctions. Applicants for pensions in 1877 were refused for joining a strike five years earlier.(39) A church, school, and library were also provided at Beckton. Following an amalgamation with the Imperial Company, the sick funds were reconstituted in order to promote a single corporate identity. In 1872, the Indoor Society catered for waged employees at the works of the old Imperial Company, the Outdoor Society for the Imperial's fitters and mains-layers, and the Workmen's Society founded by the G.L.C.C. in 1830 paid benefits to the Chartered's employees. The last fund being insolvent, its members were transferred to the Indoor and Outdoor societies.(40) A Sick and Burial Fund was founded at the South Metropolitan in the 1842, and a pension scheme in 1855.(41) The S.M.G.C. also provided Christmas gifts, and one week's paid holiday after a year's employment or two week's paid holiday after two years at the company. But all those granted holidays had to visit the country or the seaside in order to counter the debilitating affects of retort-house work.(42)

Both labour and capital had to be planned during the rationalisation of the industry in the 1870s. The S.M.G.C. built workers' houses when its works were relocated.(43) The G.L.C.C. constructed homes at Beckton, otherwise "the operations of the Company could not be carried on advantageously on such a site". Some workers had to live nearby to cope with emergencies like foggy weather.(44) The houses were let to workers from 1872 "subject to the Enquiries to be made by the Superintendant... as to their character being satisfactory".(45)

Labour disputes were rare in the industry, but not unknown. Strikers had been instantly dismissed at the Chartered as early as 1834.(46) It was the harshness of work rather than wages which proved the major cause of labour problems. Stoking was an arduous trade carried out in intense heat and smoke. Twelve hour days were normal, and, to enable the change-over of shifts on Sunday, men had to work twenty-four hours. Thorne, the gas-workers´ leader, recounts how it took three to four days "to feel normal again" from such long stretches of "inhuman labour". Foremen were employed to check meters and to increase the efforts of teams lagging in output.(47) In 1867, delegations from four G.L.C.C. works requested that the working-day be cut from 12 to 8 hours,(48) but the directors would not accept such a rise in labour costs.(49) When wage increases were agreed by the Metropolitan companies in 1871 as a result of reported labour agitation, many companies axed their annual and monthly holidays. No "increase in the working expenses per 1,000 feet of gas sold" occurred because "you may pay higher wages and get more work".(50) Further agitation in 1872 induced the G.L.C.C.´s directors to grant additional wage increases. The station engineers had advised them on the damage a strike would cause. But shorter hours and a six day week were refused, and an unsuccessful strike, led by the men at Beckton, followed.(51) Strikers were sacked and those living in company houses were evicted.(52) Parts of London were in darkness for six hours, ten weeks passed before production levels were restored, and £30,000 in profits were lost. All the companies met to make preparations against future workers´ combinations. One works superintendant, aware of losses in productivity, wanted to re-employ the strikers, but the directors refused out of principle. The new men were asked to sign weekly contracts of employment. By having to give seven days´ notice before leaving their work, the gasworkers effectively renounced sudden strikes and their chief bargaining counter. The strike leaders were prosecuted.(53)

Gas employers objected to labour unions. Yet, the secretaries of Metropolitan gas concerns met regularly in order to hold down wage-levels. When the men at the G.L.C.C. in 1865 had requested a wage of 3/6d a day, representative delegations of the "two classes" of men from the retort-house and the yard were summoned to the Court and informed of its decision.(54) Workers could petition for an increase in wages but the directors´ decision was non-negotiable. Attempts to form a union in 1872, 1884 and 1885 failed.(55) The strike in 1872 was denounced because the tie of master and man, forged by "patriarchial care", had been broken.(56) Employers were entitled to respect from their employees because of "the position in which they are placed".(57) The Journal of Gas Lighting concluded in 1889 that it was an attribute of the status of an employer that he could dismiss his workers without giving reasons. Only salaried staff had contracts setting out conditions for the termination of employment.(58) Gasworkers were expected to show the same discipline and loyalty required of other national services like the Army and Navy. But the object of management was to " bind them to your house by the stomach (rather) than by the legs ".(59) The total authority of employers to hire and fire, a labour surplus, high wages, and sickness and pension schemes were all designed to produce a well-disciplined and cooperative workforce.

When the National Union of Gas and General Labourers was formed on the 23rd April 1889 to reduce the hours of labour, stokers had been complaining of overwork for nearly a quarter of a century.(60) London's gas employers were surprised by the union's solidarity,(61) and so, by May, agreed to an 8 hour day. The number of retorts to be loaded per shift was reduced from 76 to 72 on the further insistence of the men. George Livesey of the South Metropolitan, however, made these concessions to gain time for the enlisting of black-leg labour.(62) Unlike other employers, he would not agree to a closed shop, and, on the 5th September, a strike was called at the S.M.G.C.(63) Strikers were immediately sacked. Livesey publicly declared that the union should not interfere with management, but the G.L.C.C. opposed a calling of the joint committee of Metropolitan gas directors to discuss the issue. Indeed, the G.L.C.C.'s Court gave the station engineers full power to discuss "Labour management" with the union "for the maintenance of order and work". The union was best organised at the G.L.C.C., although it remained unrecognised there.(64) Blacklegs at the S.M.G.C. did not obtain an "ordinary system of working" till January 1890. The strike, which cost the company £250,000, did not end till the 4th February 1890, and full gas pressure was not restored till the 13th.(65) By June, the London gas companies had begun to impose monthly contracts of work as an anti-strike tactic. Men at the G.L.C.C. were reputed to "down tools" 2-3 times a week. The company also began to build up coal stocks, and applied to the government for assistance. Troops at Chatham were made ready to replace any strikers at Beckton.(66)

The Journal of Gas Lighting remarked during the strike that there was "a stir in the minds of gas directors" about new machinery.(67) Water gas, the inclined retort, stoking machinery, automatic loading, and vertical retorts were installed in the 1890s and early 1900s.(68) By 1908, numbers in the retort-house had fallen by 50%. New machinery lessened the employers' dependence upon the stokers' work-skills at "the point of danger".(69) By 1910, 2 or 3 men could achieve the output which had once required 12 workers.(70) But Livesey at the South Metropolitan also founded in October 1889 "a special system of Profit-sharing" as a means of averting strikes. S.M.G.C. foremen had been profitsharers since 1886, and workers already received weekly bonuses once their shift produced above a standard output. A means of maintaining supervisory control was transformed into an all-encompassing labour strategy. By offering workers the right to a division of the profits, the scheme changed the company's constitution, and a permissory Act of Parliament had first to be obtained.(71)

Livesey believed that the absence of a firm bond between employers and men was ultimately responsible for the dispute in 1889. He - at least avowedly - preferred copartnership labour to new machinery as a means of countering industrial strife.(72) Profitsharing was suited to the gas industry. It marked, firstly, the end of discretionary paternalism as the "old social habits and personal relationships of the workers underwent a radical change" due to the growth in the size of companies. Welfare could be placed on a more orderly footing. Secondly, it was an extension of the sliding-scale arrangements introduced, for one, at the S.M.G.C. in 1876 for the benefit of consumers. Higher dividends were paid only if prices were reduced. Workers´ bonuses likewise would be paid when dividends increased, prices fell, and productivity improved. The 1889 scheme set a bonus of 1% of annual wages for every 1d reduction below the price of 2/8d charged for 1,000 cubic feet of gas. The price in 1899 was 2/3d. Workers´ capital could not be withdrawn for five years and was deposited with the company at 4%. To become profitsharers, the more permanent men had to sign on for 12 months, and effectively renounced participation in sudden strikes. Temporary employees committed themselves for 3 months.(73) Workers were not only enticed by the bonuses, but by the offer of security of employment.

The Profitsharing Committee, established in 1889, consisted half of employers´ nominees and half of elected workers. Labour relations and industrial welfare were institutionalised and taken from the sole control of the station engineers. The Committee administered the various provident funds, and discussed work-conditions and pay. Managerial autocracy was tempered by a degree of consultation, although the directors retained an ultimate veto. A worker could take any grievance to the Profitsharing Committee,(74) which appointed a Safety Committee in 1892. The cooperation of the workforce was recognised as integral to the enforcement of safety-procedures. A jury of twelve workers adjudicated on the causes of accidents and granted compensation payments. After the passing of the 1897 Workmen´s Compensation Act, an Accident Fund was established which enabled the company to contract out of the legislation.(75) The Profitsharing Committee also administered the Superannuation Fund.(76) In 1898, profitsharing at the S.M.G.C. added some 7-8% or 5d to 7d a day to wages, and the South Metropolitan produced gas 1/- per ton of coal cheaper than the average. S.M.G.C. men did not work to union rules, and ignored stipulations about the numbers of charges to be made per shift. The efficiency and energy of South Metropolitan workers were generally recognised and attributed to the profitsharing scheme,(77) which became copartnership in 1898 with the election of two worker-directors. A Copartnership Committee was formed in 1899. Significantly, the staff obtained the right to elect a

director only in later years.(78)
    Makins, governor of the G.L.C.C., objected to the "hybrid
species of Director" because to him the interests of employer
and worker were inherently opposed and the social barrier was
insuperable. Managerial authority had to be total if industry
was to be efficiently run.(79) Management was responsible for
profits and losses, and the worker had merely to offer
faithful service.(80) The characters of the two chairmen were
contrasted. Livesey was the "the prophet, the projector, the
pioneer", Makins´ approach was conservative. Livesey believed
that Makins´ views were representative of gas employers and
unsuited to the modern gas industry. Before 1889, employers
were "regarded as the fathers of their workpeople" and labour
relations could be conducted informally. Trade unionism had
challenged the institution of mastership, and only "the
argument of the pocket" could win back the allegiance of
workers. Workmen would no longer be treated as deferential
servants. The chief question was how "to give responsibility
to everyone in society - without changing their status".(81)
Livesey´s answer was to make workers "property-owners" in the
business that employed them. They would as a result also
become better citizens.(82) In 1906, Livesey adopted the
language of reform to decry the "serious inequalities of
wealth which abound in the existing social system". But only
copartnership could "distribute wealth in the most efficient
manner". While the working-class had failed themselves by a
lack of providence, employers were culpable by not helping
them to become property-owners.(83)
    The G.L.C.C. founded a non-contributory pension fund in
1895 for regular employees. It was modelled upon a scheme at
the Great Eastern Railway where Makins was a director. It was,
moreover, "a kind of set-off to Mr Livesey´s profitsharing
scheme" because "it will have the same effect" in "that the
men will like the service of the company better". The
Secretary, Field, believed that every advantage given to the
men reflected upon the company. He denied that the G.L.C.C.
was dominated by the Gasworkers Union because it refused to
meet its representatives, but union strength probably deterred
the company from introducing profitsharing in 1889. Great
reliance was still placed on the fact workers could voice any
grievance to the station engineers.(84) A worker was
compulsorily retired at 65, and received a pension of a third
of his wages of 35s a week after 25 years´ service, if he had
"a good record as a workman". The inadequacies of the
Provident Fund continued to be covered by the company, and
various sports and social clubs were founded at Beckton in the
1890s. It was admitted that the motive behind the company´s
greater interest in welfare since the labour strife of 1889
was to offset the gradual enforcement of stricter
discipline.(85)
    By 1900, four companies other than the South Metropolitan

offered profitsharing contracts. In 1908-9, nineteen gas concerns introduced profitsharing or copartnership schemes. Eight more followed this example between 1910-12. By 1913, gas companies accounted for 33 of the 133 profitsharing schemes listed by the 1912 Royal Commission.(86) Although the gas industry was particularly suited to profitsharing, there is no clear reason for its sudden expansion within 4 years. Livesey had publicised profitsharing as a solution to the railway dispute in 1907. Strikes, moreover, occurred in provincial gas companies throughout 1912-13 over the questions of minimum wages and maximum hours.(87) Many companies concluded that their existing pension and provident clubs were insufficient to meet the new situation. Whereas "sick, pension, and other funds had not cured disaffection amongst the workers", profitsharing bonuses had the advantage of being paid presently and constantly.(88)

The Journal of Gas Lighting also believed that the Liberal government elected in 1905 was committed to "class" legislation. The Gas Labourers Union was still campaigning for an eight hour day, when the Liberals passed the "socialistic" 1908 Mines (Eight Hours) Act. It increased the price of the coal used for producing gas, and set a precedent for other industries. Gas companies also feared the municipalisation of public utilities. The Progressive-controlled London County Council began purchasing tramway companies after 1891, and the Metropolitan Water Board was formed in 1903. Spreading the ownership of gas concerns amongst workers was a counter to demands for public purchase.(89)

Moreover, gas companies had not generally sought statutory authority for industrial welfare, despite being regulated by Act of Parliament. Those companies which had altered their articles of association to undertake profitsharing and copartnership schemes were in this sense exceptional, and the legality of other aspects of welfare in the industry was questionable. Some concerns, therefore, began to seek specific statutory permission for benefit funds. The Brighton and Hove Gas Company was granted its Benefit Funds Act in 1912. The legislation was seen as systemising and assuring the free pensions which had been available at the company for forty years. The aim was to establish "rights" and replace discretionary benefits. Six other gas companies applied for similar legislation in the same year, although in reality there was little fear of Parliament halting welfare benefits.(90) Other gas employers responded by introducing profitsharing schemes which legalised and systemised their provident payments.

At the G.L.C.C., the succession of Makins by Corbet Woodal as Governor in 1908 was significant. Woodal had a more progressive outlook to labour relations, and introduced copartnership in three other concerns where he was a director.(91) Woodal was determined to rescue the company from

the "impertubable conservatism of the old Board". He was
critical of the "Manchester School" view that cheap production
depended upon cheap labour. Woodal's ideal was "that every
industry and every firm shall be united in the pursuit of its
own corporate welfare". The rights of humanity as well as
capital had to be protected, particularly within the anonymity
of a large joint-stock enterprise.(92) Autocratic management
was depicted as anachronistic. By 1912, Woodal's chief success
was declared to be the statesman-like "way in which he has
humanised the whole corporate life of the vast century-old
institution......."(93) He established a complaints procedure
which the men could use without fear of victimisation.(94)

Although the G.L.C.C.'s pension scheme was central to its
industrial relations policy, the company had not calculated
its costs. Faced with increasing losses by 1908, the G.L.C.C.
had to implement economies,(95) and it was hoped to replace
the expense of guaranteed pensions with copartnership.
Copartnership was established at the G.L.C.C. on the 9th
October, 1909.(96) Employees received a half per cent bonus
for a 1d fall in the price of gas. £5 had to be accumulated
before half of all bonuses above that figure could be
withdrawn, and the remainder had to be invested in company
stock. The scheme applied to regular employees and to winter
hands who agreed "to work well and faithfully". Temporary
workers were given their bonus on the 30th June if they
promised to return the following winter and left half of their
bonus on deposit with the company. A copartnership committee
of 18 members appointed by the directors and 18 elected by
copartners with 5 years' service was charged with
administering the scheme.(97) Social and educational life at
Beckton was extended by the Copartnership Committee with the
provision of a rifle club, boy scout units, and football,
cricket, and swimming teams.(98)

The G.L.C.C. was, in addition, concerned that the 1908
Old Age Pensions Act would undermine company retirement
allowances. Relieving old age poverty and copartnership were
viewed as a single question on the grounds that retired
workers who possessed capital would not require pensions. The
1908 Act was opposed as the possible first instalment of a
larger policy which could stifle the industrial pension and
benefit funds which united employers and employees.(99) While
the companies at first intimated that they could not afford
the burden of state and industrial pensions, they never
seriously considered the abandonment of private
provision.(100) Nor did legislation seriously weaken the
effectiveness of old age allowances. The G.L.C.C. merely
reduced their pensions by 5s a week to ensure that workers in
retirement received the state pension and an aggregate,
average allowance of 13s.(101) In a attempt to reduce costs,
the General Manager of the Chartered together with the
Copartnership Committee on the 15th March, 1910 proposed

replacing discretionary pensions by a contributory system. The suggestion was declined by the Board because of the possible resentment from the men, who would have to begin making payments. The company, therefore, failed to tackle the problem which the increasing cost of generous, ex gratia pensions presented. Indeed, the maximum allowance was increased in December 1910.(102)

When the National Insurance Bill 1911 was enacted, the Governor of the Chartered presided at a meeting of the provident societies. They agreed unanimously to contract out.(103) The two societies were amalgamated and the rules were revised to accord with the Act. A Supplementary Society was also founded and was supported by a 1d donation per member from the Court. Members petitioned for widows and orphans' benefits to continue, and the company agreed with the proviso that workers contribute an extra 1d per fortnight to the Supplementary Society.(104) A committee of management and twelve sub-committees were appointed. They tackled the detailed tasks of administering medical and sanatorium benefits, stamping medical cards, and appointing doctors to the Society's panel. Woodal gave his wholehearted support to the Act, calling it a "blessing and Godsend to the poor and sick". The secretary of the old Outdoor Society assumed that role for the new Approved Society, while his counterpart in the Indoor Society became Treasurer.(105) A committee representing all grades of employees at the S.M.G.C. agreed that the existing Sick Fund could not be an Approved Society and established the Employees (1912) Fund in its place. The Copartnership Committee was empowered to act on behalf of workmen in Approved Society matters. The Sick and Burial Fund was continued by the company in order to pay supplementary benefits.(106)

* * * * *

Good wages and welfare payments encouraged faithful service amongst stokers. Company provision remained on the whole discretionary and non-contributory, due to the industry's reliance on casual labour. Welfare did, however, contribute to the establishment of a "core" labour-force. Permanent stokers were the main beneficiaries of company provision, because their role and numbers in the retort-house made them crucial to the maintenance of gas supplies. The expansion of the Metropolitan gas industry in the 1870s left companies increasingly vulnerable to strikes by stokers whose physical efforts alone sustained output. Labour management and the granting of welfare benefits remained autocratic and often ad hoc. Livesey's response to the 1889 strike was ruthlessly to smash the union at the S.M.G.C., and to initiate a profitsharing scheme. Company provision was increased at the South Metropolitan and the G.L.C.C. after the strike, and set benefits began increasingly to be given as a right. Moreover, the decline in the use of casual labour in the 1890s furthered the systemisation of welfare and its extension to Winter workers. The industry's twin strategy of introducing new technology and extending welfare provision after 1889 undoubtedly undermined the National Union of Gasworkers. In 1891, it was 60,000 strong; by 1908, it members numbered 32,318.(107) Yet, the effectiveness of profitsharing and copartnership as an anti-strike tactic is difficult to measure. Strikes, in any case, had been and continued to be rare in the gas industry. But profitsharing and copartnership did improve the stability of employment and the workers' economic security, and they established representative institutions within the company. The lack of employment rights and labour's inability to influence and negotiate work conditions, pay, and hours undoubtedly contributed to industrial strife in general during this period.(108) Whereas profitsharing and copartnership assumed only a small importance in most industries, market circumstances enabled them to become a major influence in the administration of industrial welfare in the gas industry.

(iv) THE EXTENSION OF WELFARE PROVISION, 1914-1939

In August 1914, the Gas Light and Coke Company established a fund to provide for the dependants of employees sent as territorials in the London Rangers to France. Full compensation was paid for any loss of wages while on active service.(109) By September, the Copartnership Committee had founded the "G.L.C.C. War Distress Fund". It was financed by a subscription of one quarter of all copartnership bonuses.(110) The South Metropolitan received over a thousand letters during the War from men at the front. Many expressed hope of returning to the company and appreciation of the help given to their families.(111)

War-conditions, however, threatened the industry's copartnership agreements. As the price of gas increased, dividends which were paid according to a sliding-scale were squeezed, and some companies ceased to pay profitsharing bonuses.(112) The government, moreover, assumed the right to fix wages, and gas workers received the substantial advances of other munitions workers. By 1918, gas employers were seeking to resume total control over the determination of wage-rates,(113) but the government established a Joint Industrial Council.(114) Membership of the gas workers' union had increased, and stoppages, involving the G.L.C.C., occurred in September 1918 over the employment of non-union workers.(115) Labour shortage during the War had enhanced union bargaining power. The Coalition Government hoped that Joint Councils would reduce industrial strife by ensuring workers had negotiating rights. Collective bargaining and official company recognition strengthened the unions as representative organisations, and helped prevent unofficial strikes. The Councils were intended, therefore, to encourage union membership. Because of this, Carpenter of the S.M.G.C. argued for the founding of an independent federation of gas concerns, which would institute bargaining with workers outside any state system of councils.(116)

The Gas Industrial Council was appointed in 1919, and wage negotiations began in October 1921. Awards were automatically made according to a sliding scale based on a cost-of-living index.(117) But employers continued to rely on company provision instead of collective bargaining, and this reliance influenced the final form of the industry's joint councils. The Whitley structure consisted of one central and many regional and works committees.(118) The regional committees were appointed to draw up the constitution of their respective works committees. They generally failed to do so, because the employers opposed the possible interference of unions in management at the level of the shop-floor.(119) The works committees formed in London during 1919 were established by the companies as an extension of copartnership.(120) They were chaired by the station engineers,(121) and their function was advisory only. The introduction of these committees, indeed, was designed to pre-empt and forestall the proposed state system of Whitley councils. They were meant to improve efficiency by utilising the experience of workers, who in turn would be educated about the problems of management.(122) Carpenter founded independent works committees at the S.M.G.C. and its subsidiary, the South Surburban. They were effectively works branches of the central Copartnership Committee, which made it clear that it did "not recognise the claim of any other body or organisation to interfere with this Committee's powers or decisions" about conditions of employment at the company.(123) Carpenter preferred industrial welfare because he believed Whitley to be merely two adversaries facing each other. By 1922, he pointed out, South Metropolitan workers owned £500,000 in capital, and both union and non-union employees signed copartnership agreements despite the limitations they set on the freedom to strike.(124) Even sports promoted a "feeling of part-ownership" because they demonstrated the employer's concern for his worker's social life and not just for his worktime activities. Consequently, sports grounds were more effective, in terms of labour relations, if they were sited some distance from the works.(125)

At a G.L.C.C. Copartnership Committee meeting in July 1919, both employers and employees recognised that copartnership, pensions, and double holiday-pay promoted mutual understanding. Although copartnership bridged the gap between capital and labour, it was held that the works committees to be established at every plant would increase day-to-day cooperation. The Deputy Governor in July 1919 hoped "that the Works Committees might take the place of the Whitley Council and all the difficulties of the Company could then be worked out round that table, and it would be very gratifying for the Governor to be able to meet the various demands as they arose instead of referring them to arbitration or Government Departments".(126) Works committees could make representations to works management, and through the central Copartnership Committee to the directors. Suggestions on work-methods were particularly encouraged.(127) Yet, Copartnership Committee meetings in this period were dominated by the Governor, Milne-Watson. The numbers voting in copartnership elections, the commissioning of Milne-Watson's portrait, or the sending of congratulations to the winners of company awards were typical of its discussions.(128) Milne-Watson attributed the industry's good industrial relations to the existence and the expansion since 1918 of welfare.(129) It was claimed that supplies were retained throughout the General Strike of 1926 because of the good feeling engendered by company provision.(130) If, as Milne-Watson said in 1928, "Copartnership is the vehicle by which (the 'family spirit' in industry) can be reached", its concrete embodiment was the pension funds, benefit schemes, distress funds, and the sports associations gathered around the copartnership scheme itself. They gave workers "an opportunity of taking part in the activities of the Company" without actually interfering in management. Welfare benefits built up that degree of worker loyalty which was essential to any large-scale company.(131)

Increased company provision at the G.L.C.C. in the 1920s involved the creation of a central catering department which took charge of canteens previously organised at each station and office.(132) New sports grounds and medical facilities were established.(133) Gas companies could also be exempted from the Unemployment Insurance Act 1920 if they guaranteed jobs for life, but this onerous condition was unacceptable.(134) The G.L.C.C. decided, nonetheless, that its Employees Insurance Society should make arrangements with the National Federation of Employees' Approved Societies to found a supplementary society under the Act. The Federation was headed by Henry Lesser, who had previously administered the South Metropolitan's provident societies. Weekly subscriptions of 2d secured 7/6d in addition to state benefits for fifteen weeks of unemployment. 4s was available to men out of work for another ten weeks. All unemployment benefits, basic and supplementary, were received from the society rather than from the employment exchange.(135)

An Employees Benefit Fund was established in 1920. It replaced the Employees Insurance Society which had provided additional benefits under the 1911 National Insurance Act.(136) Due to inflation after the War, subscriptions and benefits had to be revised.(137) The G.L.C.C. believed that the introduction of the Employees Benefit Fund was appreciated because the company "know how valuable is the feeling of security and independence which membership of such a Society can ensure". All workmen under 45 could join, and contributions, matched by the company, were set at 3d a week. Benefits included the payment of doctors´ fees and medicines, and guaranteed sick allowances of 18s for thirteen weeks, 10s for a subsequent thirteen weeks, and 6s for the next twenty-six. Death benefits of £14 or £6 for members or wives and widows were also available, and widows´ and orphans´ allowances were provided. The company paid the Fund´s administrative costs.(138)

In 1919, the G.L.C.C. spent some £23,000 on voluntary and non-voluntary pensions "because you get far better work out of a man if he feels that you are going to treat him well when he goes".(139) A contributory G.L.C.C. (Non-Staff) Pension Fund was finally established in 1921.(140) The firm´s 1,000 pensioners became its responsibility, but their allowances continued to be funded by the company. Contributions were set at 1s a week, and the company donated £50,000 to start the fund. Retirement was set at 60 after 40 years´ service, with employment before 1921 being taken into account.(141) The company was concerned about the effect of the 1925 Pensions Act upon the Fund.(142) The G.L.C.C. committed itself, therefore, to generous contributions, totalling £11-12,000 per annum, in order to induce workers to retain membership of the Fund. The Court and the Copartnership Committee agreed that employees should pay full amounts to both company and state funds, and so receive two pensions.(143)

By 1925, the S.M.G.C.´s Copartnership Committee administered the accident fund, hospital treatment, a provident society, an unemployment insurance scheme, and a superannuation fund.(144) The company had set up a supplementary fund under the 1920 Unemployment Insurance Act, and benefits were collected from the company´s pay-office.(145) The S.M.G.C. founded an Approved Society under the 1925 Pensions Act, called the Copartnership Insurance Fund, at a cost of £3,000 per annum. Discretionary pensions for those not covered by the Act continued to be paid under the Employees (1912) Fund at the largesse of the Court.(146) The Employees Widows and Orphans Fund, whose company contributions were ended after 1925, was wound up in 1930, but money to help in needy cases could still be obtained from the Livesey Bequest.(147) Copartnership rules were altered in 1929 to allow those employed "for periods of uncertain duration" to participate in the scheme. They agreed to remain "sober, honest, (and) industrious", and to perform all work allotted to them. But the agreements could be terminated with a week´s notice.(148) Savings bank, social, medical and sports club facilities were all extended in the 1920s.(149)

In 1931, Industrial Welfare believed that "No industry has done more for welfare than the gas industry", and praised the G.L.C.C. for realising that industrial success depended "on the keen co-operation of all who are in the company's service". Its employees by 1931 held £850,000 in shares.(150) Actuarial valuations of the Approved Society in 1935 led to increases in benefits. Convalescent accommodation, medical and surgical appliances, and opthalmic treatment were also made available.(151) Because welfare at the G.L.C.C. in 1937 was a "considered", all-embracing policy, the absence of hospital benefits was regretted. 65% of its employees subscribed to the Hospital Services Association or the Hospital Saturday Fund, but the company wanted to involve the other 35%. The Employees Benefit and Hospital Society was established to expand the provision of convalescent homes, sanatoria, surgical appliances, spectacles, ambulance services and visiting nurses. Its rules were drawn up by a sub-committee of the Copartnership Committee, and its administrative costs were borne by the firm. The scheme was thought to round "off the work of the Company with regard to welfare...." A new pension scheme in 1939 allowed over-55s to begin subscribing.(152)

* * * * *

The basis of company provision was largely determined before 1914, and only extended during the Inter-War period. The early introduction of works committees forestalled government interference through Whitley Committees and merely continued the tradition of copartnership. Industrial welfare was highly systemised in the gas industry because it was composed of large companies and had a managerial structure which dealt with the complexities of its operations. Indeed, by 1937, the Chartered had 50,000 employees, about one-fiftieth of the breadwinners in the Home Counties. Its welfare schemes, therefore, were calculated to affect 125,000 people.(153) The need for loyal and efficient service in an essential supply service was reflected in the industry's commitment to company provision.

(v) CONCLUSION

The development of industrial welfare in the gas and railway industries has parallels. Monopoly enabled them to finance a variety of relatively generous schemes. Both sought to maximise the returns on large-scale investments by minimising work-disaffection, and transport and fuel supplies were particularly vulnerable to strikes. Unlike railways, however, even the world's largest gas company, the G.L.C.C., did not require a divisional managerial structure till the 1930s. But gas companies were large-scale businesses by contemporary standards. It was primarily the continuance of seasonal employment for some workers which encouraged the retention of discretionary welfare in the 19th Century, despite the existence of some contributory schemes. As a result of the 1889 strike, welfare was gradually systemised and eventually came to match the size of gas companies and its departmental management. The copartnership system finally adopted at the South Metropolitan so effectively resisted trades unionism and increased productive efficiency that it was generally introduced throughout the industry by 1914. The S.M.G.C. was regarded as more efficient and innovative than the G.L.C.C, and Livesey directly attacked Makins´ competence.(154) Worker share-ownership, "participation" in management, more secure employment, and increased welfare facilities provided an answer to the industry´s special vulnerability to strikes.

NOTES

1. Cf. D.A.Chatterton "State Control of the Public Utilities in the Nineteenth Century: the London Gas Industry", Bus.Hist. (1972), pp.168-78. Cf. also M.Falkus "The Early Development of the British Gas Industry, 1790-1815", Econ.H.R. (1982), 2nd ser., vol.xxxv, pp.217-234; "The British Gas Industry before 1850", Econ.H.R. (1967), 2nd ser., vol.xx, pp.494-518; "The Development of Municipal Trading", Bus.Hist. (1977), vol.xix, pp.134-161.
2. Cf. C.Singer et. al., A History of Technology (1954-78), Vol.IV, ch.9.
3. J.Reeson Acts Relating to the Supply of Gas and Water by Companies and Local Authorities (1902), pp.115-21.
4. Chatterton (1972), pp.168-78.
5. PP 1867 (C.18-I) lviii 497, Letter No.24.
6. PP 1867 (C.520) xii 1, p.3.
7. GLCC The History of the G.L.C.C. (1912), pp.38-42.
8. PP 1860 (C.78) iii 485, p.501; PP 1875 (C.281) xii 1, Qs.4568-5590.
9. PP 1867 (C.520) xii 1, Letter regarding 1860 Act.
10. PP 1867 (C.18-I) lviii 565, Letter No.24; PP 1867 (C.520) xii 1, p.3; PP 1875 (C.281) xii 1, Qs.19-23.
11. Hansard, 13 May 1875, 5th ser., vol.224, cols.611-6.
12. PP 1867 (C.520) xii 1, p.3.
13. PP 1867-68 (C.49) cxv 459.
14. Hansard, 13 May 1875, vol.224, cols.619-621.
15. Chatterton (1972), pp.168-78; PP 1899 (C.294) x 19, note 50.
16. Journal of Gas Lighting, 14 Feb 1871, p.105; 28 Feb 1871, pp.144-5.
17. South Metropolitan Gas Company Co-partnership Almanack(1909).
18. GLCC (1912), p.99.
19. B/NTG/2117.

20. PP 1875 (C.281) xii 1, Qs.300-11.
21. PP 1899 (C.294) iv 19, Evidence of G.Livesey.
22. B/NTG/2084, Evidence of Beck to Commons, 1867; B/NTG/2085, note 64.
23. GLCC (1912), p.79.
24. Reeson (1902), pp.513-6.
25. PP 1875 (C.281) xii 1, Qs.6639-6688,6791-2.
26. Ibid, Qs.216-20.
27. PP 1899 (C.294) x 19, Board of Trade Returns, 25 July 1876.
28. Chatterton (1972), pp.168-78.
29. S.Everard The History of the Gas Light and Coke Company (1949), p.279.
30. Ibid, pp.277-8.
31. B/S.Met.G./111/17/1, 17 May 1916.
32. Everard (1949), pp.311-313,333,349-351.
33. F.A.Popplewell in S.Webb & A.Freeman Seasonal Trades (1912), pp.184-5 notes that the difference in the numbers employed in the industry between the busiest and slackest weeks declined from 53.4% in 1885 to 20.4% in 1906.
34. Journal of Gas Lighting, 17 Sept 1889, pp.541-2; W.Thorne My Life's Battles (1925), p.36.
35. Journal of Gas Lighting, 21 Jan 1890, p.105.
36. Ibid, 14 Aug 1888, pp.286-7.
37. B/NTG/2021-2051; B/GLCC/38/1, 6 May 1887; Everard (1949), pp.116,121.
38. PP 1899 (C.294) x 19, Qs.2475-78.
39. B/GLCC/38/1, 20 May 1887.
40. Everard (1949), pp.207,240,266-7.
41. PP 1899 (C.294) x 19, Q.3482.
42. Thorne (1925), p.51.
43. C.Carpenter Industrial Copartnership (1927), p.51.
44. PP 1899 (C.294) x 19, Q.3040.
45. B/GLCC/147.
46. Everard (1949), p.123.
47. Thorne (1925), pp.37-38.
48. B/GLCC/29/2, 1 & 25 Oct 1867.
49. Everard (1947), p.165.
50. B/GLCC/29/2, n.12.
51. PP 1899 (C.294) x 19, Appx. no.15.
52. Everard (1949), pp.209,244; Journal of Gas Lighting, 12 Feb 1895, p.303; B/GLCC/147.
53. B/GLCC/22/2, 5,6,13, & 20 Sept 1872; Journal of Gas Lighting, 17 Dec 1872, pp.1027-8,1031-33.
54. B/GLCC/29/2, Court Minutes, 15 & 26 Sept 1865.
55. Thorne (1925), p.61.
56. Journal of Gas Lighting, 17 Dec 1872, p.988.
57. Ibid, 14 Feb 1879, p.49.
58. Ibid, 1 Oct 1889, pp.633-4.
59. Ibid, 17 June 1890, p.1115.
60. Ibid, 16 April 1889, p.707.

61. Thorne (1925), pp.35-37,51-52,64,66.
62. Journal of Gas Lighting, 17 June 1890, p.1115.
63. Cf. J.Melling "Industrial Strife and Business Welfare Philosophy: the Case of the South Metropolitan Gas Company from the 1880s to the War", Bus.Hist. (1979), pp.163-179; E.Hobsbawm "British Gas Workers, 1873-1914" in Labouring Men (1964); R.A.Church "Profit-Sharing and Labour Relations in the Nineteenth Century", I.R.S.H. (1971), pp.2-16.
64. B/GLCC/38/1, 20 Sept 1889; Thorne (1925) pp.106-109.
65. S.M.G.C. Copartnership Almanack (1909); Carpenter (1927), p.23; Journal of Gas Lighting, 21 Jan 1890, pp.99-100.
66. Journal of Gas Lighting, 3 June 1889, p.1019; 17 June 1889, p.1115; 24 June 1890, pp.1164-5; 7 Oct 1890, pp.735-6,746.
67. Journal of Gas Lighting, 22 Oct 1889, p.589.
68. Ibid, 4 March 1890, p.377; Copartners Magazine, March 1911, pp.36-7; PP 1899 (C.294) x 19, Qs.1744-49,1873-76. Cf. C.E.Brackenbury Modern Methods of Saving Labour in Gasworks (1900); Popplewell in Webb & Freeman (1912), pp.176-7.
69. Journal of Gas Lighting, 23 June 1908, pp.791-3.
70. Popplewell in Webb & Freeman (1912), p.178.
71. PP 1912-13 (C.6496) xliii 853, Report on Profitsharing and Labour Copartnership.
72. Journal of Gas Lighting, 23 June 1908, pp.791-3.
73. Carpenter (1927), pp.12-14; Journal of Gas Lighting, 27 Nov 1889, p.998, & 17 June 1890, p.1115; PP 1912 (C.6496) xliii 853, Appx.2.
74. Carpenter (1927), pp.46-7; PP 1912 (C.6496) xliii 853, pp.51-2.
75. Industrial Welfare, Aug 1922, pp.305-8. Cf. Ch.9, s.(ii).
76. PP 1912 (C.6496) xliii 853, pp.51-2.
77. PP 1899 (C.294) x 19, Qs.1060-64,1734-47.
78. Carpenter (1927), pp.3-7,16-17,51-54.
79. Journal of Gas Lighting, 26 Feb 1895, p.427.
80. Ibid, 14 Jan 1890, pp.57-58.
81. Ibid, 12 March 1895, pp.527-8,541-2; 26 Feb 1895, p.415.
82. Carpenter (1927), pp.2-7,101.
83. Journal of Gas Lighting, 6 Nov 1906, p.375.
84. PP 1899 (C.294) x 19, Qs.2456-89,3807-44. Costing £25,000 a year, the scheme added one-third of a 1d to the price of 1,000 cubic feet of gas.
85. Everard (1949), p.280.
86. Carpenter (1927), Appx; PP 1912 (C.6496) xliii 853.
87. Journal of Gas Lighting, 1912 & 1913, passim.
88. Ibid, 9 Feb 1909, p.153.
89. Ibid, 25 Dec 1906, p.865; 28 Jan 1908, pp.217-8,223; 31 March 1908, pp.217-8.
90. Ibid, 7 May 1912, pp.348,379; 13 Jan 1914, p.101.
91. Ibid, 15 Dec 1908, p.914. Woodal was chairman of the

Tottenham and Edmonton Gas Company, and a director of the Bournemouth and Croydon companies.

92. Copartners´ Magazine, May 1911, Supplement: Address by GLCC Governor to the Labour Copartnership Association.
93. Ibid, Aug 1912, p.114.
94. Ibid, June 1911, p.82-83.
95. Journal of Gas Lighting, 11 Feb 1908, p.337.
96. B/GLCC/48/2, 9 Oct 1909.
97. Copartnership, Feb 1909, p.18; Journal of Gas Lighting, 19 Jan 1909, p.519.
98. Copartners´ Magazine, July 1912, p.102; Jan 1911, p.15.
99. Journal of Gas Lighting, 18 Feb 1908, p.223; 12 May 1908, p.345; 11 Aug 1908, p.298.
100. B/GLCC/44/1, 31 July 1908.
101. Ibid, 6 Nov 1908.
102. B/GLCC/45/1, 4 Nov 1910; 30 Dec 1910.
103. Ibid, 28 July 1911. Cf. Ch.9, s.(iii).
104. Ibid, 8 & 22 March 1912; 14 June 1912.
105. Co-Partners Magazine, May 1914, pp.66-8; June 1914, pp.81-2.
106. B/SMetG/111/16/1, 4 Feb 1912; 29 May 1912; 28 Aug 1912; 8 Oct 1912.
107. Popplewell in Webb & Freeman (1912), pp.160-1. There were 80,000 workers in the industry by 1907. 18,000 were reported to be involved in profitsharing and copartnership schemes (cf. pp.156,158-9).
108. Cf. J.E.Cronin Industrial Conflict in Modern Britain (1979), pp.93-96.
109. B/GLCC/46/1, 5 & 6 Aug 1914.
110. Ibid, 4 Sept 1914.
111. NCEO Archive, MSS/200/B/3/2/C140, Pt.1: C.Carpenter Copartnership of the South Metropolitan Gas Company (1922), p.17-21.
112. Journal of Gas Lighting, 28 Aug 1917, pp.364-5.
113. Ibid, 12 Feb 1918, pp.283-4.
114. On the Whitley Joint Industrial Councils, cf. R.Charles The Development of Industrial Relations in Britain, 1911-1939 (1973); also, Ch.9, s.(iv).
115. Journal of Gas Lighting, 17 & 24 Sept 1918, pp.524,567.
116. Ibid, 26 Feb 1918, p.384; 2 April 1918, p.13.
117. Cf. PRO LAB2/458/IR173/1925, Gas JIC, 21 March, 2 Dec 1925; Report of Chief Conciliation Officer (London and S.E.), 9 Jan 1925; & Memo. from C.C.O. (S.Wales & S.W.), 27 Nov 1925.
118. Cf. T.Williamson "Trade Unionism and Negotiating Machinery in the Gas Industry" in F.E.Gannett & B.F.Catherwood (eds) Industrial and Labour Relations in Great Britain (1939).
119. LAB/2/458/IR139/3/1921, Gas JIC, Memo., 9 July 1921.
120. Ibid, Position re. Works Committees, 23 Sept 1921.
121. Industrial Welfare, Jan 1931, pp.44-5.

122. Journal of Gas Lighting, 15 Dec 1920, p.628.
123. Ibid, 25 Feb 1919, p.376; 4 March 1919, p.438; 18 Aug 1920, p.354.
124. Carpenter (1927), pp.18,21-2,100,104.
125. Journal of Gas Lighting, 9 Dec 1925, pp.644-5.
126. Copartners´ Magazine, July 1919, p.84.
127. LAB2/458/IR139/3/1921, Extract from Gas World, 11 June 1921.
128. Copartners´ Magazine, passim.
129. PRO LAB2/458/IR173/1925, Gas JIC, Note. Cf. Williamson in Gannett & Catherwood (eds) (1939).
130. Journal of Gas Lighting, 5 May 1926, p.266; 19 May 1926, pp.335-6.
131. Ibid, Sept 1928, pp.335-40.
132. B/GLCC/50, 16 Jan 1920.
133. Copartners´ Magazine, July 1921, p.129; April 1929, p.99.
134. Journal of Gas Lighting, 15 Dec 1920, pp.630-1.
135. Copartners´ Magazine, Jan 1921, pp.3-4; June 1930, pp.226-7; April 1930, pp.134-5; B/GLCC/48/1, 22 Oct 1919.
136. Copartners´ Magazine, April 1930, pp.134-5.
137. Ibid, March 1925, p.69.
138. Ibid, Feb 1929, p.39,64.
139. PP 1919 (C.410) xxvii 299, Qs.4336-4454. Departmental Committee on Old Age Pensions.
140. B/GLCC/48/1, 15 July 1921.
141. Copartners´ Magazine, Dec 1922, pp.236-237; B/GLCC/48, 21 Nov 1919; 19 Nov 1920.
142. B/GLCC/50, 16 Oct 1925. Cf. Ch.9, s.(vi).
143. Copartners´ Magazine, Jan 1926, pp.13,16; B/GLCC/50, 13 Nov 1925.
144. PRO BT55/2, The Gas Industry.
145. B/SMetG/111/18/1, 13 Oct, 10 Nov 1920; Industrial Welfare, March 1923, p.81.
146. B/SMetG/111/20/1, 24 March & 29 Dec 1926; Industrial Welfare, March 1927, pp.75-8.
147. Ibid, 2 & 16 April 1930; 14 Sept 1932.
148. B/SMetG/111/21/1, 6 Jan 1929.
149. B/SMetG/111/18/1, 24 Dec 1918, 2 April 1919, 16 March 1921; B/SMetG/111/20/1, 24 March & 29 Dec 1926.
150. Industrial Welfare, Jan 1931, pp.44-5.
151. Copartners´ Magazine, Jan 1935, p.9; Aug 1937, pp.458-9.
152. Ibid, Jan 1937, pp.3,14-5,18-9; July 1938, p.309; & Journal of Gas Lighting, 20 Oct 1937, p.210.
153. Ibid, Jan 1937, p.3.
154. 1899 (C.294) x 19, pp.285,331. From 1876-99, the G.L.C.C.´s gas fell in price from 3/9d to 3/- per 1,000 cubic feet, while that of the S.M.G.C. decreased from 3/2d to 2/2d. The capital employed per 1,000 cubic feet fell respectively from 20/3d to 12/6d, and from 10/1d to 8/10d.

Chapter 4

THE DEVELOPMENT OF COMPANY-BASED LABOUR POLICIES IN THE IRON
AND STEEL INDUSTRY

(i) INTRODUCTION

The neo-classical labour market was epitomised by the
steelworkers' job-insecurity and the continual adjustment of
their wages in accordance with steel's selling-price. As iron
and steel workers were often hired, not by employers, but
through gangers and subcontractors, managerial responsibility
for work-organisation was indirect. A reliance upon export
markets induced the industry to be competitive and susceptible
to trade cycles, but it was its atomised structure of small
and medium-sized companies which made it vulnerable to
overproduction. Unstable profits reduced the funds available
for welfare expenditure, while a fluid workforce undermined
its necessity. But the mere payment of wages could not solve
all the labour-management problems faced by steel employers.
The history of industrial welfare in the industry shows that
employers were more acquainted with industrial realities than
economic theory, and had a varied approach to the management
of their workforces. Moreover, the establishment of integrated
enterprises in the steel industry during the 1930s - as a
means of increasing profits and rationalising competition -
was matched by a corresponding development in company-based
labour strategies.
The history of industrial relations in the steel industry
has emphasised the role of collective bargaining.(1) But it is
a mistake to see the employers' association rather than the
company as the key unit determining the structure of economic
activity or industrial relations. Iron and steel companies
often agreed to wage increases even if they undermined the
rates set by regional associations.(2) Steel employers,- like
others - were principally concerned with the operations of
their own companies. Their vested interests and those of
shareholders often prevented cooperative action despite the
benefits that rationalised competition could have achieved.
Company-based labour management and industrial welfare,
therefore, were important to steel companies.

* * * * *

Section (ii) of this chapter analyses the relationship between the economic development of the steel industry in the years 1870-1914, the founding of internal labour markets, and the practice and purpose of industrial welfare. Section (iii) investigates the type of welfare practised before the Great War, while section (iv) assesses the changes induced by the War-period. Section (v) looks at the connections between capitalisation, the Tariff, and the systemisation of welfare by steel companies.

(ii) MANAGEMENT AND WELFARE

Changes in the internal management of steel companies can only be explained if the need for integrated production and the broad difference between the structures of the heavy and light steel sectors are first understood. Mass-production steel works were established in Britain during the twenty years following the final development of the Bessemer-Siemens process in the 1860s. By 1900, however, plant compared unfavourably with the large-scale, technically-integrated units established in Germany and the United States. Only one company in Britain but ten in Germany produced 30,000 tons of steel or more per annum. British rerolling continued as a separate trade. Modernisation such as the introduction of mechanical handling or charging occurred at a slower rate, and output per head was consequently low. The world production of basic steel trebled by 1900, yet increased by only 50% in Great Britain. The phosphoric ores of the East Midlands were left unexploited. Although outdated by the mass-production of steel, wrought-iron remained a large part of British output until World War One.(3) But British steel exports continued to expand until 1914, and only their share of the world export market declined. Traditional British markets gradually exploited their own iron ore resources, and tariff barriers were put up. Britain's early primacy was in many respects fortuitous, and changes in world markets were beyond the control of British producers.(4) Yet, by the 1920s, the British steel industry experienced an absolute fall in output, caused principally by its continued failure to invest in large-scale enterprise and to reorganise the anarchy of its capital structure. Too many goods were being produced for too few customers by an unnecessary number of small companies, each unable to reap the benefits of returns to scale. A Board of Trade report in 1918 had argued for the necessary reorganisation of the industry into plants of over 300,000 tons capacity per annum.(5) Large vertically-integrated concerns involved in flow-processes like steel-making could maintain the fullest utilisation of expensive capital. They could organise production to prevent bottle-necks at the various process-stages. More importantly, coordination made savings in the use of heat by rapidly moving iron and steel between each stage in production.

It has been argued by historians and not least by steel employers in the 1920s that the lack of investment was a result of costly state welfare schemes and high wages.(6) But the vested interests of a fragmented industry proved unwilling to rationalise on a scale adequate enough to make new investment worthwhile. The National Federation of Iron and Steel Employers, founded in 1918, favoured collective ore-buying, selling and exports, but failed to implement any of these policies because of district jealousies and competitive rivalries. Historical circumstances had left the British steel industry with obsolete but not worn-out capital equipment. Marginal concerns could still accrue returns for their fixed, capital costs, although their overall profitability remained low. Shareholders would not agree to plant closures which resulted in the downward revaluation of their stock. The uncertainty of economic life and the trade cycle proved too risky for employers to consider investment in integrated production and the latest technology. Although businessmen believed that recovery depended on an increase in exports, it is probable that a stimulus to the domestic economy and the countering of import penetration contained the answer.(7)

Indeed, the growth of consumer markets between the Wars established thriving concerns in the production of tinplate, galvanised sheet, and tubes. Rearmament in the 1930s rescued the heavy steel companies of the North East and Scotland. These factors and the 1932 Tariff meant that British steel producers in 1937 surpassed their 1929 output by 40%. Given expanding markets and higher profits, light steel producers, like Richard Thomas´ and Stewart and Lloyds, sought to concentrate production. From 1922 to 1939, Richard Thomas moved from holding 22% of tinplate production to 49%. By 1932, Stewart and Lloyds made 72% of British tubes. They proved, therefore, more willing to establish the managerial structures familiar to large companies. But sheet, tinplate, wire and tubes composed only 28% of steel tonnage in 1920 and 36% in 1937.(8) Heavy steel producers remained unrationalised, and used the increased demand created by the Tariff to sustain an outdated and atomised capital structure. Dorman-Long, Consett Iron and Steel, Colvilles, and other North Eastern and Scottish firms, consequently, remained less progressive with respect to management.

Chandler has noted the link between market strategy and managerial structure. New corporate companies, created through amalgamations, supplanted the market mechanism by a managerial hierarchy which could directly coordinate production between process-stages. Traditional economic theories assumed that output expanded to meet demand, and that only when demand was

saturated would prices fall as firms began undercutting each
other to increase their own output. Yet, firms with a large
market share could control supply, limit competition, and
influence prices. Profit-maximisation, the single motive of
the entrepreneur in the hypothetical case of perfect
competition, gave place to oligopoly or sales-maximisation.
Moreover, market and price mechanisms were not necessarily the
best means to achieve the efficient allocation and utilisation
of resources. Chandler's thesis is based on the proposition
that far more economies result from the careful coordination
of production and distribution than from merely increasing the
size of the producing and distributing units.(9) Corporate
companies, though rarely without competitors, sought to
replace the market mechanism with the long-term planning of
their own production. Being less prone to external economic
factors, managerial hierarchies within large companies could
exercise greater "discretionary behaviour".(10) Consequently,
the rise of the corporate economy in the 20th Century affected
the internal organisation and market strategies of many steel
companies.

With the exception of railways, research into managerial
development has, however, concentrated on the "new", expanding
sectors.(11) This factor is reflected in Chandler's
description of the "ideal" or "advanced" managerial model,
which consists of the large-scale, decentralised,
multi-divisional enterprise. Such an organisation has a
general office which oversees the whole company. The next
level of the hierarchy, the division, handles one major line
of products, or a set of services in a particular geographical
area. Divisional executives are responsible for the financial
success of their unit. The division itself has a central
office and administers a number of departments, each of which
is concerned with a major function like manufacturing,
selling, accounting, or research. Each department has its own
headquarters. Only the central office decides on strategic or
entrepreneurial decisions about policy and procedures. It
allocates the men, money, and materials on the basis of a
long-term market strategy. Managerial decisions which are
tactical and concerned with day-to-day operations are taken by
the divisions and departments.(12)

But the multi-divisional enterprise was not suited to the
market circumstances of the British steel industry. Companies
involved in chemicals, food processing and electricals
integrated horizontally with other concerns, and, therefore,
gained control over many different but related products. They
were, in addition, presented in this period with the
technological opportunities for product differentiation, and
there were advantages in pooling the high costs of research.
Those companies competing for consumer markets often took over
others in order to gain access to their distributive outlets.
Obtaining returns-to-scale and planning the factors of

production at each process-stage necessitated an adequately-large and stable market. In sum, the chemical, food processing, and electrical industries expanded their markets by introducing new products, taking over the production of other goods, or by increasing the area of sales. The manufacture of many varied products required separate factories and management. The selling of consumer goods required an independent sales network which could assess changing tastes, market and advertise effectively, and build up brand loyalty. Such a sales network, often spread over a large area, required regional administrative centres.(13) Distinguishable products or regions, and separate manufacturing and distributive units moulded well into a structure of semi-autonomous divisions.

Williamson questions the idea that multi-divisional organisation, rather than the multi-departmental, can be accepted as the "modern" organisational structure. Generally, the multi-divisional structure was founded upon the economic growth which has occurred since 1945. Expansion in the Inter-War years mostly increased the number of company departments, and not the number of divisions. Within the multi-departmental form, the general office directly concerns itself with coordinating different departmental tasks like production or distribution, and there are no semi-autonomous divisions.(14) The steel industry in the 1930s began to integrate vertically rather than horizontally. Management was centralised to improve the lines of command and communication. It was better coordination between each process-stage within a single, integrated works, and not the allocation of responsibility to company divisions, which produced savings like those to be gained in the use of heat.(15) In a country the size of Britain, the full economies of integrated production could only be achieved if a single works produced for a national market, and so geographical dispersion within companies was inappropriate. There were no new steel products or markets. British steel companies made only a few capital goods for only one or several buyers who were industrial producers themselves, and a more centralised structure could easily deal with a few, large customers. A multi-divisional form would have coped better with a varied, changing mass market - quite unlike that of steel companies. Contacts with shipbuilding, engineering, railway, canning or automobile companies were jealously protected by steel companies. Consequently, the steel industry in certain regions became specialised. The companies of the North East, for example, concentrated on manufacturing ship-plates to meet the demand of the region's shipbuilding industry.(16)

Steel company amalgamations from 1914 to 1939 eventually encouraged the adoption of the corporate management structure most appropriate to the industry's markets. Moreover, company-based industrial relations policies were also increasingly geared towards the needs of the corporate business. Chandler and Williamson have emphasised the importance of company objectives being determined by a process of internal bargaining within the firm. But the balance of personal, administrative or group pressures within a company restricted its scope of choices, and included the workers´ ability to hinder production or to strike. Employers were in a position to minimise class-conflict, and could limit the workers´ ability to combine or attempt to retain their loyalty. Labour requirements, moreover, had to be met. Administrative consequences followed once companies decided to cope, for example, with the problem of sickness or the aspiration of workers to have a say in the running of the firm. Sick benefit clubs or works councils could be established.

Internal labour markets were an example of the exercise of "discretionary behaviour" or planning in the area of labour management. A "core" of permanently employed workers in a competitive industry could be sheltered as far as possible from fluctuations in trade. An internal labour market was also the minimum number of workers required to sustain a level of output which, in failing to make adequate profits, could help the redemption of capital charges. The larger the company and the greater the scale of capital investment, the greater was the need to secure labour and keep expensive investments fully utilised. Trained and experienced in often firm- or machine-specific skills, "core" workers were differentiated by management from the "pool" of residual, non-permanent workers and treated accordingly. They represented a lost investment if labour-turnover or work-disaffection were at high levels. Employers might maintain employment amongst "core" workers - even when it was in the short-term unprofitable to do so - in order to retain their proven skills and loyalty.

Internal labour markets were expanded in the iron and steel industry due to the transformation from manual to mass production technology. New techniques established a category of semi-skilled machine operatives. But a one-time steelworker and writer on the industry in 1933 denied that Scientific Management had substituted traditional reliance upon the experience and good judgment of workers.(17) Semi-skilled workers substituted for skilled and unskilled alike, and, rather than producing an easily-replaceable lumpenproletariat, the new technology made it more expensive in the aggregate to lose labour. Steel companies had to pay for the six-month-long training of the new semi-skilled, and better wages and welfare benefits were offered as insurance against their leaving once trained. The old apprenticeship system had placed the responsibility for new recruits upon sub-contractors or leading-hands, who controlled the allocation of all jobs according to a "seniority" system. By undertaking training as an overhead, management assumed direct control over job-allocation and employment.(18) Moreover, the semi-skilled, unlike the skilled, did not have the tradition of participating in craft-based friendly societies. Changes, therefore, in the nature of work and employment induced steel companies to reassess their welfare policies.

Two phases can be discerned in the history of industrial welfare in the steel industry from 1870 to 1939. Before the introduction of integrated production in certain steel sectors, company provision was based on sporting and social clubs, unsystematic sick clubs in receipt of a voluntary subvention, or on ex gratia pensions. Subsidised sports associations and social clubs became common in iron and steel and other companies during the Post-War boom. Employers tried to consolidate the larger workforces they had inherited as a result of amalgamations during the Great War. Recreation alleviated the boredom and arduous nature of work, and social amenities were necessary among those communities which formed around the more isolated steel factories. Sports and social clubs, and ex gratia benefits were seen as expressing a team spirit and encouraging loyalty.(19)

With the increasing concentration of capital in the years around 1930, steel companies began to support joint contributory pension and sick-pay schemes which, by implication, demanded a commitment from and to individual employees. Old age pension, sick pay, and profitsharing schemes, pledged to the automatic payment of benefits as a right of participation, were large administrative tasks requiring bureaucratic procedures and friendly society rules. The extension of internal labour markets led companies increasingly to underwrite the financing of benefits. Large corporate enterprises undertaking massive capital investments sought to safeguard expected rates of return by planning the numbers and stability of their workforces on whose cooperation the full and efficient use of new plant would depend. Pensions helped reduce labour-turnover, and sick pay minimised the dissipating effects of illness upon efficiency and output.

Oligopoly and monopoly, or high profit margins provided either the labour market stability or the revenues necessary for systematic company provision. But the welfare practices of small steel companies absorbed into larger corporations by the 1920s had at first continued unaffected. Provision within constituent companies was often merely continued on an uncoordinated, works basis. Systemisation was undertaken because of the reorganisation of management rather than occurring merely because of increased company size.

* * * * *

The increasing scale of welfare expenditure in the steel industry stemmed from changes in markets, production technology, and company and managerial organisation. But even the small companies which remained typical of the British steel industry during this period had to deal with the recalcitrant problems of employed labour. Employers required industrial welfare as a means of instilling loyalty. Where housing was in shortage, or when state pensions and sick pay were unavailable or insufficient, employers often had little choice but to finance industrial welfare if the correct quantity and quality of labour was to be maintained.

(iii) INDUSTRIAL WELFARE IN THE STEEL INDUSTRY, 1870-1914

The development of collective bargaining from the 1860s onwards confirmed that the replacement of small-workshops by factories was ending the master-craftsman relationship.(20) J.S.Jeans of the Iron Trade Employers Association supported collective bargaining in order to contain organised labour, and its growing threat to capital and profitability.(21) Carr and Taplin view the "paternalistic" attitudes of iron and steel employers as workable in a period of non-unionised labour and as outmoded after the formation of conciliation boards.(22) But industrial "paternalism" describes a firm owned by a single employer or family that might also dominate the social and political life of a factory community.(23) It existed quite naturally among the large number of small and medium-sized businesses in the steel industry which survived into the 20th Century. Harry Brearley in 1933 tells how steelworkers were brought up to regard their employers "with awed respectfulness".(24)

Paternalism at the Coalbrookdale Iron Company is associated with the Quaker convictions of the Darbys, yet labour efficiency was a greater influence than philanthropy. After Alfred and Abraham Darby had inherited the firm in 1830, Abraham concerned himself largely with works management, while Alfred concentrated upon labour relations. The control of family groups over the organisation of work was broken up, and "trustworthy and skilful foremen" were appointed in their place. They made regular reports to the company offices, and, instead of employing and paying workers through gangers, men were enrolled directly with the company. The gang system was seen as inappropriate for a firm of over 2,000 workers. Pool Hill Estate was purchased in 1838 to provide cottages for the expanding labour force. In 1840, Alfred Darby helped revise the rules of one works´ sick club in order to place it on a "sound financial basis". It had been voluntarily founded by workers and had 200 members, but Alfred wanted to establish it as a company fund open to the whole labour force. Its contributions were deducted from wages, and, along with donations from the fines levied for bad work and breaches of company rules, Alfred also contributed regularly on behalf of the company. The club soon accumulated a surplus. It was able to give a monthly subscription to Alfred Darby´s school, established in 1846 for the workers´ 700 children who were compelled to attend until the age of twelve. The company also provided a Friends Meeting Place and rooms for the Literary and Scientific Institution.(25) It was because the sick club was a vital institution to the workers that the company assumed responsibility for its continuance. Industrial discipline and welfare were the twin means adopted by the autocratic Darbys to instill cooperation amongst their workforce.(26)

The Carron Company in Scotland, on the other hand, deliberately maintained a tradition of "family employment". Trusted gangers employing their relatives and friends formed a reliable and local labour force. "The Company's own direct interest was particularly responsible for this stability, but in other fields the workers showed their own initiative, though they were helped by the Company. These were in the provision of schools (or of educational and social facilities generally), in the friendly society and in the cooperative store." Welfare was a mixture of direct company involvement and encouragement of working-class self-help. The Carron Founders' Society, established in 1814, revised its rules in 1839. For subscriptions of 16s in the first year and 12s in following years, members were entitled to 5s a week sick pay for six months, 4s for the next year, and 3s subsequently. A funeral grant of £3 10s to members or their widows was also paid. The employers gave the Society two shares in the Carron Company as its main source of income. Free coal and housing were also available to the workforce.(27)

Until the middle of the 19th Century, it was possible for the majority of iron and steel producers to know their workers personally and to live "in their midst". Paternalism meant establishing "a kind of 'family feeling'". The authority of the Wortley Ironworks' employers, for example, was based on their personal standing amongst workers in the village of Wortley.(28) Likewise, the ironmasters of Middlesborough, a city which was created by the iron industry of the mid-19th Century, dominated local politics. Henry Bolckow, John Vaughn, Isaac Wilson, Edgar Gilks, W.R.I.Hopkins, and Thomas Vaughn were all mayors and often members of Parliament for the borough. Henry Bolckow endowed Middlesborough with schools, and built an infirmary in 1867 primarily for the use of iron workers. Joseph Pease, in 1870, paid for a school which could hold 600 pupils. The rapid growth of the city in the 1860s caused a housing shortage. Ironmasters in the surrounds of Middlesborough established factory villages like New Marske, Lingdale, Hulton, Lowcross, North Ormesby and Skinningrove. Bernard Samuelson erected 500 cottages on the South Bank. These villages were the recipients of employers' patronage. Alexander Cochrane, for example, financed the construction of a cottage hospital at North Ormesby.(29)

Another North Eastern firm, the Consett Iron Company, drew up a report in 1871 noting the "great want" of cottage accommodation in the city. It concluded that the men could erect houses themselves, if suitable land was offered and the help of a building society secured. To support the local community, donations were given to churches and chapels, schools, a hospital for sick children, and a band.(30) When the Consett Company's articles of association were revised in 1900, it was formally acknowledged that money could be used to establish or support any institution which could benefit employees, ex-employees, or their dependants. Pensions and allowances were also permitted under the new articles of association.(31) In 1908, a Workmen's Club was founded, and rooms for reading and recreation were set aside at the works.(32)

The Coltness Iron Company likewise supported a wide variety of welfare services for its workers. From 1850 onwards, it made deductions from the men's wages for house-rent, medical attendance, and payments to the friendly society or savings bank.(33) Smiths of Coventry and Lincoln built the village of Blairhall, and donated money to hospitals and convalescent homes which would receive their men. The company set up a savings association, and began supporting a sick club which the workers had originally financed themselves.(34) At Archibald Kenrick and Sons of West Bromwich, membership of the Mutual Benefit Society for funerals, incapacity, and long-term sickness was a condition of employment. Contributions were taken from wages, and a committee of fifteen workers administered the funds. Rights to benefits were controlled by strict rules. Thirty visitors were elected at every annual general meeting to keep a constant check on all claimants. Recipients not at home before dusk were fined 5s and had their sick pay suspended. The company supervised the accounts, bore the expense of administration, and held the funds at 5% per annum. Kenrick's underwrote the payment of benefits, and, in return, had the power of veto over any decision or change of rules made by the Society. Surplus funds were used for payments to hospitals and doctors, and for donations to a Benevolent Fund which helped in cases not covered by the Mutual Society. Medical aid, accident compensation, and pensions were all available by 1902.(35)

The paternalistic traditions of small firms were most clearly evident in the South Wales tinplate trade. In a largely unmechanised process, the profitability of the mills relied largely on the skill of its workers. It paid employers, therefore, to keep local labour-pools intact, even if works were run at a temporary loss and wages of 21 to 26s had to be met.(36) The comprehensiveness of welfare provision in South Wales was said to be epitomised by the Dowlais Ironworks, which, by employing nearly 9,000 people, was one of the country's largest firms by the mid-19th Century. The trustee of the firm, G.T.Clark, said that the workforce was organised through fifty self-administered benefit societies. 2d in contributions was compulsorily stopped from weekly wages. Rooms were provided free for friendly society meetings, and the company distributed the benefits which included sick allowances, funeral expenses, and accident cover. Another 2d was deducted to pay for schools and doctors, and a self-supporting medical fund began receiving company aid when it failed financially. Workers were encouraged to erect their own cottages, since Clark believed it was beneficial to management and workers if the men felt that their home-life was independent of the company. Houses were, however, built free on company land with 99 year leases. Clark accepted that only by giving workers a "substantial voice" could difficulties be effectively resolved. He claimed that all disputes at Dowlais were settled fairly by the heads of department whom every worker had the right to approach. The men could appoint representatives to voice general grievances, and informal negotiations bred a "family" atmosphere. Conciliation and arbitration boards were seen as unnecessary. The private ownership of a firm was preferred to shareholding, because it encouraged greater responsibility among board members and enhanced the standing of employers amongst the workers: the manager of a joint stock organisation "has not the power that a man who stands alone has, and that creates difficulty" when labour disputes had to be settled.(37)

By 1847, cottages and amenities like reading rooms had been established at the Morfa works at Llanelly, the Llwydarth works at Maesteg, and Players' at Clydach. Schools are known to have existed at the Aberdulais, Maesteg, and Margram works. In 1882, deductions for medical aid and education were taken from the wages of rollerman at Gower's Penclawdd works.(38) The housing estate which developed in the vicinity of the Blaenavon Coal and Iron Company necessitated the active involvement of English general managers like John Paton in the recreative and social activities of the workpeople.(39) The company had appointed a surgeon and a physician by the 1860s.(40) The South Wales, Monmouthshire, and Gloucstershire Tinplate Workers, which itself had no provident funds, acknowledged in 1892 that 90% of tinplate workers belonged to friendly societies. The union supported the introduction of state-funded retirement, because "....it is alleged that pensions derived from funds organised by and under the control of employers practically result in forfeiture of independence, since, as a rule, a probable claimant upon such a pension fund cannot change his employment without loss".(41) Richard Thomas' had by 1888 hired a recreation ground for the use of their employees, who needed leisure facilities amongst the homes they rented from the company. A Housing Accommodation Fund was established in 1891.(42) In 1911, the company gave £25 per annum to provide one quarter of the wages for a nurse at the Lydney works in South Wales. By 1912, the directors were discussing profitsharing as a means of retaining their workers' loyalty, and were helping workers purchase their homes with loans worth four-fifths the price of a house.(43)

Like the Dowlais Iron Company, the directors of tube manufacturers Lloyd and Lloyd of Birmingham accepted petitions of grievances or requests from their men. In 1859, the workers asked for a "day's enjoyment out somewhere Similar to those given by other Tube manufacturers", with the expenses of the trip and wages being paid by the company. In 1867, the men petitioned their employers to support a sick club, expressing their willingness to contribute to it through deductions from their wages. The company founded the Albion Tube Works Sick Society to cover illness, funeral expenses, and the death of members, wives, or children. The company had, therefore, responded to the expressed needs and anxieties of the workers themselves. The Society fined its members 2d for not attending meetings. After three days' illness, workers had to obtain a medical certificate to be entitled to six months' full sick pay. Half-wages were given for the following twenty-six weeks. Collections were held to help those recently widowed. Seven members were elected to be in charge of the scheme, and they regularly visited the recipients of benefits at home to prevent fraud. Beneficiaries had to be at home before 9.00 p.m. during the Summer months and before 7.00 p.m. in the Winter. Scales of benefits were adjusted to match the money available.(44)

Stewart and Lloyds was formed by an amalgamation in 1903 of Lloyd & Lloyd and Stewart and Menzies Ltd. As the company proved a successful competitor in an expanding market, it soon developed a policy of company provision in advance of most steel companies. Labour management within the new company was reorganised by the chairman, John Graham Stewart, and welfare became the concern of the new board of directors. "One of the first steps in Welfare Work was inaugurated in 1908 .... (A) handsome two-storied building was erected for the use of workers and people living in the village of Clydesdale, Mossend, and comprises a Billiard Room, Gymnasium, Baths, Reading and Reference Rooms, Warehouses and Laundry". In 1913, the Board discussed the introduction of a contributory pension scheme, but eventually decided on the less systematic Employees Benefit Fund. The Fund depended wholly on company subventions for its finances, and dispensed ex gratia benefits. But the very existence of a company fund for all workers was the first example of a single, centralised welfare policy at Stewart and Lloyds. It replaced the paying of benefits on a works basis and according to the traditional practices of the constituent companies. By May 1914, the Fund was bestowing sick-pay, pensions, and death grants to the dependants of members.(45) It became an increasingly important institution at Stewart and Lloyds, and in many respects presaged those companies which placed industrial welfare on more ordered basis some twenty years later.(46)

* * * * *

The scale of welfare provision in the iron and steel industry could not match the expenditure of public utilities. But sick societies were a common feature amongst steel companies, and industrial housing was necessitated by the geographical isolation of many firms or the general lack of homes which workers could afford. Housing maintained the supply of labour, and, along with benefit societies and recreational facilities, helped the retention of workers for as long as companies required them. Welfare remained on the whole ex gratia, although there were contributory schemes, and Stewart and Lloyds formed a company-wide and standardised fund. It was a successful, expanding firm with a large market share, and it sought to retain workers through more systematic provision.

(iv) WORLD WAR ONE AND STATE INTERVENTION

The First World War forced the government to undertake the full management of the war economy. By 1916, the Ministry of Munitions controlled supply, production, prices, and wages in the steel industry. Centralised direction of the economy encouraged governmental interest in the efficiency of munitions workers. Reports stressed the need for adequate lighting and heating, for hot food provided at canteens, and for measured rest-periods.(47) Richard Thomas', for example, established canteens at their Llanelly, Abercarn, Lydney, and Endlogan works in 1916, and their costs were compensated by relief from Excess Profits Duty.(48) The expansion of production to meet war needs also brought labour shortages. Company housing schemes were undertaken with the financial help of the state to attract workers to certain sites, and welfare benefits maintained contacts with ex-employees on active service in the expectation they would return to their place of work.

The Ministry of Munitions promoted the construction of industrial housing amongst companies involved in the production of weapons. The Clyde, Coventry, and Barrow were recognised as the most acute areas of housing scarcity. The Ministry aided Beardmores, Colvilles, and Stewart and Lloyds in the building of 350 homes for Glasgow steelworkers, and Colvilles later built another 250 at Glengarnock.(49) Samuel Fox and Company constructed a village of 364 cottages near their Sheffield works with the stated purpose of attracting workers.(50)

Further industrial housing was required to match the labour requirements of the Post-War boom. Government grants were chanelled into the Public Utility Societies established under the 1918 Housing Act. Richard Thomas' sponsored the

Margram Cooperative Homes Limited to serve its Margram and Port Talbot works. This public utility society was constitutionally bound to provide small holdings and allotments, and to support educational and recreational activities. Thomas' also helped finance the Crymlyn Burrows Housing Society.(51)

The Consett Iron Company's housing scheme let houses on condition that strict rules, affixed in each home, were followed. Tenants were financially responsible for damages, and an official or workman could enter homes at any reasonable time to examine or repair the premises. Gardens, hedges, and fences had to be kept in good order. Moreover, the "Water closet and bath must be kept clean and used only for the purposes for which they are intended".(52) Dorman-Long, which had tried to cope with Middlesborough's housing shortage since the 1870s, had, in 1891, established a House Accommodation Fund to offer homes at cost-price. From 1917-21, the company invested much capital in building Dormanstown, near Redcar, and its labour policy was largely concentrated on providing for the pool of workers it had created. The company took expert advice from the Welsh Garden Cities Limited, which had built homes for Fox's of Sheffield and the Birmingham rubber-manufacturers Dunlops, and had experience in negotiating with government departments. In 1917, the company agreed with the Ministry of Health upon a 300-home scheme. Dormanstown became a Public Utility Society in 1919, and a recreation ground, athletic club, public hall, garden nursery, school, church, and tennis club were built. A doctor was hired by Dorman-Long for the benefit of the town's inhabitants. By 1920, the company had built a Club House, and bought cinema equipment for use in the village hall.(53) Aware of the fact that housing investment brought a poor return of between 2-5%, Dorman-Long, nevertheless, was prepared to invest in Dormanstown because of the overriding need to increase the size of its workforce. With the coming of the slump in 1921, however, Dorman-Long was shedding labour.

Benefits had been paid during the War to the dependants of employees on active service in order to ensure that, on demobilisation, their labour skills were not lost to their companies. The Consett Iron Company started payments to the dependants of such employees in August 1914. Private Edward Coxon thanked the company for the 12s per week given to his wife. The benefits were, he stated, a comfort to him in his absence, especially in "these days of increased prices of the means of subsistence".(54) Richard Thomas' in 1915 founded an Employers' and Employees' Joint War Relief Fund.(55)

At the outbreak of War, Stewart and Lloyds decided to grant 6s each week to those wives of husbands who had joined up and 1s for each of their children under sixteen. By September, 1,125 workers had volunteered to join the armed forces, and they had 494 dependants costing the company £223 per week. In calculating benefits, the directors took account of the official separation allowance, but guaranteed a minimum income. When the War had not ended by Christmas, these allowances became the responsibility of the company's Employees Benefit Fund. The directors, consequently, donated £10,000 to the society in 1915. By 1916, the fund was costing Stewart and Lloyds £20,000 per annum. An investigative committee was asked in 1918 to overlook welfare policy. In May, the Board appointed the committee to act as its advisors on welfare matters.(56) The duties of the Employees Benefit Fund were expanded so that, by the end of the War, it operated as the Board's central welfare organisation. By 1922, the Fund still required a company donation of £12,000, a sum which greatly exceeded the pre-War subvention.

The Parliamentary voice of iron and steel employers had been noticeably weak before the Great War. As a highly competitive industry, it required a say in matters like import duties and social legislation because of their affect upon prices and costs. But the very intensity of competition militated against the creation of an effective employers' association. The National Federation of Iron and Steel Manufacturers was established in 1918 only through the insistence of the government, which at the time was formulating plans of industrial reconstruction and needed the industry's cooperation. The N.F.I.S.M. objected to the Iron and Steel Trades Confederation's suggestion in 1919 that unions be made responsible for collecting Workmen's Compensation contributions and paying the benefits. The Federation argued that, as accident compensation was paid by the employers, they should retain control over its administration. They opposed proposals to discuss accident prevention with the unions on the grounds it would constitute an interference in management. But the Federation supported the idea of "Committees of Employers and Workpeople" collecting joint contributions for supplementary accident benefits because it would encourage class cooperation.(57)

In 1918, proposals had been put forward for the reorganisation of industrial relations through Joint Industrial Councils. The N.F.I.S.M. preferred to retain the industry's well-established system of collective bargaining.(58) Yet, two Joint Industrial Councils were eventually established, one in the Iron and Steel Wire trade, the other in tinplate production.(59) Sir Peter Rylands, one-time F.B.I. President, led the Iron and Steel Wire Manufacturers' Association which in 1919 proposed to introduce one week's holiday with full pay. The N.F.I.S.M. was concerned about setting a precedent for the whole steel industry, and persuaded the I.S.W.M.A. to abandon its plans.(60) In 1923, the Iron and Steel Wire J.I.C. objected to "the inclusion of workpeople's savings, Friendly Society, Joint Benefit and Superannuation Benefits for the purpose of calculating their Income as affecting the right to enjoy the Old Age Pension....." from the state. Both the Steel Wire employers and their union counterparts were eager to encourage voluntary initiatives in industrial cooperation and welfare, and they opposed a Bill in 1923 proposing to enforce the formation of J.I.C.s in unorganised industries. Industrial relations were harmonious, and the Amalgamated Society of Wire Drawers nominated Rylands to continue as chairman in 1923 despite the fact it was their turn to head the Council. The J.I.C. opposed in 1924 the repeal of contracting out under the 1920 Unemployment Insurance Act. It had drafted a scheme, and felt its existence would have been justified if it had been able to administer unemployment benefits.(61) The J.I.C. was, therefore, a supporter of the right to contract out under the 1925 Contributory Pensions Act.(62)

Paid holidays in the wire trade were finally introduced in 1938 following general government legislation. The Iron and Steel Trades Employers Association, created in 1922 to coordinate the views of employers on industrial relations, agreed with the various steel unions to provide seven days' holiday each year if a man had been employed at a company for the previous fifty weeks. The scheme proposed also to encourage cooperation between employers and workers at the level of the factory-floor: compulsory holiday funds were established at each works, and contributions of 1s a week were deducted from wage packets. The money saved by each worker was handed over at the beginning of a man's holiday.(63)

* * * * *

The expansion of industrial housing and employee benefit funds had been marked developments during the War. But the steel industry's Joint Industrial Councils were deprived of any role in collective bargaining. Moreover, the abandonment of Reconstruction plans by the state undermined the very purpose of the National Federation of Iron Steel Makers. Both the Federation and the J.I.C.s were able, however, to support welfare schemes which developed at a company level.

(v) THE CORPORATE COMPANY AND INDUSTRIAL WELFARE (I): RATIONALISATION AND THE TARIFF

In 1918, the Scoby-Smith Report on the reorganisation of the iron and steel industry argued for the rationalisation of ownership, the reallocation of ore-rights, and the creation of a national export-selling organisation.(64) The N.F.I.S.M. was founded in order to achieve these proposals. Yet, steel companies were anxious to abandon rather than reimpose industrial controls, and they confidently expected the high levels of production and investment to be continued by the restoration of the market's invisible hand. By 1921, steel production had returned to a system of regional price and wage regulation. But the industry found itself overcapitalised, and unable to adapt to a shrinking market. As a highly capital-intensive process, steel production could not be easily reduced to cope with falling prices. Rationalisation and the construction of integrated works required an injection of capital which companies could not hope to raise nor, given the market situation, hope to repay. Neo-classical theorists assumed that companies would respond to slumps by improving efficiency, but, instead of ruining the least efficient and reinvigorating the thrustful companies, the decline in profitability made the introduction of new technology impossible. It was a situation which led to increasing demands for tariffs to protect domestic markets. The questions of profitability, import duties, rationalisation, adequate demand, and the development of corporate companies were, therefore, inextricably interwoven.(65)

The N.F.I.S.M. had set up a Tariff Committee in 1927, but internal divisions prevented it taking a policy stance.(66) Heavy steel producers had accepted the need to rationalise behind a tariff wall. Yet, companies like Colvilles and G.K.N. were dependent upon foreign raw materials or semi-finished goods. Only after the Great Crash of 1929 were they and the Federation able to support the principle of import duties. With the backing of the industry, the National Government passed the Import Duties Act in 1932, and provided for the setting up of the Import Duties Advisory Committee. It imposed a thirty-three and a third per cent duty on iron and steel imports for two years. Promises of increased efficiency countered criticisms about the dangers to consumers of a protected market, and the continuance of the tariff, therefore, was conditional upon the rationalisation of production. Steel companies had agreed to formulate a scheme of reorganisation, despite the fact that the industry´s anarchic structure made such a condition nearly impossible to achieve. Expanding companies like the United Steel Companies, Richard Thomas´, and Stewart and Lloyds supported rationalisation because they believed that the most efficient would benefit, while Dorman-Long, South Durham and Cargo Fleet, G.K.N. and Colvilles merely wished to increase profitability and efficiency within the existing structure of ownership. Seeking to conciliate all points of view, Sir William Larke, President of the N.F.I.S.M., was unable to formulate a plan of reorganisation in the two years for which tariffs had been temporarily introduced. The British Iron and Steel Federation was established in order to by-pass wranglings within the N.F.I.S.M., but, although tariffs continued, no binding agreements on prices, quotas, or rebates for reallocated production were ever implemented. The B.I.S.F.´s constitution only mentioned price maintenance, with the result that, as demand fell, prices stayed up.(67)

Rationalisation within the industry, consequently, was

implemented by the companies themselves. Bolckow, Vaughn and Dorman-Long had joined forces in 1929, and the Lancashire Steel Company and Firth and Browns were formed in 1930.(68) But major developments followed the passing of the 1932 Import Duties Act. Changes in managerial and capital structure, moreover, shaped the industrial relations policies of steel companies. This fact was recognised in a report drawn up by the Import Duties Advisory Committee in 1937. It acknowledged that the Tariff had made possible the building of new plant on old or greenfield sites, and rationalisation had involved the rapid mechanisation and concentration of production. Works were moved nearer to ore supplies, as the relative costs of transporting steel and coal changed. The Report advised that, because of the shake-out of labour caused by the introduction of greater mechanisation, the industry should bear the costs of supplementary unemployment assistance, pensions, or compensation for loss of employment. Joint consultation was encouraged, as was the need for industrial housing.(69)

(v) THE CORPORATE COMPANY AND INDUSTRIAL WELFARE (II): 1918-1930

Industrial welfare after 1918 showed a marked continuity with pre-War company provision. The War, however, had directed attention to the issue of industrial relations. The Iron Coal Trades Review, therefore, portrayed the War as having "swept away most of the old habits of mind, much of the folly of unreasonable traditions, of high-handed autocracy, of isolated dignity and exclusiveness". British industry had undertaken research into the most scientific means of production and labour management. By following a more "human" approach, companies could instill good morale. A specialist supervisor was useful for explaining welfare proposals and avoiding misunderstandings. He or she improved efficiency and saved lost hours by the immediate provision of first aid or hospital attention, canteens, and recreational and educational facilities. The promotion of sports, argued the Review, encouraged good health.(70)

The Carron Company founded a Recreation Club in 1918.(71) The Whitehead Iron and Steel Company, likewise, set up a Sports Club by 1923. In 1926, a Welfare Scheme was established to collect from workers a 2d levy for various welfare projects. In 1936, the company streamlined its labour schemes by forming a single Sports Club and Institute. The interested participation of the men in its administration was encouraged by placing it under the direction of a Welfare Committee.(72) Edgar Allen and Company began financing a Thrift Club and Benevolent Fund in 1918, and sought to reduce work-disaffection by the promotion of sports and social clubs. A Works Sports Club was established in 1920, and the Edgar

Company-based Labour Policies in the Iron and Steel Industry

Allen Works and Sports Magazine was run by a democratically-elected committee of workers and staff. The company was proud of the fact that seven of the 1918/1919 Junior Football squad's fourteen members were still employed at the works in 1956. Limited joint consultation was allowed through a Works Council founded in 1919. Representatives were elected from each department. In 1920, a Safety Committee was introduced, and a profitsharing scheme, consisting of 20,000 £1 workers' shares offered at less than the market price, was instigated.(73) McKechnie Brothers attributed their good industrial relations partly to "the attention given by the directors to the safety and welfare of employees". A general Mutual Benefit Society had existed since 1901, but provision was extended by the establishment of a Sick and Dividend Club in 1925. The firm granted holidays with pay from 1919 onwards, yet works councils were not set up until 1939.(74) Richard Johnson and Nephew held a Victory Sports and Celebration festival in September 1919. Wiredrawers contributed 2d a week to a Sickness Fund, while ancillary workers donated 1d. The Fund also paid for hospital treatment. When the company went public in 1926, a share Trust was created in order to pay money into a reconstituted Benevolent Fund. In 1937, a pension scheme was founded with a £10,000 gift from the company.(75)

The Stanton Iron Company claimed a long tradition of industrial welfare when works committees were appointed in 1919 to encourage employer-employee cooperation. For, "Workers, too, have a code of behaviour - not imposed but agreed. They learn to work with the company".(76) By 1925, the Staveley Coal and Iron Company owned 2,000 houses, and sports clubs were introduced to cap the community's Sunday school and a cricket team which had existed since the 1870s. Team expenses and referees were paid. The Devonshire Works Mess Room had a Secretary, Treasurer, and stewards, organised a Benevolent and Convalescent Fund, and owned a convalescent home. The Warsop Main Medical Aid Fund paid doctors' bills, and the Staveley Works Sick Fund granted sick pay and made donations to hospitals.(77) There was no central direction of welfare policy, as works managers were left to administer provision according to local needs. This was true also of G.K.N., whose Smethwick Works, by 1925, had established its own Welfare Department. It was responsible for supporting social clubs, sports associations, holiday camps, a gymnasium, a works canteen, surgeries, restrooms, and the provision of trained nurses. The Castle Works at Newport organised an Institute and Club with a billiard-room, library, and canteen.(78)

The rapid growth of Colvilles during the First World War intensified the problem of good communications with the workforce. Originally, Colvilles had employed 100-200 men at Motherwell, but expanded to include 1500-2000 men throughout Lanarkshire, Ayrshire, and Stirlingshire. In 1920, therefore, the company began publishing a house journal which could develop a corporate spirit: "It is... very easy for one to feel lost amidst such a huge organisation, and sometimes to wonder what the Company is really doing, or worse still, to have no interest in the Company or its affairs. There have also grown up within the Works many organisations, not only of a Trade or Union description, but likewise of a Social nature; yet the knowledge of these and the usefulness of them is limited to the actual members, for others know little if anything about them". The Magazine Committee was elected by each works department, and the journal´s object was to prevent "unwarranted suspicions" becoming grievances. Works committees were founded for the same purpose. Colvilles hoped that "esprit de corps" would be further developed through the active participation of their men in sports and social clubs. Industrial unrest could be cured by welfare, because, rather than stemming from the activities of the lone agitator, or the selfish pursuit of large wages, its "real cause lies deeper, and will be found in the lack of sympathy, and personal interest shown by employers towards the rank-and-file of their workers". Furthermore, it was the "ever-increasing experience" of even low-paid workers and their firm-specific skills which made labour "a most important factor in industrial success". Young apprentices had to be instilled with the right attitude towards work and their employers, and welfare work was most effective on those of an impressionable age.(79)

The industrial welfare facilities which expanded during the Post-War boom found a permanent place in steel companies even during the depressed periods of the 1920s and the 1930s. William Bain of Coatbridge had established the Lochrin Welfare Football Club in 1923. A sick pay scheme was instituted in 1926 and a Pension Fund in 1928, and both were recorded as doing well "despite the depression....."(80) In 1930, Marshall and Company founded a welfare scheme which charged elected works representatives with improving sports and social facilities. In the same year, a voluntary, self-supporting sick and accident fund at the Constructional Department was turned into the Company Welfare Fund. It began providing pensions in 1934.(81) Moreover, it was in the years after the Great Crash that important developments in the welfare practices of large steel companies, like United Steel, Dorman-Long, Richard Thomas´, and Stewart and Lloyds took place.

(v) THE CORPORATE COMPANY AND INDUSTRIAL WELFARE (III), 1930-1939:

(a) The United Steel Companies

The relationship between integrated manufacture, industrial structure, corporate management, internal labour markets, and industrial welfare is most clearly illustrated by the history of the United Steel Companies, established in 1918 by the amalgamation of four concerns. Its founder, Henry Steel, was rightly convinced that the new company would exercise greater bargaining power in the securing of raw materials. Shortages had been created by the Post-War Boom of 1918-21, and economies could be obtained from buying in greater bulk. A Central Board was appointed to handle the pooling of ore and coal between companies, but the full advantages of coordinated production were not achieved because management within the constituent companies continued unchanged. Each company was responsible for its own expenditure, and investment by the subsidiaries was haphazard. Competition between the units was encouraged. A report in 1921 stated the advantages of operating as a single entity with a central staff and full-time chairman. Losses could be reduced by concentrating certain steels in those plants best suited to produce them. Capital, however, was not restructured, and, by the mid-1920s, optimistic investment in 1918-1921 had left United Steel overcapitalised. When loans of over £1m had to be redeemed in the financial year 1927-1928, United Steel found itself unable to meet even the interest charges.(82)

In 1927, the Board appointed Robert Hilton as Managing Director. He instigated the managerial reorganisation of 1928-1930, imposed central control over finance, and provided for the better planning of production between units. U.S.C.´s Head Office was moved from the headquarters of Steel, Peech and Tozer, a constituent company, and given its own building. The functions of administration, sales, and purchasing were also centralised. Statistical and accounting systems were unified, and a single store of information and data was built up. Important business, like capital expenditure, managerial appointments and financial allocations, had to be authorised by the Central Board on the recommendations of a Finance and General Purposes Committee. The boards of the subsidiaries were also reformed, with those having no seat on the Central Board or without a responsibility in branch management being retired. As a consequence of the Depression, U.S.C.´s capital in 1930 was written down by £9.75m to £11.5m. The production of railway materials, the largest element of United Steel´s business, was concentrated at the Workington Iron and Steel Company with its acid Bessemer plant. Other heavy steel products were allocated to S.P.T.´s Ickles Works, while Templeborough concerned itself with heavy carbon-steels. Samuel Fox´s Stockbridge plant was to manufacture lighter goods, and special and alloy steels. The Cleveland collieries were closed, and redundant plant like some forges at Fox´s and the tyre-mills at Workington were scrapped. There were difficulties, however, over the calculation of "depreciation rates" upon which government compensation for War-time losses was based. These problems and the vested interests of some shareholders in the subsidiaries halted the transfer of shares to the new single entity of United Steel. S.P.T. remained a separate company till 1931. The plants at Scunthorpe were not integrated into U.S.C. until 1946, while Samuel Fox remained legally independent into the 1950s. Due to the U.S.C.'s financial situation, major capital development was forestalled until 1933-1934, and peaked in 1937-1938 with the building of an integrated plant near to basic ore supplies at Appleby-Frodingham in Lincolnshire.(83)

Yet, "The reconstruction of United Steel in 1928 produced not only a reorganisation of its management and its production structure, but also the first ventures in those aspects of management which are additional to the primary activities of buying, manufacture and selling which have now come to be regarded as important and essential parts of management responsibilities. The most important of these internal ventures were labour relations....."(84) A staff pension scheme was begun in 1928, and indicated the company's new commitment to establishing a large managerial hierarchy. U.S.C.'s policy towards its labour-force, however, relied upon works councils. Workers' pensions were not introduced until 1935. The works councils were closely linked with managerial reorganisation in 1928-1930, while the pension scheme was connected with the capital developments of 1934-38. Just as management was centralised and systemised, works councils were charged with operating on a uniform basis at plant and company level. They sought to imbue loyalty to U.S.C. by regularising the rights and conditions of workers on a company-wide basis. The councils, for example, took over the administration of the varied welfare schemes organised at once-independent works. They instilled a "tradition of mutual confidence", cooperation, good feeling, safety-consciousness, and two-way communications between employer and employee. The provision of pensions, on the other hand, eased the shedding of old and inefficient workers when more mechanised techniques were being introduced. U.S.C. saw the replacement of labour as a permanent source of economy because machinery was less troublesome. There was also a greater need to reduce labour-turnover amongst men trained in the new techniques. Only welfare benefits like pensions could ensure loyalty, which was considered a prerequisite to "smoothness of operation" in "ancillary operations" like the charging of new machinery.(85)

Works councils, as well as managerial reorganisation, were introduced by Hilton. Safety First and Suggestions Committees were also appointed. Each plant had it own works council able to send members to a central representative body. Works councils provided workers with insight into the administration of the company. They allowed labour "to take their part in the management of welfare services and similar functions". The Appleby-Frodingham Works Council had forty members, and an Accident Prevention Committee, a Canteen Committee, a Sick and Dividing Club, a Coal Committee, and a Benevolent Society. It managed welfare buildings like the Athletics Club. Moreover, "The Council is kept regularly in touch with proposed developments of the Works, or changes in practice by the Works Manager, who regularly attends their meetings". The Council at Appleby-Frodingham superseded a joint sports committee established in 1922. It had deducted 1d per week from pay-packets, although the wages of groundsmen were paid by the company. The enthusiasm for sports facilities was illustrated by the fact that, during a stoppage in 1921, workers had given up their time to lay pitches and carry out repairs.(86) Indeed, one of the guiding principles behind changes in welfare practice was to put "Social Organisation" completely under the control of the men. Although sports and recreation clubs relied upon U.S.C.'s financial assistance, they were considered more effective if the initiative of members could be encouraged.(87) The Workington Welfare Hall was registered as a company in 1929 and its directors were elected by ballot.(88) By 1935, every branch works council at U.S.C. had its benevolent sick society.(89) In the ten year period between 1938-48, United Steel spent £335,000 every year on welfare facilities.(90)

When George V in 1935 requested that on the occasion of his Silver Jubilee workers should be granted a day's holiday, U.S.C. instead decided to donate a day's wage bill to establishing a Convalescent and Holiday Home for Appleby-Frodingham workers, and cottage homes for employees retiring from S.P.T., Fox's, and Workington. This decision, however, was reached after great argument within the company. United Steel had calculated that just paying the £10,000 in wages was cheaper than losing a day's production as well. The directors were also opposed to dividing the money equally between the men, on the grounds that the £10,000 was consequently frittered. The cash grant was allocated to the works councils, who were to ballot the workers on the use to which the money should be put, although the Managing Director had the final say in the matter. The only question asked of the men was whether they wanted a convalescent home or retirement cottages. U.S.C. hoped for savings from not having to continue donating to private convalescent homes. But workers were discontented at not receiving a day's holiday. The opportunity of the Jubilee was used to extend industrial welfare policies. To the directors, a permanent institution for the benefit of employees would help "display the corporate and family spirit" during the Jubilee.(91)

The provision of amenities and the temporary alleviation of sickness did not need the central planning and extensive financing of a pension scheme. The company, consequently, dithered in 1935 over the prospect of providing workers' pensions. The central Works Council, meeting in October that year, pressed for their introduction but their request was at first refused.(92) Nevertheless, a deal with the Legal and General Assurance Company was soon signed and, by the end of 1935, 1,500 had joined the new pension scheme. By 1937, 90% of the workforce were contributors, and membership was a condition of employment for workers joining the firm.(93)

(b) Dorman, Long & Company

The steel companies of the North East coast, unwilling to sacrifice their individual interests for the regional industry as a whole, resisted the creation of large-scale units of production. By continuing to invest heavily in declining sectors like ship-plates and engineering after the War, costly mistakes were made. Managerial practices, interest groups within firms, rigidities of plant, and financial burdens merely increased their reliance on these declining sectors throughout the 1920s. Production overlapped between and within North Eastern companies, and bottlenecks at different process-stages continued. Although by 1923 Dorman-Long had consolidated all the concerns it had absorbed in recent years into a single company, little restructuring of plant followed. The amalgamation of Dorman-Long with Bolckow-Vaughn in 1929 led only to the closing of the Carlton Ironworks.(94) Dorman-Long, consequently, remained backward in developing corporate management, and did not establish during this period extensive internal labour markets systems or comprehensive welfare services.

The formation of "Welfare Committees" had been discussed in 1918, although a system of "works committees", acting as trustees for the sports and social clubs, was not actually appointed till 1928. Welfare, therefore, continued at first to be organised on a works basis and the practices of previous companies were continued. The Britannia and West March Ironworks, for example, levied 1d a week for the services of a doctor. Another 1d in deductions went to the North Riding Infirmary, where workers would be treated if they had obtained an admission ticket from the company.(95)

It seemed fairer in 1924 to extend the rights of the Bell Brothers Workmen's Savings Fund to all Dorman-Long employees than to abolish the institution altogether.(96) Dorman-Long recognised, nonetheless, that the maintenance of previous welfare schemes created anomalies. Because the sports and social clubs had developed haphazardly, the Board in 1930 commissioned a report on all the associations "run mainly for the benefit of employees of the company...." Three boys' clubs, a sports club, two workmen's institutes, and three workmen's clubs were investigated.(97) A more centralised direction of welfare facilities was recommended, but no action was taken until 1935. This was partly because of the drain of the economic depression on available resources, and partly because the direction of welfare policy could not be finalised while the company dithered over whether to grant pension rights to all its employees or not.

In 1920, Dorman-Long had established a contributory pensions scheme for "officers", a category which included staff and foremen. Members had to be under 55 years when they joined and had to agree to joint contributions. Its principal purpose was to ensure that managers and supervisors did not join a union. The scheme was open only to those who were not members of labour organisations, and those unwilling to join had to submit a written explanation to the directors. The company, in addition, began making annual donations to a special fund, which could at the discretion of the directors help officers in circumstances not covered by the pension scheme.(98) By 1922, "all those who were paid upstanding wages and not by the day or hour" were encouraged to join the contributory pension scheme, because, like officers, they were permanent employees. But the Board's Pension Committee generally accepted the recommendations of local managers that long-serving men, if they were not members of the pension scheme and even if they were hourly-paid employees, should be granted at 65 years of age ex gratia allowances from the special fund. Awards were not given on any systematic basis. One labourer, for example, was granted 5/- per week in 1922, while another at the Redcar furnaces was awarded 10/-. A 78-year-old metal carrier at Samuelson and Company received 10/- for 39 years' service, while a labourer at Dorman-Long's Sheet Department received a similar amount after only ten years at the works. In 1923, the Pension Fund was responsible for 212 people at a cost of £8,711 for the year.(99)

The company estimated that the 1925 Old Age Pensions Act would cost it some £12,000 per annum, and the Board was determined to make savings in welfare provision to defray the extra costs. It reduced its contributions to the Pension Fund, and deducted £500 a year from the special fund also. After 1925, only staff members could join the Pension Fund. It was hoped that these measures would save a total of £5,000 per year.(100) Yet, Dorman-Long felt obliged to honour the welfare commitments undertaken by Bolckow, Vaughn when it was bought out in 1929. The "ex-officials" of Bolckow, Vaughn had to be included in Dorman-Long's pension scheme, but the discretionary "Workmen's Allowances amounting to £2,087" were also confirmed. This decision, to be reviewed annually, affected 160 men. Moreover, the Pensions Committee at Dorman-Long had in fact continued since 1925 to make discretionary awards to workers. The perceived advantages of cost-cutting had not surpassed the value of welfare in industrial life. Every claim for benefit had to be individually assessed, and this cumbersome procedure was revised in 1931. It was decided that grants of 5s would be automatically awarded for fifty years' service, and that they would be reduced to 2/6d when a beneficiary or his wife became eligible for a state pension. All "border-line" cases, however, would continue to be assessed by the Committee on an individual basis.(101)

By 1934, Dorman-Long had established a Pensions Office in order to wind up the Pension Fund and to provide all pensions on an ex gratia basis and according to the 1931 guidelines. Dorman-Long's limited profitability and its failure to construct an integrated works meant that it had a small "core" of permanent workers. It had little reason, therefore, to sustain a systematic pension scheme. With the dissolution of the company pension fund, however, it was thought necessary to place other welfare activities on a uniform basis. Savings could also be made. Dorman-Long appointed a Welfare Office to streamline the wide variety of sports, social, and benevolent clubs. In 1935, all donations made by individual works to convalescent homes were channelled into three institutions at Redcar, Dinsdale, and Leeds.(102) In the following year, the newly-appointed Welfare Officer was instructed to found an Employees' Provident Fund to incorporate the many benevolent societies at the various works. The new society provided sick pay and hospital treatment. It was headed by a Workmen's Committee, although the Welfare Officer became the Honorary Secretary and Treasurer. Dorman-Long agreed to supplement the men's contributions of 4d a week by 10% of its total income. Membership of the Fund was made a condition of employment for all new recruits to the company. Each situation of hardship was reviewed independently, and Dorman-Long was not committed to maintaining its financial assistance which had been its chief objection to continuing the Pension Fund.(103) An Employees' Sports Committee was founded in 1936 to organise activities on a company-wide basis, and the Welfare Officer was a given a central directing role because of the apathetic attitude of works managers. Grants were given to promote sports associations and inter-company competitions between works. In cases like Cleveland where there was a limited number of sporting leagues, the intervention of the Welfare Officer was crucial.(104)

As Dorman-Long failed to rationalise its plant, it did not establish the more extensive internal labour markets of other steel companies. But as demand expanded in the later 1930s with the increase in government armament contracts, Dorman-Long systemised its sports clubs and non-contributory benevolent societies. Such provision instilled loyalty and helped alleviate work-disaffection. Unlike contributory pensions, it was not intended to reduce labour-turnover.

(c) Richard Thomas and Company

Whereas the United States tinplate industry largely concentrated upon the manufacture of autobody sheet, no single item dominated British output. As companies were contracted to a number of suppliers, rollers required the adaptability provided by small-scale machinery. Rolling, consequently, remained a separate trade to the production of tinplate bar. The nature of the domestic market hindered the development of integrated tinplate works. A fragmented industrial structure caused overproduction, and many works were under-utilised. Richard Thomas´ profits and prices throughout the 1920s were undercut by the comparatively low costs of entry into small-scale tinplate manufacture. Cheap imports added to economic instability. Only Baldwins, who obtained contracts to supply Anglo-Persian Petroleum and Shell, were able at Elba to build an integrated tinplate unit in the 1920s. Yet, as the selling price of tinplate bar increased after 1925, rollers were keen to develop permanent links with suppliers. Moreover, greater company size improved the purchasing power of tinplate producers. During the late 1920s, Richard Thomas´ began buying out rivals and established a dominant position in the British tinplate industry. But, on the whole, its plant remained unrationalised. The scale of losses at Redbourn was so great that there was no prospect of paying dividends on Ordinary Shares at Richard Thomas´ while production continued there on old lines. William Firth who gained control of the company from the Thomas family was convinced that Redbourn should be scrapped or developed into an integrated basic Bessemer plant at a cost of £2.5 million. Only the greater market security provided by the imposition of import duties in 1932 allowed Thomas´ to concentrate production as well as ownership. Under pressure from the government, the company agreed to build the new plant at the inland site of Ebbw Vale where unemployment was high. Relative costs favoured Redbourn with its proximity to Lincolnshire´s basic ores. Ebbw Vale was designed to produce 250,000 tons per annum of high grade steel. It was equipped with a large rolling mill, and had guarantees of orders from customers like Morris and Austin.(105)

Richard Thomas´ had acquired the Redbourn works in 1906. By 1921, the Redbourn Village Society owned 238 houses.(106) There were official Sick Clubs and others spontaneously and independently organised by the men. All employees could join the main self-managed Sick Club. Benefits included sick-pay and death grants to widows, and administrative costs were covered by the company. The Workmen´s Hospital Fund, founded in 1910, gave donations to the unemployed, to a Nursing Fund, an Aged and Poor Fund, and a convalescent home.(107) In 1925, welfare facilities were extended at Llanelly by the founding of a club with billiard rooms, a gymnasium, bowling greens, and tennis courts.(108) The Abercarn Welfare Fund was established in 1931. Levies were set at 2d per week and they were intended to continue the traditional welfare services set out in the previous owners´ articles of association. Drawn up in 1875, they stated that the employers should promote the welfare of workers through their support for clubs, provident societies, hospitals, and churches.(109)

While Thomas´ remained a conglomeration of small companies, industrial welfare was uncoordinated. One exception to leaving welfare in the control of individual works was the profitsharing scheme established in 1921. 7.5% dividends were distributed. Industrial relations would be improved, "as every Employee Shareholder in the Company had an additional interest in helping to save the profits, and the scheme also encourages better work and tends to the advancement of the joint interests of the Company and its employees". Close cooperation between employers and employed was particularly necessary in the tinplate industry "for the human element enters into that industry to an exceptional degree". Small-scale tinplate manufacture was dependent upon the skills and loyalty of its workforce. Richard Thomas´ claimed to have "recognised that fact". House-loans and a Welfare Inspector "to look after the training of the boys" were also envisaged as part of a comprehensive, company-wide welfare policy.(110)

Richard Thomas´ had founded an Officers and Staff Pension Scheme by 1921,(111) and it was the trade union side on the Tinplate Joint Industrial Council which in 1926 first argued for the introduction of workers´ pensions. The I.S.T.C. repeated their proposals in 1929 and 1933, but the employers would not countenance the costs.(112) Opinions within the industry were altered, however, once William Firth began in 1934 to give the idea his support. Firth was motivated by changes in the labour management requirements of the Ebbw Vale works. Large-scale, rationalised production required a more permanent workforce suited to the skills of the continuous, integrated process which was replacing the old "hand mills".(113) Pensions would help ease out those least adaptive and proficient in the new techniques. Firth offered to give £25,000 of his own money to start the scheme if other employers would match the sum. Firth was a member of the Provisional Management Committee appointed by the 1935 annual meeting of the J.I.C. to draw up the rules of the pension fund. Death benefits were also to be provided by the scheme, which was completely private and did not rely on the services of an insurance company. It was decided that companies should contribute a levy of one and a quarter pennies per box of steel ingot produced. A 2.5% levy on wages would also be needed to accrue the £125,000 in benefits expected to be paid in 1936. But negotiations over the scheme lasted three years. It was finally decided that works could join the scheme if 80% of their men had agreed by ballot to become members by 24th September 1937. Only John Player and Son, with a contributory fund of its own, was excluded from the operation of the scheme. Trades unions had complete control over the administration of the pensions, but rules could not be revised without the permission of every contributing employer. Benefits were made payable by July 1938.(114)

Firth circularised employers in 1937 urging their agreement to the plans. He argued for the introduction of pensions on a number of grounds apart from those of humanity. Improvements in trading conditions over the next few years would make labour restive. It was commercially sound to retire men who were 65 and, consequently, the least efficient. A lack of industrial provision would bring increased state involvement. Administrative and financial responsibility for the scheme lay with the unions. Moreover, the payment of pension contributions was merely an accepted and natural element of wage-costs. Firth also contended that tinplate employers were fortunate in having moderate labour leaders like Ernie Bevin. As advocates of pensions, their authority had to be upheld.(115) The unions, undoubtedly, helped gain the men's acceptance of the pension scheme. Resistance to the 2.5% levy on wages was illustrated by the 5,000 tinplate workers who struck unofficially in April 1936. The Welsh Plate and Sheet Manufacturers Association was determined not to make concessions to rank and file dissent, and, with the cooperation of the union, contributions were first collected in 1937. The union also agreed to suspend retirement at 65 for the two years after 1938, because demand was expanding so fast that there was a shortage of skilled labour.(116)

By 1938, therefore, sports and social amenities, sick pay, medical treatment, and profitsharing were available at Richard Thomas', and, because of the restructuring of its capital and the expansion of an internal labour market, the company introduced old age pensions.

(d) Stewart and Lloyds

Stewart and Lloyds revised both production and labour management in 1918: "The unification of management had to be considered owing to the various methods and systems which in each case were the result of many years experience...." at different works. Because Stewart and Lloyds was a large company dominating the manufacture of steel tubes in Britain, it required a more central direction of decision-making and the systemisation of procedures. Its Employees Benefit Fund was given the role of unifying the organisation of welfare provision. It was supervised by the Board's Employees Benefit Committee, and paid ex gratia sick pay, pensions, and death benefits. It was concluded, however, that all aspects of reorganisation would take years to achieve, and, indeed, production and management were not comprehensively rationalised until 1931. Stewart and Lloyds concluded that "a greater measure of consolidation of British Tube Tonnage" was needed to "ensure economy and to provide conditions of manufacture essential to large output as now used or being developed". Once the decision to concentrate production at Corby was taken, it was clear that Stewart and Lloyds would have to undertake a more rigorous streamlining of management than had been previously attempted. The size of the Board was cut, and decision-making was finally moved to the centre: "The reorganisation (is) to be designed to fit in with the Centre Department situated in London". Some sub-committees to the Board were wound up, and the details of the business were transferred from many part-time directors to a small body of professionals. A.G.Macdiarmid was appointed General Managing Director and he and five Managing Directors formed an executive committee. Sub-committees, like the Transfer Committee, the Special Salaries Committee, and the Employees Benefit Committee, were considered useful and important enough to be continued.(117)

During the 1920s, local works remained responsible for organisations like the Clydesdale and Vulcan Welfare Clubs. They "entered deeply into the tissue of local life, providing recreation, religious instruction, choral singing, bowls, badminton, and billiards". The Vulcan Welfare Club owned a hut where dinners and dances were held, and had a Holiday Fund and Safety First Committee. Carfin Hall, near Clydesdale, catered for cricket, bowling, tennis and football. In 1928, the Clydesdale works established a Benevolent Fund to supplement the central Employees Benevolent Fund. It replaced the old Works Friendly Society which had included only skilled men as members. The new society's constitution and rules were agreed by "accredited representatives" of the Welfare Club and Works Friendly Society, and the scheme covered sickness, accident and death. 4d a week was deducted from wages to provide 12s for the first twelve weeks of sickness, 9s for the next, and then 5s for an unstipulated period. Death benefit was set at £6 and £3 for a deceased worker and wife respectively.(118)

The Stewart and Lloyds Employees' Trust Limited was formed in 1923 to undertake any project for the benefit of employees. 60,000 company shares secured a permanent source of funds for general welfare projects. In 1924, 20,000 40s shares were freely distributed by the Trust to all employees at Stewart and Lloyds.(119) A share held for four years received an annual bonus of 1s, and an extra 1/6d was given to any shares held for five years or more. Stewart and Lloyds also agreed to compensate the men for any part of their dividends that were taxed. The company were careful in stating that wage-levels would be unaffected by the scheme, and employees were given the same rights as Ordinary shareholders. The Trust was prepared to advance loans to help workers and staff purchase further shares, and, in 1924, Stewart and Lloyds lent the Trust £20,000 at 4% to purchase more shares from the company. By May 1924, 33,058 shares had been issued to workers.(120)

When it was decided to develop the greenfield site of Corby, it was realised that "the problems of labour and trade union relations would be urgent and difficult". After some procrastination, it was finally decided that workers' trades unions would be recognised. But "every endeavour was to be made to settle a works difference locally at the works without reference to a neutral committee". Staff unions were never countenanced. The building of the plant and a community entailed a huge transfer of men and materials. The local authority had to assist in the construction of houses, and Stewart and Lloyds received local government subsidies for the building, by 1937, of 2,253 houses. The company provided shops, and, by 1938, a Welfare Hall and Sports Ground. Traditional practices were continued, for "It had always been the practice of the Company at its older works in Scotland and in England to encourage sports and communal activities of all kinds among its employees. It was realised from the start that assistance on an even more liberal scale might be given at Corby". The work of the trust established by J.G.Stewart at Clydesdale in 1908 was transferred to Corby. A Welfare Supervisor was appointed to oversee the various recreational associations, although detailed administration was left to the workers' committees. The Odeon (Corby) Limited was created in association with Odeon Cinemas and a picture-house was opened in 1936. A boys' club, gymnasium, and swimming pool were particular needs fulfilled by the company.(121)

(v) THE CORPORATE COMPANY AND INDUSTRIAL WELFARE (IV): SUMMARY

Despite amalgamations between steel companies during the Great War, the managerial sructure of the industry remained largely unchanged. As a consequence, sports associations, social clubs, and sick benefit societies, which increased markedly in the years after 1918, were independently organised at individual works. When the Tariff was implemented in 1932, steel companies in expanding sectors of the industry began to tackle the financial and productive inefficiencies of an anarchic capital structure. Corporate managements were founded to administer the large companies which were established, and labour management practices had to be revised. As management became more systematic and centralised at United Steel in 1928, industrial welfare provision was placed on a more unified basis by the appointment of a corporate system of works councils. Capital reorganisation at Richard Thomas' and United Steels in the 1930s increased their "core" of company-trained workers, and pension schemes were founded as a means of reducing labour turnover. Due to the early dominance of Stewart and Lloyds in the tubes trade, its Employees Benevolent Fund had been attempting to systemise company provision since the end of the Great War, and its finances were secured by the creation of a trust fund in 1923. Pensions had been available at Stewart and Lloyds since 1913, and they remained throughout this period ex gratia for historical reasons. Dorman-Long, which rationalised neither plant nor management, continued with the provision of unsystemised benefits.

(vi) CONCLUSION

Industrial welfare was an important aspect of industrial relations in the iron and steel industry, and ex gratia benefits were suited to the circumstances of small and medium-sized companies. Competitive rivalries and low profitability hindered the establishment of internal labour markets and the systemisation of company provision, particularly in the heavy steel sector. The development of company structures and welfare in the industry was, therefore, pre-empted by the chemicals trade in the 1920s. But the evidence of this chapter does reveal a link between managerial restructuring and the systemisation of industrial welfare, and markedly so in the case of tinplate and tube concerns. However, the example of United Steel - which was engaged in most types of steel production - most clearly illustrates the link between capital and managerial organisation and welfare.

NOTES

1. Carr & Taplin (1962), chs.vii,xvii,xxv,xxvii,xli; J.Porter "The Iron Trade" in C.Wrigley The History of British Industrial Relations, 1875-1914 (1982), pp.253-265.
2. Carr & Taplin (1962), pp.73-4,145-6,149-50,279-80, 287-8.
3. T.H.Burnham & G.O.Hoskins Iron and Steel in Britain 1870-1930 (1943), pp.17-8,39-40,42-5.
4. S.Tolliday "Industry, Finance, and the State: An Analysis of the British Steel Industry in the inter-war years" (Camb. Ph.D., 1979), pp.14-16. On the role of British entrepreneurship and the steel industry, cf. D.N.McCloskey Economic Maturity and Entrepreneurial Decline (1973); L.G.Sandberg & D.N.McCloskey "From Damnation to Redemption: Judgments on the Late Victorian Entrepreneur" in D.N.McCloskey (ed) Enterprise and Trade in Victorian Britain (1981); & L.G.Sandberg "The Entrepreneur and Technical Change" in R.Floud & D.N.McCloskey (eds) The Economic History of Britain since 1700, Vol.II (1981), pp.99-120.
5. PP 1918 (C.9071) xiii 423, p.20.
6. Burnham & Hoskins (1943), pp.49,206-7.
7. Tolliday (1979), p.31.
8. Ibid, pp.14-15,31,41.
9. Chandler (1973), p.13.
10. Cf. O.E.Williamson Markets and Hierarchies (1975).
11. Namely the motor car, chemical, tobacco, electrical,

and distributive trades.
12. Chandler (1973), pp.13-14.
13. Ibid, pp.2,9,11.
14. O.E.Williamson in A.D.Chandler & H.Daems (eds) Managerial Hierarchies (1980), p.187.
15. Chandler (1973), pp.44,326,334.
16. Tolliday (1979), pp.35,42,382.
17. H.Brearly Steel-Makers (1933), pp.vii,85.
18. H.Gintz "Effects of Technological Change on Labour in Selected Sections of the Iron and Steel Industries of Great Britain, the United States, and Germany, 1900-1939" (London Ph.D., 1954), Abstract, & pp.90-92,98.
19. A.G.P.Elliot "Company Welfare Benefits" in G.L. Reid & D.J.Robertson Fringe Benefits, Labour Costs, and Social Security (1965), pp.300-9.
20. Carr & Taplin (1962), pp.9-10,63-70,73,75,77,136, 139,277.
21. J.S.Jeans Conciliation and Arbitration in Labour Disputes (1884), pp.16,24.
22. Carr & Taplin (1962), p.66.
23. Cf. Ch.1, ss.(i),(ii).
24. Brearley (1933), p.82.
25. A.Raistrick Dynasty of Iron Founders: the Darbys of Coalbrookdale (1953), pp.256,258-60,262-3; A.Raistrick The Coalbrookdale Ironworks (1975), p.11. For another firm in the traditional iron-making areas of the 18th Century, cf. L.T.C.Holt Waterloo Ironworks: A History of Taskers of Andover, 1809-1968, pp.109-111.
26. Cf. E.P.Thompson "Time, Work Discipline and Industrial Capitalism", Past & Present (1977), pp.56-97.
27. R.H.Campbell Carron Company (1961), pp.231-4. The provident fund was wound up in 1911 with the passing of the National Insurance Act.
28. C.R.Andrew The Story of the Wortley Ironworks (1952), pp.54-5. Cf. S.Pollard The Genesis of Modern Management (1965), p.235 on factory villages in the iron and steel industry.
29. B.J.D.Harrison "Ironmasters and Ironworkers" in C.A.Hampstead (ed.) Cleveland Iron and Steel (1979), pp.234-6,240. On the lives of iron workers and their families, cf. F.Bell At the Works (1985, 1st edn. 1907), esp. pp.xvii,85-141. Lady Bell was the wife of Sir Hugh Bell of Bell Brothers, a leading Middlesborough firm. On Middlesborough, cf. also P.D.Stubley "The Churches in the Iron and Steel Industry in Middlesborough, 1890-1914" (Durham M.A., 1979).
30. British Steel Corporation 218/7, Directors´ Minutes, 7 March 1871; 1 Dec 1874; 29 Nov 1875; 31 March 1896. Also, Consett/7/1753, 25 July 1900.
31. BSC 1066/13/9, General Meeting, 11 Aug 1900; Extraordinary G.M., 1 Sept 1900.

Company-based Labour Policies in the Iron and Steel Industry

32. Ibid, 7 April 1908; 7 July 1908.
33. J.L.Carvel The Coltness Iron Company (1948), pp.57-8.
34. A.Muir 75 Years: A Record of Progress: Smith's Stamping Works (Coventry) Ltd; Smith-Clayton Forge Ltd (Lincoln) (1958), pp.39-41.
35. BSC 29/12/2, Stewart and Lloyds, Rules of the Mutual Benefit Society....of..Kenrick & Sons (1882). Cf. R.A.Church Kenricks in Hardware, A Family Business (1969), pp.280-302; & "Family and Failure: Archibald Kenrick and Sons Ltd, 1900-1950" in B.Supple Essays in British Business History (1977), pp.103-124.
36. W.E.Minchinton The British Tinplate Industry (1957), pp.108-111. The Dowlais, Cyfartha, Aberdare, and Plymouth companies are quoted as keeping workers on "uneconomically" in PP 1867-8 (C.3980-I) xxxix 1.
37. PP 1867-8 (C.3980-I) xxxix 1, Qs.10,041-10,132. The Dowlais Ironworks was later merged into the conglomerate Guest, Keen, and Nettlefords, which inherited in 1896 playing fields from the previous owners of its Smethwick works. Cf. Gwent R.O., D.409.25, GKN Ltd An Outline History of this Group of Companies.... (1925). Re. Nettlefords, cf. J.L.Garvin The Life of Joseph Chamberlain, Vol.I (1932), pp.65-66; & D.Judd Radical Joe: a Life of Joseph Chamberlain (1977), p.22. Cf. also, G.M.Young Stanley Baldwin (1952), p.22; & A.W.Baldwin My Father: the True Story (1956), pp.25-26,77. Like the Dowlais company, William Clay, manager of the Mersey Steel and Ironworks, promoted company-backed friendly societies and company bargaining procedures in the 1860s as an alternative to trades unionism. Cf. PP 1867-8 (C.3980-I) xxxix 1, Qs.11,141-11,290.
38. Minchinton (1957), pp.111-113. The Melingriffith works' benefit club was founded in 1782, and the employment of generations of local labour there was seen as promoting cooperation and work-discipline.
39. Gwent R.O., D.751.356, Minute Book, 1846.
40. E.J.Davies The Blaenavon Story (1975), pp.37,52.
41. Industrial World, 17 June 1892, p.7.
42. BSC 271/3/31, Directors' Minutes, 30 Aug 1888, 18 Feb 1891; BSC 312/1/40, Rent Book, 1st entry on 30 June 1902.
43. BSC, 271/3/31, Directors' Minutes, 11 Jan 1911; 12 July 1912.
44. BSC 39/12/1, Letter to Messrs Lloyd & Lloyd, 6 July 1859; BSC, 29/12/2, Letter from workers, 1887; Rules of the Sick Society for the Workpeople employed at Lloyd and Lloyd, Albion Tubes Works (1888), established 1867.
45. BSC 39/7/3, Notes on the History of Stewart and Lloyds, 1919; BSC 65/1/3, Minute Book, 27 May 1913, 20 May 1914.
46. Cf. ss.(iv),(v).
47. Cf. PP 1914-16 (C.8133) xxix 289.

110

48. BSC 271/3/31, Directors´ Minutes, 25 Aug 1916. Cf. Whiteside (1980), pp.307-331.

49. Ministry of Munitions, Vol.V (1919), pp.44-5,55-6.

50. BSC 003/2/1, History of S.Fox & Co. Ltd (typed).

51. BSC 271/2/22, Rules of the Margram Cooperative Homes Ltd (1919); BSC 271/2/114, Crymlyn Burrows Housing Society Rules (1924); BSC Consett/7/1745, Memo., 4 March 1921. Cf. Ch.9, s.(iv).

52. BSC Consett/7/1745, Consett Iron Company Regulations and Conditions of Tenancy of Company´s Houses.

53. BSC 271/3/31, Directors´ Minutes, 18 Feb 1891; Letter from W.G.C. Ltd, 12 Feb 1917; 12 May 1917; BSC 1066/21, Housing Committee Minutes, 9 Sept 1919; 1 June 1920; 6 Oct 1920; 22 Nov 1920.

54. BSC Consett/7/1746, Memo., 8 Feb 1915; Letter from Private Coxon, 24 March 1915.

55. BSC 271/3/31, Directors´ Minutes, 22 Dec 1915.

56. BSC 65/1/3, Directors´ Minutes, 21 Aug 1914; 23 Sept 1914; 21 Oct 1914; 4 March 1915; 8 March 1916; 9 May 1918; 26 Jan 1922.

57. BSC 802/6/5, Parliamentary Committee, 6 Nov 1919.

58. BSC 802/6/35, CCWA, 22 Jan 1920.

59. For the Tinplate J.I.C., cf. s.(v)(III)(c).

60. BSC 802/6/5, NFISM Parliamentary Committee, 6 Nov 1919.

61. PRO LAB2/1012/IR111/1924, ISWMA JIC, Annual Report 1923-24; Memo., 18 Aug 1924, and Memo. from Chief Conciliation Office (NW Area), 9 July 1924; LAB2/2/1017/IR233/1923, Memo. by C.F.Walthers, 23 July 1923.

62. Cf. Ch.9, s.(v).

63. ISTEA Agreement with regards to holidays (1938), p.5 and passim. Cf. also F.Stones The British Ferrous Wire Industry, 1882-1962 (1977), pp.87-9,96-7,184-5,291.

64. PP 1918 (C.9071) xiii 423.

65. Andrews and Brunner (1954), pp.xii,67-8, 73-4,77,393.

66. Iron and Coal Trades Review, Dec 1927, pp.179-80.

67. Carr & Taplin (1962), pp.439,471-2,478,495-6,499; Tolliday (1979), pp.425-6,447-66.

68. R.S.Sayers The Bank of England 1871-1944 (1976), pp.315-6,322; T.Firth & J.Brown Ltd 100 Years of Steel (1937), p.70.

69. PP 1937 (C.5507) xii 423.

70. Iron and Coal Trades Review, 9 Dec 1921, p.840.

71. Campbell (1961), p.324.

72. WISC Group News, May 1948, pp.5-8.

73. Edgar Allen Magazine, Feb 1956, pp.55,58,260,267.

74. J.D.McKechnie The McKechnie Story (1965), pp.23-24. Contributory pensions were introduced by 1946.

75. M.Seth-Smith Two Hundred Years of Richard Johnson and Nephew (1973), pp.119,121,124,145,193.

76. Unity, Jan 1929, pp.312-3.

77. BSC 39/90/3, Synopsis of Stavely Coal and Iron Company Ltd and Subsidiary Companies, March 1925; Staveley Works Club, 31 Dec 1926; Barrow Hill Memorial Club, 31 Dec 1925; Ringwood Club, 30 June 1929; Devonshire Works Mess Room, 31 Dec 1926; Warsop Main Medical Aid Fund, 31 Dec 1926; Staveley Works Sick and Accident Fund, 31 Dec 1926. Cf. also Sunday School, General Fund; and Barrow Hill Works Fund, 1872.

78. Gwent R.O., D.409.25, GKN Ltd An Outline History of this Group of Companies.... (1925).

79. Colvilles Magazine, Jan 1920, p.131; Aug 1920, p.131.

80. W.Bain & Co. Ltd Lochrin's One Hundred Years: the Story of William Bain and Co. Ltd of Coatbridge (1959), p.50.

81. Marshall News, Autumn Number, 1930, pp.9,90.

82. Andrews & Brunner (1951), pp.119-121,123-4; R.Peddie The United Steel Companies Ltd, 1918-1968 (1969), pp.13-15.

83. Andrews & Brunner (1954), pp.119-20,156-8, 162-5,167-9,208,234.

84. Peddie (1969), pp.18-19,26.

85. Andrews & Brunner (1951), p.355; BSC 888/14A/1, USC: 5th Annual Week-end Conference of Representatives of Works Councils, 4-6th Oct 1935, pp.1,10-11,15,21.

86. Peddie (1969), p.26; G.R.Walshaw & C.A.J.Behrendt The History of Appleby-Frodingham (1950), pp.140-141; BSC 159/5/1, History of Appleby-Frodingham: An Outline (1950), pp.140-141.

87. BSC 159/1/7, Memo., 9 March 1938.

88. Ibid, Workington Welfare Hall, Articles of Association (1929).

89. BSC 888/14A/1, USC: 5th Annual Week-end Conference of Representatives of Works Councils, 4-6th Oct 1935, pp.1,10-11,15,21; BSC 159/1/4, USC: Cottage Trusts, 1935-39, Memo., 3 Feb 1936.

90. Andrews & Brunner (1951), p.318.

91. BSC 159/1/4, USC: Cottage Trusts, 1935-39, Poster for Works; Memo., n.d.; Memo., 1 May 1935; Memo., 21 May 1935; Letter to Cllr. Townsley, 4 May 1935.

92. BSC 888/14A/1 USC: 5th Annual Week-end Conference of Representatives of Works Councils, 4-6th Oct 1935, p.20.

93. Journal of Gas Lighting, 3 Feb 1937, p.263. The Park Gate Iron and Steel company established a Pension Fund to commemorate the Silver Jubilee. It was administered by a sub-committee of its works council. Pensions were set at 3d for every year's service, and the company could revise or disband the scheme at will. Cf. BSC Consett/7/1753, Rules for the Park Gate Company Pension Fund (1950).

94. Tolliday (1979), pp.65,71,74,81-88,125-6,132,140, 152,160-1.

95. BSC 271/3/31, Directors' Minutes, 25 Feb 1918; 17 Dec 1919; BSC 1066/12/2, Memo., on Cleveland Works Social and Athletic Club, 24 Nov 1941; BSC 1107/11/1, Britannia and West March Ironworks Rules, 4 May 1920.

96. BSC(UK)/SEC/3/102, Directors' Minutes, 9 April 1924.

97. BSC 1107/11/1, Memos., 2 April 1930; 28 Oct 1930; 6 Nov 1930; 1 Nov 1930; 8 Nov 1930.

98. BSC(UK)/SEC/3/1&2, 7 Sept 1920; BSC 1100/6/1, Dorman-Long Pension Fund, Book of Application Forms; BSC(UK)/SEC/3/1&2, Directors' Minutes, 7 Sept 1920.

99. BSC 1066/13/1, Pension Committee Minutes, 1 Sept 1922; 18 Dec 1922; 16 March 1923; 1 May 1923; 19 Oct 1923.

100. BSC CHM/SEC/1/1-3, 5 May 1925; BSC 1066/13/1, Pension Committee Minutes, 27 Oct 1925.

101. BSC(UK)/SEC/3/1&2, Directors' Minutes, 7 Sept 1920.

102. BSC 1066/12/2, Letter from Pensions Office to Industrial Welfare Society, 17 Sept 1934.

103. Ibid, Welfare Donations, Memo., 5 Sept 1935; BSC(UK)/SEC/3/1&2, Directors' Minutes, 17 Jan 1936; BSC 1066/12/2, Welfare Donations, Memo., 1 Aug 1936 & 17 Nov 1936; BSC 271/3/31, Directors' Minutes, 9 Feb 1939 & 9 March 1939.

104. BSC 1066/13/1, Employees Sports Committee, 16 March 1938; BSC 271/3/31, Directors' Minutes, 17 Jan 1936; Letter from Welfare Officer to Cleveland Works Sports Club, 28 Oct 1937; Memo., 7 Sept 1939; & BSC 1066/12/2, Welfare Donations, Memo., 3 June 1939, Cleveland Works Sports Club.

105. Tolliday (1979), pp.164-181,183,191-7,200,211,218, 221. Cf. Ch.7, s.(vii).

106. Ingot, May 1951, p.3.

107. BSC 271/2/103, RTB Redbourn Works, Scunthorpe, Memo., 4 October 1945. By 1940, Thomas' were contributing £50 to the Hospital Fund with a total income of £360. The Fund was the basis of the company's contributory pension scheme founded in 1948.

108. BSC 312/1/8, Accounts for 1930,1931,1932,1936,1940; Abercarn Old Age Pension Fund, Accounts, 1948; AGM, 21 Dec 1925, pp.4,10-11.

109. BSC 312/1/1, Abercarn Welfare Fund, 5 Sept 1931; BSC 312/3/4, Memo. of Association of the Abercarn Tinplate Company Limited (1895).

110. BSC 271/3/37, A.G.M., 20 Dec 1921, pp.2-3; AGM, 21 Dec 1925, pp.4,10-11.

111. Ibid, AGM, 20 Dec 1920; 271/2/6, Memo., on future of Staff Pension Scheme, 8 June 1939. The fund was insolvent by 1939. Benefits were reduced, and its business was transferred to an assurance company.

112. A.Pugh Men of Steel (1951), pp.406,444,487,492, 498.

113. B.S.Keeling & A.E.G.Wright The Development of the Modern British Steel Industry (1964), pp.15-16.

114. BSC 271/2/50, Rules of the Tinplate Trade Superannuation Fund (1937); Memo., 30 Jan 1936; Letter from Welsh Plate and Sheet Manufacturers Association, 6 March 1936; Memo., 1 July 1936; Memo., 1935; Explanatory Note on Main Points of the Scheme, by H.C.Thomas.

115. Ibid, Circular from Sir Wm. Firth, 4 May 1937.

116. Ibid, Extract from Western Mail, 27 April 1936;

Circular from W.P.S.M.A., 8 April 1936; Rules of the Tinplate Trades Superannuation Fund (1937); Circular from W.P.S.M.A., 5 May 1937.

117. BSC 39/7/3, Notes on the History of Stewart and Lloyds, 1919; BSC 65/1/3, 3 Feb 1931; 15 Dec 1931; 2 Feb 1932.

118. BSC 39/7/3, Clydesdale & Vulcan Welfare Club, Annual Report, 30 Sept 1928.

119. BSC 39/2/2, Memorandum and Articles of Association of Stewart and Lloyds Trust Ltd (1923); Letter from Secretary to Directors, 20 March 1924.

120. BSC 65/1/3, Directors' Minutes, 22 & 27 May 1924.

121. F.Scopes The Development of Corby Works (1968), pp.110-8,129-31,237; BSC 39/7/3, Clydesdale & Vulcan Welfare Club, Annual Report, 30 Sept 1928.

Chapter 5

SYSTEMATIC MANAGEMENT AND WELFARE IN THE CHEMICALS INDUSTRY

(i) INTRODUCTION

The chemicals industry underwent extensive rationalisation from the 1890s onwards, and two companies, I.C.I. and
Unilever, came to dominate British chemical output. Moreover,
they both became recognised exponents of all-embracing
industrial welfare schemes. The expanding demand for chemical
products in the 20th Century and a secure domestic market
enabled the industry to enlarge the funding and extent of
company welfare. Provision was, therefore, greater than in
"old", contracting staples like steel.(1) Given the degree of
attention paid to company organisation and management in the
chemicals industry, it is not surprising that welfare was also
highly systemised. The chemicals trade was not truly a "new"
industry, since the production of chemicals had been essential
to many textile, glass, and paper making processes throughout
the 19th Century. Consequently, 20th Century chemical
companies inherited traditions of small-firm Victorian
paternalism.
    I.C.I was formed in 1926 by the amalgamation of Nobels,
the British Dyestuffs Corporation, United Alkali, and Brunner,
Mond. At its founding, it controlled 40% of Britain's chemical
output, and was the country's largest company in terms of
capitalisation.(2) The careful co-ordination and long-term
planning of production within a large firm brought
efficiencies, avoided bottlenecks at various process-stages,
and obviated the dangers of over-competition amongst many
rivals. Research and development, a costly item in the
chemicals industry, could be pooled and centralised. The
amalgamation in 1926 brought together paint, dyestuffs,
fertiliser, alkali, explosives, and metals interests, and the
technological opportunities of the industry entailed further
product differentiation. The variety of processes and markets
made the creation of semi-autonomous divisions or groups a
practical administrative necessity. I.C.I. took its model from
Nobel Industries, which in the early 1920s had found the right

115

balance between the authority of top and middle management. From the outset, I.C.I. established a headquarters in control of purchasing, personnel, publicity, investment, and legal and taxation matters throughout the four constituent companies. A single system of accountancy was introduced, and research and development resources were amalgamated. Sufficient central authority allowed plant to be rationalised on the basis of reports about the viability of each works. During 1928-1931, responsibility was devolved to eight boards in control of product divisions or groups. Each group controlled its own finance and capital investment but was accountable to the main board for its performance. It was by the 1930s a rare example of the "modern" multidivisional, decentralised corporation. McGowan, who succeeded the first chairman Alfred Mond in 1930, insisted, however, on direct control over pricing policy. Therefore, the groups which were responsible for their own success or failure paradoxically had little say over the price-levels of their products.(3)

As I.C.I. approached the question of management in a systematic and planned fashion, its labour policies are important to the history of industrial welfare. It adopted the paternalistic practices of Brunner, Mond,(4) but altered them to suit its different size and structure. The reorganisation of welfare at I.C.I. was contemporaneous with the restructuring of management, and the organisation and comprehensiveness of the company's schemes were aspects of systematic management in general. I.C.I., therefore, provides an important test case.

The advantages of multidivisional enterprise applied even further to Lever Brothers, which joined with the Dutch Margarine Union in 1929 to form Unilever. Soap manufacture became an increasingly technological enterprise involving diversification into oil-milling, alkalis, rosin, perfumes, glycerine, and candles. Lever Brothers, however, remained principally a soap concern in control by 1921 of 158 associated and unintegrated companies. The authority of its founder and sole Ordinary shareholder, William Lever, substituted for formal organisation. Control over the associated companies, like Gossages, Knights, and Crosfields,(5) depended upon the extent of Lever's individual stake in them. Yet, by 1924, Lever controlled some 90% of British soap output.

But even Lever in the early 1920s had come to recognise that his vast expanding conglomeration required managerial restructuring. The parlous state of the company's finances, attributed to the inability of one man singly to control so large an organisation, made managerial reform inevitable. Reorganisation was undertaken by Francis D'Arcy Cooper, who joined the Board in 1921. Special sub-committees dealing with manufacturing, finance, and the West African raw material interests were formed. The many companies were reorganised according to regions, but, in 1923, it was decided to group companies by product. As commercial rivalry between the three major producers, Levers, Crosfields, and Gossages, was especially intense in export markets, an Export Trade Board was set up as a means of joint consultation. But, even if Lever lost some of his direct influence, he remained firmly in charge till his death in 1925, continuing to believe that rivalry between the associated companies produced incentives and overall benefits.(6)

One element of the reorganisation of the early 1920s was the greater autonomy given to Lever Brother's Port Sunlight works. The prospect of a slump in 1920 led to a call for greater efficiency and a reduction in manpower. Lever had always taken a direct personal interest in the works and its model village, but in 1922 the administrative headquarters of the company was moved from Port Sunlight to Blackfriars in London. Consequently, a General Works Manager was appointed at Port Sunlight.(7) He was backed by a new Management Committee intended to create a "self-contained unit". The irregular engagement and discharge of workers was stopped, quality supervision and stores control were reorganised, and cost accounting methods were revised. A Staff Officer was given charge of the new Service Department which took over control of welfare from Lever himself. Its duties were "all domestic matters connected with the Works and Village".(8) The professionalisation of management did not finally occur until the chairmanship of D'Arcy Cooper, who succeeded Lever on his death in 1925. Cooper increasingly delegated day-to-day affairs so that he could concentrate on long-term or strategical issues. Administration was increasingly transferred and centralised at London. Cooperation throughout the company in product-development, advertising, and market research was secured by the appointment of special committees.(9)

The commercial advantages of soap and margarine producers cooperating rather than competing over the securing of oils underlay the decision to amalgamate with the Dutch Margerine Union in 1929. Moreover, the rapid demand for margarine from the 1900s onwards had forced the British and Dutch firms into rivalry for retailing outlets.(10) Unilever, like its predecessors, was engaged in the production of numerous goods, wholesaling, transport, and retailing - but on a far greater scale.(11) Cooper soon established himself as Unilever's chief executive. His main objective was to found a single, unified company. In 1931, London became Unilever's headquarters, and voting on the board according to groups representative of the two old companies was ended. Capital expenditure was controlled centrally, and Cooper was able to close works and rationalise plant throughout the 1930s. Salaries and accounting were standardised. The problem was recognised to be the establishment of sufficient degrees of headquarters control and freedom of action in middle management. Divisional responsibility was shared according to product and geography, a decision which reflected the organisational problems of a worldwide chemicals, soap and foods group.(12) This hybrid organisation, however, undoubtedly obfuscated the division of managerial responsibility within the company.(13)

Just as Lever had controlled commercial management personally, the extensive welfare expenditure of Lever Brothers was based upon the trusts and benefices he established. Funded from his private fortune, company provision was non-contributory and, in many respects, paternalistic. His efforts, moreover, were concentrated upon Port Sunlight, and management and welfare in the associated companies were largely unaffected by their takeover by Lever. Contributory schemes bestowing rights to benefits for the company as a whole were introduced by the more professionalised management of Cooper. Industrial relations became more clearly a question of company organisation rather than personal philanthropy.

Welfare and labour policies in the chemical and soap industries have been investigated in Charles Wilson's history of Unilever and in the biography of I.C.I. by William Reader.(14) There is, however, justification for specifically studying industrial relations in these giant concerns, especially as the standard works contain gaps in their accounts of industrial welfare.(15) Outlining the development of company provision was not their chief objective, and neither, therefore, can adequately explain the purpose of industrial welfare nor its systemisation without tracing their link with managerial structure. I.C.I.'s reputation as a well-managed enterprise makes its study important. By becoming in 1930 Britain's largest company in terms of capitalisation, Unilever and its labour management are of natural interest.

(ii) IMPERIAL CHEMICALS INDUSTRIES

I.C.I.'s welfare policy was crucially influenced by Brunner, Mond, a firm established in 1873 by John Brunner and Ludwig Mond. It was Brunner, however, who gradually assumed the running of the company, and he was its chairman till one year before his death in 1919. As a Unitarian, John Brunner believed that employers were given by God custody of their workers' moral and material well-being. He, therefore, opposed social legislation which interfered with company provision, and so placed the state as an intermediary between employer and worker. Brunner was prepared to negotiate with local unions but believed that national collective bargaining was a threat to his personal standing with his men.(16)

Brunner, Mond built houses in the village of Northwich in Cheshire near to its Winnington Works. Fines and instant dismissals were slowly replaced by a more sophisticated labour policy which established a settled community of workers. Northwich became a company village, and Brunner was elected the M.P. for the area in 1885. Both Brunner and Ludwig Mond mingled socially with their workforce, and Brunner was president of the Workers Sick Club at the Winnington factory. The fund was administered by an elected committee, and contributions of 4d a week were deducted from the men's wages. The company paid the doctors' fees and medicine bills, kept the Club's accounts, and held its funds with interest. The company school, built in 1886, furnished a well disciplined and settled labour-pool. A Workmen's Club was established at Northwich in 1877, and provided a number of indoor games, a library, reading room, and sports ground. The tee-total Brunner forbade the sale of alcohol at the Club. Workers were first granted a week's paid holiday in 1884 on condition they missed, unless for reasons of sickness, no more than ten days' work during the previous year.

In 1897, sick pay was increased to 10s a week. Brunner supported the Workmen's Compensation Act of that year, but stressed how his company had paid accident compensation since 1881 without considering who was at fault. The goodwill imbued was held to be incalculable, and men attended the works surgery for the slightest abrasion because prevention reduced any "consequent suffering to the men and cost to the firm". All compensation was paid by Brunner, Mond itself, which refused to buy a policy with an insurance company. By assuming direct responsibility for accidents at the factory, the company hoped to increase the workers' loyalty. Pensions were introduced in 1899, and Brunner decided that no-one over 30 years would be employed. All pensioners, therefore, required a record of long service. Recipients of these allowances, which were a personal benefaction, were placed upon the Mond Pension List. Because of the Shops Clubs Act 1902, which stipulated rules and rights to benefit under contributory schemes, the company took over the Workers' Sick Club and began paying benefits without contributions. Double holiday pay was provided from 1902 onwards. In 1911, an Approved Society was created under the National Insurance Act, and supplementary benefits were also provided. The company in 1913 guaranteed sick pay for the first 26 weeks of the National Insurance scheme, when participants were accumulating contributions and were not entitled to state benefits.(17)

A General Works Council was appointed in July 1918, and works committees chaired by local managers were founded a month later.(18) In 1920, the works committees at Middlewich and Sandbach suggested that a copartnership scheme be founded. The directors opposed the idea because of the fall in trade and profits, but two directors and members of the Brunner family were willing to sell 10,000 shares to set up a Stock Purchase Scheme. Although the numbers who could be placed upon the Mond Pension List were limited, when two men retiring in 1920 were clearly deserving of a pension, the list was merely extended. The works committees supervised various provident societies like the Benevolent Fund. At the Winnington works in 1920, the Fund paid out nearly £152 in sick and death benefits. An annual company donation matched the total contributions of the men over the previous twelve months. Although Brunner, Mond already contributed to hospitals on behalf of its workers, each works committee in 1921 was placed in charge of a branch of the new Hospital Fund. An extra 1d a week towards provident contributions paid for its benefits.(19)

Labour policy at I.C.I. was based upon personal contact, improving the status of workers, increased financial and job security, consultation, and copartnership. Sir Alfred Mond, who took charge of Brunner, Mond in 1925, was directly responsible for labour matters, and Lloyd Roberts, I.C.I.´s first Chief Labour Officer and the architect of its welfare policy, had been employed at Brunner, Mond since 1916. Lloyd Robert´s Labour Department was given the remit of initiating schemes and systemising the welfare provision already established by the four constituent companies. I.C.I.´s sucess was seen to depend upon good labour relations, as well as rationalisation, capital development, management selection, and research. The company´s labour policy, revealed on the 7th October 1927, was designed to dispel the notion "that the trend towards great amalgamations will widen the gap between employers and workers". The central aim was to win men´s loyalty by providing security and status, and these advantages were seen as having the potential to undermine trades union and "class loyalties". Cooperation between managers and workers was essential to a modern enterprise. For Mond, a successful labour policy entailed predicting the demands of labour and granting them before they were sought.(20) He believed that I.C.I. as a large employer could set an example in industrial relations for the rest of British industry. Mond, indeed, held the view that "large and well-organised concerns" should handle all state health and unemployment benefits.(21)

Security was to be given through the staff grade system, and status through a share ownership scheme. They were both introduced in 1928. The grading scheme was intended to establish an internal labour market. Brunner, Mond had secured continuity of labour by drawing on generations of workers from its company village. At I.C.I., hourly workers with five years´ service were promoted to a permanent status and paid weekly wages. All staff grade workers were entitled to one month´s dismissal notice, full payment for bank holidays, and, for six months in any one year, full sick pay less state benefits. For, "It stands to reason that a man who doesn´t have to worry what is to become of his wife and children if he should be ill is freer to devote himself to his work". Such promotion was totally at the discretion of the directors, and a worker was judged upon keenness, team spirit, skill at work, economy in the use of materials, general tidiness at his job, time-keeping, and length of service. Permanent workers also had the right to purchase I.C.I. Ordinary shares at 2/6d below the mean market price. But, because share prices were depressed during the early 1930s, profitsharing was abandoned in 1934.(22) Long Service Awards of watches and medals, which had been awarded at Brunner, Mond, were continued by I.C.I. Alfred Mond saw the subsidised I.C.I Magazine founded in 1928 as a tangible symbol of harmonious industrial cooperation.(23)

Contact and communication were to be established through the works councils founded in 1929. They promoted a spirit of cooperation, increased contentment and efficiency, and gave employees greater responsibility for working conditions.(24) I.C.I. wanted to disprove the notion it was "a soulless organisation which reduces its workers to the level of easily replaceable machines". The works council scheme sought to establish "scrupulous fair and open methods" of management and consultation.(25) Equal numbers of managers and elected workers sat on the monthly works councils. A General Works Council represented the Group and a Central Works Council consisted of delegates from the Groups. All of them were purely consultative bodies, dealing with safety, sport, recreation, and health and welfare matters. They had no right to information, and the decisions of local managers and directors were final.(26)

I.C.I. gave £50,000 to set up the Directors Benevolence Fund under the control of the Central Works Council. Its purpose was to supplement existing schemes and to fill gaps in company provision. The Fund, the I.C.I. Bravery Awards, and the Safety Committees all date from the beginning of the works council scheme.(27) It was clear from the first meeting of the Central Council that the works committees had a specific and essential role in the provision of welfare. They were designed "to take over a number of activities which already exist in some works in connection with benevolent funds and other funds of that character". A hierarchy of councils could provide the administrative machinery needed to operate any systematic company-wide welfare scheme. Moreover, gaining the active participation of works´ council representatives in their administration reduced fears - particularly amongst independent shop clubs - about company control and patronage. To avoid conflict with the organisers of these existing, voluntary funds, the works councils sought to co-opt them.(28)

In 1929, I.C.I. located three types of funds at its works: hospital schemes and benevolent funds - each with set contributions - and yearly sick clubs where income varied according to necessity and the surplus was divided every Christmas. At one factory, a works council proposed to replace whip-rounds for cases of hardship with a "'rationalised' benevolent scheme". Slate or "money" clubs with no financial reserves offered little guarantee of security in times of need. I.C.I. agreed to aid these clubs with subventions. But, apart from the Alkali Group, where a "comprehensive" fund had already been established, most societies still had limited membership and inadequate benefits. While some workers paid 1d or 2d a week, others at smaller works gave 1s. Offering the company's help for provident organisations on a works basis, therefore, was an inadequate solution. A larger fund and better management could secure greater benefits for smaller contributions.(29)

The I.C.I. Workers' Friendly Society, consequently, was inaugurated on the 1st January 1930 as a company-wide fund. A central society was intended to instill a sense of identity and loyalty to I.C.I., and membership was a condition of employment for actuarial reasons. The company had to provide £50,000 to start the fund. Its trustees and General Management Committee were elected, but it was administered through the works council system. I.C.I. agreed to give 1d a week to every member. Men contributed 3d a week and women 2d in return for respectively 10s and 7/6d sick pay for thirteen weeks. Benefits for a subsequent three months were set at 5/- for both sexes, after which time workers could apply to the Directors' Benevolent Fund. Death grants of £10 for a male worker and £7 for his wife, and £7 10s for a female worker were also offered. Hospital provision was the responsibilty of works committees, which could add 1d to general contributions for the extra insurance cover. Local works committees could recommend workers to the Society for discretionary pensions.(30) The Friendly Society became insolvent by 1931. Its dissolution was proposed in favour of funds for each group within I.C.I. In a ballot of members, the idea was defeated. Lloyd Roberts wrote that it was "a matter of congratulation that members have strongly upheld the principle that every I.C.I. man shall receive the same treatment as another, no matter where he works..." Contributions, however, were increased to 4d for men and 3d for women.(31) Works councils, nonetheless, continued to encourage voluntary funds like the Billingham Life Benefit Society. It was self-supporting and provided benefits supplementary to the compulsory funds, although the company paid the administrative costs.(32)

The I.C.I. Sports Association was formed in 1930. Just as provident provision was centralised, the Association was founded to coordinate works sports activities throughout the company. Clubs were largely independent associations with elected committees, although their facilities were usually either provided or funded by the local works. The new Association was an affiliated organisation, and did not directly interfere in the administration of any sporting organisation. Indeed, Group Labour Managers stressed the value of leaving clubs to rely on the enthusiasm and interest of their members. But, because sports competitions were "not organised in accordance with any defined Company policy", I.C.I. was divided into six geographical areas within which annual inter-area competitions in fifteen sports would take place. National competitions would also be held, and the whole scheme cost £4,800 per annum. The Association was discontinued in 1932, partly for reasons of cost, but mostly because it seemed anomalous to be dismissing workers while paying the expenses of sports teams to travel around the country. Reports from labour managers in Scotland, the North West, and North East, however, stated that the Association had encouraged participation, and that their areas would have been devoid of sports facilities but for its existence. It had established a bond between management and workers, encapsulating "the I.C.I. spirit". National competitions, in particular, had increased interest and membership. 25% of the employees of Muntz´s Metal Company, or 100 people, participated in some sport. By 1933, therefore, £650 was made available to the Labour Department to encourage competitions between neighbouring works.(33)

To provide pensions, a Workers´ Voluntary Fund was set up in 1930, which the company administered free of cost. But ex gratia pensions and gratuities were paid by I.C.I. according to a fixed table of benefits. The central Labour Department established a Pensions and Assistance Funds unit to process applications. After being employed for 15 years, a worker received as a gratuity two weeks´ wages for each year of service. A pension of 10s a week for a male worker and 7s for a woman were provided for service of between 15 and 24 years. 12/6d and 9/6d per week were available respectively for employment of between 25 and 34 years. 15s and 12s were paid to workers with 35 years´ service, and £1 and 15s for over 40 years. The whole scheme cost £100,000 a year.(34) Gratuities were also available for workers certified by the Medical Department as too unwell to continue in work. By 1930, lump-sum payments were made an instrument of plant rationalisation, as older workers were replaced with either fitter and younger men or new machinery. Gratuities varied according to works and Groups, but the Welfare Department in 1930 came to view them as too costly. General guidelines, therefore, were drawn up, which generally reduced the levels of the awards. Where a works was closed, gratuities had often been paid to all those with five years´ service. The qualification period was increased to ten years. Where greater efficiency was sought and an ill or incapacitated worker was to be retired, he needed 20 years´ employment to be entitled to a benefit. If, however, a worker was between 60 and 64 years, he needed half that period of service. I.C.I. justified these changes on the grounds that all gratuities were discretionary.(35)

A typical central works council agenda consisted by 1931

of discussion of the many provident and recreational associations, "and everything appertaining to the welfare of the employee".(36) By providing the administrative means to organise a whole spectrum of welfare provision on an ordered, company-wide basis, works councils matched the rationalisation of production and management. As Lloyd Roberts commented in 1930: "Whatever steps our commercial and technical experts may devise for the restoration and maintenance of our trade, their efforts will be to a large extent stultified in the absence of rationalised relations between the human factors in production". He did not apologise for the word "rationalised", as labour relations depended on planning and organisation.(37) By 1931, welfare expenditure equalled 8.33% of the wages bill. A report concluded that "It has been the aim of the Central Labour Department throughout to lay a greater stress on the attainment by the workers of a sense of status and security rather than on a mere rate of wages, and it is believed that I.C.I. workers now fairly generally accept this view".(38)

In 1934, £1,000 was allocated to the establishment of works dental clinics. The Labour Department believed that neglected teeth and oral sepsis were a major cause of illness through gastritis, ulcers, and even "mental disturbance". Treatment took place in the company's time. By 1937, I.C.I. hired the services of six dentists.(39) The company still calculated, however, that it lost from 1936-37 3.5m working hours through 5,000 individual cases of sickness among 46,000 workers. A male worker lost an average 8.2 days per year and a woman 11.3, while the figure for staff was 12.1 days. Sickness was viewed as "disorganisation and loss of efficiency to the Company", and work-conditions and medical treatment were considered an important element of business management.(40) I.C.I. employed 5 full-time and 30 part-time medical officers. 15 more were paid according to their hours of attendance. There were also 19 full-time nurses, 19 full-time and 57 part time ambulance room attendants, and 705 first-aid attendants.(41)

From 1936-37, I.C.I. paid £3,000 in ex gratia pensions. By 1937, 71% of all employees had been pensioned, and the company decided to establish a contributory and compulsory scheme to pay supplements to the 1925 Pensions Act. I.C.I. agreed to donate a sum worth 3% of the gross weekly wages bill to the fund. Moreover, the company compensated the society for all employment before 1937 when it could have received no contributions, including that at I.C.I.'s antecedent companies. Full pensions, therefore, could be paid upon the society's founding. A cash lump sum was given to the relatives of any members who died before receiving their pension. The contributory scheme replaced all old age, retirement, and out-of-work gratuities.(42)

* * * * *

Brunner, Mond had funded a comprehensive, but

paternalistic, welfare policy. I.C.I., however, adopted a planned policy of institutionalised welfare based upon semi-independent friendly societies which administered schemes according to set rules and pre-determined benefits. Favoured with the advantages of oligopoly, I.C.I. established a large internal labour market, and the Staff Grade Scheme was a means of appointing permanent workers. Only these workers - defined by the company as those who could be expected to stay with the company till retiring age - were compelled to join welfare schemes. Temporary workers only became members of the Workers' Friendly Society and on a voluntary basis.(43) The works councils were an institution for the centralised administration of every aspect of industrial welfare. The Labour Department, however, formed policy and had the final authority. Yet, the contributory element of the Workers' Friendly Society made sick pay a right. Even the Labour Department's table of ex gratia pensions and gratuities was viewed in 1933 as a half-way house to a prospective contributory pensions society.(44) Knowing the full costs of systematic pension provision, however, I.C.I. did not introduce such a scheme until 1937. In sum, I.C.I. adopted Brunner, Mond's traditions in labour management. But they did not remain wholly intact.(45) Paternalism was unsuited to the size and structure of I.C.I., and as much attention was paid to reorganising welfare as management and research. Capital and management were rationalised between 1928-31, and welfare was generally standardised throughout the new corporate company simultaneously. Pensions were the only exception, but plans were made during this period for their introduction. The contributory pension fund was finally founded after redundant labour, which would have been eligible to improved benefits, had been shed in the early 1930s.

(iii) UNILEVER

   William Lever's labour policy was intended to gain the cooperation of his workers through promoting the "unitary ideal" of the company and by maintaining for them a degree of economic security. Lever drew from his Congregationalist beliefs when he argued that industrialists had a moral responsibility for their workers. Employers were "trustees" of their firms, although benevolence and unrealistic generosity, he argued, would ruin a company. Welfare was part of business organisation and had to be paid for through higher productivity. To meet his moral and business commitments, Lever was an advocate of "prosperity sharing", which he defined as the spending of profits by employers on the workers' behalf. Lever believed that workers would merely fritter any bonuses paid to them directly. Better housing and social amenities were presented as a means of distributing profits on a "fair" basis. Consequently, Lever´s welfare schemes often appeared paternalistic and sometimes autocratic.(46)

The model village of Port Sunlight, begun in 1888, was central to Lever´s scheme of "prosperity sharing".(47) Port Sunlight was intended to provide workers with the opportunities to enjoy life. Workers who endured long stretches of labour and bad housing had little reason to give an employer faithful service. Good home conditions and social amenities were meant to "Socialise and Christianise" business relations and revive the "close family brotherhood" of the Victorian small firm. The management at Port Sunlight was convinced that their esprit de corps was unsurpassed by any other firm.(48)

The Village Council was established in 1896, and had a number of sub-committees to run the social and sporting facilities, schools, shop and sick society. Education was available for all children at Port Sunlight. The Council was elected but its role was purely advisory and it depended upon the company to finance its ventures.(49) At the factory itself, employees could only submit recommendations through a suggestions box. The Works Committees, founded in 1899, consisted of managers and foremen only.(50) By 1901, the Village Council was promoting at least fifteen sporting, social, educational and religious associations,(51) and they all enjoyed the free use of company lands and buildings.(52) By 1905, the 3,000 inhabitants of Port Sunlight were served by a park, allotments, church, two schools, a public hall, a restaurant, gymnasium, open-air swimming-pool, numerous sports grounds and club-houses, an inn, theatre, concert hall, library and a cooperative store. There were some 600 houses which had cost £350,000 to build. The average rent, taken directly from wage-packets, was 6s a week for homes considered to be worth 10/6d.(53)

In 1905, Lever Brothers formed a Holiday Club to be run by an elected committee of employees. Members who had been employed for the previous year were eligible to one week´s paid holiday. Contributions were stopped from wages and amounted to one hour´s pay per week, to which the company added 4% interest. Long Service Awards of gold watches were introduced in the same year for workers with 15 years´ service. The Employees Benefit Fund was, however, the largest welfare measure introduced in 1905. It was managed by four trustees appointed by the company and by four elected employees. The Fund was wholly financed by Lever Brothers, and it provided sick pay, accident compensation, and pensions for employees and widows. Pensions were given to men of 65 years with 15 years´ service. Women were granted a pension at 60.(54) By 1907, the Employees Benefit Fund supported eighteen pensioners, and the benefits were revised "to make (the Fund) thoroughly sound". Pensions would be given after 20 years´

service, and the amount paid was reduced. The Fund had an income of £5,801 in that year. £5,200 of this sum was donated directly by the company and the rest came from its investment of £15,000 in Lever preference shares. Its expenditure, however, amounted to only £785.(55) A Cottage Hospital was opened at Port Sunlight in 1907.(56)

Two years later, Lever introduced profitsharing, although its payment of cash bonuses contravened the principles of "prosperity sharing". The company, however, was becoming larger and as a welfare policy Port Sunlight could not be repeated. Lever had to find another means of winning the loyalty of workers outside the village, and called Copartnership "The New Relationship". He hoped profitsharing would increase efficiency and counter work-disaffection. Copartnership Certificates entitled workers to dividends but not to shares, and every copartner in return signed a contract agreeing not to waste time nor materials. Three members were elected to a Copartnership Committee from each of the four "classes" of directors, managers and foremen, salesmen, and general staff. After the 5% annual dividends had been paid to shareholders, the remaining profits were divided equally between the Ordinary shareholders and copartners. £100,000 was distributed to employees in the first issue. By accumulating certificates in each year, a worker could finally add 5% to his annual wages. All certificates could be withdrawn by Lever at any time and the record of every worker was assessed before being invited to be a copartner. Strikers immediately lost their copartnership rights. It was because the productivity and reliability of every potential copartner was assessed that Lever felt able to call his new scheme "prosperity sharing". Profitsharing would, he claimed, have paid bonuses to good and bad workers alike. Not finding the capital, the copartner, argued Lever, "must admit the logic of the control and management of the business resting in the hands of those who represent the capital, namely, the Board of Directors".(57) Lever did not believe, therefore, that copartnership would abolish the wages-system or interest on capital. The system obtained the "more equal distribution of wealth", but, if it failed to increase output, improve quality, reduce waste, and prevent strikes, "it is perfectly obvious that Co-partnership is absolutely useless as an implement of production".(58)

Between 1917-23, Lever introduced compulsory education for all Port Sunlight employees between 14 and 16 at the company's Staff Training College. A recreation ground, a holiday camp, a dental surgery, maternity home, and an opthalmic clinic were built. A Recreations Association was formed as a federation for existing clubs.(59) Rationalisation and changes in management influenced the administration of industrial welfare. The Service Department, which increasingly took over the control of welfare at Port Sunlight from Lever, was founded in January 1922. Its remit was to develop the human element at the factory, improve a worker's home life, and increase labour efficiency. It was responsible for all aspects of welfare at the works and the village, including the Health Insurance Approved Society. It expanded company provision, and established a "core" labour force. For, in 1922, its first duty was to reduce the large numbers of temporary workers employed since the beginning of the War. The Department was charged with dismissing these "undesirables" and forming "a minimum permanent and reliable staff, the main object of which is reduction in costly labour turnover". Indeed, labour stability was the "foundation of successful finance". Recruits were asked to register with the Service Department and casual labour was stopped from queuing at the factory gates. Grading and the distinction between permanent and casual employees were essential to an internal labour market. A monthly assessment of each individual was made by foremen and managers on personal characteristics like reliability, punctuality, and co-operation. The employee's status and chances of promotion depended upon the results of the assessment. Despite strong opposition from unions and workers, grading eventually gained acceptance, and employees could make appeals about their assessment to a Workers' Representatives Committee.(60) Lever Brothers recognised that labour mobility and casual employment limited the possibilities of industrial welfare: it was unprofitable to invest in temporary workers.(61)

Industrial disputes had been caused at Lever's by redundancies and short-time during the Post-War Slump. In September 1922, a Works Advisory Committee, elected by copartners, was established by the Service Department as a means of evaluating shop-floor opinion. But Lever also offered to guarantee certain workers security of employment or income.(62) Permanent employees were allowed to join the new Life Assurance and Unemployment scheme. An internal labour market could be built upon the perception that "There is a legitimate aspiration on the part of all workers to have a monetary interest in the industry in addition to wages. They are seeking greater security of tenure.."(63) In addition, there was "fear of unemployment, fear of sickness, and the fear of death, the way it will leave our widows and dependants".(64) These were the "Three Ghosts" which Lever saw as haunting workers, and which his welfare policy aimed to lay. Every copartner was given a free life assurance policy, its benefits varying with individual grades and responsibilities. Lever Brothers, however, could change the terms of the policy at will. A sum would be paid to the dependants of all participants when deceased. Moreover, if they found themselves on short-time or without employment, they were assured of a sum which together with state benefits would pay half a worker's standard weekly wages. A copartner who was sick for seven days would receive the same rates, although his or her situation would be reassessed every four weeks. Temporary workers could be dismissed at the end of the day, while permanent employees were entitled to one week's notice. Unemployment pay tackled the first great fear, sick pay the second, and life assurance the third, and pensions under the Employees Benefit Fund catered for the fear of old age.(65)

The dependence of welfare at Lever Brothers upon the personal philanthropy of its owner was illustrated by Lever's decease in 1925. His will made provision for the continuation and creation of independent trusts in control of preference shares with which to fund welfare benefits. But Cooper wanted to make welfare provision an integral part of the company's organisation. He claimed that the position of the Employees Benefit Fund was insecure because it relied upon 8% Preferred Shares which, after Ordinary stock, would be first to suffer any economic set-back. The company would not guarantee benefits over which it had no control. Lever Brothers were advised by lawyers that they were entitled to the accumulated assets of the Employees Benefit Fund but the company wanted to avoid an acrimonious legal battle with the trustees. An equitable compromise was agreed. It was accepted that the trustees had a legal right to the funds and would continue to administer them. The assets reverted, nevertheless, to the company. With control over the company's welfare schemes, Lever Brothers could begin to standardise company provision. By 1927, Group Life Assurance was extended to all associated companies except Gossages and Watsons which had their own schemes.(66)

Lever himself had been the driving force behind copartnership, and it was abandoned on the formation of Unilever. But, generally, welfare after the amalgamation was increased, and placed upon a systematic and contributory basis. Benefits, consequently, became rights. Wilson sees the introduction of contributory schemes as a reflection of the leading role being assumed by professional managers at the expense of owner-employers. Paternalism was anachronistic, and employees in more democratic times were in position to assume direct responsibility for their own sick pay and pensions.(67) A company-wide staff pension scheme, however, was for Unilever an investment in its managerial resources. The management of a large, highly-diversified enterprise required an increased administrative structure, and a shortage of managerial skills would have placed limits upon economic growth. Pension schemes helped in the retention of staff, and a contributory system was the only secure means of financing adequate benefits.(68) A staff Union Superannuation Fund was formed in 1931. It replaced the Employees Benefit Fund at Lever Brothers for all salaried employees, and was made a condition of employment for new recruits.(69) Unilever agreed to donate £1,100,000 to the Superannuation Fund in place of contributions for service before its founding, and the company continued to donate some £100,000 a year. Far from the scheme being independent, therefore, Unilever ensured it was an integral part of its staff management.(70) A Pensions Officer was appointed to administer the Fund.(71)

In 1929, the consolidation of the new company coupled with an economic downturn lead to the closing of works.(72) Out-of-work payments and pensions, therefore, became important for a company that wished to retain its reputation for fair dealing.(73) Ex gratia pensions for workers were increased in 1932. It was considered an expense of rationalisation, but the cost would be, said Cooper, "counterbalanced by (the) corresponding savings".(74) Unilever supported a variety of pension schemes by that date, costing the company, in addition to the staff fund, about £450,000 per annum. This sum equalled an extra 10s a ton on the price of soap and margarine. As the expense of ex gratia pensions was burdensome, the Pensions Officer was asked to draw up a contributory scheme for all workers. He calculated that a contributory pensions scheme would cost Unilever £1,000 a week. Yet, Unilever wanted to place pension and provident provision "upon a uniform basis..." throughout the new international company. An all-embracing Union Provident Fund was founded to oversee all forms of industrial welfare for workers, and its trustees were appointed by the Board. Membership of the Fund was a condition of employment. Within the British half of Unilever, Approved Society and Pensions sections were set up. The differing levels of state benefits between countries necessitated such a division of administration.(75) With regard to pensions, the Fund was "a common-sense solution of one of the most difficult problems facing large-scale industries to-day, and maintains the tradition in regard to industrial relationships which has characterised the firm's policy in the past".(76) Contributions to the Fund were set at 1s a week to which the company added 2s to each individual account but Unilever reserved the right to alter its donation at will. Workers retired at 60 years, or earlier if there was a valid reason like illness.(77)

In 1935, Unilever established a branch of the Hospital Services Association. Workers at Levers and at associated companies like Planters Foods, the Bromborough Margarine Works, Brooke and Company, and the road transport firm S.P.D. were allowed to join. A Management Committee decided on the level of contributions in return for benefits of 7s a day to cover hospital fees, allowances for operations, consultants' bills, convalescent treatment, ambulance services, nursing treatment, and surgical appliances.(78)

* * * * *

Wilson argues that welfare policy under Lever was based upon Port Sunlight and copartnership, and that pensions and sick pay were introduced by Unilever.(79) In fact, pensions and sick pay had been provided directly by the company in the 1890s. After 1905, they were paid through the Employees Benefit Fund. Welfare under Lever remained paternalistic, and was dependent upon productivity and profitability. It helped companies to cope with the "human factor". After its formation in 1929, Unilever's management and structure needed to be reorganised. Contemporaneously, welfare provision for workers became based upon contributions, actuarial calculations, and rights to benefits. Wilson, however, overlooks the workers' Union Provident Fund. The systemisation of welfare was possible because of the central managerial organisation established under Cooper. An internal labour market, pensions and other benefits were an investment by a corporate company in its workforce. It reflected the exercise of greater planning over the whole production process.

(iv) CONCLUSION

I.C.I. and Unilever emerged as amongst Britain's largest companies, worth by 1930 £77m and £132m respectively. Both employed over 50,000 people. I.C.I. is distinguished by its attention to management, and, through its Labour Department, it administered a planned and unitary welfare policy. Unilever's benefits were comparatively less systemised and unified across its many concerns. Memoranda drawn up by I.C.I.'s Lloyd Roberts in 1931 imply that its welfare was an anti-union strategy, and a way of cheapening wages and labour. Unions, however, accounted for only 30-40% of I.C.I.'s workforce when welfare schemes were initiated in 1928, and, during the Great Depression, their postion was weakened. Lloyd Roberts was probably justifying welfare expenditure to McGowan, who assumed control in 1931 and who was less convinced of the value of company provision than his predecessor. In practice, I.C.I.'s welfare benefits were their own justification.(80) They did, however, produce a contented workforce, and I.C.I., like Brunner, Mond before it, remained free of major industrial disputes. Lever's dislike of unions was well known, and, during a dispute in 1911, strikers' copartnership certificates were removed. But Lever's labour relations policy was a comprehensive and calculated means of man-management and organisation. It was not, as some claimed, merely a ploy for generating publicity and advertising soap.(81)

NOTES

1. Cf. Ch.1; & Ch.4, s.(ii) for an analysis of welfare strategy and expenditure.
2. W.J.Reader I.C.I.: A History (1970), Vol.I (1970),

pp.249-327,451-466; W.J.Reader "I.C.I. and the State, 1926-45" in Supple (ed.) (1977), pp.227-243; A.E.Musson The Growth of British Industry (1978), pp.216-221.

3.   Hannah (1979), pp.81-86.

4.   This is not to say that other chemical companies had not adopted "progressive" labour policies. Nobel Industries had developed welfare and safety measures in order "to cultivate a sympathetic understanding between the management and the workers". Cf. I.C.I. I.C.I. Ltd and its Founding Companies: the History of Nobel's Explosives Co. Ltd and Nobel Industries Ltd, 1871-1926 (1938), p.94. Cf. also the British Cyanides Corporation in PP 1920 (C.544) xxxiii 765, and Whiffen and Sons at the Greater London R.O.

5.   The type of paternalistic provision made famous by Lever Brothers at Port Sunlight had parallels with Joseph Crosfield and Sons of Warrington. As important employers in the town, they saw themselves as natural leaders of their community, endowed Warrington, and patronised local building societies and charities. As Quakers, the Crosfields assumed from the 1860s a moral responsibility for their workers, but did not see welfare as philanthropy because it bound together employers and workers in mutual interest. From 1922 onwards, Lever Brothers terminated Crosfield's welfare schemes and extended its Copartnership and Employee Benefit Fund to the company. Cf. A.E.Musson Enterprise in Soap and Chemicals: Joseph Crosfield and Sons Limited, 1815-1965 (1965), pp.149-56,316-9.

6.   C.Wilson The History of Unilever, Vol.I (1954), pp.213-5,244,246-7,269-71; BB6, "Rationalisation".

7.   Wilson, Vol.I (1954), pp.266,272-3,276.

8.   BB6, "Lever,- Management and Labour"; "Reorganisation at Port Sunlight, 1921-22"; "Port Sunlight Local Board".

9.   C.Wilson "Management and Policy in the Large-scale Enterprise" Lever Brothers and Unilever, 1918-1938" in Supple (ed.) (1977), pp.124 140; Wilson, Vol.I (1954), pp.296, 299-300,302. Cf. also BB6, "Reorganisation of Top Management, 1925"; "Report of Technical Commission, 1925"; "Beginnings of Market Research, 1926".

10.   Mathias in Supple (ed.) (1977), pp.141-162.

11.   Wilson, Vol.II (1954), pp.263,269,307-316.

12.   Reckitt and Colmans, formed in 1937, was another example of a large company engaged in chemicals and food. Reckitts had principally been a producer of polishes and cleaning agents, and Colmans had originally been a mustard company. They were both extensively involved in building factory villages, education classes, sick clubs, sporting facilities, pension funds, medical services, profitsharing and works councils. Cf. B.N.Reckitt The History of Reckitt and Sons Limited (1951), pp.ix,33-4,39-40,52-3, 59-63,76-7,91; & J. & J.Colman The First Fifty Years of the Carrow Works Council, 1918-68 (1968), passim; W.Ashworth "British

Industrial Villages in the 19th Century", Econ.H.R. (1950-51), pp.378-387.
13. Wilson, Vol.II (1954), pp.307-11,381; Channon (1973), pp.172-3.
14. Wilson, Vols.I & II (1954); Reader, Vols.I & II (1970, 1975).
15. Wilson overlooks the development of pension and sick pay schemes before 1914, and, during the period of the 1930s, he concentrates on staff welfare policy. Several works deal with welfare at Brunner, Mond but not in a comprehensive fashion, and the descriptions of the development of its welfare practices need to be drawn together.
16. Reader, Vol.I (1970), p.233; S.Koss Sir John Brunner: Radical Plutocrat (1970), pp.x,1-2,4,23,24-5,33-8,40-4,46-7, 144,152-4.
17. Koss (1970), pp.x,1-2,4,23-5,34-8,40-4,46-7,144, 152-6; Hansard, 29 Nov 1906, vol.164, cols.1037-9; Chemical Trade Review, 16 May 1908, p.459; B.Didsbury "Cheshire Saltworkers" in R.Samuel (ed.) Miners, Quarrymen, and Saltworkers (1977), pp.182-7; J.Goodman The Mond Legacy (1982), p.33; 8/4A, General Works Council Minutes, 29 Oct 1920; 9 Feb 1921. Cf.9, ss.(ii), (iii).
18. I.C.I. Works Council Scheme: Fiftieth Meeting of Central Council (1960), pp.3-7; I.C.I. Memorandum on Labour Relations (1961), p.14.
19. 8/4A, General Works Council Minutes, 29 Oct 1920, 9 Feb 1921, 22 Oct 1921; Works Benevolent Fund.
20. Cf. H.R.Northrup Boulwarism (1964): General Electric of America's labour policy encapsulated this principle.
21. Industrial Welfare, Oct 1927, pp.317-9; Reader, Vol.II (1975), pp.11,57,60-1,63-4,137.
22. Reader, Vol.II (1975), pp.62-4; ICI Magazine, May 1928, pp.511-12; I.C.I. Memorandum on Labour Relations (1961), p.31. I.C.I., however, renewed profitsharing in 1954.
23. ICI Magazine, May 1928, p.413; Jan 1928, pp.3,8-10.
24. Ibid, Feb 1929, pp.125-6.
25. I.C.I. Imperial Chemicals Industries: A Short Account of the Activities of the Company (1929), pp.30-1.
26. Reader, Vol.II (1975), p.61.
27. I.C.I. The Works Council Scheme (1960), p.7.
28. Minutes of the Central Works Council, 18 April 1929; 20 Nov 1929; 20 Nov 1930.
29. ICI Magazine, July 1929, p.4; Sept 1929, pp.240-2; Oct 1929, pp.356-8.
30. I.C.I., Minutes of Central Works Committee, 18 April 1929, 20 Nov 1929, 20 May 1930, 20 Nov 1930; ICI Magazine, Dec 1929, pp.566-577; May 1930, pp.487-8; 135/33A, Memo., 6 Sept 1932, & Rules of I.C. (Workers) Friendly Society (Revised 1933).
31. ICI Magazine, Dec 1931, pp.552-3; 135/33A, Memo. from Labour Department, 12 Aug 1935.

32. 53/6/6, Rules of Billingham Life Benefit Society;
First Annual Report for year ending 31 July 1936.
33. ICI Magazine, Jan 1928, pp.21-33; April 1929,
p.378; 87/33A, Circular, 16 Jan 1928; W19/4A, Memo. to Lord
Melchett, 20 May 1931; Report on ICI Sports Association, May
1931; Letter to L.Roberts, 13 Nov 1935; Handbook: ICI Sports
Association; W19/4A/1B, Memo., 16 Dec 1946.
34. ICI Magazine, Dec 1929, pp.568-9,579-80; Reader,
Vol.II (1975), pp.68-69; 18/33A, Memo., 10 May 1933.
35. 10/4A, Memo., to Hon. Henry Mond, 28 Jan 1930; Letter
to Hon. H.Mond, 27 Jan 1930; Circular cancelling Circular 93:
Payments to Redundant Workers; Payments to Discharged Workers,
Central Labour Department, 14 April 1930; 18/33A, Memo., 10
May 1933.
36. ICI Magazine, March 1931, pp.209-11.
37. 8/4A, Talk given by R.Lloyd Roberts, Chief Labour
Officer of I.C.I., at I.W.S. Conference, 7 Sept 1930.
38. Reader, Vol.II (1975) pp.67-8; 155/33A, Memos to
Chief Labour Officer, 22, 27 & 28 Feb 1933.
39. 78/33A, Memo., 2 March 1934.
40. 29/33A, Memo., 29 Dec 1938. L.Johnman "The Largest
Manufacturing Companies of 1935", Bus.Hist. (1986), pp.239
gives a figure of 49,706 ICI employees for 1935.
41. 29/33A, Sickness Investigation, 21-6-37; ICI Medical
Service.
42. ICI Magazine, June 1928, pp.507-8; Dec 1929,
pp.568-9,579-80; 53/6/6, Letter to Pensions and Assistance
Funds Department, 26 Aug 1937; 11/33A, Memo. from Labour
Department, 1 May 1936.
43. 44/33A, Memo., on Casual Labour, 27 Feb 1934; Memo.,
13 Feb 1934; Memo., from General Labour Manager, Ayrshire, 20
March 1934; Memo., from Central Labour Department, 31 Jan
1934.
44. 18/33A, Memo., 10 May 1933. Cf. Reader, Vol.II
(1975), p.68.
45. Cf. Reader, Vol.II (1975), p.60, where a contrary
opinion is stated.
46. Wilson, Vol.I (1954), pp.142-7,293-6; Progress, Oct
1902, pp.101-2.
47. Cf. Prices of Bromborough The History of Prices of
Bromborough, 1854-1954 (1954), pp.6,34-5,37; & Alan Watson
Price's Village (1966), pp.46-7. Price's model village was
built during the 1850s, and was Lever's inspiration for the
construction of Port Sunlight. It was served by community and
medical facilities, and numerous provident societies. The
Wilson brothers, the founders of welfare at the firm, had once
been employed at New Lanark where Robert Owen had gained fame
as an enlightened manager. Lever bought Prices out in 1919.
48. Unilever, Internal Memorandum, Evolution of Working
Conditions at Port Sunlight; Progress, Sept 1902, p.323;
A.G.M., 6 March 1902. However, as Port Sunlight consisted of

tied cottages, management also had a powerful means of deterring labour unrest.

49. Port Sunlight Monthly, Jan 1896, pp.1,32; Feb 1896, p.34; March 1896, p.66; April 1896, p.98.

50. Unilever, Evolution of Working Conditions at Port Sunlight.

51. There were 24 by 1911.

52. Port Sunlight Monthly, June 1896, pp.161-2; Progress, 1899-90, p.viii; 1901, p.viii; Sept 1902, pp.321-2; Dec 1902, p.468.

53. Wilson, Vol.I (1954) pp.144-6,147,149; B.Meakin Model Factory and Villages: Ideal Conditions of Labour and Housing (1905), pp.426-33.

54. Unilever, Internal Memorandum, Evolution of Working Conditions at Port Sunlight. The amount paid was set at one eightieth of the sum earnt by an individual in his or her last twelve months multiplied by the number of years´ service.

55. Progress, April 1908, p.56; A.G.M., 8 March 1907. The Employees Benefit Fund´s assets stood at £37,505 in 1911.

56. Unilever, Internal Memorandum, Evolution of Working Conditions at Port Sunlight.

57. Wilson, Vol.I (1954), pp.151-8; W.P.Jolly Lord Leverhulme (1976), pp.90,92; Unilever, Internal Memorandum, Evolution of Working Conditions at Port Sunlight; Progress, July 1909, p.76; Oct 1909, pp.109-110; A.G.M., 10 March 1911.

58. W.Lever Copartnership and Efficiency (1912).

59. Unilever Evolution of Working Conditions at Port Sunlight.

60. Unilever, Evolution of Working Conditions at Port Sunlight; BB6, "Reorganisation at Port Sunlight, 1921-22"; Progress, Sept 1922, pp.147-8,153-4; LBL/1, Lever Brothers Employees Handbook (1923), pp.24,29-34,42,45-55.

61. Progress, Sept 1922, pp.165,172-5.

62. Ibid, pp.221-3.

63. Unilever Evolution of Working Conditions at Port Sunlight.

64. W.Lever Copartnership: Laying the Three Ghosts: Unemployment, Sickness, Death (1922). Cf. Ch.1, s.(ii)(d).

65. Unilever, Evolution of Working Conditions at Port Sunlight; Unilever Employees Handbook (1937); Progress, Sept 1922, pp.156-7.

66. Lever Brothers, Directors´ Minutes, 8 July 1925, 13 Jan 1926, 3 Feb 1926, 10 Feb 1926, 24 Feb 1926, 25 Aug 1927. In 1928, the sickness and unemployment scheme was extended. All employees were guaranteed not to lose more than four and a half hours´ wages in any week if they were placed on short-time. Those unemployed for a whole week received three-quarters wages less four and a half hours´ pay for a period of twelve weeks. Those with fifteen years´ service obtained full wages less the four and half hours´ deduction if out of work for a week, and those on sick pay enjoyed the same

conditions. In 1936, a standard week was introduced. The company agreed to pay the difference between that standard and the hours worked (minus any state benefits received). All those without work for a full week would have their unemployment benefit supplemented to ensure no loss of income. Sick pay was available on the same basis for thirteen weeks in every year. Full pay was also given to the victims of industrial accidents. Cf. Unilever, Internal Memorandum, Evolution of Working Conditions at Port Sunlight; & Employees Handbook (1937).

67. Wilson, Vol.II (1954), p.384.

68. Ibid, pp.382-4.

69. Unilever, Evolution of Working Conditions at Port Sunlight.

70. Directors' Minutes, 1 Jan 1931.

71. Ibid, 3 Sept 1931.

72. BB6, "Closing of Factories", 1929.

73. Directors' Minutes, 17 Sept 1931; 10 Dec 1931.

74. Ibid, 28 Jan 1932.

75. Ibid, 5 May 1932, 6 Oct 1932, 13 Oct 1932; 8 Dec 1932, 15 June 1933; CPPS, Rules of Union Provident Fund (1932).

76. Progress, Jan 1933, pp.21-2. Progressive welfare policies were, in fact, a tradition of the industry, which included associated companies like Crosfields, Watsons, Thomas', Pears, Knights, and Prices, as well as Lever Brothers. Cf. CP 14, Note on History of Industrial Policy in Lever Brothers' Business.

77. CPPS 9, Rules of Union Provident Fund (1932).

78. WH4, HSA (Jan 1935).

79. Wilson, Vol.II (1954), pp.382-3.

80. Reader, Vol.II (1975), pp.57-8,65-70, 119-20,299.

81. Wilson, Vol.1 (1954), pp.144-56,275-7; Vol.II, pp.382-4.

Chapter 6

THE LABOUR QUESTION IN THE BREWERIES

(i) INTRODUCTION

Industrial welfare provided brewing employers with a formidable means of managing their labour force. The industry remained composed of small family firms, and company provision was notably paternalistic. In 1936, over 77% of brewing companies had less than £1m in capital, although some large firms had emerged.(1) Welfare encouraged the personal links between employers and employees which small-scale production made possible. Gratuities could be bestowed on an individual and _ex gratia_ basis, and their effectiveness depended upon the standing and reputation of the brewing dynasties within firms.

Paternalism, of course, was not unique to brewing. Within the small business characteristic of the Victorian economy, gratuities commonly won the deference employers needed for the exercise of authority over their workers. Because work-discipline was easier to maintain amongst established and settled communities, small factory owners and family partnerships were willing to finance housing, social amenities, and sick clubs. Generations of workers grew up in the expectation of working with their parents. _Ex gratia_ welfare was illustrative of a very personal style of management, and changes in the size and structure of companies undermined paternalism. Brewing was one of the earliest examples of capitalist production, and firms had been established in all large industrial centres by 1800 in response to the creation of urban markets.(2) But there was little innovation in production methods throughout this period, and amalgamations could not have brought returns to scale. Corporate management was not, therefore, introduced into the brewing industry,(3) and brewing provides an interesting case-study of a trade proud to retain its paternalistic practices and a tradition of "family employment". Its history has parallels with the wool and worsted, footwear, and pottery trades.(4)

Dominated by the brewing industry, towns like

137

Burton-on-Trent and Tadcaster in Yorkshire became epitomes of industrial paternalism. Even London breweries established self-contained communities like those at Pimlico and Mile End. Special factors increased the opportunities for industrial welfare in the industry. The lack of foreign competition made employment and company provision secure within brewing firms. Moreover, as labour constituted a small proportion of total costs, brewers could retain men even during a slack period. Pensions or annuity payments, and half-wages during sickness were common features of brewery employment.(5)

The families which remained in control of brewing companies were a significant feature of the industry. Yet, between 1886 and 1900, brewing firms converted into joint stock companies. 260 breweries went public, and £185 million in shares were issued. Brewers accounted in 1905 for eleven of the United Kingdom's largest fifty companies in terms of market capitalisation, and, by 1930, the figure was still as high as eight.(6) A number of firms in London and Burton had become leaders within the industry. London brewers had expanded by the early 1800s to meet the size of the capital's market, while the laying of the railways presented openings to brewers like those in Burton. They were able to sell their beer, with its distinctive flavour, to urban markets and it soon won widespread popularity. Advertising was, consequently, particularly important to the Burton producers, and they were the first to introduce trade-marks. Commercial brewers continued to replace local and domestic producers throughout the 19th Century because their products were of a better quality. But an expanding demand and a free and open licensing policy continued to allow new brewers to enter the market. Restrictive licensing was reintroduced in 1869, and the 1870s marked the beginning of a fall in the demand for beer which continued into the Inter-War period. The need to secure outlets against the affects of shrinking demand and increasingly restrictive licencing forced brewing firms to buy public houses. Smaller breweries were often bought out merely because of the value attached to their tied premises. Investment in public houses increased from £30 million to over £200 million in the thirty years after 1870. By 1900, only 10% of public houses were independent. Perhaps three-quarters of the industry's capital consisted of licensed premises during this period. Capital was floated in order to buy property, not to finance the rationalisation of beer production, and there was no incentive to make management more professionalised. Indeed, most of the capital raised on the stock exchange was in the form of debenture or loan shares, and the brewing families retained ownership as well as managerial control.(7)

The continuance of the small, privately-owned family firm shaped labour policies. Ex gratia welfare proved an adequate means of managing brewing workers. While other employers introduced collective bargaining to cope with the rise of

trades unionism, brewers opposed the appointment of workers'
intermediaries. Labour relations were never discussed by the
brewers' associations, and a workforce fragmented by the low
concentration of firms had a weak bargaining position.
Settling labour problems within the firm increased the
influence of employers and their discretionary benefits over
the attitudes and actions of their workers.

(ii) BREWERY PATERNALISM

Ex gratia welfare was well established in the brewing
industry by the mid-19th Century. It was only threatened
during the years 1913-1914, when newly-formed unions
challenged the employers' authority. But, despite increasing
unionisation after 1914, traditional welfare practices were
continued and extended. They helped produce a labour force
which remained at work even during the General Strike of 1926.

Guiness', the noted stout producers, became the United
Kingdom's largest brewers under the stewardship of Benjamin
Lee Guiness in 1835-1858. He introduced death benefits and
discretionary pensions of between 2s and 6s per week. Medical
attendance and free medicine were available, and hospital and
convalescent home bills were met. Housing was built to
accommodate workers, and excursions were held.(8) Mitchell and
Butlers of Birmingham began a non-contributory pension and
gratuity fund in 1869. Men were eligible at 60 years of age
and if employed for 20 years. A sports ground was laid in
1879, and later a recreation club was founded. Mitchell and
Butlers promoted the company fire brigade, established in
1882, because "it is worthwhile from the employers' point of
view to do whatever he can to make his employees proud of the
Company".(9) When Boakes began to pay bonuses to their men in
1886, it invited staff and workers to a luncheon. Employees
returned a vote of thanks. The traditional excursion was also
organised on their behalf.(10) John Smiths of Tadcaster was
"the centre of industry in the town". By the 1890s, the firm
had some 200 "steady, decent, trustworthy men". The
proprietors, Henry and Frank Riley-Smith, wanted an efficient
workforce, and were particularly anxious, ironically, to
encourage sobriety. "The firm have fully recognised their
responsibility, and felt it their task to promote their
employees' general good, and consequently, in this brewery,
only one common interest exists between masters and men".(11)

By 1893, Burton had 31 breweries employing 8,000 workers.
It was a brewing town, often electing a brewer as its Member
of Parliament.(12) An excursion organised jointly between
Messrs Salt & Company, Beard Brothers, Eversheds, Bell &
Company, Hill & Son, and Nunnelly & Company was held in
1886.(13) Nearly all the 60 men and foremen at the Abbey
Brewery were members of a self-supporting sick fund, and they

had formed cricket and football clubs.(14) But it was Bass and
Allsopp which dominated the Burton brewing industry. Michael
Thomas Bass built a vicarage, chapel, Sunday school, and
workmen's institute there. As M.P. for Derby for 33 years, he
endowed the city with a public library and baths, and a
recreation-ground costing £3,000. A church, schools, and a
literary institute with library, reading room, and billiard
room were constructed at his estate of Rangemore, which later
became the country seat of his son, Lord Burton. It was
believed that, during his life, Bass spent some £200,000 on
such patronage.(15) Samuel Allsopp & Sons is known to have
constructed workmen's houses and provided mess rooms at its
works.(16)

The other large brewers were to be found in London, where
Barclay, Perkins & Whitbreads were the major producers of the
19th Century.(17) By the 1890s, Barclay, Perkins employed at
Southwark 700 workers "for whose comfort, health, and
recreation they have attended to liberally in every way". A
cricket ground was laid at Dulwich, and special arrangements
were made with local railways to provide employees with cheap
transport to work. A scripture reader and a surgeon were paid
to attend at the brewery, and a benefit club provided sick
pay.(18) Whitbreads was credited with spending large amounts
on employees' welfare. Annual beanfeasts were held in the
1870s. By the 1890s, the firm began providing free medical
attendance and half wages for men who were sick. The scheme
replaced the contributory sickness and burial fund founded in
1866. Annuities, pensions, cricket and games clubs, sports
equipment, a kitchen and cafe were also available.(19) The
"family tradition" in Whitbread was conceived as involving not
only the active interest of the brewers in the welfare of
workers, but also the long-service given to the company by
individuals and their families.(20)

The authoritarianism which was often an element of
paternalism was demonstrated by the Quaker Sampson Hanbury of
Truman, Hanbury & Buxton. In the 1830s, he decided to employ a
teacher and compelled his workers to learn to read and write
on pain of dimissal. Welfare provision was the direct concern
of members of the firm's four controlling families. Pensions
were at first bestowed directly by the partners upon retired
or injured workers if they could not be found alternative
employment. The Black Eagle Benefit Club was established in
1841, however, to take over the awarding of benefits. In the
1890s, "Many social functions took place at the brewery, for
the employees did not commute and the firm became the pivot of
their existence. The men looked to the company to provide
their entertainment and security; it was their local club, for
hours were long and they lived nearby". A Workmen's Hall,
adjoining the head brewer's residence, contained a library and
reading room, a mess room fitted with cooking apparatus, and
an allowance room where the workers could obtain their free

beer. Edward North Buxton became chairman in 1897, "and a special place is reserved for him in the long memories of East Enders for whom he did so much".(21)

Charringtons at Mile End did much "for the comfort and well-being of all the employees". The firm had a "well-organised" Sick Fund and a Convalescent Fund, allowing "masters and men (to) unite in (their) management, the partners taking office with the men". Charringtons constructed "a long row of very excellent cottages, occupied by workmen, selected from the ranks for good service and good conduct", and brewers and heads of department also lived on site.(22) The partners of another Mile End firm, Mann, Crossman, & Paulin, resided near the brewery too. Beanfeasts, excursions, and Christmas gifts were common occurrences, and, after becoming a joint stock concern in 1901, the company continued to boast of the way "personal and family associations" had been retained.(23)

Weekly pensions at Watneys of Pimlico were given to most loyal and long-serving workers or their widows, while others might receive gratuities. Granted at the discretion of partners or directors, their amounts varied. James Withers, a drayman, could have expected a pension of 15s a week for 27 years' service. He was only awarded 12s, for at one time "disposing of beer in the town" where he was making deliveries. A widow of another drayman received a £10 gratuity on the grounds that, although her deceased husband had been "fairly stupid" and had six offences against his name, he had become "fairly good" after receiving a warning from a partner. Awards were given for accidents and deaths at work. Sick pay at Watneys, however, was granted through the contributory Brewery Sick Club to which the firm gave subventions.(24)

Special provision was made for draymen, because the arduous nature of their work left them particularly prone to accidents and illness. Carrying casks of perhaps two hundredweight, draymen frequently suffered from broken limbs or hernias. Bronchitis, arthritis and rheumatism were occupational diseases. Being on call to meet demands for beer, the hours of those employed in the supply department, like draymen or the horsekeepers, were long and irregular. Draymen could be at the brewery an average of 92 hours in a slack week. Hard work forced them to retire between the ages of 50 and 55, unless they could be transferred to another department. Pensions, consequently, were necessary due to the nature of their employment. The loyalty and reliability of draymen were encouraged by breweries insuring them against the short and long-term risks of their job. The "yard" men at Watneys, therefore, had their own Yard Club. Total benefits could not exceed the subscriptions paid to the fund, although the directors considered cases where this occurred.(25) During the 1890s, beer was available to all workers at meal times in the allowance room, and Watneys owned a street of model houses abutting on to the works. There were 91 dwellings housing 546 people. Its community was served by a club, library, and bagatelle-room. Another 100 people were accommodated at Brewers Street.(26)

By 1911, brewery welfare was extensive enough for the Brewers´ Journal to argue that the National Insurance Bill could undermine company paternalism. Social legislation was depicted as relieving brewers of the responsibilities they had freely assumed. Workmen were considered better cared for under the existing system.(27) Guiness´ sacked their 4,000 employees, and re-employed them only after they had signed a formal contract. It stipulated that "any payment which may be made to any employee in the nature of sick allowance or pension will be purely gratuitous, and in granting it the board will take into account the benefits derived from the Insurance Act". The discretion exercised by the brewers was an important element of the industry´s paternalistic welfare.(28)

Some brewers claimed that the extra costs imposed by the Insurance Act, coupled with increases in licensing duties in 1911, had undermined profitability and the finance available for welfare. Some of the smaller breweries undoubtedly announced the cancellation of excursions or the termination of company sick pay. The principal reason, however, was the particularly sharp fall in the demand for beer during the Edwardian period.(29) It affected wages as well as welfare with the result that the general labour unrest of these years occurred in the brewing industry also. One of the partners at Bass, Ratcliff, & Gretton came to acknowledge how the cutting of company benefits, reduced wages at a time of high prices, and redundancies had brought about a spate of strikes.(30)

Russell & Wrangham introduced profitsharing in 1911 as a response to a strike threat. Shares were awarded to all those who had been employed for three or more years.(31) Throughout 1913-14, strikes for increased wages were reported at the Northern Brewery Company Limited, Peter Walker & Sons, Showells Brewery, Messrs Shipstones & Company, and at a number of firms at Burton, London, and Bradford.(32) Employees seeking an increase of 6d an hour and overtime pay formed "A Brewery Labourers´ Branch of the Workers´ Union" in October 1913. Their membership spread in Burton, Nottingham, and Bradford especially.(33) In February 1914, a National Union of Brewery Workers was founded in London. Meeting with some initial success, they sent officials all over the country to enlist support.(34)

The employers´ policy of giving benefits and gifts to a quiescent and grateful workforce on an informal brewery-to-brewery basis was challenged by the creation of unions. Their aims and ideals opposed the traditional authority of brewers. The N.U.B.W.´s leader, Ed Pratt, declared class war aginst the "the brewery kings".(35) Workers were accustomed to petitioning their employers for a wage increase. The firm would privately discuss the issue, and make a non-negotiable decision.(36) The N.U.B.B.W., however, wanted to bargain as an equal, and was conscious of the results of welfare capitalism. It saw brewery workers as "serfs" and demanded that they think and act for themselves by combining "like all other workers".(37)

Burton brewers jointly negotiated with the brewing union, and agreed to an average wage of 23s for a 54-hour week. The Brewers´ Journal, however, urged employers to adopt the "excellent tactics of Messrs Watneys" and to refuse to talk to unions. "Sympathy and kindliness between employer and employed had not been excelled in any other industry" and "....it is quite obvious that when there is an alien organisation, those who avail themselves of this kind of intervention must in future forego any of the privileges which belonged to the old regime". Improvements in pay and conditions at Watneys were conceded in July 1914, however, because workers were "solid on their Association being recognised". But those who had actually joined the union were eventually sacked and replaced by "free labour" on the next day.(38)

The labour shortages of the Great War "cheated (brewers) of one of their best weapons of defence, namely, the right to employ other men in place of those who decide to go on strike". Employers, like those at London and Burton, were forced to agree to collective pay agreements at a district level.(39) In June 1915, however, the industry was placed under the control of the Central Control Board. It was empowered to grant war bonuses to meet the rapidly rising cost of living. From the 3rd March 1915 to the 5th February 1919, workers at Huggins and Company, for example, recieved total increases of 17s a week,(40) and awards continued to be made until the Control Board was disbanded in 1921.(41) Confronted with increased trades union strength, the industry had to consider the question of Whitley Councils. It was recognised that the policy of buying peace through high wages could not be continued indefinitely. The Brewers Society reported that employers would have to establish a means of consulting their employees. The industry was concerned that trade unionists, once given representation on joint councils, could claim some credit every time employers improved conditions. The industry not only objected to the Whitley Act´s interference in pay-bargaining, but to the very determination of wages on a national basis. A national Joint Industrial Council was successfully opposed, but, because district bargaining was already established, district councils were accepted. The Brewers Society supported proposals for the founding of works councils, if their constitutions were independently agreed by each brewer and if their tasks were confined to issues like improving production-methods, conditions of employment, works discipline, profitsharing, sick clubs, and social activities.(42) In fact, the employers´ opposition to works councils ensured that they were not established in breweries, and, when district committees became during the slump of the early 1920s instruments for imposing wage-cuts, they gradually lost credibility as a means of joint determination.(43)

Despite reductions in their standard of living, most brewery employees remained at work during the General Strike of 1926. A weakened trades union movement and threats of dismissal were contributory factors.(44) Much, however, was accredited to the type of firm prominent in brewing. While other industries had concerns so large that they had become a "sort of semi-military organisation...", only ten or so breweries in 1921 employed 1,000 or more workers. The brewing industry was said to treat its employees as individuals. Goodwill could not be established by the mere payment of wages. The industry promoted a mixture of social and athletic clubs, sick pay, works committees, bonuses, pensions, profitsharing, gratuities for labour-saving suggestions, convalescent homes, and house magazines. "A few words of friendly counsel, as a rule," said the Brewers' Journal, "proved sufficient to restore (the) better judgment" of workers when strike action was contemplated. "It is one of the cherished traditions of the Brewing Trade that the industry should be a model employer, and in this case the fruits of that wise policy have been the general and steadfast loyalty of brewery employees."(45) No worker struck at Courages because of "the kindness and goodwill of the Directors".(46) The personal relations of small-scale industry and welfare retained industrial peace.

The philosophy underlying this policy was outlined in a comprehensive document drawn up in 1926 by Warre S.Bradley of Watney, Coombe, and Reid, called "Industrial Welfare in Practice". The principle behind company provision was "to effect a closer relationship between the worker and the employer, and that was even more possible in small concerns than in large businesses". Watneys spent heavily on welfare because willing service was considered worth the cost. The firm had organised a non-contributory pension scheme, so that a worker "receives (a pension) as a gift from his employer, or it would be more accurate to say as a reward for long and faithful service". These two attributes should determine the scale of the pension awards, which could be altered or terminated at the pleasure of the Board. Men could retire between 60 and 65 years, and women at 50. "Now an employer who provides his people with this safeguard forges the first and, perhaps, the greatest link in the chain which binds them to the employer's business as loyal and faithful servants. Not a chain of slavery, but a chain formed of such links as good will and gratitude......" Moreover, because pensions would only be awarded for continuous and faithful service, they would not be given to one-time strikers. Therefore, pensions "will often be the means of staving off a disastrous strike".

The pension was transferable to widows, because a wife would then be more anxious that her husband worked hard, stayed at his job, and did not strike.(47)

The "next step" was to provide a means of reward for long service which, in contrast to pensions, operated during the employees' working life. At Watneys, men with three years' service received a bonus of 2s a week; eight years entitled a worker to 4s; 11 years to 5s; and over 14 years' employment brought 6s extra. The money was placed into a company savings bank at 4% interest, and was paid in a lump-sum to the men every quarter as a reward for good conduct during the previous three months. Furthermore, Watneys in 1926 introduced a profitsharing scheme, called a "prosperity gift". Wage earners received "until further notice" a bonus when share dividends reached above 10%. When between 10-15%, a bonus of one week's wages would be paid annually to all workers who had been employed for one year. When the figure was between 15-25%, 2 weeks' pay would be granted, and, if over 25%, 3 weeks'. The dividend was 17% in 1925. It was considered important that all bonuses were given separately from wages so it was obviously a gift and not "earned". For a similar reason, management made it clear that sick and accident pay, awarded in addition to Health Insurance and Workmen's Compensation, was ex gratia. Sports, and recreational facilities were believed to encourage efficiency, health and individual effort. The company sports club had its own ground and 1,800 members. Watneys also had a convalescent home in Surrey for the use of its workers.(48)

Friary, Holroyd and Healey's Breweries also attempted to secure the loyalty of their men when it organised a pension scheme in 1922. It was "entirely gratuitous on the part of the company" and restricted to non-union employees.(49) By 1927, John Courage's had introduced a Savings Bank and a Sick Fund. A Sports Club Hall was situated next to the the brewery, and catered for indoor games like billiards as well as outdoor pursuits like football. Membership cost 2d a week.(50) By 1931, Mitchell and Butlers had founded a recreation club, and allowed their men a week's paid holiday every year.(51)

Mr Harry Whitbread in 1924 stated that Whitbreads was one of the most successful companies in the City, "due to the efficient and loyal support of an unusually capable staff". Their methods were called "old-fashioned and our business is managed more on family than Limited Company lines. Far from denying this, I assert and rejoice in it, and I believe it to be one of the causes which contribute materially to the welfare and happiness of those who are working for you and with you...." The good feeling existing in the works was "due to the fact that the Directors were human beings and regarded all employees as such, and they had the welfare of the men at heart, whether in connection with their work or their play". Through the firm's house magazine, the personality of Harry Whitbread as an understanding and caring employer was carefully cultivated. Great stress was laid upon the value of all kinds of sport in connection with the company, and social events were supported because they induced good feeling. They brought together all classes of employees. Sports and games clubs were associated with the London Breweries Amateur Sports Association and its leagues and competitions. Whitbreads also established a savings bank and a benefit club. With no systemisation of management or welfare, there were different benefit clubs at each store or depot. But they all received company support. At the brewery itself, 95% or 570 of its employees were members of the Hospital Savings Association. 3d a week guaranteed free hospital, opthalmic and dental treatment. In 1926, Whitbreads issued 300 vouchers to employees seeking hospital treatment, and 80 claims for other treatment were met. Workers also received pensions. In 1936, the canteen at the brewery was replaced by a modern cafeteria with more adequate eating facilities.(52)

(iii) CONCLUSION

Welfare in brewing companies expanded during the 1920s, particularly in large companies like Watney, Coombe, and Reid. Yet, the discretionary nature of brewery "welfare", as it was often called in the 1920s, was not markedly different from the brewery "paternalism" of the 19th Century. Company provision helped fulfil the material needs of workers and encouraged their loyalty to a firm. But the welfare provided at the discretion of employers also carried a threat of intimidation and discrimination. George Middleton, M.P. for Carlisle, could, nevertheless, embarrass the government in 1931 when he sought Parliament's permission to found a pension scheme for brewery workers in his constituency. The industry there had been nationalised during the Great War in order to encourage sobriety amongst munitions workers. The point was that "For some time past they have been making unfavourable comparisons between the interest which the private employer took in the old workers and the indifference with which the Government treats them".(53) Management was strengthened by meeting the real material needs of workers.

NOTES

1. K.H.Hawkins & C.L.Pass The Brewing Industry (1979), p.49. There were 4,482 breweries in 1910; 2,889 in 1920; 1,418 in 1930; and 885 in 1939.
2. Ibid, pp.14-20. Cf. also P.Mathias The Brewing Industry in England, 1700-1830 (1958).
3. Channon (1973), pp.92,94,96,99. Corporate enterprises were not formed in the brewing industry till the late 1950s.

The Labour Question in the Breweries

The Labour Question in the Breweries

4. Cf. Ch.7, ss.(ii),(ix).
5. D.M.Knox "The Development of the London Brewing Industry" (Oxf. B.Litt., 1956), pp.123-4,134-5. Labour costs were about 12.5% of total costs during 1920-1930. Cf. J.Baxter "The Organisation of the Brewing Industry" (Ph.D., 1945), pp.311,359.
6. Hannah (1979), pp.102-3,187-92.
7. Hawkins & Pass (1979), pp.20-22,25,27-8,34-5,37-9, 40-2,44,50.
8. P.Lynch & J.E.Vaizey Guiness's Brewery in the Irish Economy, 1859-1876 (1960), pp.232-238.
9. Unity, Jan 1931, pp.199-202.
10. Brewers Journal, 15 Sept 1886, p.346.
11. A.Barnard Noted Breweries of Great Britain and Ireland, Vol.III (1889-91), pp.36-7,46.
12. Brewers Journal, 15 July 1892, p.291.
13. Ibid, 15 June 1886, p.152.
14. Barnard, Vol.I (1889-91), pp.330,340.
15. Ibid, pp.46-7,49,60; Brewers' Journal, 15 Sept 1870, p.200. By 1891, Bass had the largest ale and bitter brewery in the world, covering 145 acres.
16. Ibid, p.127.
17. However, London firms like Ind Coope in 1856; Charrington in 1872; Mann, Crossman, & Paulin in 1872; and Truman, Hanbury & Buxton in 1873 opened Burton breweries.
18. Barnard, Vol.I (1889-91), p.272.
19. Knox (1956), p.135.
20. B.Hill Whitbread's Brewery (1947), pp.36-7.
21. Truman, Hanbury, & Buxton Trumans the Brewers (1966), pp.22,25,33-4,38-9,44-6,52; Brewers Journal, 15 March 1872, p.567; Barnard, Vol.I (1889-91), pp.216,225. By 1891, the company employed 150 men.
22. Barnard, Vol.I (1889-91), p.304.
23. H.Jones Albion Brewery, 1808-1958 (1959), p.73.
24. Westminister City Library Archives Dept, 789/208, Register of Pensions, 10 Feb, 3 March & 7 April 1892; Ibid, 789/7, Minutes of Cobham Brewery, 30 Aug 1922.
25. Ibid, 789/208, Register of Pensions, 1860-1898; Knox (1956), pp.134-5.
26. Barnard, Vol.I (1889-91), p.367. Watneys employed about 400 men in the 1890s.
27. Brewers Journal, 15 May 1911, p.260; 15 Dec 1911, p.660.
28. Ibid, 15 Jan 1913, p.8.
29. Brewers Journal, 15 April 1908, p.233; 15 April 1909, p.214; 15 June 1909, p.349; Brewing Trade Review, 1 May 1911, p.212.
30. Brewing Trade Review, 1 Dec 1913, p.575; 1 Nov 1913, p.494.
31. Brewers Journal, 15 May 1911, pp.260-1.
32. Brewing Trade Review, 1 May 1913, p.239; Brewers

Journal, 15 May 1913, pp.544,548; 15 Feb 1914, p.63; 15 July 1914, p.386.

33. Brewers Journal, 15 Oct 1913, pp.544,548.

34. Ibid, 15 Feb 1914, p.63.

35. Brewing Trade Review, 1 June 1914, p.329.

36. Cf.Westminister Archives Dept, 789/138, Watney, Coombe & Reid, Minutes, 10 Oct 1890.

37. Brewers Journal, 15 Feb 1914, pp.444-5.

38. Ibid, 15 Feb 1914, p.76; 30 July 1914, p.365; 15 Aug 1914, pp.436-7; 15 Feb 1915, p.63.

39. Ibid, 15 Feb 1915, p.63.

40. Westminister Archives Dept, 789/3, Huggins and Company, Minutes, 3 March 1915 to 5 Feb 1919.

41. Brewing Trade Review, 1 Sept 1919, p.255; 1 May 1920, p.142; 1 June 1920, p.193; 1 July 1920, p.233; Brewers Journal, 15 Jan 1921, p.13.

42. Brewers Society, Minutes, 20 March 1919. Cf. Brewing Trade Review, March 1919, pp.76-80.

43. Brewing Trade Review, 1 May 1920, p.142; 1 July 1921, p.263; 1 Aug 1921, p.332; 1 March 1922, p.122; 1 Aug 1922, p.320.

44. Ibid, 1 Sept 1926, p.331; Brewers Journal, 15 May 1926, pp.193-4.

45. Brewers Journal, 15 Feb 1921, pp.49-50; 1 June 1926, p.203.

46. J.Courage & Co. The Development and Growth of the Company's Brewery (1933), p.53.

47. Brewers Journal, 15 Dec 1926, pp.559-61.

48. Ibid; Industrial Welfare, Jan 1931, p.95; Brewing Trade Review, 1 Oct 1926, pp.344-5.

49. Brewing Trade Review, 1 March 1922, p.105.

50. J.Courage & Co. (1933), p.53.

51. Unity, Jan 1931, pp.199-202.

52. House of Whitbread, Jan 1924, pp.41,45; May 1924, p.19; July 1925, pp.43-45,47; October 1925, p.19; July 1926, p.19; Jan 1927, pp.40-1,44,46-7; April 1928, pp.48-9; Jan 1936, pp.23-24; April 1936, p.82.

53. Brewers Journal, 15 May 1931, p.288.

Chapter 7

THE PLACE OF INDUSTRIAL WELFARE IN BRITISH INDUSTRY

(i) INTRODUCTION

The previous chapters have emphasised the connection between market strategy and industrial structure in various industries. Managerial bureaucracies replaced unfettered markets with the coordination of raw material extraction, production, and wholesaling within a single enterprise. Such companies, in other words, exercised greater "discretionary behaviour". Objectives could be decided by a process of internal bargaining within a firm. The accumulation of "discretionary profits", which were net profits minus the minimum return to dividends acceptable to shareholders, increased the opportunities for and the scale of welfare.

Greater profits were, firstly, a result of the creation of monopolistic or oligopolistic companies, which enjoyed higher profit margins through their control over prices and output. Secondly, large-scale and standardised production and the use of flow-production techniques brought returns to scale. Thirdly, internal labour markets, based on the need to retain skills acquired at an employer's cost, depended upon the stability of the product market or the levels of capitalisation in production. The better utilisation of what were often firm-specific skills increased labour productivity. Fourthly, those industries which grew in the 20th Century either through technological innovation or through meeting the demands of new, mass consumer markets experienced better profit margins. The last source of higher profits, the conscious integration and organisation of economic activity within large firms, is seen by Chandler as central to the fullest exploitation of all these developments. Therefore, two principal factors upon which the corporate company came to be based - oligopoly or monopoly, and managerial structure - moulded developments in industrial welfare. The emergence of corporate managerial structures led to the systemisation of industrial welfare strategies.

* * * * *

The Place of Industrial Welfare in British Industry

Yet, it must be remembered that certain industries continued to rely heavily upon casual labour, and did not require the sort of managerial structures which could coordinate a settled workforce. They, therefore, had little incentive to invest in industrial welfare, although there were exceptions to the general rule. The shipping industry founded an accident insurance society in 1893. On the strength of the benefits it paid, it successfully campaigned to be excluded from the 1897 Workmen's Compensation Act, despite the high accident rate amongst mariners.(1) While it was acknowledged that welfare and profitsharing little affected the lives of casual labourers, the cost of labour turnover could be reduced by enlisting the loyalty of a "cadre of permanent employees".(2) As a result of often bitter disputes in the docks industry from the 1889 onwards, sick allowances and schemes which supplemented employers' liability payments were established. Docks companies specifically differentiated between permanent employees and "casuals", with discretionary pensions sometimes being paid to the former.(3) Welfare and permanent employment were often anti-union tools - permanently employed supporters of London's 1911 dock strike, for example, were replaced by "free labour". Many dock companies invested in sporting, social and canteen facilities, particularly during and following the Great War.(4) The employment of "core" workers at the general builders G.F.Trollope's in the 1860s was noted as a common practice of the industry. Discretionary benefits were paid in large and small firms throughout this period. John Laing, for example, had by the 1930s canteens and lodging facilities, and an ex gratia fund for permanent employees covering sickness and old age, widows and orphans pensions, and paid holidays.(5)

Moreover, certain industries continued to be generally composed of relatively small-scale producers. They likewise did not require corporate management structures, nor systemised welfare policies. As in the case of brewing, paternalism was an important presence in footwear manufacture, and ranged from sick pay, profitsharing, and social facilities.(6) The first question of concern to the Boot and Shoe Joint Industrial Council in 1920 was a joint contributory Holiday Provision Scheme, and it drew up a plan for a supplementary fund under the 1920 Unemployment Insurance Act.(7) At Clark's - a comparatively large firm in the industry - extensive provident and social facilities in the factory village of Street in Somerset were provided by the 1880s. They were designed to retain valuable work skills. Expansion and the securing of retail outlets against the encroachments of competitors in the Inter-War years stabilised output and employment-levels. From 1925 onwards, a contributory pension scheme catered for this growing internal labour market. In 1933, Labour Management and Welfare Departments were appointed. A Welfare Worker supervised provident and leisure facilities, while a Labour Manager administered employment and promotion matters.(8)

The pottery industry also contained small-scale, paternalistic employers like Josiah Wedgwood, Royal Doulton, and Frederick Bralys. The Morgan Crucible Company, moreover, had by 1929 founded an elaborate system of welfare.(9) Other "materials users" equally inherited paternalistic traditions from the 19th Century. The City Saw Mills, a timber company, organised sick pay and pensions by 1938.(10) Bryant and May, the match-makers, initiated an extensive welfare strategy as a result of the famous strike at its works in 1888.(11) By 1924, the company organised profitsharing, pensions, non-contributory life assurance, voluntary unemployment benefits, athletics, and canteen facilities. Its policy towards a largely female workforce was supposedly encapsulated in its slogan "Brotherhood".(12) Small firm paternalism survived within the units which formed Wall Paper Manufacturers Limited in 1899. After the Great War, initiatives in welfare came from the Joint Industrial Council which WPM dominated. The Council was encouraged by the 1925 Pensions Act into collecting equal and joint industrial pension contributions. Unemployment benefit was supplemented by 50%, and holidays with pay were introduced.(13) The paper-makers Robinsons of Bristol, and Dickensons provided every form of welfare by the 1920s, often on a contributory basis.(14) Sir David Russell of R.Tullis, however, upheld the value of discretionary, ex gratia benefits as a means of personally rewarding only deserving and efficient workers.(15) Examples of welfare provision could also be found at the Metal Box Company, the tin-can manufacturer.(16) Hans Renold, the chain makers, adopted the extensive industrial welfare practices of its German parent-company,(17) and the activities of the well-known welfarist company of Pilkingtons, the glass-makers, have been recounted by Barker.(18) A "materials user" like pottery manufacture continued the paternalism of personal and direct relations with workers. This was also true of works belonging to WPM, but, despite its lack of a corporate structure, its near monopoly enabled it to finance major welfare expenditure. Although Robinsons, Dickensons, and Pilkingtons remained controlled by their founding families, they were in the 1920s expanding, profitable, and well-managed businesses with oligopolistic power. Like WPM, they had the means to finance extensive company provision. They differed from Metal Box, a badly structured company which often funded welfare amenities for its poorly-paid, casual and largely female workforce following threats of investigation from its wages council. Contributory pensions at Pilkingtons, Renolds, WPM, Dickinsons, and extensive provision at Robinsons were significant steps in industrial welfare.

In contrast to casual trades and small-scale manufacture, the internal labour markets established in monopolistic public utilities necessitated the provision of extensive welfare services. The profitsharing and welfare policies of the St Marlyebone Electric Supply Company in 1913 aimed to rid workers of their worries about their economic security in the event of sickness, accidents, and death. Housing was also provided. Such "Applied Psychology" was based on the principles of the "model employer" George Livesey of the South Metropolitan Gas Company.(19) The London Electricity Supply Act 1925 allowed profitsharing schemes to be founded without each company having individually to seek Parliamentary permission.(20) Extensive welfare services were also available in local and municipal transport concerns. Many tramway companies had founded friendly societies by the 1890s.(21) The North Metropolitan Tramways Provident Society in 1904 collected weekly subscriptions of 6d in return for 17/6d a week sick pay over a three month period and for 8/9d in the following quarter. The company donated 6s per member every year, and £200 were awarded as a death benefit.(22) The London Traffic Combine, a holding-company incorporated in 1902 to coordinate London's transport services, held that industrial welfare for its 46,000 workers was second in importance only to questions of wages and hours. Social, sporting, and cultural associations, convalescent homes, sick pay, and discretionary pensions were available. When London Transport was formed in 1933, it inherited and continued the large number of welfare facilities promoted by the Combine. The L.T. Sports Association coordinated the activities of sporting clubs throughout the new company, and a Chief Welfare Officer was appointed in 1937. Friendly societies were numerous, and the Benevolent Fund, which helped in all cases of financial distress, had 68,000 members.(23)

* * * * *

This chapter mainly analyses welfare in major competitive industries not covered in the previous case-studies. It does not generally rely on company records and each section is necessarily a short space in which to cover an industry. The evidence presented, however, does correlate with the preceding chapters. Sections (ii), (iii), (iv) and (v) review the histories of industrial welfare in the staple industries of textiles, coalmining, shipbuilding, and engineering, and complement Chapter 4 on iron and steel. Sections (vi), (vii), and (viii) detail events in the "new" industries of electrical engineering, motor cars, and food and tobacco, and reference to the chemicals industry in Chapter 5 may prove useful. Section (ix) will draw comparisons between industries outlined in this and previous chapters.

(ii) TEXTILES

Pollard shows that many cotton firms tried from the 1830s

to create a settled, cooperative labour force. That decade marked the success of mechanisation and capitalist production over domestic outwork in the cotton industry, and saw a brief end to over fifteen years of economic upheaval and depression. Employers had to build houses alongside their factories in order to accommodate workers. They provided sick and accident clubs, libraries, chapels, sporting facilites and institutes for the communities which formed around their expanding businesses. Under such circumstances and particularly within the many factory villages that were established in isolated areas, it was impossible to separate work-discipline and community life.(24)

Large concerns like the Strutts, however, had built houses for their workers as early as the 1790s, and constructed community schools and churches soon afterwards. Indeed, the Strutts claimed that the worst excesses of insanitation and overwork occurred in less profitable and less wealthy small workshops. Having trained their workers in factory production, the firm did not want them to leave for other employers. A Sick Club was established in the 1820s. Arkwright at Cromford found it necessary to offer employment and housing to whole families in order to convince them to move from Nottingham, Derby or Manchester.(25) Paternalism was also an essential feature of other factory villages established in the early part of the 19th Century, like David Dale and Robert Owen's New Lanark, Kirkman Finlay's Deanston village, Samuel Gregg's Quarry-bank mill, the Evanses at Darby Abbey, and the Peels' settlements at Bury.(26) The early factory masters had to overcome the reluctance of labour to working in mills, particularly when they were located in remote countryside for the sake of adequate water power. David Dale had imported pauper apprentices to New Lanark.(27) McConnel and Kennedy, William Hollins, and Ashworth and Company were amongst those which established factory communities in the 1830s,(28) and Samuel Greg still regarded the "restless and migratory spirit" of his workers as one of his main problems as an employer.(29)

Joyce has traced the development of small-firm paternalism and its influence on Lancashire's cotton mills during the middle of the 19th Century.(30) Trade cycles and the limited resources of small producers, however, limited the effectiveness of paternalistic practices.(31) Joyce also argues that the arrival of the limited company caused the decline of paternalism.(32) In the sense of paternalism meaning the personal involvement of an owner-employer in the life of a local community - whether in a village or in a district within a town - this is undoubtedly true. Large combinations were formed in the cotton spinning and finishing trades by the late 1890s, but production and control remained in small units, and did not reap some of the benefits of returns to scale exploited in the United States.(33) Chandler,

153

nevertheless, points out how the main emphasis in textile management was on improving the methods of machine-tending rather than on company organisation,(34) and changes in the structure of management in Britain were equally few.

English Sewing Cotton was formed in 1897, and the paternalistic traditions of each of its constituent companies were continued.(35) Even before the publicity for industrial welfare during the First World War, cotton employers were urged to finance company provision as a prophylactic against the resentment caused by the monotomy of work.(36) The Textile Manufacturer in 1919 reflected that early paternalism in manufacturing, if "not exactly comparable with modern ideas of welfare work", had provided the operatives with educational facilities, recreation, and better housing. Such practices had, consequently, been continued by small firms like Messrs Burgess, Ledward & Company, which had just begun providing dining, rest and recreation rooms, and bowling, tennis, cricket, and football grounds.(37) Although it was felt by 1920 that the cotton industry had ignored developments in welfare for nearly two decades, Tootal, Broadhurst & Lee, Richard Howarth & Sons, Kelsall & Kemp, John Bright & Brothers, Bannerman & Sons, as well as Burgess, Ledward & Company, were quoted as notable exceptions.(38)

The cotton industry, deemed die-hard supporters of laissez-faire, had not reacted wholly unfavourably to the Liberal welfare reforms. Undoubtedly, Sir Charles Macara, President of the Association of Master Cotton Spinners, was instrumental in founding the Employers Parliamentary Association in 1911, which orchestrated an unsuccessful campaign against Lloyd George's National Insurance Bill. Macara viewed it as damaging to labour-intensive industries like coal and cotton.(39) The Textile Manufacturer also condemned the damage that the 1911 Insurance Act might do to the industry's competitiveness, but it believed cotton employers would surmount this difficulty. By acquiring the benefits of a healthier workforce, they would not "regret having contributed their full share to that end".(40) During the Great War, Messrs Eccles at Darwen, Dugdale and Company, Messrs E.Heyworth, and W.D.Coddington and Sons installed canteen facilities, and working conditions continued to be improved after 1918.(41)

One of the large combines, J. & P. Coats, from its founding in 1896, established statistical, and buying and selling departments. The lines of communication between the central office and the branches were delineated, and accounting procedures were standardised. In addition, company welfare was increasingly directed centrally and eventually placed on a more orderly footing. Coats developed what they saw as a proud record of "conditions of working and welfare....." In 1919, the company introduced profitsharing, and, in 1920, a contributory pension scheme began providing allowances of 30/- for its women workers at 56 years.(42) Another combine, the Amalgamated Cotton Mills Limited founded a profitsharing scheme in 1920.(43) The Fine Cotton Spinners Association, created in 1898 out of 30 firms, in 1919 set aside £100,000 to provide pensions for its 25,000 workforce. The aim was to encourage "assiduous and whole-hearted service", and it enabled the company to have its pick of job-applicants. The Association believed that, by meeting the demands for economic and social security amongst its workers, it would secure industrial peace.(44) Tootal, Broadhurst and Lee, which remained a loosely-run federation throughout the Inter-War period, nonetheless, initiated profitsharing in 1919, and in 1923 established a contributory Pension Fund. Opera and sports societies were also supported by the company.(45) The Spirella Company of Great Britain advocated a Scientific Management which took account of the importance of the human element. By the late 1920s, works committees, death and sick benefits, pensions, sports and recreation clubs were available at the firm.(46) In 1920, moreover, the Cotton Reconstruction Committee took charge of a fund to pay accident allowances above those due from Act of Parliament.(47)

* * * * *

In 1923, Industrial Welfare concluded that leading employers in the textile finishing trades, the "combines" established in the 1890s, had pursued a very enlightened policy in regard to the well-being of their workpeople. The Bradford Dyers Association, for example, had by 1920 introduced copartnership and sick pay. By 1925, it had founded a pension scheme for staff and operatives as an approved society under the recently-passed Pensions Act.(48) The Bleachers Association in 1926 felt that since their founding in 1900 they had been able to establish better working conditions because of the market strength amalgamation had given them. Costs between the various branches could be compared and economies made. Horizontal amalgamation had allowed the new company to be sure of its sellers' market. Its very size allowed its directors "to develop certain welfare schemes...which would have been impossible, or in any case difficult, for the individual firms to have carried out". Concern for the human side of industry was seen as contributing in large measure to the success of the company. Its housing stock, much of it inherited from the efforts of local and once independent firms, was improved. The customary retirement allowances available from works managers were replaced after a grant of £325,000 to a central Superannuation Fund. It was non-contributory, remained under the complete control of the directors, and paid discretionary pensions to men with 50 years' service. Special help was available for those in financial need because of sickness, and sporting facilities were further developed.(49)

* * * * *

155

The Linen Thread Company, formed in 1898, also continued the paternal practices of the firms which composed it. By 1914, model villages at Hilden, Gilford, and Kilburnie contained schools, medical facilities, and community centres.(50) As early as the 1790s, the flax-spinners Marshalls of Leeds had encouraged its men to form a friendly society covering sickness and death. From the 1830s, labourers were granted holidays. Fans and blowers regulated working conditions, and changing rooms, stoves, and baths were provided. A surgeon, dispensary, admittance to an infirmary, allotments, schools, and library were other advantages.(51) Factory villages had existed, moreover, in Ulster's linen industry since the 18th Century.(52) John Martin's, near Shingley - at first a cotton mill - became a linen firm in 1845, and had an established industrial community. Founded in 1846, the firm of Quaker J.G.Richardson built Bessbrook in Newry, with its numerous educational and social facilities, as a model village. The Liddles constructed Donaghcloney in the 1870s.(53)

* * * * *

Being less mechanised than the cotton trade, Joyce argues that the labour demands of the woollen and worsted industry in Yorkshire were different and did not favour the development of industrial paternalism.(54) But it is the implications of the employment-relationship in any context and the need for income-maintenance which explain the necessity for industrial welfare.(55) Indeed, Sir Titus Salt of Bradford was famous for the practice of paternalism. His mills had good lighting, ventilation, and heating, and Saltaire from the 1860s was served by a public-dining hall, church, schools, baths and washhouse, almshouses, infirmary, club and institute, and a park. The village's 600 houses had cost a total of £100,000 to build. Samuel Akroyd's constructed the Halifax suburb of Akroyden.(56) Benjamin Gott's woollen mill and the Worsley complex of enterprises were further examples of paternalism in the woollen and worsted industry.(57) Profitsharing as adopted at Thomson's of Huddersfield in 1886 derived from George Thomson's Ruskinite philosophy. The scheme succeeded because it genuinely sought to involve workers in the management of the firm through a committee of elected directors. A Provident Fund provided pensions and sick pay.(58) Taylors, which dominated the town of Batley, had a wholly different and autocratic view of industrial welfare. A Sunday school and a Temperance Hall instilled the moral views of the employers. In the 1860s, a hospital, maternity home, Christmas gifts and socials were bestowed on Batley. The firm adopted profitsharing for the whole workforce in 1896, but control of the scheme was not given to the workers. The town's remoteness limited labour turnover and made profitsharing an effective anti-union tool. A Workers' Benefit and Sick Fund was founded in 1903.(59) In 1892, Messrs Martin of Huddersfield and Kay &

Crowthers of Lockwood established mill committees in order to improve communication and to reduce the possibilities of a strike,(60) a policy still favoured by wool and worsted employers in the 1930s.(61)

* * * * *

Beginning as silk-spinners and producers of fine crepe, Courtaulds emerged as one of Britain's foremost companies by exploiting the development of rayon. The Unitarian Courtauld family believed it exercised a stewardship over its labour force. Its workers were subjected to strict industrial discipline, but the firm rejected the notion of obtaining the greatest level of output for the cheapest wages. Samuel Courtauld spoke of a "Social Economy" which bound employers and workers. The value of work skills was recognised, and Courtaulds, rather than sacking workers during a decline in trade, preferred to retain labour by putting them on short-time. Fetes and social functions were held for workers. Hostels were available for the many young girls employed at the Courtauld factories. The firm also built cottages, and provided schools, libraries, workmen's clubs, provident societies, a hospital, and a convalescent home. Pensions were paid directly by the partners until 1897 when an ex gratia fund was established. Paid holidays were given by the 1890s. Even after Courtaulds became an international enterprise, the founding family remained firmly in control. Welfare, consequently, remained discretionary.(62) Examples of extensive welfare can also be found amongst other silk firms. John Heathcot of Tiverton, Devon had founded by the 1920s sick pay, pensions, profitsharing, and works councils. The schemes were intended to remove fears of destitution amongst the workers, and the firm's manager, John Amory, believed that the actions of Liberal Progressive employers like themselves had complemented the work of Campbell-Bannerman and Asquith in government.(63) Ford, Ayrton dominated the village of Low Bentham and provided extensive benefits and community facilities.(64) The North British Rayon Company created a public utility society in 1919 to provide industrial housing at Jedburgh.(65)

* * * * *

Industrial welfare in the textile industries was with few exceptions ex gratia. It enabled firms which faced volatile or declining markets to trim expenditure according to resources. The holding-company structures which were formed in cotton spinning and the finishing trades sought to consolidate their workforces by expanding outlays on welfare. Centralised discretionary pensions and copartnership funds appear to have been seen as interchangeable policies in the 1920s. They supplemented but did not replace the traditions of small firm paternalism, because the operations of the units within holding-companies generally remained untouched by changes in ownership. Textile industries remained unrationalised, and companies did not have the managerial structures nor the internal labour markets which would have induced them to invest heavily in systematic welfare expenditure.

(iii) COALMINING

Although the ownership of the coalmining industry remained anarchic and fragmented throughout this period,(66) coal-owners did cooperate in the provision of industrial welfare. The strategical importance of coal as an energy source and the need to pacify and cooperate with a cohesive and well-organised workforce moulded coalmining´s industrial relations and involved the government directly in matters of strikes, hours, and wages. The work-experience and skill of the miner was important in a largely unmechanised industry, and the 1887 Mines Act required a man to have two years´ employment before he could work alone underground. The community welfare of the industrial village, the permanent relief societies established in the 1870s, and the Miners´ Welfare Fund founded in 1920 were the three major elements of the industrial provision which developed in the coalmining industry to cope with its special circumstances.

* * * * *

Benson has pointed out that company villages were not necessarily the norm for many miners.(67) A tradition of "free" houses in Durham and Northumberland, however, had grown with the "binding" system which was abolished in 1844.(68) Some of the earliest reading rooms and lending libraries provided for mining communities appear to have been eventually closed. But the colliery communities established in the 1860s, during a sustained period of economic growth, survived intact. The success of the Mickley Colliery Workingmen´s Institute, providing lectures, concerts, and a library, depended upon the active interest of the company agent.(69) Denaby Main, built wholly by the local colliery, had schools, churches, a hotel, sports, water and gas supplies, an operatic society, and a large hall. Such paternalism was not a symptom of good industrial relations, but of the need to contain bitter class-conflict.(70) The Colliery Guardian praised the social facilities made available by Mercer and Evans to cope with the urban expansion of Wigan and Ashton-in-Mackerfield. It argued that "kindness" rather than wages won the cooperation of workers, because a bond beyond the cash-nexus militated against strikes and established mutual obligations. Festivals and celebrations gave expression to paternalistic relations at the firm.(71) Mining companies continued throughout the 19th Century to construct industrial homes either to attract workers to the location of isolated coal-seams or to overcome shortages in urban housing. The model Woodlands Colliery Village, near Doncaster, was built by the Brodsworth Main

Colliery in 1907.(72)

Under the Coal Mines Act 1911, a two-thirds vote by miners could compel employers to install pit-head baths. Yet, the Wharncliffe Silkstone Colliery had put up wash-houses in 1902.(73) By the 1900s, nearly every coalfield had its own miners' institute.(74) The institute at Kelty, although administered by miners, was a personal gift from the company chairman. The Fife Coal Company wanted to involve workers in the running of welfare facilities, and began to encourage individual house-ownership. Cooperation and good home conditions improved industrial relations, whereas a sense of dependence on the part of the workers was perceived by the company as detrimental.(75) After the Great War, the Housing Department was reorganised and a Housing Manager was appointed. In 1927, a Convalescent Home was established for aged and infirm workers.(76) After 1918, Harden Collieries began laying a new village with an institute, theatre and church. The Brodsworth Company constructed a jointly-administered workmen's club with a wide variety of social facilities. Emerson Bainbridge, Sanquhar and Kirkconnel, William Baird, and the Maltby and Rossington Colliery, which spent £5,000 on an institute, also expanded their community welfare in the 1920s.(77)

During the Inter-War period, owners in the expanding coalfields of the East Midlands sought to ensure their investment by the building of company villages. They were convinced that colliery houses and the provision of numerous social and sporting facilities enabled them to exercise influence over their miners. 54% of the colliery housing erected between 1918-25 was constructed in the East Midlands. Paternalism and welfare encouraged deferential behaviour. It, therefore, helped George Spencer to establish the Nottinghamshire Miners Industrial Union, which during its brief existence from 1926-1937 practised the principles of mutual cooperation rather than conflict with employers. The Nottinghamshire coal-owners also generally refused to recognise the official union and prevented it from collecting dues at the pits.(78)

* * * * *

The founding of permanent relief societies from the 1870s onwards demonstrated that the traditional pit-club was unable to provide adequate accident provision. They were small, accumulated no reserves, and set subscriptions with little calculation of the potential liabilities involved.(79) Colliery employers had granted relief to injured employees or their widows, and company clubs had in some cases been extended to cover medical treatment and ordinary sickness. The Alloa Colliery fund paid for school-fees, medical care, christening bonuses, widows' allowances, sick pay and pensions in return for contributions of 8d per week. In 1869, Messrs Grouchett and Sons' men thanked their employer for his "kindness in introducing the system of assuring the colliers of the firm..." against accidents.(80) Joining the provident fund at the Staveley Company, as in many clubs, was a condition of service, and its workers' committee by 1880 was in charge of £65,000. The company preferred joint mutual funds rather than taking out a policy with an insurance firm.(81) Employers usually controlled pit-clubs, and could arbitrarily refuse payment.(82)

As colliery funds were usually actuarially unsound, relief for the victims of major accidents depended upon public appeals. In 1861, The Colliery Guardian depicted pit-clubs as an outdated hinderance to labour-mobility and suggested the formation of a national and financially-viable institution. The men had to take the initiative and support themselves but, "Having done so, they will find abundant assistance flow towards them from their employers".(83) After the Oaks disaster in 1862, some West Yorkshire colliery-owners tried to establish a county-wide friendly society, but the majority was content to rely on individual pit-clubs. The size of benefits which an employer felt obliged to pay after another tragedy in 1875 finally persuaded the Yorkshire industry of the advantages of actuarially-calculated schemes. By enlisting contributors and determining benefits, they would, at least, place a ceiling on any awards to be made. It was felt that a 20% donation to a joint, independent fund would establish industrial goodwill, and the West Riding Miners' Permanent Relief Fund was founded.(84)

By 1892, the Northumberland and Durham Miners' Permanent Relief Fund Friendly Society, founded in 1862, had 108,000 members, and provided allowances for widows and orphans. A superannuation fund, begun in 1874, paid pensions to men over 60 or to any unfit to work. Income came from members' contributions, donations from employers, charitable subscriptions, and investments. Members of the Monmouthshire and South Wales Permanent Provident Society, which covered accident compensation, were generally members of other friendly societies catering for sick benefits and pensions, but the Society began organising a contributory pension scheme in 1899.(85)

110,000 miners contracted out of the 1880 Employers Liability Act through the relief societies of which they were members. Colliery employers argued that they could not afford to pay both donations to the funds as they stood and liability under the Act. They wanted through contracting out exclusion from the terms of the legislation.(86) The miners' leader, Burt, believed that coal-owners were willing to increase contributions in order to fund contracting out, because it was cheaper than paying liability and implementing strict safety procedures.(87) In all cases except that of the Northumberland and Durham Fund during the 1880s, employers remained represented on the societies' committees. In the North East, the miners rejected in a ballot the employers' suggestion to contract out. As a consequence, the employers transferred their indemnity to insurance companies. Before the ballot, some two-thirds of employers had participated and subscribed 12.5% of the Fund's income. Following the vote, some owners withdrew altogether and the remainder provided 5.7% of the contributions. The Society was put into debt. Employers were, however, involved in pit clubs that collected "smart" money to cover the early weeks of injury which, under the Act, did not entitle victims to compensation.(88)

Events in other coalmining regions occurred differently. The North Staffordshire organisation altered its rules to suit the Act. A local miners' leader himself obtained changes in the rules of the Lancashire and Cheshire Society in case the employers established an alternative masters' relief fund. Owners' contributions were, as a consequence, increased by 10% to 25%, and allowances for accidents were improved by 2s to 10s a week. But the agreement was ended after a strike was called on another issue. Company-based contracting-out through pit-clubs became common in Yorkshire and South Wales. Pit-clubs could also pay benefits which were supplementary to awards made under the Act or by permanent societies. In an agreement with the North Wales Fund, local employers increased their donation from 10% to 25% and allowances from 6s to 7s. Contracting out became a condition of employment in West Lancashire.(89) Colliery-owners, therefore, had good reason to be prominent opponents of the controversial 1893 Employers' Liabilty Bill which proposed ending the right to contract out.(90)

The permanent relief funds expanded rapidly because of an essential administrative convenience. Employers normally allowed them to deduct contributions directly from wage-packets. By 1892, therefore, some 275,000 miners were members of a permanent society. The West Riding Miners' Permanent Relief Fund grew in membership until 1908. In that year, the Yorkshire Coal Owners Mutual Indemnity Company Limited, which had contracted out of workmen's compensation legislation and was separate from the permanent relief fund, halted the fund's collection of contributions direct from wages.(91) The relief funds were incorporated into the 1911 National Insurance Act as Approved Societies.(92) Moreover, sick and pension pit-clubs continued into the 20th Century. Company benefit societies at the Fife Coal Company in 1904 collected subscriptions for sick and accident pay, death grants, and funeral expenses.(93) Messrs Newton & Chambers helped in cases of accident, sickness, and widowhood. Pensions were available at 65 years.(94)

* * * * *

Welfare provision in coalmining was changed greatly by legislative interference after the Great War. The Miners' Welfare Fund was established in 1920 to coordinate industrial

welfare in the collieries.(95) It was set up by Act of
Parliament as a pallid alternative to nationalisation, and was
financially supported and controlled by the employers. The
Sankey Report in 1919, commissioned in order to stave off
industrial strife in the coalfields, proposed either
nationalisation or "joint control". Lloyd George, unwilling to
countenance nationalisation, agreed to a diluted form of
"joint control" through two channels. Pit representation
committees would discuss industrial welfare but not actual
management. Miners, however, would be able to elect a number
of directors to Area Boards which could consider production
matters and wages. The industry was to be regulated through
the Department of Mines at the Board of Trade, a National
Board, Area Boards, and District and Pit Committees. Pit
committees were directly financed by the owner, while higher
bodies were paid out of a tonnage levy.(96) A central Miners
Welfare Fund would cooperate with these bodies to try and
improve miners´ social conditions which were held to be the
seed-bed of their militancy.

The Government was suggesting, therefore, a traditional
formula of works committees and industrial welfare. The
employers, however, ensured that the miners were denied a
voice in production matters and given a minimal say in welfare
provision. The 1920 Act stated that if within one year of its
passing joint committees were not appointed they would be a
dead-letter. Following industrial strife in 1920-21, the
owners refused to found district joint committees. The Miners
Welfare Committee was legally obliged to consult with these
joint committees before it could allocate any funds, and their
absence held up grants in 1921. By September, the Secretary of
Mines suggested that ad hoc joint "District Welfare
Committees" be appointed as an alternative. Their
constitutions were determined locally, and were never placed
on a regular footing. The 1927 Statute Law Revision Act
repealed legislative mention of the joint councils, "thus
emphasising the purely voluntary character of the machinery
which had been set up for the assistance of the Miners´
Welfare Committee".(97)

Originally, the Miners´ Welfare Committee was to
determine the allocation of grants but from the outset it
merely acted on the recommendations of the District Welfare
Committees.(98) This decision was defended on the grounds that
it was the best way of obtaining work-face cooperation.(99)
District Committees, in their turn, dealt with applications
from the colliery committees which organised institutes,
sports, and recreation at the pits.(100) The Miners´ Welfare
Fund was based on the legislated provision of industrial
welfare as a right to miners. Yet the Committee decided in
1922 that claims under £500 would not be investigated in
detail on the grounds that "It was clear that the mining
community would derive benefit from such a scheme, even if it

was under the Company's ultimate control".(101) The Fund had become so decentralised that it served the interests of the colliery companies. Evan Williams, President of the Mining Association of Great Britain, in 1932 argued that it was the joint committees at company-level which had been the Fund's one success, and he objected to the notion of a centralised, statutory fund.

That many employers agreed with him was illustrated by the welfare work carried out by companies in addition to the Fund.(102) Early in 1920, the M.A.G.B. contacted the Industrial Welfare Society to discuss the promotion of schemes. The Society received a £2,000 grant from the Welfare Fund in 1923 for its work in collieries, and District Boards independently added to this amount in their areas.(103) Ashington Colliery, an employer of some 10,000 miners, dealt with the I.W.S. direct. It funded its own welfare activities and used M.W.F. grants to build pit-head baths only. The colliery provided recreation grounds, and its model village of Lynemouth was served by a local hall and cinema.(104) It was recognised that an essential advantage of the Fund was its ability to concentrate its resources on "backward" employers. In the 1920s, the Mining Association, therefore, favoured the private I.W.S. replacing the state's central Miners' Welfare Committee as the Fund's administrators in order to promote such a policy. The Fund, in any case, was heavily dependent on the advice and professional services of the Society.(105)

The statutory scheme was jeopardised by the Great Depression. Some owners questioned whether they could afford to pay for the Fund, and the M.A.G.B. argued for a reduction in the levy to half-penny a ton. Williams stated, however, that: "I am not going to deny for one moment that as between the owners and the men the welfare schemes have been worked in the best spirits" and probably contributed to the comparative peacefulness since the 'war' in 1926". One large combine in Yorkshire, in particular, felt that the welfare expenditure had significantly benefited industrial relations. Williams' argument was that profits had been squeezed too hard, and that schemes could be extended by employer-union negotiations without the interference of the state.(106) The Fund continued its work in the 1930s, however, financing aged miners' homes, clinics, holiday centres, and institutes.(107)

* * * * *

Industrial paternalism was a feature of the mid-19th Century coalmining industry, and the inability of separate companies to cater for the large numbers of victims caused by individual and large-scale tragedies necessitated cooperation on a regional basis. Actuarial and contributory permanent relief funds, which were later extended in order to provide sick pay and pensions, existed despite coalmining's atomised industrial structure. But over-competition limited the commitment of owners to these societies, and community welfare and company-clubs remained discretionary and arbitrary in their application. Faced with the powerful position of the Miners´ Federation after the War, government and employers agreed to a statutory welfare fund. But owners preferred the colliery-based arrangements suited to an industry composed of small and sometimes marginal firms.

(iv) SHIPBUILDING

The general introduction of steel ships from the 1870s onwards transformed shipbuilding. Due to the considerable capital costs involved, firms in the industry were by 1900 large in comparison to those in other staples. Few, though, were public companies.(108) By 1939, the industry had achieved a greater degree of rationalisation than cotton textiles or coalmining, but the operations of individual yards remained untouched by corporate management.(109) Yet, the problems of running even one large yard did induce changes in works organisation and labour management.

The fluctuations in the market for ships during this period were a consequence of the changing levels of demand in international trade. But the sharpness of the economic cycles in the shipbuilding industry was further increased by the capital costs involved in constructing even a single ship. The loss of a contract could ruin a firm, and a shipbuilder was, therefore, normally in a weak market position. A highly capitalised industry which produced large single products was especially vulnerable to excessive competition. Moreover, shipbuilding was basically an assembly-operation, and coordination between each stage in production was essential. Cost-control and production planning, therefore, drove shipbuilding companies towards a form of centralised, multi-functional management with common features throughout the industry. An Estimating Department prepared tenders with information from the Costing Department, while a Works Department was in charge of operations. Management had to coordinate the flow of output, allocate capital and labour resources between departments, and balance the levels of work between them. Cost-controls at every level of production facilitated the drawing up of tenders and increased competitiveness. The board issued detailed operational guidelines, and oversaw a hierarchical management. But the economic vicissitudes of shipbuilding hindered the development of internal labour markets. Employers did try, however, to maximise their supervisory control over yards as a means of reducing labour-costs, and incentives and sanctions were used to encourage loyalty and long-service. Cooperation enhanced the coordination necessary for the assembly of ships.(110)

The shipbuilding industry invested heavily in industrial housing as a solution to labour-supply problems. Palmers

Shipbuilding and Iron Company so dominated Jarrow that it was
called "Palmer's Town". In the 1860s, the company sponsored a
building society for its workers, and, by 1900, nearly half
the town was owned by them. Charles Palmer, Jarrow's first
mayor and its M.P., built a hospital in 1870 and staffed it
with a resident doctor and nurses. It was financed and
administered jointly with the workers.(111) Palmers
established profitsharing in 1903, and, by 1906, supported a
club, canteen and brass band.(112) Because Glasgow's high
rents were proving prohibitive for shipyard workers, Alexander
Stephens and Sons developed a ten acre site to house skilled
men. William Denny and Brothers owned homes in the 1850s,
founded Dennystown, and funded friendly societies and accident
clubs. John Brown's gave precedence to supervisory workers in
its allocation of cottages, and so its housing policy helped
the imposition of industrial discipline. Glasgow's shipbuilding firms, in addition, often awarded houses firstly to
"regular" workers. By 1905, Beardmores in expectation of naval
orders was planning the construction of new homes,(113) and
the Ministry of Munitions, concerned about ship production
during the Great War, subsidised industrial housing in Glasgow
and Barrow.(114)

The comprehensive labour strategy developed by A.F.Hills,
General Manager of the Thames Ironworks Company, revealed the
link between labour-costing and welfare in a highly
competitive industry. After a strike in 1889, he proposed
dividing profits above 10% equally between shareholders and
workers. The workers rejected this proposal, but a Good
Fellowship Scheme was founded in 1892. It was differentiated
from profitsharing or the payment of individual bonuses. The
management, in consultation with workers, would distribute to
each department the value of the savings they had collectively
made from each contract costed at trade union rates. Each
section had its own Fellowship Council and they met monthly to
hear the production results, and the successes and failures of
each department. In 1895, Hills received a workers'
testimonial for introducing an eight hour day, which he
claimed was the result of the efficiency produced by
Goodfellowship. Bonuses were distributed twelve times a year
as a constant reminder to the men of the scheme's advantages.
£80,000 was paid in benefits by 1903.(115)

By reducing unit-costs, Goodfellowsip encapsulated the
principles of Scientific Management. Assessing the performance
of each department required extensive bookkeeping, and the
company acquired accurate information on the prime cost of
each contract and the profitability of each department and
worker. By 1894, 300-400 men had been dismissed at the request
of other workers who were asked to criticise their work-mates'
efficiency. The scheme, indeed, was intended to instill a
self-regulating discipline. Goodfellowship broke down the
sub-contracting system, in which the ganger could reward

himself undeservedly, and replaced it by managerial measurement and reward. The scheme was also meant to restore the company's traditional "friendly feelings" after so much strike bitterness. Hills realised that "the prosperity of any individual organisation depends as much upon discipline as upon good will; and I further learned that the interest of the individual workman must be guarded and encouraged for the securing of the common interest of all". A judicious mixture of discipline and goodfellowship would produce a "corporate patriotism". In 1895, the company began publishing The Thames Ironworks Gazette as a means of communication between workers and management, because, in the interest of industrial morale, workers had to be confident that the company was well administered.(116)

Dramatic and choral societies, a boat club, science classes, a cycling club, an Art and Literary Society, a Temperance League, social clubs, athletic and football associations, bands, and a cricket club were supported by the company. By 1895, so many clubs had been formed that a Federal Council was appointed to coordinate their activities. The company was concerned that these groups would dissolve as quickly as previous institutions. The company also organised joint pensions and sickness insurance schemes. Hills believed that industrial provision would make the introduction of state pensions unnecessary. The company's donations accumulated after 25 years to provide an old-age income. The combination of three schemes - sickness, pensions, and goodfellowship,- was seen as a sufficient guarantor of peaceful industrial relations. A joint Accident Fund was introduced in 1895 to cover Employers' Liability. Another fund in 1900 gave aid to the widows, wives, and children of employees who had gone as reservists to the Boer War.(117)

Developments at the Thames Ironworks were reflected in other shipbuilding firms. Denny & Brothers set up an Accident Fund Society in 1875, although it was disbanded in 1880 with the enactment of Employers Liability.(118) In 1878, Sir Joseph Armstrong had established a savings bank. The company also provided two-thirds of the contributions to an accident fund, which was organised by a committee of workers and which contracted out of the 1880 Employers Liability Act. Incapacity pay was awarded whether the accident was the worker's fault or not. A profitsharing scheme was extended to the new, amalgamated company of Armstrong-Whitworths when it was formed in 1896.(119) In 1900, Sir Christopher Furness' South Durham Shipbuilding and Iron Company introduced a copartnership scheme and a works council into its Hartlepool shipyard. The company was seeking a cure for its constant labour strife, but the scheme was abandoned within a few years.(120)

The Dublin Dockyard Company exemplified the link between shipbuilders' industrial welfare and labour supply. Founded in 1901, it needed to attract immigrant workers from the Clyde.

It was calculated that "Economical operating depends in great measure upon the harmonious working of all factors of production", and that the "personal element factor" was crucial. Welfare was the main means of coping with work-disaffection. A building with sleeping cubicles, social hall, and dining room, and a non-sectarian social club were constructed, and private firms were allowed to erect homes in the yard. Apprentices' class fees were paid. Subscriptions for an Accident Fund created by the workmen in 1911 were deducted directly from wages, and in 1920 the company agreed to donate annually 50% of the total contributions. The Fund contributed to those local hospitals which treated the company's workers, and a separate fund provided for their families.(121)

The demand for labour during the Great War concentrated the minds of employers on housing and apprenticeship schemes. But amalgamations and expansion between 1914 and 1918 also intensified the problems of managing large enterprises which employers like Hills, Palmer, and Furness had tried to solve before the War. Messrs Denny claimed to be amongst the first "to put their scheme for the welfare of their apprentices on a definite basis by the appointment of a welfare supervisor and the provision of suitable premises". These schemes led naturally to similar provision for adult workers. Canteens had been established at all large yards like Barclay, Curle and Company, Fairfields, and Harland and Wolff by 1918.(122) Directors and partners had become involved in ad hoc negotiations with labour. This was considered inefficient, "partly because it involves the use of big men on small occasions and partly because it lacks the solid basis of the sound organisation of Labour affairs". Labour Directors were appointed to maintain industrial relations and to keep employers informed.(123)

Welfare, therefore, began to be organised more formally during the War. Barclay, Curle had hired a welfare supervisor in 1916 and its Welfare Department by 1919 provided a recreation room for boys and apprentices, a lecture room, and various outdoor sports. The supervisor vetted job applicants and kept personnel records. The welfare officer in shipbuiding usually had a particular pastoral responsibility for apprentices. By 1919, The Shipbuilding and Shipping Record reported that most yards in the Clyde had welfare departments. The workers' search for better conditions and a role in management were diverted into copartnerhip and works committees. It was thought that efficiency depended upon a "happy industrial atmosphere", and cloakrooms, heating, ventilation, and refreshments added to the physical health and psychological contentment of workers. But factors outside the works - recreation as well as housing - were not "left to chance".(124)

An industry requiring a large number of apprentices had

an interest in instilling industrial discipline and cooperation at an impressionable age. To William Beardmore, welfare promoted an esprit de corps and class goodwill. By 1917, he saw sport as integral to apprenticeship training, and created the Patriotic League in Sympathy with Boy Welfare. The League became the Boys´ Welfare Association in 1918 and the Industrial Welfare Society in 1919. It attracted the support of shipbuilding employers who wanted to ensure that industry rather than the state controlled welfare matters. Boys at Beardmores were placed under a Superintendant Supervisor. The firm founded a Labour Bureau, and a welfare department which organised athletics and youth organisations. Help was given for doctors´ bills, medicines, and rents. In 1917, a self-managed Workers´ Relief Fund superseded the Local Relief Fund, which had helped the dependants of employees on active service, and its remit was extended to aiding sick workers and donating to hospitals and convalescent homes on their behalf. A Holiday Fund was established in the same year. In 1923, Beardmores appointed works councils "which were to be co-partners with the management in the oversight of production".(125)

William Beardmore, to whom welfare was an arm of industrial efficiency, wanted British industry to study carefully "the first principles of the production of material in bulk". The Science of Motion Study could eliminate the unnecessary movements of each worker. Lessons in "science and technics, designs, and manufacture, volume and economy of production, and finally, the relation of both employer and employee to all of these" had to be learnt. Technology had to be developed with the realities of industrial relations in mind, and welfare gained the cooperation management needed to minimise labour-costs. Beardmore also argued that overcompetition in the shipbuilding industry prevented it making satisfactory profits.(126)

Scotts paid similar attention to work-planning in their yards. Central managerial control over men and materials reduced overlapping. Moreover, the company carried out an "enlightened policy in their treatment of apprentices and young tradesmen". A supervisor was responsible for a boys´ club, a gymnasium, baths, lecture hall, recreation and study rooms, and outdoor sports. By 1918, a club room was made available to adult workers, who could join a number of friendly societies.(127) Messrs A.Stephen and Son established a Welfare Department during the War. The Department was originally intended to cater for workers during working hours only but it gradually expanded its activities into sport and recreation. It directly employed the apprentices and kept careful records detailing their timekeeping and conduct. Each work-shop was supposed to have a "systematic" approach to passing on labour-skills to apprentices but special supervisors were appointed to oversee training. A Savings

Scheme offered 5% interest, and a works magazine was designed to keep employees in touch with welfare activities.(128) By 1919, John Brown's, Napier and Miller, Yarrow's, Fairfield's, Simmons and Company, and Denny Brothers were reported to have set up welfare departments.(129) Swan, Hunter and Wigham Richardson in 1918 built a technical school and welfare institute for apprentices, and organised sports for them.(130) The men at Armstrong-Whitworth's Scotswood yard had by 1918 subscribed £125,000 to funds "supported by the Works Committee".(131) Palmers in 1919 built a hostel with a dining hall for 800 men, who were able to use its football pitch, laundry, and sitting-rooms. Profitsharing was reintroduced at Palmer's in 1919.(132) William Gray's established a profitsharing scheme in the same year,(133) and later founded a recreation ground, institute and a £38,000 convalescent home.(134)

* * * * *

The coordination of process-stages in shipbuilding and the imposition of effective cost-controls required the systemisation of management in the industry. Although costing procedures were mainly abandoned in 1916-21 due to the inflated demands of war-production, they were soon reimposed. Yet, the scope for corporate management still remained limited by the scale of shipbuilding operations.(135) Welfare, nevertheless, became centrally directed within firms, and played an important role in the industry's labour management. Cooperation and loyalty to a firm was important to the process of shipbuilding. The expansion of the industry on the Clyde, moreover, caused problems of labour supply and housing which were particular to the region and influenced the scale and nature of welfare provision in the industry.(136) The ordering of welfare into special departments and the increase in facilities set a pattern which continued largely unchanged throughout the Inter-War years. But the extreme fluctuations of trade in shipbuilding prevented the formation of extensive internal labour markets in companies and, therefore, the establishment of long-term welfare projects like pension schemes.(137)

(v) THE ENGINEERING INDUSTRY

The engineering industry's complex machinery and skilled labour could be better utilised through improved shop-floor organisation rather than corporate management.(138) Its fragmented structure produced over-competition and low profitability, and so reduced the opportunities for large-scale capital investment.(139) Therefore, the manual skills of the workforce, passed on through a self-regulated apprenticeship system, were essential to production. The employers attempted to exert some control over output by trying to undermine the value of the worker's craft. Rather than introducing line-production methods or Taylorism, they enforced non-apprenticed labour, piece-rates, and regular overtime. After the defeat of the Amalgamated Society of Engineers in the lock-out of 1897, this exercise of managerial prerogative was enshrined in the "Terms of Settlement" the following year. But the employers' success was partial and temporary, and the workforce maintained its sense of craft.(140) Good wages and high labour mobility reinforced the engineers' independence, and encouraged the formation of trade union friendly societies. The welfare benefits provided by the A.S.E. helped it retain members against the employers' efforts to exercise greater workplace control, and company schemes, therefore, were often designed as an anti-union strategy. Welfare policies, moreover, often had specific aims like gaining the loyalty of foremen, and that of the rapidly-expanding numbers of apprentices and women workers during the Great War whose employment diluted traditional practices.(141)

Tangye Brothers of Birmingham was a prominent company which recognised the value of retaining direct control over labour matters. In 1871, Tangyes disagreed with Sir W.G.Armstrong's opposition to the Nine Hour Day, and stated that it would deal with labour questions internally rather than through an employers' association. Tangyes believed that welfare maintained its labour supply. It was a means of organising the workforce and was seen as complementing the company's placing of apprenticeship on a regular footing in the 1900s. Tangyes had, by the 1860s, established a school and a mess hall serving cooked meals. A sick visitor appointed in 1871 soon revealed the need for more medical treatment if men were to return quickly to work. The Works Dispensary, founded in 1877, was managed by the company until 1895, when a workers' committee with the power to appoint medical officers took control. In 1883, Richard Tangye replaced the four provident societies with a single self-administered organisation. Costs were lessened and standard benefits introduced. Members of the new Sick Club automatically joined the Accident Fund which contracted out of the 1880 Employers Liability Act. For, "...they wished to tie in their new responsibility with the other welfare schemes". Tangyes paid generously even in cases of accidents caused by the victims themselves. Profitsharing was begun by 1891.(142)

Salters, another prominent Birmingham firm, organised works outings, and dramatic and choral societies existed in the 1870s. A Compensation Committee inquired into the circumstances of each accident and made awards. A Works Committee advised on conditions at work. Pensions were introduced in 1901, and an Approved Society was established under the National Insurance Act "so that instead of belonging to a vast impersonal concern, they had their own Society, entirely self-governed..." It was the duty of shop-mates to visit sick employees and check against fraudulent claims. The premises of the Works Club, built in 1859 with a library, reading room, recreation room and dining room, were improved in 1919. A Welfare Committee took over its administration. In 1928, a social centre with playing-fields was opened at the Salters' old family home.(143)

The Engineer in 1918 felt that insufficient attention had been given to works committees as a method of dealing with wages, conditions, and "the social side" of industry. William Fosters, Listers, John Wrights, Boxfoldia, and Beckett, Laycock and Watkinson introduced recreational facilities after the War. But the chief cause of industrial unrest was assumed to be labour's lack of social security, and pensions were particularly important in attracting and keeping workers.(144) Allen and Sons, which had built the workers' village of Queens Park at Bedford in the 1890s, established in 1918 a non-contributory Annuity Fund to provide allowances after 25 years' service.(145)

In 1919, a Works Director at Vickers felt that, despite its rapid growth, the company had managed to retain the "human touch". Workers, nonetheless, had to recognise their status and accept managerial authority. A house magazine kept employees in touch with management, and men with long service were awarded a gratuity of £10. The Sheffield Works Swimming Club was open to all workers, and a works club, sports club and canteen were founded at a Coventry subsidiary. The Welfare Supervisor at the Erith Works had at his disposal funds for the promotion of welfare activities.(146) Vickerstown was a company village which supplied houses for its workers. The Sentinel Works (1920) Limited, a public utility society, had a tenants' committee to organise various community facilities.(147) Short Brothers of Belfast founded Shortstown, and Rouston and Hornsby of Lincoln were granted £10,000 under the 1919 Housing Act to construct Swanpool Garden Suburb to accommodate 3,000 workers.(148)

Smith's Dock Company believed that welfare was the only means of solving human problems in industry. Company provision was not concerned with "'getting on' but with life" in its broadest sense and "its vital essential is that everybody wishes and works for the well-being of everybody else". By 1919, indoor and outdoor sports, lectures, and canteens were provided and administered by the men. Smiths also had a savings bank scheme. The Employees' Hospital Committee paid donations to local institutions on behalf of the men, and a Yards Benevolent Fund gave further assistance.(149) John Brown's had formed a sports club in 1903 at their Atlas and Norfolk Works as a means of encouraging esprit de corps. In 1938, a welfare officer was appointed to coordinate the activities of the many works sports clubs. John Brown's assisted them financially, because "The value of such an

171

institution in large industrial concerns is almost impossible
to over-estimate". The board believed, nevertheless, that the
clubs had to be self-administered if they were to thrive.(150)
* * * * *
Industrial welfare in the engineering industry mainly
concerned a minor investment in recreation and work-
conditions, and generally operated on an ad hoc basis. Welfare
was often provided for specific groups like foremen or
war-time dilutees as a means of reinforcing supervisory
control.(151) The industrial and managerial structures for the
establishment of internal labour markets and company-wide
welfare strategies did not exist, although there were
exceptions like Tangyes and Salters.

(vi) THE ELECTRICAL GOODS INDUSTRY

The technological development of electrical goods was a
costly and time-consuming process. Production was equally
complex, and required large outlays of capital in machinery
and raw materials. The manufacturers of electrical goods were,
therefore, the first non-monopolistic concerns extensively to
raise external capital. Moreover, the variety of electrical
goods produced necessitated the decentralisation of
responsibilities between company departments which could
concentrate on a particular line of products. Yet, the
production, marketing, and obtaining of materials both for
standardised switches and lamps, and for non-standardised
turbines and generators called for close scheduling within and
between departments. Electrical goods could be composed of
many pieces that had to be manufactured separately and then
assembled. Commercial departments and sales outlets were also
essential to the promotion of consumer goods. Capital
requirements, and the demands of coordinated production and
marketing led to the establishment of large companies and
sophisticated managerial structures. By 1914, the British
market was dominated by British Thomson Houston, the General
Electric Company, and Siemens. They also limited competition
between themselves through an effective system of national and
international cartels.(152)
Hirst, G.E.C.'s founder, began his business as a retailer
and diversified vertically into manufacturing in order to
safeguard his supply of a full-range of electrical goods. The
company had an early conception of the problems of management.
A Supplies Department in the 1880s anticipated
consumer-demand, coordinated with the manufacturing units, and
standardised designs. Hirst responded to a rapidly growing
demand by beginning construction of the Witton works in
Birmingham in 1900. He wanted to concentrate all G.E.C.'s
production there, but different goods were dependent for their
production on existing and specialist local labour skills.

Output at the Hammersmith lamp works, for example, had been
delayed for a year after its opening in 1894 because each
operative had to be taught and trained in 40 or more different
tasks. G.E.C. eventually decided, therefore, to establish
geographically and functionally-separate works throughout the
country. Independent and authoritative heads of department in
charge of each works had to be appointed. "They became, in
effect, managing directors of their particular
undertaking......" but they had to work within the general
policy of the board.

Hirst did, however, centralise marketing in 1900, but its
complexities grew with the expansion of electrical household
goods in the 1920s. Selling was eventually decentralised
through branches and sub-branches which were "complete
self-acting sales centres, with warehouses and showrooms,
under the charge of expert salesman and technical men". G.E.C.
was set upon a clearly-formed policy: "The object of
rationalisation is to co-ordinate all the sections of an
industry, to acquire full command over raw materials, to
establish an effective selling organisation, and to make the
streams of production flow steadily through the well-cut
channels of distribution for the adequate service of the
largest possible demand".(153)

Social events had been held for employees at G.E.C.'s
Manchester works in the 1880s. Its contributory, self-
administered Sick and Benefit Society was founded on the
initiative of the work's employees, but it became the basis of
a company-wide Benevolent Society. The Witton works was built
"as a complete industrial community, with houses and shops for
its own workpeople and with the highest possible amenities in
the way of sports grounds, clubs and open spaces". Its
"Magnet" Club had a gymnasium, large hall, dining, rest, and
billiard rooms, and was served by a seven acre playing-field.
Indeed, each G.E.C. factory in the 1900s developed "a centre
of social life". In 1920, a Contributory Pension scheme was
inaugurated and funded by 4% deductions from wages and equal
company donations. A Benevolent Pension Fund, established by a
grant of £108,000, provided ex gratia allowances for those too
old to join the contributory scheme. G.E.C. claimed that, as a
competitive firm, it could only pay average wages. But
"Regular employment; comfortable, healthy houses; good food;
reasonable hours of labour - these and similar prime
necessities may be ensured to the wage-earner. It is clear,
however, that the higher amenities of life do not lie within
the economic range of the individual at this level." G.E.C.,
therefore, provided the capital to build up a "co-operative
system of dealing with sickness, unemployment, and...pensions,
by uniting the resources of workers, employers, and taxpayer".
Welfare provision was dependent on the mutual and interlinking
assistance of the state and the company. Because provident and
recreational associations were under the charge of workers'

committees, G.E.C. was deemed a contented "democracy". Welfare and employer-worker cooperation developed the "G.E.C. spirit".(154)

In 1872, Werner Siemens formally adopted a systematic labour policy at his British works. Its principles were derived from the practices of its German counterpart. The firm was determined "to be a paternal employer". But such a relationship "was not to be a soft one; it was based upon the ordinary industrial discipline of the period....." Every year awards and bonuses were paid for loyal service. Invalids received financial assistance, and a pension scheme and an endowment fund for widows and orphans were founded. But the "simple unselfconscious paternalism" which was natural in 1900 was considered out of place by 1920. A welfare officer was appointed to bring a "modern" approach to the company. Provision after the War consequently differed from the "personal kindliness and organisational indifference" of previous years.(155)

The British Westinghouse Company, which became Metropolitan-Vickers during the War, combined in 1928 with British Thomson-Houston to form Associated Electricals Industries. But A.E.I. continued to operate as two separate companies and had no central office or functional organisation.(156) British Westinghouse built workers´ houses at Trafford Park, which, although it provided homes for workers, was not held to be a model village. In the early 1900s, the company imported American foremen to introduce their own production methods. Dismissals were frequent, and labour turnover was fast. "Yet in a few years this chaotic youth developed to an ordered maturity, thanks to a spirit of cooperation engendered above all by a man - P.A.Lange - and an organisation - the British Westinghouse Engineers´ Club." Membership of the Club, which organised sporting and social events, was open to trained engineers or apprentices. The company provided the Club with premises in 1907. British Westinghouse began an Approved Society in 1912 to supplement National Insurance payments, because it disliked the prospect of outside interference in matters of sick pay. In 1912, the Engineers´ Club was opened to all male employees, and the word "Engineers" was dropped from its title. "...thenceforward it played an ever-increasing part in developing a ´Westinghouse spirit´ throughout the organisation". New premises were opened, and a house magazine was first published in 1913. Works and staff committees were formed in 1917, and they dealt with every aspect of employment not within the remit of an employers´ association. The works committee promoted industrial welfare schemes, as well as providing a platform for the discussion of grievances. A Suggestions Scheme was started in the same year. In 1921, a contributory Works Benevolent Fund began helping in cases of accident, sickness, and widowhood. Membership was a condition of employment for all "clock" employees. The fund replaced Westinghouse's many shop clubs, and by 1949 it had paid out over £210,000 in sickness and accident benefits alone. The company donated £100 a month to the fund, yet did not assist the staff provident scheme. An Accident Prevention Committee, and a debating society were established in 1925. A thrift scheme was begun in 1926 offering a rate of 4%. In 1928 the company began a "special grants account" to provide ex gratia pensions in return for long service. For 1d a week and 1d for his wife, a worker could join the hospital scheme. The company added £500 per annum to these subscriptions.(157)

Brush Electrical Engineering in 1887 founded a profitsharing scheme. Participants were individually selected by the directors. The project only lasted for a few years, but another scheme automatically open to all employees was introduced in 1926. It aimed to give "employees a direct and continuing interest in their work and in the success of the company". Profits above a 10% dividend were distributed in stock or cash. A Copartnership Council organised the scheme, a sick room, the sports club, and the Hospital and Benevolent Fund.(158)

* * * * *

The electrical goods industry is a clear example of how capital-demands, research and development, the need for effective marketing, and work-scheduling between departments brought about the establishment of decentralised corporate management. The experiences of G.E.C., Siemens, and Metro-Vick proved the advantage of retaining "core" workforces and their skills. Although companies continued to employ many casual, female workers, the loyalty and cooperation of the labour force was crucial if bottlenecks in the industry's capital-intensive flow-production processes were to be avoided. British Westinghouse attempted to introduce line-production methods, but had to abandon fully-fledged Taylorism in favour of a welfare strategy. Company provision was transformed from conciliating only the most highly skilled workers - the engineers - into an all-embracing corporate strategy. The reliability of all workers within the scheme of production had become important. Managerial planning, crucial to the manufacture of mass-produced electrical goods, enabled welfare administration to be systemised. G.E.C., in comparison to A.E.I., English Electric, and Siemens, was the most rationalised concern. It had adopted a unified company approach to all forms of company provision by 1914 with the object of meeting material and recreational needs unfulfilled by the state or the market. Siemens, nonetheless, had devised a positive welfare policy in the 1870s. Recreational facilities at Metro-Vick by the time of the First World War were organised effectively, but provident societies were not placed on a regular footing until the 1920s.

The Place of Industrial Welfare in British Industry

(vii) THE MOTOR CAR INDUSTRY

The production of cars is associated with Henry Ford´s advocacy of absolute managerial authority, direct control over the rate of work, and mechanisation. But Lewchuck shows that before 1939 British car employers relied on payment-by-results rather than on line-production methods to control output. He also concludes that the car-manufacturer Morris was personally uninterested in industrial welfare.(159) Lewchuck, however, seems to be referring to the industry´s poor work-conditions, for Morris did personally fund a number of "external" welfare schemes.(160) When managerial reorganisation was implemented by L.P.Lord in the 1930s, welfare schemes were also removed from the direct control of Morris and placed on a more secure financial footing. The efficient flow of production between units was improved by an appropriate welfare policy as well as by the requisite managerial structure.

During the 1920s, the British motor car industry was dominated by the Big 3 of Morris, Austin, and Ford. But Morris Motors quickly overtook Fords as Britain´s largest firm through aggressive pricing and efficient standardised production. When market demand was affected by taxes on car horse-power and falling consumer incomes, the Big 3 failed to respond to changing conditions. Other competitors, like Singer, Standard, and Hillman-Hunter, stimulated demand for the smaller car from 1926-27 onwards. But over-competition in an atomised industry rocked profit-stability. Manufacturers tried to overcome the problems caused by the high income elasticity of demand for cars by adopting in the 1930s product market strategies.(161)

Employers like Morris and Austin were engineers rather than managers. By 1921, Austins was crippled by its investment in its large 20 horse-power car, and was not allowed by its creditors to invest in a smaller model until Engelbach was appointed Production Manager. Low-price cars developed in 1926-27 brought good returns, negotiated the company through the Slump without crisis, and funded the installation of continuous production methods in the early 1930s. The company, therefore, expanded through growth rather than integration with other concerns, and its management continued without radical change despite its increased size. In 1928, Fords also finally abandoned relying on the sales of a large car. The company intended that its new works at Dagenham would mass produce 8 to 10 h.p. models. Fords captured 50% of the 8 h.p. market in 1934, but its investment was, nonetheless, wrongfooted in the late 1930s when increasing product competition reduced the market for low priced cars. Morris´ experiences of mass-production during the First World War led him to conclude that efficient production could be best achieved by purchasing parts through specially-contracted small suppliers. Managerial problems were, therefore,

176

minimised. But, from 1919 to 1926, the capacity of his suppliers in engines, bodies, sheet, radiators, cylinder block castings, and carburettors was outstripped by Cowley's expanding demand, and bottlenecks held up production. Morris at first responded by financing or building additional shops under the management of his suppliers, but he was eventually forced to buy them out. Moreover, the company diversified into taxis and ambulances by purchasing in 1923 Wrigley Limited, and into the higher-priced market by taking over Wolseleys in 1926. The number of process-stages and products under Morris' direct control had, consequently, grown.(162) Yet, Morris continued his costly policy of encouraging competition between different works often engaged in making the same parts. He also ignored until 1928 arguments for a low-priced model to counter Austin's challenge. The market for Morris' 11.9 h.p. car collapsed during the Slump, and the company did not recover till 1935. Morris himself shunned board meetings, and yet was unwilling to consult or delegate authority. It was Lord, as managing-director from 1933-36, who reorganised the company into coordinated component groups, built up the capacity to produce new models, adopted a central marketing strategy, restructured the capital, and installed assembly-line techniques with moving tracks and conveyors.(163)

The direct control of Morris over production matters was reflected in his approach to industrial relations. Before 1914, Morris still owned a small company and personally organised socials and concerts. He provided generous club and sports facilities, but was anxious that work and leisure were kept as separate activities. Sports facilities were greatly expanded during the 1920s. By 1927, the Athletic Club at Oxford had a building worth £30,000 and a membership of 2,000 out of 2,700 workers. There were also concerts, whist-drives, lectures, a dramatic society, canteen, and brass band. Dental and medical services with X-ray, radiotherapy, and massage units were also available. The Morris Employees Benefit Scheme was founded in 1926, and the life insurance scheme gave £100 to a bereaved wife or dependant mother.(164) Wolseley Motors had established an Athletic Club in 1903 and provided provident benefits which were continued after the firm's take-over.(165) Pressed Steel, which as an Oxford sheet producer gradually came under Morris' control, published a house magazine from 1928 onwards, paid donations to a local hospital, and ran works dances, sports meetings, and a rifle club.(166)

At first, Morris gave donations to hospitals in Coventry, Birmingham, and Oxford if they would receive sick or injured workers. But hospital donations and the Benefit Fund were superseded by the reorganisation of the 1930s. Professional management at Morris', established under Lord, had replaced the founder's ad hoc methods. In order to promote and retain managerial resources, staff were provided with pensions in 1935. Workers were offered holiday pay after five years' service, a contributory Provident Fund, and a Savings Club. The Benefaction for Employees, a trust created by the setting aside of Ordinary shares in Morris', reduced labour turnover. Benefits were given according to length of service, sex, and age, if workers had been employed for more than a year. In 1936, it paid out £111,799 when the total wages bill was £3,116,841. The Trust's board had representatives from every Morris factory.(167) In 1939, one manager at Morris' concluded that, although a living wage was the primary instrument for guaranteeing industrial peace, the company considered it important to provide good working conditions and leisure facilities if the best possible production results were to be obtained. The aim was to build up a corporate loyalty. "The principle underlying this policy is that it is an employer's duty to see that his workers are happy, not merely from altruistic motives, but because he knows that a happy man is going to produce better work than a discontented one. The greatest factor which the average working man has to fight against is fear; fear of losing his job; fear of ill-health; fear of old age and its attendant possibility of being thrown on the industrial scrap heap." Morris' welfare schemes were designed "to give to their workers a sense of security".(168)

With the expansion of demand during the First World War, Austin's needed to attract labour. The company obtained the help of the Ministry of Munitions in 1917 to build 250 homes near Longbridge on "garden suburb lines". By 1918, amenities included a village hall, clubrooms, steam laundry, and an Anglican Mission. Austin believed it was important to maintain the skills of his workforce whom he continued to employ even during a moulders' strike in the winter of 1919-20. Profitsharing was introduced in 1932.(169) The Leyland Motor Company, which after the Great War faced a labour shortage, received a government subsidy of one-third of the cost of building housing near Preston.(170)

In 1918, Rolls Royce began developing comprehensive welfare services. The workers proved hostile to the introduction of profitsharing, but agreed to a Welfare Fund in its place.(171) In 1934, every employee with one year's service at Vauxhall Motors received a share of 1% of company profits, a sum which amounted to £66,000. By 1937, Vauxhall Motors consulted workers through works committees. The Vauxhall Recreation Club had a canteen, which was used also as a theatre, cinema, dance-hall, and an area for indoor sports. By 1939, the profitsharing scheme paid bonuses on an incremental scale after 6% had been issued in dividends.(172)

Lucas' was an electricals manufacturer which came to specialise in motor-car parts. In 1907, Harry Lucas set up a Savings Bank to supplement a Sick Society. Works committees on health, canteens, and even effluent were appointed after

the Great War. The ad hoc Sick Society was replaced by a
Benevolent Fund with an elected committee. It depended on
subscriptions of 1d a week and donations from the company. By
1924, a Welfare Officer and a Safety Superintendant had been
appointed. Sports were expanded in the early 1920s and later
placed under the charge of a full-time organiser. A Death
Benefit Fund was formed in 1928 after Lucas donated £8,000
with the stated object of winning the loyalty of its
workforce. A widow would receive a grant of £100, and the
fund's solvency was guaranteed by the company. Full-time
doctors, a dentist, and nursing staff, and a girls' rest home
were financed. With the fall of profits in 1933, Lucas decided
against introducing a profitsharing scheme, but placed
£100,000 of dividends into a general welfare fund called the
Lucas Workers' Shares Bank. It provided, for example, £10,000
in 1932 to found the Work People's Old Age Fund. During the
1930s, the Work People's Holiday Fund collected 1s a week from
the men and the company added 50% of total donations. A Hard
Luck Fund was created in 1937.(173)

* * * * *

The need to attract and retain a workforce in the early
1920s was an important factor in the development of the car
industry's welfare policies. Housing schemes and sports
facilities were of particular concern. Weak, personal
management, however, militated against the systemisation of
company provision, while its industrial structure and
profit-instability reduced the possibilities for large outlays
on welfare. There were, for example, no systematic and
contributory pension schemes for workers. But, undoubtedly,
large-scale capital investment and managerial reorganisation
in the early 1930s did increase the scope and necessity for
industrial welfare in the car industry. The introduction of
line-production methods and managerial reorganisation at
Morris' was matched by the founding of a contributory
provident scheme whose finances were secured through a
permanent benefaction administered by an elected workers'
committee.

(viii) FOOD AND TOBACCO

It was a common characteristic of food, drink, and
tobacco companies that sustained growth depended on securing
the brand-loyalty of consumers. A stable market facilitated
decisions on the rate at which to produce
quickly-deteriorating goods. It regularised returns on capital
and allowed oligopolistic pricing to be introduced.
Comprehensive retailing and wholesaling services, and
widespread advertising were well established in Britain by
1914.(174)

* * * * *

179

Managerial staff at Cadburys were recruited, trained and allocated clearly-defined duties, although the firm remained predominately a family concern in this period. Managers ran separate departments through committees and answered directly to the Board. Reorganisation began in 1915 "with the objects of centralising production control and maintaining an even flow of work, daily, and weekly, through the factory". By the 1930s, Cadburys had developed a coordinated system of production, distribution, and retailing to cope with the problems of quickly turning over consumer-perishables.(175)

In 1912, Edward Cadbury argued publicly with Scientific Management theorists. He rejected the assumption that workers would unquestionably accept repetitive work because of their low mentality. He argued that efficiently-organised production required the workers´ cooperation.(176) Cadburys sought the loyalty of their employees by funding industrial housing, sports events, socials, cultural societies, and provident provision. Bournville Village was founded in 1895, and a Savings Fund in 1897. From 1900, a Medical Department with a works doctor and a dental clinic was established, and a Sick Benefit Scheme was begun in 1902. Shop-floor works committees existed from about 1900, and were credited with being primarily responsible for the firm´s good industrial relations. Day continuation classes, under the supervision of the Works Education Committee, originated in 1906, and, along with youth clubs, instilled "social education". In the same year, a contributory Pensions Scheme was introduced for men, and in 1911 for women. Every male employee under 50 joined the pension fund, while the remainder continued to receive discretionary allowances.

Two works councils, one for men and one for women, were created in 1918 to coordinate all aspects of welfare. They replaced the many shop-floor committees with a single, unified structure because "With the growth of the business the old order of the intimate relation of master and man had inevitably, through the sheer scale of modern works organisation, either to disappear or yield to a new order". The Welfare Fund was created in 1923 by the company setting aside a block of Ordinary shares. The Fund, for example, financed a Short Time Scheme designed to help workers during the seasonal fall in trade. Family allowances were set at 5s a week for each third or subsequent child, and a contributory Sick Benefit Scheme supplemented National Health Insurance. Pensions continued to be seen as the company´s most vital scheme and its benefits were improved by additional help to bereaved widows. The Rowheath Recreation Ground was laid in 1924.(177)

Like the Cadburys, Joseph Rowntree viewed his company as a Christian trust. An eight hour day was established in 1896, for, as B.Seebohm Rowntree put it, adequate leisure time and the opportunity for "recreation and self-expression outside the factory" were essential to industrial efficiency. Clubs organised a large variety of sports, hobbies and pleasure pursuits. A Self-Help Medical Club begun in the 1890s distributed medicines, and Sick and Funeral Societies existed by the early 1900s. A works doctor was appointed in 1904, and later a full-time dental staff was employed. Continuation classes for boys were augmented in 1905 by a Domestic School for girls, and all workers under seventeen were obliged to attend some form of education at the company. Along with after-care committees and lads´ clubs, they aimed to safeguard "the transition from the discipline of school to the comparative freedom of industrial life".

Joseph Rowntree in 1904 devoted half his industrial wealth to founding charitable trusts. The Village Trust financed the construction of New Earswick and its assets were reposed with a Village Council. A joint Pensions Scheme, inaugurated in 1906, provided incomes worth half the average wages earnt by any individual in his or her final five years of work. In 1917, Rowntrees granted widows´ benefit, and gave, by the 1920s, additional unemployment allowances in the belief that state benefits were inadequate. In B.S.Rowntree´s view, industry´s efficiency depended upon the quick transfer of labour to profitable trades and, therefore, upon the availability of labour reserves. But the lack of economic security within such a system was to him also the main cause of labour unrest. He argued that, if the capitalist claimed the profits as the right of the risk-taker, he could not leave the worker a victim of commercial failure. He supported unemployment insurance by industry, because it made each trade responsible for its own labour pool. Rowntree introduced profitsharing in 1923 not as a means of giving financial incentives but in order to develop worker participation. Labour would no longer accept industrial autocracy although " there must be some one in supreme control, and there must also be discipline..... " In other words, although a joint Appeals Committee judged breaches of factory rules, the directors at Rowntrees retained an unquestioned veto in all matters. The Committee, moreover, had no jurisdiction over dismissals due to individual inefficiency or falling trade, which were considered matters of production and, therefore, of concern to managers only. Factory discipline merely worked better if employees were at least consulted.

In 1917, Seebohm Rowntree stated that "organised Welfare work" had its origins in the fact that "industry, which used to be conducted in small units, is now more frequently conducted in very large units, and the attempt to create a good working environment which was often made quite informally in the small unit, must be organised, lest it be overlooked, in the increasing complexity of the unit". Wages and conditions were dependent on technical achievement and sound business organisation, and the responsibility for securing the conditions for industrial peace rested with the employer.(178)

The confectioners Clarke, Nicholls and Coombs had a profitsharing scheme in 1890. By 1920, another fund provided sick pay, death grants, pensions, and marriage bonuses of £5 for women with five years' service. The aim was to promote good relations and continued service but all benefits were a gift given without rights.(179) Pascalls invested in sporting and recreational facilities by the 1920s.(180)

* * * * *

Another Quaker employer, Huntley and Palmers, employed a schoolmaster in the 1860s as a means of training juvenile workers. Being the largest employer in Reading, they faced a low labour turnover and paid minimal wages. "Deserving" employees received bonuses, and ex gratia pensions, amounting to £2,750 in 1898-99 and £6,350 in 1913-14, were given for 50 years' service. Socials, a canteen, and library facilities were provided. The Sick Fund was considered the firm's most important amenity. All adult employees contributing 6d weekly received 12s a week when sick. Sports were encouraged from the 1870s onwards. All welfare benefits at Huntley and Palmers remained discretionary, and an ad hoc approach was matched by managerial weaknesses. In 1921, the firm exchanged shares with Peek, Freens in order to found Associated Biscuit Manufacturers.(181) Peek, Freens paid the administrative expenses of its sick club, in existence since the 1860s, and the wages of a doctor.(182)

* * * * *

James Robertson and Sons, preserve manufacturers, was also a family business. By 1929, it gave discretionary pensions according to status and length of service. 10s bonuses were given on marriage, and workers were allowed one week's holiday. Money was granted to several sports and recreational societies. A visiting doctor was employed, and a Benevolent Fund was bestowed on the firm by the partners. The Workers' Representation Committee was considered largely responsible for harmonious industrial relations.(183) Chivers, another preserve manufacturers, built the model village of Histon, near Cambridge during the 19th Century, and W.P.Hartley of Liverpool constructed Aintree.(184) By 1920, Hartleys had introduced profitsharing and extended sports and recreational facilities.(185)

* * * * *

In 1925, it was noted that welfare work, namely sports and club-houses, had existed in the flour-milling industry before the Great War. Joseph Rank, for one, had purchased a sports ground for his mills at Birkenhead, and works committees after 1914 were considered essential as the size of firms increased.(186) Given the demand for labour immediately after 1918, the employers agreed to the establishment of a Joint Industrial Council in the hope of minimising the bidding up of wages. But rationalisation continued to concentrate production in the larger mills. In 1929, the industry, therefore, created a company which would with the aid of levies buy out superfluous mills. But the employers felt obliged to compensate long-serving workers, who were traditionally retained in milling companies, but whose labour they now intended to shed. An industry-wide pension scheme was introduced in 1930, which would pay 10s at 65 years. Moreover, annuities were available for those made redundant.(187) Hovis Limited in 1929 provided paid holidays, discretionary pensions, sick pay, profitsharing, sports facilities, and a Savings Association.(188)

* * * * *

By acquiring the exclusive use of the Bonsack cigarette-making machine in the 1880s, Wills soon came to dominate the tobacco industry. In 1900, the Imperial Tobacco Company was formed from most of Britain´s leading firms as a protective measure against the competitive threat from America. Wills owned 60% of Imperial´s capital.(189) Tobacco companies, on the whole, adopted loose holding-company structures, and a degree of rivalry between the constituent companies of Imperial continued. But the tobacco industry had become a highly concentrated industry at an early date, and oligopoly was strengthened by restrictive agreements in the 1930s.(190)

The Willses, as Congregationalists, believed they had a duty to the less fortunate. Wills from the 1870s provided cooking facilities, and adequate breaks and meals at subsidised prices were available in the 1880s. Pensions were granted by the 1870s, and profitsharing was introduced in 1889. Annual outings, fetes, and entertainments were familiar features, and employees from 1895 with one year´s employment were given one week´s paid holiday. A permanent matron was engaged in 1889 to deal with minor sickness and injury, and a works doctor was appointed in 1895. It became such a frequent practice to supplement the Sick Club that in 1899 Wills decided to place its funding on a formal basis. Contributions to the Club guaranteed sick pay equal to three-quarters of a weekly wage. The Wills Convalescent Home was opened in 1889 and a Savings Bank offered 3.5% interest. The Willses were disappointed that their men failed to save their profitsharing payments, and decided in 1899 to retain a third of any bonus. These savings were used to provide a gratuity when a man reached 60 years, changed employment, faced exceptional hardship, or left a widow. Ex gratia pensions, which continued to be paid, commonly amounted in this period to 10s a week. Cricket and football clubs, a brass band, lending library, and evening classes were subsidised. Wills´ welfare policies, being the most generous amongst tobacco manufacturers, were adopted by others within the Imperial group.(191) Carreras and Rothmans, like Gallahers, remained independent of the combine, however. Rothmans in 1904 were involved with the Tobacco Trade

Athletic Association which catered for cricket, snooker, darts, athletics, table tennis, and football.(192) Carreras developed sporting and social activities in the 1920s.(193)

* * * * *

Industrial paternalism is associated with the religious commitment of Quaker employers and particularly with Cadburys and Rowntrees. It does not follow, however, that their welfare practices were uncommon. Quaker views on the responsibilities of the employer were no different to those of Congregationalists, Unitarians, and many other businessmen who were Nonconformists. Workers at both firms had no say in production matters. Their involvement in the organisation of welfare schemes was constrained by a managerial veto, and continuation classes and youth clubs were used to discipline a young, largely female, workforce. Huntley and Palmer was a Quaker employer and yet it was often investigated by Wages Councils. Its ungenerous and unprogressive welfare schemes were merely a reflection of general managerial malaise, while Rowntrees and especially Cadburys were more systematically organised and more concerned about company provision. It is probable that the influence of Quaker goodfellowship was minor in comparison to the demands of labour management. In 1949, Seebohm Rowntree confessed that, despite "his absorbing interest in the welfare of workers", he saw it as a "part, and only as a part, of the wider problem of the management of industry..."(194) Although total labour costs were minimal in comparison to total capital at Wills, welfare was paid for by the stream of profits its market position provided. Both the tobacco trade and the food industry, therefore, are good illustrations of the connection between market, managerial structure, oligopoly, labour management, and industrial welfare.

(ix) CONCLUSION

The five chapters on the railway, gas, steel, chemicals, and brewing industries during the years 1846-1939 have emphasised the material fact that the incidence of high levels of industrial welfare expenditure depended on the ability of companies to find the required outlays. Railway and gas employers, as monopolies, were able to spend extensively on industrial welfare. Yet, the organisation of company provision was largely determined by a systematic approach to management, which as large enterprises the complexities of their operations required. The growth of company size in other, more competitive industries from the 1890s onwards induced changes in their managerial structures, and ex gratia paternalism was also increasingly systemised into corporate labour management. Large amounts of capital and the necessity for flow-production, scheduling, or coordination increased the employer's reliance upon the cooperative worker. In the interests of optimum efficiency, labour turnover and work-disaffection had to be minimised. Bureaucratic means replaced the personal in relations between employers and workers. The industrial welfare established in the 19th Century differed, therefore, from the type of company labour management later used to obtain the better administrative organisation of the workforce.

Until 1914, the staple industries of steel, textiles, coalmining, shipbuilding, and engineering consisted largely of small and medium-sized firms, owned and administered by single employers or partnerships. They share similarities, therefore, in the early development of their industrial welfare. Steel, textiles, and coalmining sought to attract workers to new locations, and contained many examples of industrial villages. Employers had to foster a sense of community between themselves and their workers, and paternalism was a common feature of British industry in the 19th Century. It was central to the industrial relations of the textile industries. Coalowners also cooperated voluntarily in the funding of mutual benefit societies, and, during the 1920s, they had legal responsibilities for the Miners' Welfare Fund. Shipbuilders, although concentrated in ports and urban centres, nevertheless built houses in order to attract the right sort of labour. From 1890-1918, the shipbuilding industry was centralising management and promoting the type of company-based welfare policies suited to the requirements of their heavily-capitalised businesses. Company provision, especially from 1918 onwards, assisted in maintaining work discipline and reducing labour turnover. The engineering industry's structure and the sort of labour it employed militated against heavy expenditure on welfare. Ex gratia company provision, however, was available in many engineering firms.

The iron and steel industry realised in the 1920s that their continued lack of profitability derived from their failure to rationalise and invest in plant of the size used by international rivals. The construction of large-scale works in the 1930s necessitated planning for the coordination of various flow-processes and the type of management that would facilitate it. The internal labour markets that were created needed to be trained and maintained, and systematic welfare policies had an important place in the emergence of corporate labour management. Other traditional trades like certain materials users remained under family management. Those with expanding markets, however, such as Robinsons and Dickensons in paper, Pilkingtons in glass, and Hans Renold in chain-production, did not prove deficient in management, and organised welfare provision effectively. Even the adoption of holding-company structures brought changes in the nature of welfare provision. Certain textile firms in the finishing and spinning trades, in particular, increased outlays on welfare, while the oligopoly exercised by the Wall Paper Manufacturers enabled it significantly to expand its welfare expenditure.

The success of the high technology or "new" industries depended on oligopolistic controls over product markets and effective multi-functional management. High margins financed the growth of these expanding industries, and the electrical engineering, chemical, and some food processor companies were amongst the earliest systemisers of management. Although chemical and food processor companies had a long tradition of paternalism, welfare in all these industries altered with the changing structures of the companies and their markets. Like the chemical trade, management in electrical engineering needed to coordinate a variety of products and a sales organisation, and much thought and effort was placed in slotting labour into the scheme of production. Food and tobacco, on the other hand, did not rely on technological innovation as a market strategy. They did, however, attempt to balance production with consumer demand. The organised management this required was noticeably successful in the case of Cadburys. The motor car industry was not as highly concentrated as other "new" industries, nor its management so systemised. Industrial welfare in motor car production did not, therefore, match the provision of chemicals and electricals companies, and certain food and tobacco concerns.

Despite the comparatively greater commitment of large companies to industrial welfare, it would be wrong to assume that the small firm or partnership epitomised the practices of the profit-maximising capitalist. Industries which retained a highly atomised structure, like those involved in brewing, footwear, wool and worsted, and pottery, confronted economic reality and not theory. They granted unsystematic and discretionary benefits, because, whatever the size of the company, welfare was a means of coping with the ever-present prospect of class conflict. Paternalism particularly suited small productive units.

Industrial welfare was often crucial to the management of labour, and, although levels of company provision varied, examples could be found in every sector. The place of industrial welfare in British industry was extensive and pervasive.

NOTES

1. Liberty Review, 24th Feb 1894, p.193; Hansard, 26 March 1906, 4th ser., vol.154, cols.913-914.
2. J.Ramage "Profit-Sharing and Co-Partnership in Great Britain" in Gannet & Catherwood (1939), pp.261-62.
3. The introduction of welfare benefits was a common strategy adopted by certain London dock, gas, and match

companies to counter the "new", general unions formed in the late 1880s. Cf. Ch.3, esp. s.iii; & Bryant & May below.

4. PP 1892 (C.6708-V) xxxv l, Qs.4590,6906-7155; J.G.Broodbank History of the Port of London (1921), p.448 & ch.26, s.8; PP 1899 (C.9203) xxxiii 871, Qs.143-223; Shipbuilding and Shipping, 6 Feb 1919, p.169; Industrial Welfare, May 1921, pp.191-2.

5. A.D.Webb "The Building Trade" in S.Webb & A.Freeman Seasonal Trades (1912); PP 1867 (C.3980-I) xxxix l, Qs.2880-2947; Master Builders Association Journal, Feb 1898, pp.15-16, 31; PP 1920 (C.544) xxiii 765, pp.119-20; R.Coad Laing: the Biography of Sir John W.Laing, C.B.E., (1879-1978) (1979), pp.68,93,95,141; Team Spirit, Nov 1946.

6. Shoe Manufacturers Monthly, July 1904, p.78; July 1908, pp.67-71; May 1911, p.13; Oct 1911 p.183; May 1911, p.20; June 1911, p.34; Feb 1919, p.267;Jan 1920, pp.298-300; Feb 1920, p.331; Jan 1925, p.285; Nov 1933, p.183; Jan 1934, pp.239-40; Shoe and Leather News, 15 May 1919, p.342; E.O.Greening A Pioneer Copartnership, being the History of the LeicesterCooperative Boot and Shoe Manufacturing Society Ltd (1923).

7. Magazine of the Boot Manufacturers´ Federation, 1 Dec 1919, p.24; 1 Feb 1920, p.72; 1 March 1920, p.96. Cf. Ch.9, s.(v).

8. L.H.Barber Clarks of Street 1825-1950 (1950), pp.13-15,19,21-23,58-60,74-5,77,152.

9. N.McKendrick "Joseph Wedgwood and Factory Discipline", H.J. (1961), pp.30-55; D.Eyles Royal Doulton, 1815-1965 (1965), pp.35-6,121; Morgan Crucible Co Ltd Battersea Works, 1856-1956 (1956), pp.13,33,36-7; Unity, Jan 1929, pp.312-3.

10. J.L.Carvel One Hundred Years in Timber: The History of the City Saw Mills, 1849-1949 (1951), pp.145-7. Cf. also Melling (1980), pp.227-230.

11. Cf. n.3.

12. East London Observer, 9 July 1921, p.4; 21 May 1924, p.4; 10 Feb 1934, p.8.

13. Wall Paper Manufacturers Ltd WPM: The Pattern of a Great Organisation (1949); Unity, Oct 1929, pp.455-7.

14. E.S.& A.Robinson & Co Robinsons of Bristol, 1844-1944 (1947), pp.67-8; PP 1920 (C.544) xxiii 765; Unity, Sept 1929, pp.403-5.

15. C.D.M.Ketelbey Tullis Russell: The History of R.Tullis & Co and T.Russell & Co Ltd, 1809-1959 (1967), pp.232-37.

16. W.J.Reader Metalbox (1976), pp.28-31.

17. B.H.Tripp Renold Chains: A History of the Company and the Rise of the Precision Chain Industry, 1879-1955 (1956), pp.29,94,96; Chandler (1976), pp.39-40; Unity, May 1930, pp.72-5.

18. T.C.Barker Pilkington Brothers and the Glass Industry

(1960), pp.179-181,215.
19. A.H. Seabrook The Management of Public Electric Supply Undertakings (1913), pp.11,15,19-20,22,23-24,26-7; C.Carpenter Industrial Copartnership (1927), p.14.
20. PP 1890-91 (C.6267) lxxviii 15; Electric Railway and Tramway Journal, 2 Jan 1914, p.7; 16 Jan 1914, p.49; 13 Feb 1914, p.112; 3 Jan 1919, p.2; 10 Jan 1919, p.7.
21. P.S.Bagwell in Wrigley (1982), p.246.
22. East London Observer, 6 Feb 1904, p.5.
23. Unity, Nov 1930, pp.167-170; H.A.Clegg Labour Relations in London Transport (1950), pp.154-66.
24. S.Pollard "The Factory Village in the Industrial Revolution", E.H.R. (1964), pp.513-531; The Genesis of Modern Management (1965), pp.234-5.
25. R.S.Fitton & A.P.Wadsworth The Strutts and the Arkwrights, 1759-1830: A Study of the Early Factory System (1958), pp.193,246-254.
26. Pollard (1964), pp.513-531; S.D.Chapman The Cotton Industry in the Industrial Revolution (1972), p.55.
27. Chapman (1972), p.53.
28. C.H.Lee A Cotton Enterprise, 1795-1840: a History of McConnel and Kennedy, Fine Cotton Spinners (1972); R.Boyson The Ashworth Cotton Enterprise: The Rise and Fall of a Family Firm, 1818-80 (1970); F.A.Wells Hollins and Viyella: A Study in Business History (1968). Cf. also S.Pollard & J.Salt (eds) Robert Owen: Prophet of the Poor (1971), pp.149-153.
29. Quote in Chapman (1972), p.54.
30. Joyce (1980), esp. pp.xiv-xxi. Cf. Ch.1, s.(ii)(c).
31. Dutton and King (1982), pp.59-74.
32. Joyce (1980), p.136.
33. A.F.Lucas Industrial Reconstruction and the Control of Competition (1937), pp.50-51.
34. Chandler (1977), p.69. On this issue, cf. M.W.Kirby "The Lancashire Cotton Industry in the Inter-War Years: a study in Organisational Change", Bus.Hist. (1974), pp.145-159.
35. English Calico Ltd English Sewing Cotton Company Ltd (1958), p.5.
36. Textile Manufacturer, 15 Dec 1912, p.397.
37. Ibid, 15 Feb 1919, p.32. Cf. also Melling (1980), pp.269-292.
38. Textile Manufacturer, 11 Sept 1920, p.256.
39. C.Macara Recollections (1922), pp.217-225.
40. Textile Manufacturer, 15 July 1912, p.217.
41. Ibid, 27 March 1919, p.335; Unity, May 1920, p.7.
42. P.L.Payne "The Emergence of the Large-scale Company in Great Britain, 1870-1914", EHR (1967), pp.519-542; J.& P.Coats Ltd The News Reel, June 1947, pp.10-11,23; PP 1920 (C.544) xxiii 765; Textile Manufacturer, 15 May 1920, p.542.
43. Textile Manufacturer, 30 Oct 1920, p.440.
44. Ibid, 15 June 1919, p.160; 19 June 1920, pp.683-4.
45. Hannah (1979), p.87; Textile Manufacturer, 15 Sept

The Place of Industrial Welfare in British Industry

1919, p.257; Unity, Aug 1930, pp.120-122.
46. Unity, Feb 1929, pp.328-30.
47. Textile Manufacturer, 31 July 1920, p.98.
48. NCEO Archive, MSS 200/B/3/2/C645 Pt.1, Correspondence
with BDA, 9 & 13 June 1925; PRO LAB2/716/186/1920, Memo. on
works committee.
49. Industrial Welfare, June 1923, pp.154-7; Bleachers
Association Concerning the Bleaching Industry (1926),
pp.36-37,46-49.
50. Linen Thread Company The Faithful Fibre (1956). Cf.
also Industrial Welfare, May 1920, pp.156-7.
51. W.G.Rimmer Marshalls of Leeds, Flax-Spinners,
1788-1886 (1960), pp.80-1,105-6,108-9,119-21, 216-17.
52. Cf. D.G.Lockhart "The Linen Industry and the
Advancing of Towns and Villages in Ireland, 1700-1750",
Textile History (1977), pp.183-5.
53. Meakin (1905), pp.419-20.
54. Joyce (1980), pp.xx-xxi.
55. Cf. Ch.1, ss.(i), & (ii)(a)(c)(d).
56. Owen (1965), pp.381-386; Pollard (1964), pp.513-531;
Meakin (1905), pp.416-17;Ashworth (1950-1), pp.378-7. Cf. also
T.Balgamie Life of Sir Titus Salt (1877); A.Holroyd Saltaire
and its Founder (1871); & J.G.Reynold Saltaire: an
Introduction to the Village of Sir Titus Salt (1977), & The
Great Paternalist: Titus Salt (1984)
57. Pollard (1965), p.235.
58. R.B.Perks "Real Profitsharing: William Thomson & Sons
of Huddersfield, 1886-1925", Bus.Hist. (1982), pp.156-74.
59. S.Pollard & R.Turner "Profit-Sharing and Autocracy:
The Case of J.,T.,& J.Taylor of Batley, Woollen Manufacturers,
1892-1966", Bus.Hist. (1976), pp.4-34. Cf. also T.C.Taylor One
Hundred Years: Records, Recollections, and Reflections (1946);
G.A.Greenwood Taylor of Batley: A Story of 102 Years. (1957).
60. PP 1892 (C.6708-VI) xxxiv 1, Qs.4898-99,4902-3,5048.
61. D.R.H.Williams Textile Factory Organisation and
Management (1934), pp.49-50. Examples of industrial welfare
can also be found in other areas of the woollen industry. Cf.
A.Plummer & R.E.Early The Blanket Makers, 1669-1969: A History
of Charles Early & Marriot (Witney) Ltd (1969), pp.78-9,83,
104,123,147-8,159-60; W.Ross Crombies of Grandholm and Cothal,
1805-1960 (1975), pp.135-138. The carpet-makers John
Crossley's of Halifax built the suburb of West Hill Park (cf.
Owen (1965), pp.381-2). Cf. also J.N.Bartlett Carpeting the
Millions: the Growth of Britain's Carpet Industry (1978). On
welfare in the West Riding textile industry, cf. Melling
(1980), pp.296-325.
62. D.C.Coleman Courtaulds: an Economic and Social
History (1969), Vol.I, pp.230-60, & Vol.II, pp.155-70,429-59;
C.H.Ward-Jackson A History of Courtaulds (1941), pp.45-6,
50-1,60.
63. W.Gore Allen John Heathcot and his Heritage (1958),

pp.126,145,148-9,151-5,161,166-7,181-2.
64. E.R. & J.H.P.Pafford Ford, Ayrton & Company Ltd, Silk Spinners (1974), pp.2-3,7,14,48,53-55,58.
65. NCEO Archive, MSS/200/3/2/C591. Memo. on housing conditions. Cf. Ch.9, s.(iv).
66. Cf. M.W.Kirby "Government Intervention in Industrial Organisation: Coal Mining in the 1930s", Bus.Hist. (1973), pp.160-73.
67. J.Benson British Coalminers in the 19th Century: a Social History (1980), pp.82-88. Cf. also M.J.Daunton "Miners' Houses: South Wales and the Great Northern Coalfield, 1880-1914", I.R.S.H. (1980), pp.143-175; & "Down the Pit: Work in the Great Northern and South Wales Coalfields, 1870-1914", Econ.H.R. (1981), pp.578-597.
68. H.F.Bulman Coal Mining and the Coal Miner (1920), p.247.
69. Colliery Guardian, 26 Jan 1861, p.51. For examples in other pits, cf. Ibid, 9 March 1861, p.154; 28 Dec 1861, p.438; & Gwent R.O., MISC MSS 1147, The Tredegar Iron and Coal Company, 1873-1923. On early 19th Century colliery paternalism, cf. G.Mee Aristocratic Enterprise: the Fitzwilliam Industrial Undertakings (1975).
70. J.MacFarlane "Denaby Main: a South Yorkshire Mining Village" in J.Benson & R.G.Neville (eds) Studies in the Yorkshire Coal Industry (1976), pp.112-3,115,117.
71. The Colliery Guardian, 26 Jan 1861, p.53; 2 Feb 1861, p.72.
72. Ashworth (1950-1), pp.378-87; & GLRO, LCC Housing Sub-Committees, Presented Papers No.9. On the Dixon Iron and Coal Company, Lanarkshire, and Briggs & Company, Yorkshire, cf. Melling (1980), pp.344-369.
73. Bulman (1920), p.252.
74. Benson (1980), pp.152-3.
75. K.Durland Among the Fife Miners (1904), p.109.
76. A.Muir The Fife Coal Company Ltd (1953?), pp.82-84. Cf. Gwent R.O., GKN Archive, D.409.21.
77. Bulman (1920), pp.265,271-2,274,277-8,282,284,286-9, 304,307,312-3.
78. R.J.Waller The Dukeries Transformed: the Social and Political Development of a Twentieth Century Coalfield (1983), pp.75-130,189-207,254-260,275-280.
79. E.Welbourne The Miners' Unions of Northumberland and Durham (1923), pp.83-4.
80. Iron and Coal Trades Review, 20 Oct 1869, p.575.
81. Colliery Guardian 4 June 1880, p.901.
82. Benson (1980), pp.177-201.
83. Colliery Guardian, 2 Feb 1861, pp.71-72.
84. PP 1892 (C.6078-I) xxiv 1, Qs.2468-2539.
85. Ibid.
86. Colliery Guardian, 4 June 1880, pp.892,897.
87. R.N.Boyd Coal Pits and Pitmen (1895), p.236-7.

88. PP 1892 (C.6708-I) xxxiv 1, Qs.2468-2539.
89. Ibid, Qs.8264-8328,8504-62.
90. Colliery Guardian, 9 June 1893, p.1061; 17 May, p.985; 31 May, p.1098; 7 June, p.1132.
91. J.Benson "The Establishment of the West Riding Miners' Permanent Relief Fund" in Benson & Neville (eds) (1976), pp.92-102.
92. Colliery Guardian, 2 Aug 1912, p.246. Cf. Ch.9, ss.(iii).
93. Durland (1904), pp.131-5.
94. Colliery Guardian, 29 March 1912, p.632.
95. POWE 1/47, Annual Report to the Board of Trade 1923.
96. Hansard, 18 Aug 1919, 5th ser., vol.119, cols.1996-2003,2007-8; Ibid, 30 June 1920, vol.131, cols.479, 482-3,487-94,585-7.
97. POWE10, BX3/3. Committee of Inquiry, Paper No.2, Origin of District Welfare Committees, 1932.
98. Ibid.
99. POWE1/45. Circulars of MWF, 1921-23. Cf. statement by C.S.Mason, South Wales Organiser of the IWS to the Central MWF Committee: POWE 1/47, 1st Annual Report 1921-22, pp.8-9.
100. POWE10, BX3/3, Committee of Inquiry, Paper No.7.
101. POWE1/1. Miners Welfare Committee Minutes, 28 March 1922.
102. POWE10, BX3/3. Committee of Inquiry, 23 March 1932.
103. Industrial Welfare, June 1920, p.203; POWE1/1, Miners' Welfare Committee Minutes, 27 Feb 1923.
104. Industrial Welfare, Feb 1923, pp.35-40; Unity, Dec 1930, pp.184-186.
105. POWE1/1, Miners' Welfare Committee Minutes, 3 Feb 1921; 29 May 1923.
106. POWE10, BX3/3. Memo. on the M.W.Committee, Paper No.22, 1932; Evidence of MAGB, 23 March 1932.
107. POWE1/10, Miners' Welfare Committee Minutes, 24 Jan, 21 March, 16 May, 19 Sept 1939.
108. J.R.Parkinson The Economics of Shipbuilding in the United Kingdom (1960), ch.1.
109. Lucas (1937), p.58.
110. A.Slaven "Strategy and Structure in the Shipbuilding Firms on the Clyde" in A.Slaven & D.H.Aldcroft Business, Banking, and Urban History (1982). The usefulness of maintaining a skilled workforce was illustrated by the effects of the Great Slump. Sir Maurice Denny of Denny Brothers in 1937 noted that fewer apprentices had been trained in the 1930s and that men redundant for many years were not immediately employable. The result was a bottleneck in production. He put four priorities before the shipbuilding industry: achieving a steadier level of production; cutting costs; recruiting and training labour; and preserving industrial peace. Cf. Sir M.Denny The Shipbuilding Industry: Rapid and Substantial Improvement: the Shipyard Labour

Situation (1937).
    111. M.Dillon Some Account of the Works of Palmers Shipbuilding and Iron Company Limited (1900), pp.8,11-14.
    112. Palmer Record, Sept 1903, p.27; May 1904, pp.126-7; Oct 1906, p.104. On the challenge of Pete Curran to the political dominance of the Palmer family in Jarrow, cf. A.W.Perdue "The Liberal and Labour Parties in North-Eastern Politics, 1900-14: the Struggle for Supremacy", I.R.S.H. (1981), pp.1-24.
    113. J.Melling "Employers, Industrial Housing, and the Evolution of Company Welfare Policies in Britain's Heavy Industry: West Scotland, 1870-1920", I.R.S.H. (1981), pp.255-301. Cf. also Melling (1980), pp.33-106.
    114. Ministry of Munitions (1919), Vol.V, pp.44-5,55-6; Cf. also Shipbuilding and Shipping Record, 3 Jan, p.19; 27 June, p.707; 5 Sept 1918, pp.240-1.
    115. Thames Ironworks Gazette, June 1903, pp.8-10,25, 99-101.
    116. Ibid, Jan 1895, pp.1-2,23-4; June 1903, pp.99-101.
    117. Ibid, Jan 1895, pp.5,8,14,18-21; Jan 1896, pp.26,32; 1 June 1896, p.834; 31 Dec 1900, p.48; PP 1893-4 (C.6795-IV) xxxii 1, Qs.24,893-25,140, Royal Commission on Labour.
    118. Denny & Bros Denny, Dumbarton, 1844-1950 (1950), p.13.
    119. PP 1893-94 (C.6894) xxxii 1, Q.25,495; PP 1920 (C.544) xxiii 765.
    120. W.G.Willis South Durham Steel and Iron Company Limited (1969), pp.5,10,17.
    121. J.Smellie Shipbuilding and Repairing in Dublin: A Record of Work Carried out by the Dublin Dockyard Company, 1901-1923 (1935), pp.i,61-81,168-69,177.
    122. Shipbuilding and Shipping Record, 5 Sept 1918, pp.240-1.
    123. Ibid, 7 Feb 1918, p.138.
    124. Ibid, 1 May 1919, p.556; 22 May 1919, p.653; 29 May 1919, p.745; 25 Sept 1919, p.360; 18 Dec 1919, pp.716-17.
    125. Forge News, 4 Sept 1917, pp.2-3; 18 Sept 1917, p.1-2,4; 4 Oct 1917, p.2-3; Beardmore News, 6 Nov 1917, p.2; 19 March 1918, p.2; 28 May 1919, p.6; 18 Oct 1917, p.2; Shipbuilding and Shipping Record, 28 Aug 1919, p.246; J.R.Hume & M.S.Moss Beardmore: the History of the Scottish Giant (1979), pp.206-7. Cf. Ch.8, ss.(i),(iii) on Industrial Welfare Society.
    126. Forge News, 18 Sept 1917, p.2; 4 Oct 1917, p.2.
    127. Scotts of Greenock Two Centuries of Shipbuilding by the Scotts at Greenock (1920), p.160; Shipbuilding and Shipping Record, 5 Sept 1918, pp.240-1.
    128. A.Stephen & Son Ltd A Shipbuilding History, 1750-1932 (1932), pp.154,158-63.
    129. Shipbuilding and Shipping Record, 18 Dec 1919, pp.716-17.

130. Ibid, p.374.
131. Ibid, 29 Aug 1918, p.222.
132. Ibid, 15 May 1919, p.639; 29 May 1919, pp.691-3
133. Ibid, 20 March 1919, p.547.
134. Ibid, 22 Jan 1920, p.115.
135. Although the industry agreed in 1930 to establish the National Shipbuilders Security Limited with the object of buying out redundant berths, its success was partial.
136. Cf. Melling (1980), pp.33-106.
137. The Thames Ironworks Company is an exception.
138. Chandler (1977), pp.269-72.
139. Channon (1973), pp.150-1.
140. Cf. Zeitlin in Gospel and Littler (1983).
141. Melling in Gospel and Littler (1983); & "Non-Commissioned Officers: British Employers and their Supervisory Workers, 1880-1920", Soc.Hist. (1980), pp.183-221.
142. R.E.Waterhouse A Hundred Years of Engineering Craftsmanship, 1857-1957: a History of Tangyes Limited (1957), pp.59-60; PP 1890-91 (C.6267) lxxviii 15.
143. M.Bache Salter: the History of a Family Firm, 1760-1960 (1960), pp.82-85.
144. The Engineer, 7 Feb 1919, p.125; 8 March 1918, p.203; 31 March 1918, pp.473-5; Unity, April 1928, pp.168-9; Sept 1928, pp.248-9; June 1929, pp.393-5; Sept 1932, pp.130-1.
145. W.H.Allen and Sons, Nov 1948, p.5.
146. Vickers News, April 1925, p.217; July 1926, p.13; Sept 1926, p.352; 15 Nov 1919, p.5.
147. Industrial Welfare, May 1920, pp.156-7.
148. Works Management, Nov 1919, pp.38-44.
149. Smith's Dock Monthly, June 1919, pp.6-7; July 1920, pp.524-5; Aug 1920, p.581; Jan 1921, p.785.
150. Sir A.Grant Steel and Ships: the History of John Browns (1950), pp.52-55.
151. Melling (1980), pp.116-171.
152. Chandler (1973), pp.362-70,426-32; R.Jones & O.Marriot Anatomy of a Merger: A History of G.E.C., A.E.I., and English Electric (1970), pp.13,15-17,23,27-28,34,43-44,48-50,58-61,89-109,104-5,110-11,128-30,139-40,160,171-2; Hannah (1979), pp.110-12.
153. A.G.Whyte Forty Years of Electrical Progress: the Story of G.E.C. (1930), pp.9,11-13,17-20,23-26,32,34-42,49-54,57,59,69,70,74-76,100,102-104,108-110; Hannah (1979), pp.110-111,134-5.
154. Whyte (1930), pp.35,114-123,126-7.
155. J.D.Scott Siemens Brothers, 1858-1958: An Essay in the History of an Industry (1958), pp.247-59.
156. Channon (1973), pp.132-4.
157. J.Dummelow 1899-1949: Metropolitan-Vickers Electrical Company Limited (1949), pp.27-28,34-5, 52-5,87-91,94,204; Hansard, 14 Dec 1911, vol.v, no.32, col.2532.
158. PP 1894 (C.7458) lxxx 575; Unity, Feb 1930, pp.18-20.

159. Lewchuck in Gospel & Littler (1983), pp.82-110.
160. Cf. Ch.1, s.(ii).
161. R.Church & M.Miller "The Big Three: Competition, Management, and Marketing in the British Motor Industry, 1922-1939" in Supple (ed.)(1977).
162. Andrews & Brunner The Life of Lord Nuffield: A Study in Enterprise and Benevolence (1955), pp.87-93,95-6,99,100, 112,124-34,143,147-9,151-2,154,156,160,340-1.
163. Church & Miller in Supple (1977).
164. Andrews & Brunner (1955), pp.14-15,274,340-1; Whiting (1977), pp.162,164-6,172-3; H.A.Goddard "Profitsharing and the Amenities of the Nuffield Factories" in Gannet and Catherwood (1939), pp.268-9.
165. Vickers News, July 1924, pp.26-7.
166. R.C.Whiting "The Working Class in the ´New Industry´ Towns between the Wars: the Case of Oxford" (D.Phil. Oxford, 1977), pp.162,164-6, 172-3.
167. Andrews & Brunner (1955), pp.15,214-5,275-6; Whiting (1977), pp.161,166,172-3.
168. Goddard in Gannet & Catherwood (1939), pp.265-9.
169. R.Church Herbert Austin: the British Motor Car Industry to 1941 (1979), pp.li,lii,43,57-8, 147,152,155.
170. Works Management, Nov 1919, pp.38-44.
171. I.Lloyd Rolls Royce: the Years of Endeavour (1978), pp.20-22.
172. Ramage in Gannet & Catherwood (1939), pp.243-250; House of Whitbread, Jan 1937, pp.234-6.
173. H.Nockolds Lucas: the First One Hundred Years, Vol.I (1976), pp.139-140,209-10,191-2, 282,299,318; Unity, Jan 1930, pp.7-10.
174. Hannah (1979), pp.85,114-5,119. It is not surprising that retailers in general failed to develop welfare services (cf. for example, Melling (1980), pp.237-242), given the small scale of most traders´ businesses, and arbitrary management coupled with long hours, low wages, and high labour turnover. Exceptions, however, could be found amongst large "multiples" like Marks and Spencers, and Boots (cf. G.Rees St Michael: A History of Marks and Spencer (1969), pp.89-96,206-227; S.D.Chapman Jesse Boot of Boots the Chemists (1974), pp.159-176; & J.S.Lewis Partnerhip for All (1948), passim. By 1932, 62% of Cooperative Society employees had pension schemes (cf. Hannah (1986), p.27).
175. Cadbury Brothers Industrial Record 1919-39 (1945), pp.6,10,14.
176. Chandler (1976), pp.43,54-7.
177. Cadbury Brothers Industrial Record 1919-39 (1945), pp.62,65,67-75; & A Century of Progress (1933); Current Opinion, Nov 1922, p.24; Works Management, Dec 1919, pp.91-3; PP 1919 (C.410) xxvii 299, Report of Departmental Committee on Old Age Pensions, Qs.3909,3911,3913,3949,3951-3,3958,3961, 3963,4032,4042-3,4052; Meakin (1905), pp.433-442. Independent

of the company, the Bournville Village Trust's housing was not tied.

178. A.Briggs Social Thought and Social Action: a Study of the Work of Seebohm Rowntree, 1871-1954 (1961), pp.60-1,81,89, 91-103,128,130,144-7,155,231-3,275-6; B.S.Rowntree The Way to Industrial Peace and the Problem of Unemployment (1914), pp.34-6,56-60; Rowntree (1922), pp.3,6-7,10-17,20-48. As at Bournville, housing at New Earswick was not tied.

179. PP 1890-91 (C.6267) lxxxiii 15; PP 1920 (C.544) xxxiii 765.

180. Unity, Oct 1928, pp.264-66.

181. T.A.B.Corley Quaker Enterprise in Biscuits: Huntley and Palmers of Reading, 1822-1972, chs.7,11.

182. PP 1892 (C.6708-V) xxxv 1, Qs.232-3,242-3,245.

183. Unity, March 1930, pp.39-41; April 1930, pp.55-7.

184. Ibid, April 1932, pp.44-8.

185. Industrial Welfare, May 1920, pp.156-7.

186. E.L.Pearson Organisation and Management in the Flour Milling Industry (1925), pp.168-79,183-9.

187. L.H.Green "Labour Problems in the British Flour Milling Industry: An Experiment in the Ordering of Industrial Relations" in Gannet & Catherwood (eds) (1939), pp.120-32; Lucas (1937), pp.58-9.

188. Unity, Dec 1929, pp.488-90.

189. B.W.E.Alford "Penny Cigarettes, Oligopoly, Entrepreneurship in the U.K. Tobacco Industry in the Late 19th Century" in B.Supple (1977).

190. Channon (1973), pp.99-101.

191. B.W.E.Alford W.D. & H.O.Wills and the Development of the UK Tobacco Industry (1973), pp.279-81,284-5,288,290-93.

192. The Bulletin, Jan 1950.

193. Unity, March 1929, pp.340-1.

194. Urwick & Brech, Vol.I (1949), p.59.

Chapter 8

THE LABOUR COPARTNERSHIP ASSOCIATION AND THE
INDUSTRIAL WELFARE SOCIETY

(i) INTRODUCTION

The Labour Copartnership Association and the Industrial
Welfare Society, established in 1902 and 1918 repectively,
were organisations concerned with the coordination and
promotion of industrial welfare. Employers gave their backing
to both organisations because they required professional
advice on company provision. Financially supported by
business, the L.C.A. and I.W.S. nourished ideas and policies
which demonstrate the purpose of employer-designed welfare as
a requirement of labour management.

The Labour Copartnership Association was originally
formed in 1884 as the Labour Association for the Promotion of
Cooperative Production. Most of its founders, J.M.Ludlow,
E.V.Neale, the author Thomas Hughes, E.O.Greening, and
G.J.Holyoake, derived their principles of industrial self-help
and cooperation from Christian Socialism, although Holyoake
was, in fact, a prominent atheist.(1) In 1902, the influence
of employers within the Association compelled the choice of a
new title, the Labour Copartnership Association. The change
indicated that, instead of self-management, workers would be
urged to share in the nominal ownership of industry.
Managerial prerogative, moreover, was accepted as essential to
industrial organisation.

The Industrial Welfare Society was established following
government efforts during the Great War to boost munitions
output by the improvement of working conditions. Its founder,
Robert Hyde, was brought into the Welfare Department at the
Ministry of Munitions, which was under the direction of
B.S.Rowntree, the chocolate manufacturer. Hyde was charged
with supervising the interests of juvenile labour, and,
through visiting "model" factories, he became acquainted with
a number of important shipbuilders on the Clyde. Together they
evolved the idea of an independent Boys' Welfare Association
with the object of advancing what was described as the best
industrial practice. The large numbers of apprentices employed

196

in shipbuilding had focused much of their attention on the specific difficulties of teenage labour, but, by 1919, the scope for welfare in labour management and the demand for advice encouraged the extension of the organisation's remit and the revised name of Industrial Welfare Society.

The change in the philosophy of the Labour Copartnership Association in the years 1890-1939 illuminates the labour management strategies devised by companies. The L.C.A., with its roots originating from the industrial democracy of the cooperative enterprise, differed only nominally by the 1920s from the activities of the Industrial Welfare Society, founded by employers to preach an ameliorative approach to industrial relations within a system of managerial organisation.

(ii) THE LABOUR COPARTNERSHIP ASSOCIATION

Some of the founders of the Labour Association first met in the 1840s, when they formed links with Owenite cooperators and the Rochdale pioneers. As rich men, they were able to become the financial backers of numerous cooperatives, and, in 1850, they founded the Christian Socialist Society for Promoting Working Men's Associations. Its publication, the Christian Socialist, preached industrial cooperation as part of the universal brotherhood of man. The Society had contacts with the chairman of the Employers' Association of South Yorkshire, Henry Briggs.(2) Briggs introduced profitsharing at his Whitwood colliery in 1865 as a means of combatting nascent unionism and as a solution for recurring strikes. When Briggs failed in both his objectives, he soon abandoned his scheme.(3) Profitsharing was defined as the allocation of shares by employers to workers, while the election of employee-directors by employee-shareholders was called copartnership. The terms, however, were often confused. Ludlow, moreover, was critical of Briggs' scheme for being a bribe and contrary to Christian Socialism, but Hughes saw nothing incongruous in a combination of profitsharing and "strong" management.(4) As supporters of individualist radicalism and Gladstonian Liberalism, members of the Labour Association in 1884 were anti-statist and anti-socialist, and not anti-capitalist. The man who emerged as the Association's most forceful advocate, G.J.Holyoake, was equally vociferous in the cause of the Liberty and Property Defence League.(5) Its Liberty Review portrayed Cooperation's links with Robert Owen as a disastrous "Socialist blight", but praised the "realistic attitude" of the Rochdale pioneers because they had practised self-help and understood the ineradicable laws of the market.(6)

The Labour Association was a propaganda organisation linked to the Cooperative Production Federation, which aided a variety of self-managed workshops in the actual running of their businesses. These firms could operate in the market according to the ideals of democratic Cooperation because of their small size. Yet, from the 1890s, the L.C.A. came to accept that the pressures of competition and the demand for large-scale capital would force the replacement of shop-floor cooperation with shareholders' ownership and supervisory control. Copartnership could be supported not on the grounds of "unobtainable" equality but because it increased efficiency. An employer would "not need constant watchfulness to detect.....waste" due to work-disaffection.(7) Finding an answer to the problems of managing sizeable workforces gave rise to argument within the L.C.A. The Society in the 1890s vacillated between true industrial democracy and employers' profitsharing schemes. The original idealism of the Association led them to reject Thomas Bushill's proposals in 1894 for ameliorating the differences of employer and employee rather than erasing the dividing-line itself. Bushill, therefore, resigned from the Association and formed the short-lived Industrial Union of Employers and Employed which promoted "unity of endeavour" between capitalist and worker.(8) But profitsharing, as implemented by employers, had close similarities to the ideas of Thomas Bushill.

To the Association, profitsharing was intended to be an arrangement between equals, although workers rarely received the full voting rights of Ordinary shareholders. The differences between the theory of profitsharing and its actual practice have led to misunderstandings about its objectives. The promoters of profitsharing viewed the capitalist firm as essentially divided by class interests, which could be superseded, not through the dialectics of increasing conflict, but by allowing the "have-nots" to become minor capitalists in their own right. Accepting this definition, one commentator notes that only some 250,000 workers were by 1920 involved in profitsharing and copartnersip.(9) But such comparatively small numbers are no reason for disparaging the movement. Too much attention is paid to the actual allocation of shares. In fact, many employers recognised that the occasional payment of dividends would not win the loyalty of workers. The usefulness of these schemes rested on the joint consultation, cooperation, and complaint-channels provided by profitsharing and copartnership committees. Such works councils were usually responsible for the management of a variety of welfare schemes other than profitsharing. Profitsharing was, therefore, part of a broader practice in industry, and should not be analysed as a separate and isolated movement.

A report from the Board of Trade in 1891 revealed the diversity of meaning in the term "profitsharing". Proposals for the alleviation of industrial strife had attracted the attention of government during the many strikes of 1889-90. The report viewed profitsharing as a previously-determined scheme guaranteeing benefits before workers actually participated. An employee also had to be convinced that his efforts were an "improvable quantity" in terms of personal reward. Although the report sought evidence of the successful distribution of dividends and bonuses, it acknowledged that profitsharing was widely accepted as encompassing any means of "class cooperation", such as extra wages at Christmas or company-supported benefit funds, so long as it could be said that an employer had given up part of his profits. A wide variety of welfare schemes, it was concluded, reduced the cost of superintendence, improved the quality of work, lessened labour-turnover, and encouraged the workers to suggest better work-methods. Employers like Tangye Brothers agreed that profitsharing enhanced good industrial relations, but only because it complemented an elaborate system of benefit clubs, mess-rooms and schools.(10) One witness wrote to the Board of Trade making the observation that, if cooperation was the desired aim, and if profitsharing ranged from stockholding to benefit-payments and the building of libraries, then " there are few large employers in this country who might not claim a place in profitsharing lists ". Moreover, profitsharing schemes generally could be altered or terminated at the discretion of the employer, for "the absolute authority of the employer to deal with the workmen, irrespective of his claims in the division of profits, would appear to be indispensable" to the success of profitsharing and the company itself.(11)

During the 1890s, many types of capitalist concerns encouraged stock-holding amongst their employees, including biscuit manufacturers, McVitie and Price; Idris and Company, the soft drinks manufacturer; the Brush Electrical Engineering Company; and Peto Brothers, the general builders. Yet, it was the influence of the South Metropolitan Gas Company through the medium of its owner, George Livesey, which above all resolved the argument within the L.C.A. over its principles.(12) Livesey's opposition to trades unionism remained an embarrassment to the Association.(13) But the L.C.A., previously associated only with small productive societies, could not overlook the advantages of having the South Metropolitan and its subsidiary the Central Gas Company as members.(14) In 1898, therefore, Labour Copartnership had confirmed that the term "Labour Association" implied not only "the association of workers" but, in addition, the "association of labour with capital in a partnership".(15) Holyoake "wanted the principle of profitsharing pushed among employers, persuading them it was for their benefit".(16) The Labour Association became committed to what was termed "the transformation of capitalism".(17) In 1901, by removing its "free labour" clause from its own copartnership scheme, the S.M.G.C. was allowed to join the Labour Association.(18)

After three years of regular questioning by the Association's Executive Committee of its name and objectives, a new constitution was proposed.(19) At the 1902 Annual

General Meeting, it was advised that the organisation become the Labour Copartnership Association, "for Employers were somewhat scared by the present name, thinking it was some extreme organisation in the proposed interest of labour, not taking into account the interests of capital and consumers". Livesey seconded the motion and stressed the point that "what was wanted was the enlistment of the sympathy of employers in the work of labour copartnership".(20)

In 1905, it was claimed that "...the importance of copartnership outside the cooperative movement had come to be more and more recognised".(21) Labour Copartnership summed up the advantages of industrial participation in the sphere of labour management: "Give the worker his share of the profits in the capital, in the control, in the responsibility of his life´s work, and you afford him every inducement to look beyond a mere receipt of wages. He begins to understand the position of the capitalist, the difficulties of management, the risks and rewards of enterprise." By appreciating that work is mental as well as manual, the worker will see that mental labour "is the most important of all". Employers would then be able to impose the "discipline which is the result of conviction" rather than "the discipline which is enforced". As small workshops were replaced by large-scale plants, the ties of loyalty which had bound master and craftsman were disappearing. The increasing potential for industrial strife could be countered by state socialism or copartnership.(22) In support of the second alternative, the economist S.D.Chapman outlined the benefits of integrating Scientific Management, welfare, and copartnership: the highest efficiency possible; the "substitution of pleasant and educative forms of production for those which are monotonous or positively unpleasant or retarding to the worker´s self-realisation"; the application of productive powers to the most commendable desires; the "proper motives in respect of the relations between individuals" in a factory; and the better sharing of wealth. Where new machinery reduced skill-requirements and a man´s involvement in the planning of his job, copartnership revived his identification with his place of work.(23) Indeed, Labour Copartnership had long recognised that the proper consideration of copartnership at individual firms could replace "rule of thumb methods" in labour management.(24) The Association, moreover, was to mourn the death of F.W. Taylor, Scientific Management´s greatest advocate, as "a distinct loss upon the world of industrial organisation".(25)

To promote their new concept of profitsharing, the Association in 1905 sought the help of some eminent figure who could summon a private conference between politicians, capitalists, and labour leaders.(26) When Theodore Taylor M.P., of the well-known profitsharing firm of Taylor and Company,(27) was elected president of the L.C.A., he arranged a meeting at the House of Commons between himself, other employer M.Ps., and the trades unionist, Thomas Burt.(28) Livesey also continued to campaign on behalf of the Association. During the threatened railway strike of 1907, he argued that differences could be resolved by copartnership. Railways, like gas companies, were capital-intensive industries which could easily issue to workers shares paying the regular dividends of all monopolies.(29) As labour unrest continued to mushroom after 1911, Asquith imitated the government in 1890 and commissioned a committee of "employers and public men" to investigate copartnership as a system of industrial organisation.(30) The L.C.A. capitalised on this renewed interest in profitsharing by emphasising its versatility. Profitsharing was not a unique system but a principle "capable of varied expression".(31) Critics of profitsharing argued that it would only work in monopolies where returns were consistent enough to maintain the interest of the workforce. Supporters replied that some competitive companies had set up funds to look after profits made above those due to shareholders. Such a fund, by accumulating during good trading years, could maintain and regularise the payment of workers' bonuses even when business was bad.(32)

The First World War and talk of Reconstruction in 1915 encouraged the L.C.A. to convene an "Industrial Conference" to discuss copartnership. Sir William Lever of Lever Brothers, Charles Carpenter of the South Metropolitan Gas Company, and J.R.Clynes, the railwaymen's leader, participated.(33) In seeking to be involved at the highest level in debates about the "joint control" of industry, the L.C.A. believed it was being damaged by its association with workers' cooperatives. One spokesman "considered that the present time offered a grand opportunity to launch a wide propaganda for the adoption of Copartnership, and to insist on the right of labour to share in the profits of industry. If the L.C.A. felt hampered by its connection with the Cooperative movement then separation might be necessary." Some Association members felt that severing their contact with the Cooperative Production Federation would irreparably damage their remaining credibility with the labour movement. Nonetheless, wholly separate committees, without dual membership, were appointed so that the two organisations could be easily differentiated.(34) Whitley himself told the Labour Copartnership Association that his Committee, which had reported in 1916-17, "had naturally considered very carefully all that had gone before in the way of schemes of copartnership and profitsharing". Although his report made no recommendations on the subject, employers at a conference in 1920 stated that Whitley and factory councils, which, "to a very large extent, controlled the conditions of employment", were themselves a successful form of copartnership, even if no shares had been issued to workers.(35) The L.C.A. held talks with the National Association of Employers and Employed, which in 1917 the Federation of British Industries saw as a means of forwarding the cause of Whitley Councils. They discussed worker participation, rather than profitsharing or copartnership, as an alternative to nationalisation proposals.(36)

The 1920 Ministry of Labour Report on Copartnership and Profitsharing noted their links with industrial unrest or periods of labour shortage.(37) It discovered that Post-War schemes were often undertaken by well-known limited liability companies. They were valued because they enabled the constant involvement of workpeople in copartnership, welfare, and works committees.(38) Sir Vincent Caillard of Vickers, one-time president of the F.B.I., agreed that channels of communication eased management's difficulties. Lever Brothers, and the confectionery-makers, Clarke, Nichols and Coombs organised an annual gathering of their workers in their various factories in order to ascertain their views. Copartnership committees, like those at the Bradford Dyers' Association and the British Cyanide Company, administered benefit funds and workshop conditions.(39) Profitsharing at Ford Ayrton and Company, the silk-spinners, centred around a works council with a say in the running of non-contributory sick and pension clubs intended to "augment the National Health Benefits and to assist cases of hardship".(40) The L.C.A. asserted that the "corollary of Co-partnership is welfare work and the ultimate result of welfare work must be to enable the workers to share in the control - as the Whitley Report states it, to 'have a greater opportunity of participating in the discussion with those parts of industry by which they are most affected' - and then to share in the ownership". Welfare work itself was "proof indeed that the spirit of Co-partnership has been accepted and not only in its economic system".(41) The L.C.A. argued that its principles had been adopted in the coalmining settlement of 1920 when it was decided to divide profits on an 83-17% basis between labour and capital respectively.(42) As a reflection of their increasing involvement in any scheme of industrial cooperation, the L.C.A. decided in 1923 that the word "Labour" should be removed from their title and replaced with "Industrial".(43)

Copartnership featured in Conservative and Liberal manifestoes throughout the 1920s, and had a keen advocate in the Cabinet minister, Lord Robert Cecil of Chelwood. The Association argued that the employer should organise his business "so as to afford reasonable wage standards, security, and control to his workers....." despite the cycles in trading conditions. The Association believed that this attitude in industry had merely been given legislative effect by the passing of the Widows, Orphans, and Old Age Contibutory Pensions Act of 1925. Companies could contract out of the state scheme or establish supplementary pension funds.(44) Indeed, with the state's attitude during the Inter-War period

towards industrial cooperation being friendly but strictly
non-interventionist, voluntary initiatives rather than
government direction were the norm.(45) The L.C.A. advertised
the fact that the employers, Mond, Milne-Watson, W.Howard
Hazell, and the T.U.C. President, Ben Turner, who all
participated in the Mond-Turner talks of 1927, were prominent
members of the Association.(46)

* * * * *

Industrial Peace argued that rational industrial
organisation by "scientific methods" could be capped by
copartnership as a symbol of cooperation within large
companies.(47) Mergers during the 1920s were facilitated by
the involvement of potentially more alienated labour forces in
works councils. Sir Alfred Mond of I.C.I. believed that
copartnership introduced a "new psychology" into industry by
making employers and workers feel they were "co-workers".(48)
Worker stock-holding itself was an experiment in labour
management which met with partial success, but it was in
practice designed as only one aspect of a company's welfare
policy. Profitsharing and copartnership committees, where they
existed, tended to deal with welfare work in general. The
L.C.A., therefore, had by 1939 changed from being an advocate
of true industrial democracy into, at first, a promoter of
labour copartnership between capital and labour, and, then,
into an organisation which campaigned for industrial
participation as a means of improving labour efficiency.(49)

(iii) THE INDUSTRIAL WELFARE SOCIETY

The Ministry of Labour objected when in 1919 Robert Hyde
founded a private institution to promote the cause of
industrial welfare. Hyde's persuasiveness was acknowledged,
but he was said to have achieved few concrete results at the
Ministry of Munition's Welfare Department, with the exception
of the contacts he had forged with Scottish shipbuilders.(50)
One of these, William Beardmore of Beardmore and Company
established a welfare department at his own works in 1917 and
rallied his apprentices in the cause of the 1st Patriotic
League in Sympathy with Boy Welfare. Beardmore thought that
economic conditions after the War would be harsh, but he
believed that British shipbuilding could protect its position
by introducing modern technology. Boys' welfare would promote
the good labour relations essential to industrial success. It
was intended by Beardmore to be a means of superseding the
apprenticeship system and involving the company directly in
the training of workers in new techniques.(51) His influence
with other shipbuilders on the Clyde led to the setting up of
the I.W.S. and guaranteed its initial success.
The Society's first Council, which met in 1918 at
the headquarters of the Shipbuilding Employers

Federation, was composed of six representatives of shipbuilding firms and Hyde.(52) The formation of the Society was, nevertheless, discussed with the Engineering Employers Federation, the Federation of British Industries, and the National Association of Employers and Employed.(53) Donations were received from the E.E.F., the S.E.F., and the British Commonwealth Union.(54)

Despite the origins of the Society, the I.W.S. claimed a non-sectarian outlook in industrial relations. Many trades unionists, including J.R.Clynes, Arthur Henderson, and F.S.Button, were associated with it, but only as individuals. Although attempts were made to gain the allegiance of the Engineers, Boilermakers, and Gas and General Workers, Labour on the whole remained hostile, and the Trades Union Congress in 1932 condemned industrial welfare as an anti-union tool.(55) Yet, because welfare at the company-level often enabled employers to cooperate with their workforces, many union leaders in practice took a pragmatic attitude. As General Secretary of the Gas and General Labourers, Will Thorne recognised the advantages of negotiating with employers rather than confronting them. He was willing to be a member of the I.W.S.´s Council, but rarely attended its meetings. For the sake of retaining his name in the ranks of the Society, he was dissuaded for many years from resigning, despite the passivity of his commitment.(56)

That the Industrial Welfare Society sought to protect managerial prerogative from the encroachments of labour and the state was revealed in its early dealings with the Ministry of Labour and the Welfare Workers´ Institute. The Institute had been founded in 1913 as a professional body for welfare supervisors, and was largely composed of women engaged in industries heavily dependent upon female labour. It became, in 1931, the Institute of Labour Management.(57) The state, however, was at first perceived as the greatest threat. In 1920, the Ministry of Labour wanted the Society and the Institute to join forces, partly so "that out of the amalgamation an executive should be formed capable of really controlling Mr Hyde" who otherwise "will come to a shipwreck". During the two years after the end of the Great War, Reconstruction or large-scale government intervention in industrial and social matters was still a prospect. The Ministry held that it was "impossible" for it "to wash its hands of all responsibilty for what goes on inside the works".(58) The Society´s future, of course, depended on industrial welfare being left to private initiative, and employers´ support for the I.W.S. was in part a strategy for demonstrating that state intervention was unnecessary.

It was an outlook shared by Sir Allen Smith of the E.E.F., who opposed those within the F.B.I. in favour of a general agreement on industrial relations between government, business, and labour. His rejection of consensus and his advocacy of commercial and managerial freedom helped to ruin any hope of progress at the National Industrial Conference in 1920.(59) Engaged in the work of the I.W.S., Smith issued a circular to members of the E.E.F. recommending the work of the Society.(60) Hyde and he led a delegation which asked the Secretary of State, Horne, in March 1920, "To withdraw the Ministry of Labour from all welfare work and give the Association (sic) a monopoly".(61) By 1921, any threat of a Coalition government involving itself in the details of industrial affairs had faded with the eventual decontrol of the wartime economy.

The Ministry was certain that the Industrial Welfare Society was an organisation financed by "a large number of influential employers". One-sidedness, it was believed, would irredeemably hinder the Society in its declared aim of solving the problems of industrial unrest.(62) Yet, it was because the Welfare Workers´ Institute was an independent body that employers were opposed to it. They preferred to set the standards and determine the organisation of welfare schemes. To Hyde and many employers, the Institute was discredited by having reportedly received financial support from "labour circles".(63) The Ministry also criticised the Institute´s connections with the Labour Party, but concluded that welfare supervisors needed allies because of the cooperation given to the I.W.S. by employers.(64)

The Ministry thought that the Institute was in danger of being dictated to. On the Society´s founding, Hyde had "informed certain of the supervisors that their employers subscribed to him and that consequently they must do what he told them".(65) Hyde´s second response was to propose an amalgamation between the I.W.S. and the Institute. The Welfare Workers argued that the Society wanted to annex its connections with the trades union movement in order to improve its own credibility.(66) As Hyde was "looked upon as an employers´ man", the Welfare Workers held that amalgamation would prejudice their professional and neutral status.(67) The Society was also concerned about talks between the Welfare Workers and the Labour Party, and the N.C.E.O. was particularly worried by the notion of welfare supervisors siding with workers against management. The Institute had supported the Labour Party´s Parliamentary opposition to the introduction of a two-shift system for women and children in 1920.(68) Beardmore and Company responded to the threat of the Welfare Workers´ Institute by refusing to employ its members.(69) Hyde believed that the Institute, faced with the opposition of employers, would be unable "to further extend their operations in the direction of interference with the management of labour".(70) By 1931, the I.W.S. incorporated the advisory and promotional activities of the Institute under the Society´s name, and the new Institute of Labour Management had no direct influence over welfare schemes.(71)

The I.W.S., freed from government and independent rivals, had achieved by the early 1930s a preeminence in the coordination and encouragement of welfare activities in factories. The Society sought to promote industrial welfare on behalf of its clients, because it saw its practice as an aspect of company-based labour management. By emphasising the central role of the firm, the I.W.S. and company provision were acceptable to employers because they sought to assuage the aspirations of labour to control work-methods. They reinforced managerial prerogative. Hyde asserted that welfare work could only succeed if it arose from the shopfloor "good will and experience of employers and representatives of labour" and not from state imposition. Employers should not bestow patronage but seek "real cooperation" by using welfare as a means for both sides of industry to meet as equals.(72) Hyde argued that the giving of gifts could not establish "mutual interests" in the way a well-thought-out, and presumably contributory, scheme could.(73)

As the I.W.S. did not interfere in matters of wages and hours, it claimed it was not an anti-union body and that its views on labour combinations were kindred to the National Association of Employers and Employed.(74) Moreover, once the Whitley scheme had proved by the late 1920s a failure in private industry, the National Association began to concentrate on welfare rather than collective bargaining.(75) The Industrial League and Council, which in 1924 amalgamated with the N.A.E.E. to form the National Industrial Alliance, wished in 1923 to join with the Society because of the similarity of their outlook. The I.W.S., however, distinguished between "Labour" and "Welfare" topics.(76) But, in seeking to protect managerial prerogative, industrial welfare was very much a "Labour" issue. The I.W.S. stated that, while academics depicted welfare as an alternative to Nationalisation, Guild Socialism, or a universal system of Whitley Councils, Mr John Smith was "not greatly concerned with the exact method by which industry is controlled", but was, "however, tremendously interested in the conditions under which he follows his daily round".(77) Joint Industrial Councils had, therefore, become engaged in welfare work, and "closely allied with the welfare movement is the question of Works Committees, on which bodies the initiation and carrying out of welfare work generally and mainly devolves". Only such cooperative machinery could gain "the intelligent and careful use" of welfare facilities.(78) Rather than control over investment and production, the discussion of welfare matters demonstrated the "right relationship between management and the worker".(79) The activities of the Whitley Councils and the Industrial Welfare Society merged as they adjusted to the requirements of the firm.

As a complement to Scientific Management, the ultimate aim of I.W.S. schemes was to increase the volume of production, and talks in 1931 were opened with the British Works Managers Association on improving industrial efficiency.(80) Industrial Peace viewed welfare as "of primary importance to the employer" because full and economical use of each agent of production was possible only "in frictionless co-operation". Workers, it was claimed, could only be satisfied if the activities of the factory reflected the life of the community through sporting and social clubs and if basic needs, like sick pay or pensions, were fulfilled.(81) By 1927, the I.W.S. was involved in the type of personnel management concerned with hiring and training, and considered dropping the word "Welfare" from its title. But the name was kept intact because welfare schemes were recognisably distinct from the wage-contract and the actual task of production.(82) The Balfour Committee on Industry and Trade praised the role of the I.W.S. and the voluntary efforts of employers, and linked improvements in workshop life, industrial peace, continuity in personnel, and productive efficiency.(83) But the Committee minimised the Society's activities, mentioning only advice on canteens, clubs, heating and ventilation. The I.W.S. also helped companies in the administration of sick-pay and in planning for the never-implemented industry-based unemployment benefit clauses of the 1920 Act.(84) The Society drafted the Flour-milling Joint Industrial Council's supplementary pension scheme.(85) The I.W.S., in addition, was able to coordinate cooperation between small employers, as on the riverside in the East End of London, where £80,000 was spent on a social club, gymnasium, and theatre.(86) This type of "cooperative welfare" was demonstrated by 38 cotton mills in Lancashire which also pooled their resources.(87)

* * * * *

The Industrial Welfare Society, by 1921 funded by all branches of industry,(88) preached the "unitary ideal" of the company. Opposed by organised labour, it helped employers organise schemes which ameliorated work-disaffection and maintained managerial prerogative.

(iv) CONCLUSION

Despite the increasing mechanisation of industry in the early decades of the 20th Century, employers could not simply rely upon supervisory control and the regular patterns of flow-production to manage their labour. Management theorists, aware of the realities of industrial life, emphasised leadership rather than Taylor's simplistic notions of total industrial authoritarianism. His belief that workers were unthinking beasts of burden was rejected.(89) Edward Cadbury, the chocolate manufacturer, argued forcefully on behalf of British employers who had adjusted the demands of "objective" efficiency to suit human wants.(90) Discussion during this period and especially during the First World War concentrated on "Human Factor Psychology", industrial fatigue, and the work of C.S.Myers. Yet working-conditions during the War and the following twenty years remained poor. In the 1930s, debate focused on arguments about "Human Relations", "social satisfactions" and group cohesion on the production-line, whose chief proponent was Elton Mayo.(91) Emphasis upon Taylorism, Myerism, and Mayoism overlooks the more practical and concrete achievements of welfare schemes which did not interfere with shop-floor organisation. When the Welfare Workers Institute became the Institute of Labour Management, it was not indicative of a general abandonment of copartnership and welfare schemes in favour of management sciences as a solution to labour problems. While the Institute of Labour Management became a professional organisation for personnel managers, the I.W.S. and the L.C.A. were company-backed bodies expressing the interests of employers. Their work in many industries probably had a greater impact than the limited application of Taylorism or the Bedaux system in the 1930s.

The object of industrial welfare was to stem rank-and-file militancy and resentment by dealing with it at the level of the shop-floor. The employers' concern for workers' deep-seated worries about death, ill-health, and old-age was meant as proof of their joint interests. Both the L.C.A. and the I.W.S. sought a thoughtful approach to management, and to this end they, above all, recognised that a man's work environment and the treatment he received from his company were central to his perception of the employment-relationship and its validity.

NOTES

1. E.Bristow "Profitsharing and Labour Unrest" in K.D.Brown (ed.) Essays in Anti-Labour History (1974), pp.266-7; cf. also A.D.Murray John Ludlow: the Autobiography of a Christian Socialist (1981).
2. E.C.Mack & W.H.G.Armytage Thomas Hughes: the Life of the Author of Tom Brown's Schooldays (1952), pp.54-69,144-152.
3. Bristow (1974), pp.266-7. On Briggs & Co., cf. Melling (1980), pp.344-369.
4. Mack & Armytage (1952), p.155.
5. N.Soldon "Laissez-faire as Dogma: the Liberty and Property Defence League" in Brown (1974).
6. Liberty Review, April 1906, pp.179-181.
7. Ibid, 17 Feb 1894, pp.179-181.
8. I.U.E.E. The Industrial Union of Employers and Employed (1894).
9. Bristow (1974), p.270. This figure, taken from the PP 1920 (C.544) xxxiii 765, did not change significantly throughout the Inter-War period (cf. Ministry of Labour

Gazette, July 1930, pp.238-242; June 1934, p.194; or Aug 1939, pp.288-9). The L.C.A., though, did not accept the Ministry's narrow definition of copartnership (cf. Ibid., April 1920, p.169).
10. Cf. Ch.7, s.(v).
11. PP 1890-91 (C.6267) lxxviii 15, Report of Board of Trade on Profitsharing.
12. Cf. Ch.3, s.(iii).
13. Labour Copartnership, Feb 1899, p.26.
14. Ibid, May 1897, p.71.
15. Ibid, July 1898, p.118.
16. Liberty Review, Aug 1902, pp.87-92.
17. Labour Copartnership, Oct 1899, pp.175-6.
18. Bristow (1974), p.268.
19. LCA Minutes, 5 May 1902.
20. Labour Copartnership, Oct 1902, pp.151-2.
21. Ibid, May 1905, pp.73-75.
22. Ibid, 1 Aug 1905, pp.1-2.
23. LCA Minutes, Half-yearly meeting, 4 May 1907. Professor S.D.Chapman on "Labour Copartnership in Relation to Social Progress".
24. Labour Copartnership, 1 March 1902, p.253.
25. Ibid, May 1915, p.245.
26. LCA Minutes, 3 Oct 1905.
27. Cf. Pollard & Turner (1976), pp.4-34; & Ch.7, s.(ii).
28. LCA Minutes, 6 March & 1 May 1906.
29. Labour Copartnership, 8 Jan 1907, p.33.
30. PRO CAB 37/107, No 8, 1911.
31. Labour Copartnership, June 1912, p.82; Aug 1912, p.119.
32. PP 1912-13 (C.6496) xxxxiii 853. Report on Profitsharing and Copartnership.
33. LCA Minutes, AGM, Feb 1915; 27 July 1916; 31 July 1916.
34. Ibid, 23 Oct 1916.
35. LCA Report on London Copartnership Congress, 26-28th Oct, 1920, pp.1-3.
36. Labour Copartnership, June 1917, p.59; LCA Minutes, AGM, May 1919: Speech by Lord Robert Cecil.
37. PP 1920 (C.544) xxxiii 765.
38. PRO LAB2/716/186/15/1920, Letter, 9 Dec 1926.
39. Ibid, Memo. on Works Committees.
40. ICA Profitsharing in Practice: A Brief Outline of the Profitsharing Scheme of Ford Ayrton & Co. Ltd. (1949).
41. Labour Copartnership, Jan 1919, p.4.
42. LCA Minutes, Annual Reports, 1920.
43. LCA Minutes, 30 May 1923. The Industrial Copartnership Association later became the Industrial Participation Association.
44. PRO LAB2/1295/IR460/27. Memo. on Copartnership as a Means of Improving the Relations between Employers and

Employed, 1927.
45. Labour Copartnership, Sept 1926, pp.18-20.
46. Ibid, 1927-28.
47. Industrial Peace, Aug 1918, pp.9-12.
48. A.Mond Industry and Politics (1937), p.110.
49. NCEO Archives, MSS/200/B/3/2/C140, Pt.1, Leaflet from ICA.
50. LAB2/741/T6402/1920, Memo., 21 Oct 1919.
51. Forge News, 4 Sept 1917, p.2; 4 Oct 1917, p.2; 11 Dec 1918, p.3. Cf. Ch.7, s.(iv).
52. IWS Minutes, Council, 25 July 1918.
53. Ibid, Forward and Minutes, 1918.
54. Ibid, Finance Committee, 6 Nov 1919. Cf. Turner (1978), pp.528-551.
55. E.Sidney The Industrial Society 1918-1968 (1968), pp.6-8,11-15.
56. IWS Minutes, Council, 1918-21, passim.
57. Cf. M.N.Niven Personnel Management: the Growth of Personnel Management and the Development of the Institute (1961).
58. LAB2/741/CS204/1920, Memo., 2 March 1920.
59. Cf. R.Lowe "The Failure of Consensus in Britain: the National Industrial Conference, 1919-21", H.J.,(1978).
60. IWS Minutes, Council, 8 July 1919.
61. LAB2/741/CS204/1920. Letter from Smith, 22 March 1920.
62. Ibid, Memo., 21 Oct 1919.
63. NCEO, MSS200/B/3/2/C189, Pt.1, Letter from Beardmores to NCEO, 22 Oct 1920.
64. LAB2/741/T6042/1920, Memo., 27 Feb 1920.
65. Ibid, Memo., 21 Oct 1919.
66. IWS Minutes, Central Committee of Industrial Welfare Supervisors Associations, 17 May 1919; Meetings with Welfare Workers Institute, 1920.
67. Ibid, Memo., 21 Oct 1919.
68. IWS Minutes, Meetings with Welfare Workers Institute, 1920; NCEO, MSS200/B/3/2/C189, Pt.1, Letter to Members of the NCEO, 21 Oct 1920.
69. MSS200/B/3/2/C189, Pt.1, Letter from Beardmores to NCEO, 22 Oct 1920.
70. Ibid, Letter from Beardmores to NCEO, 10 Nov 1920.
71. IWS Minutes, Council, 19 April 1931.
72. Ibid, Annual Report, 30 June 1919.
73. Industrial Welfare, June 1920, pp.176-7.
74. Ibid, April 1919, pp.17-18. Cf. Ch.9, s.(iv).
75. Unity, 1928-32, passim.
76. IWS Minutes, Executive Committee, 7 Nov 1923.
77. Industrial Welfare, May 1920, p.145.
78. Ibid, Jan 1922, pp.9-11.
79. Ibid, March 1920, p.71.
80. IWS Minutes, Annual Report, 30 June 1927.

81. _Industrial Peace_, Jan 1927, pp.137-9; Nov 1927, pp.72-3.

82. IWS Minutes, Annual Report, 30 June 1927. The Home Office in 1931 acknowledged the good image attached to industrial welfare (cf. NCEO, MSS/200/3/2/C189, Pt.1, Home Office Welfare Pamphlet No.3 (HMSO 1931), pp.3-5.

83. _Industrial Welfare_, April 1926, pp.111-5. Cf. also PRO BT/55/2/BAL4.

84. Ibid, Sept 1920, pp.111-5,278-80; Oct 1920, pp.314,331; Nov 1928, pp.365-9.

85. NCEO, MSS/200/B/3/2/C189, Pt.1, Letter from ICA, 22 Feb 1933. Cf. Ch.7, s.(ix).

86. _Unity_, July 1921, pp.287-8.

87. NCEO, MSS/200/B/3/2/C189, Pt.1, Home Office Welfare Pamphlet (1931), p.25.

88. IWS Minutes, Council, passim; PRO LAB2/741/CS204/ 1920. Cf. Ch.7, s.(iii).

89. Gulick (1936), in Gulick & Urwick (1969).

90. Cadbury (1913) in Chandler (1979).

91. Cf. Rose (1975), passim.

Chapter 9

INDUSTRY AND SOCIAL REFORM

(i) INTRODUCTION

Explanations of the "growth" of the Welfare State during the 20th Century have in the majority of cases looked at the development of social legislation from the perspective of politics only.(1) The previous chapters have shown that welfare was also a phenomenon of business organisation. Changes in the structure of the economy, the size of companies, and the nature of management increased the possibilities of and the need for welfare. The existence of company provision throughout British industry affected the attitudes of some employers to state schemes. They realised that the workers´ fear of destitution contributed to poor industrial relations, work-disaffection, and costly strikes. The organisation of a company´s labour force required more than the mere payment of wages or piece-work bonuses. By funding social needs like housing and sports grounds, or by providing income maintenance through illness or old age, management attempted to sustain a cooperative, experienced workforce. Drawn into supporting company welfare, businessmen found state schemes more acceptable.

Employers generally resented and sometimes opposed the tax increases which paid for social legislation, and there was an ideological objection to large government. The involvement of the state in welfare provision was also seen as a regrettable interference in an important sphere of labour relations. Businessmen, however, dealt with the problems of industrial life pragmatically, and government, by enforcing funding, universality, and standardisation, could bring advantages to the provision of welfare. Employers solved their dilemma by lobbying in support of "contracting out" by which private provident societies could participate in state schemes and yet retain their independence. Government only coordinated the activities of these "approved societies" by setting standards of probity and levels of basic benefits. They operated, therefore, as part of the direct relationship

212

between employer and worker. State provision did not conflict with the interests of employers, but accommodated them. In addition, the underlying philosophy behind social reform before the creation of the post-1945 Welfare State was not to meet the needs of individuals "from the cradle to the grave" but to encourage personal providence and thrift. Government welfare was not meant to underwrite sustenance, and company schemes continued to provide the necessary additional benefits.

Before analysing the involvement of employers in welfare legislation, their ability to affect political events must be placed in context. Middlemas has looked at the relationship between industry and politics.(2) He correctly argues that politics was not a closed system and that government took account of the views of pressure-groups like employers' associations. He does not, however, asssess the degree of influence employers' organisations had over the process of government when lobbying on any particular issue. For it was the state in Britain which exerted the formative influence upon employers' associations. The Railway Companies Association was formed in 1846 in order to deal with the increasing regulation of the industry. The R.C.A. had the reputation of being an effective lobby-group but its influence in Parliament was comparatively small in relation to party political considerations.(3) The National Federation of Iron and Steel Manufacturers and the British Iron and Steel Federation were created respectively in 1917 and 1934 only at the behest of government. It was the state which sought the cooperation of the industry to carry through plans of industrial rationalisation. The staple industries, divided by competitive rivalries, were generally unable and reluctant to act collectively.(4)

It is not surprising, therefore, that attempts to set up an umbrella organisation for British industry as a whole all failed before the First World War.(5) The government proved the catalyst in forming the Federation of British Industries in 1916. The scale of state involvement in a war economy forced employers to negotiate on issues of centralised industrial planning. The Ministry of Reconstruction was founded to consider schemes in social welfare, industrial relations, and central economic planning. Without the nationalisation of industry, employers' associations like the F.B.I. were to play an important coordinating role between the state and individual companies. The Federation supported proposals for a permanent industrial parliament representing employers and unions, and advocated tariffs, an imperial trading union, and the subsidising of industries vital to the national interest. In 1917, an F.B.I. report predicted that economic conditions after the War would require extensive rationalisation and reorganisation on the part of British industry. Such changes, it argued, also needed the consent and cooperation of labour, and the report proposed a scheme of social insurance covering old age pensions, sick pay, and unemployment benefits to be funded jointly by employers and trades unions.(6) The F.B.I. in 1919 favoured the calling of a National Industrial Conference of employers, unions, and government for the discussion of industrial relations, but the officials within the F.B.I. did not necessarily reflect the attitudes of their members. In fact, employers established the National Confederation of Employers Organisations to represent them at the Conference instead, and it deliberately forestalled any prospect of agreement. The F.B.I. was left to deal with commercial matters, and by 1919 had abandoned its support for any form of state intervention in the economy. Government decontrol of industry by 1921 destroyed the major reason for many employers´ involvement in a national representative organisation. Both the F.B.I. and N.C.E.O. had few resources and no means to discipline members, and their credibility was weakened by the divisions within them. They proved ineffective as pressure groups, and seemed to exist despite having no clear purpose.(7)

Miliband argues that employers controlled the direction of government, but the influence of employers´ associations has been greater in the amending of legislation and has had little strategic input.(8) Research, administrative pressures, reforming civil servants, and not least the ambitions and electoral calculations of politicians were the important contributory factors in the passing of social legislation.(9) Employers´ reactions to Workmen´s Compensation, old age pensions, and National Insurance in a succession of Acts from 1880 to 1925 suggest that, lacking the power to halt legislation, they could only acquiesce in their passing.

Employers did, nonetheless, influence the final form of social reform. The legislative process can be restricted to "safe" issues to help gain its acceptance. Leaving industry in private hands gives significant power over investment, production, and wage-levels to employers, and this position was never seriously threatened by Parliament in this period. Employers, therefore, did not feel the need to engage widely in politics. Yet, company provision was an integral part of industrial relations, and employers naturally opposed the direct involvement of the state in this sensitive area. "Contracting out" made social reform for employers a "safe" issue. While other groups like friendly and insurance societies also lobbied hard for the right of private institutions to act as agents for the state,(10) the following evidence suggests that employers played an important part in winning concessions from government.

* * * * *

Section (ii) of this chapter deals with Employers´ Liability legislation from 1880 to 1897, and section (iii) analyses the Shop Clubs Act 1902 and the introduction of old

age pensions and National Insurance in 1908 and 1911. Section
(iv) discusses the Whitley Council scheme, housing and the
National Industrial Alliance, while Section (v) looks at the
1920 Unemployment Insurance Act and the 1925 Contributory and
Widows Pensions Act.

(ii) EMPLOYERS' LIABILITY, 1880-1906

By the 1870s, the law for compensating workers for
industrial accidents was recognised as an unfair anachronism.
The Common Law of Employers' Liability stipulated that a
worker was entitled to compensation only if he was in "common
employment". In other words, an employer had to exercise
direct supervision over the worker and, therefore, have direct
responsibility for him. The law was suited to an economy of
small workshops, and had remained unchanged despite the growth
of company size and the consequent delegation of authority to
managers and supervisors. The law was also anomalous. While
liable for accidents to passengers, railway companies were not
considered responsible for injuries to men at work. Colliery,
shipping, and railway employers were the most actively opposed
to reform of the law, because, as industries with high
accident rates, they faced the prospect of heavy costs from
compensation cases.(11)
The first signs of change were indicated by Sir Edward
Watkin, the chairman of the Manchester, Sheffield,
Lincolnshire, and South Eastern Railways.(12) As a Member of
Parliament, Watkin introduced Liability Bills in 1874 and 1875
proposing a maximum of one year's wages as accident
compensation. Many railway employers at this stage would
undoubtedly have preferred no change in the law. They ensured
that they had four representatives sitting on a Select
Committee on Employers' Liability in 1877, and the resulting
report was a conservative document opposing reform. Its
recommendations won the support of other employers'
associations.(13) Moreover, the Railway Companies Association
joined the Mining Association of Great Britain and other
employers in 1877 to lobby against a Liability Bill initiated
by Alexander McDonald, the miners' leader and Lib-Lab M.P.(14)
But there was an essential difference between Watkin's and
McDonald's Bills. Watkin's proposals had stipulated that any
judicial assessment of compensation would take into account
sums already paid by company friendly societies. It was a
suggestion which could appeal to railway companies. The law
was clearly unjust, and railway employers, like Watkin, had
already begun to provide for the victims of accidents
voluntarily. Such provision helped maintain cooperation and
discipline. Managerial orders were more questionable if
accidents suffered while working on a railway remained
uncompensated. There was, in addition, a value in aiding sick

workers to return quickly to work. When legislation became likely after the election of a Liberal government in 1880, both the R.C.A. and Watkin were agreed on the need to protect the role and existence of company friendly societies by a system of "contracting out" of any new legislation.(15)

Committed to the Liberal ideal of removing anomalies and privileges, Gladstone favoured reform of accident compensation law. At first, the new government proposed an Employers' Liability Bill which only allowed workers to sue employers whose negligence contributed to accidents at work. Consequently, "large and influential bodies of employers", representing iron and steel, building, port, railway, gas, and shipbuilding interests, in February 1880 sent a deputation to see Gladstone. They preferred to involve their men in private mutual insurance schemes which promoted class cooperation, and argued that the proposed Bill would lead to constant and bitter litigation between employers and workers. Moreover, no employer, they contended, could afford to continue with a mutual scheme if still liable under the law to civil action. Gladstone refused to abandon the Bill or to concede the principle of workers having a right to civil redress. In response, the employers sought a means to contract out of the future Act. Workers could sign an agreement with their employers by which they conceded their legal right to take employers to court in return for the security of a joint insurance scheme.(16)

The case for contracting out in the coal and railway industries was particularly strong. The former War Secretary, W.Edward Baxter M.P., on behalf of the Mining Association of Great Britain, pointed out how colliery-owners already contributed to mutual accident schemes, and that probably 113,000 out of 500,000 miners were already so covered. The others were likely to be aided by charitable funds when necessary. Most railway companies also had accident schemes, and the R.C.A. promised to match the contributions of railwaymen who contracted out. As a result of their efforts, the employers' delegation achieved a postponement of the Bill's Second Reading in May to allow time for further consultation.(17) When the Bill returned to the Commons, Thomas Knowles, M.P. for Wigan, and chairman of Pearson & Knowles Coal and Iron Company, argued that his colliery provided 10-15% of its orphans' provident society's funds. He claimed that "the people have been satisfied with it", and that the Bill had failed to acknowledge the role of private provision in coal and railway companies.(18) Railway employers, like Sir Daniel Gooch and Watkin, moved contracting out amendments. The Iron and Coal Trades Review supported them because, while employers could still be liable for accidents, private schemes would have scope to continue.(19) When Gladstone finally agreed to these amendments, Railway News came to regard the Bill as a non-contentious measure.(20)

Robert Ascroft, M.P. for Oldham, held that it was the example of the L.N.W.R. and its benefit schemes which had above all convinced Members of the need for contracting out.(21)

Employers "had several interviews" with Joseph Chamberlain who was given responsibility for steering the Bill through Parliament. He ensured that the "contracting out" clause met the business community's concerns.(22) The Employers'Liability Act 1880 allowed employers and employees to reach a mutual agreement outside the parameters of the legislation. Companies could either set up their own company schemes, or pay a premium to an insurance company like the newly-founded Employers' Liability Assurance Corporation Limited.(23) The level of compensation paid by mutual arrangements could be freely determined. The contracting out clause, however, was seen as experimental and had to be renewed in Parliament every six years. The Act also gave accident victims who were without private financial protection the right to sue. Yet, permanently disabled men did not have the financial resources to take employers to court, and temporarily injured workers still required the goodwill of their employers if they were to return to work.

In 1893, the Liberal Home Secretary, Asquith, proposed in his Employers' Liability Bill to prevent workers conceding their legal right to sue an employer even when they had contracted out. He praised the 1880 Act as a great social advance but emphasised that it had done "still more in promoting and establishing mutual insurance schemes...." The Iron Trades Employers Association, for example, had established in 1880 an insurance scheme for companies wanting to contract out. Half the miners in South Wales were compensated privately, and the Shipping Federation had set up a mutual fund in 1891. Moreover, Asquith did not consider many workers "free agents" in the matter, since agreeing to contracting out was often a condition of employment. Railway employers believed that Asquith was interfering with the right of employers and workers to settle their own differences by free contract. To them, the crucial point still was that no employer would undertake the expense of contributions to a mutual fund while the possibility of further court claims by a worker might have to be met.(24)

The Liberal Party was accused of appeasing trades unions, which opposed contracting out. Labour leaders emphasised the prohibitive expense of legal action, and they saw contracting out as a way of avoiding the greater cost of better safety-precautions at work. Trades unions wanted automatic compensation for accidents to be given as a right rather than as an element of some company welfare scheme which might undermine union loyalty.(25) Employers, however, conducted campaigns at their works to obtain the support of their employees for contracting-out.(26) Given the perceived threat to their mutual accident funds, men of the London, Brighton,

and South Coast Railway petitioned Parliament against the
Bill. W.S.B.M´Laren, M.P. for Crewe,- a town heavily dependent
upon the London and North Western,- hoped the House would
hesitate before "destroying a great system, which has been
worked for many years by both parties, and created a friendly
feeling between employer and employed". He introduced a
contracting-out amendment and was supported by a member from
another railway constituency.(27) John Burns, the dockers´
leader, refused to believe, however, that the L.N.W.R. would
withdraw its £17-20,000 per annum subscription to its
benevolent funds, because of its usefulness "against the
mischievous attacks and tactics of men like himself".(28) The
Miners Federation of Great Britain repudiated the authority of
a joint delegation from the miners permanent relief societies,
whose elected representatives claimed to speak on behalf of
miners and their interests.(29) A workers´ delegation from
Pearson, Knowles, and Company complained that the Bill would
destroy their liability fund. The Peninsular and Oriental Line
put forward similar arguments.(30) The engineers Tangye
Brothers argued that their workers preferred private provision
because "There is no delay, there is no law, and there is no
ill-feeling".(31)

During the debates, Thomas Wrightson M.P., a director of
the Cramlington Colliery and the bridge builders Messrs Head,
Wrightson & Company, stated his belief that the 1880 Act would
not have been passed "unless the power of contracting out had
been included. Many of the employers of labour would have
resisted the passing of that Act very much more strongly if
the power of contracting out had not been allowed to their
servants."(32) Indeed, the Railway Companies Association in
1893 did not organise opposition in the Commons with its
pro-government majority, because it calculated correctly that
the Lords would protect the interests of employers and reject
the measure.(33)

The Workmen´s Compensation Bill of 1897 was greeted with
a mixture of distrust and approval. It left the 1880 Act
intact and merely guaranteed automatic compensation in certain
industries even if the worker was at fault. On death, a
worker´s dependants would receive either the sum of three
years´ salary or £150, whichever was the larger. By setting
out a scale of compensation for accidents to particular
workers, it interfered directly in agreements between
employers and employees, and was, to the Iron and Coal Trades
Review, "one of the most revolutionary pieces of industrial
legislation attempted within recent years". But, it was added,
"the Bill has evoked a remarkable amount of approval from all
classes of the community".(34) Because responsibility for
accidents had no longer to be proved before a court of law,
the Bill won the support of employers who were concerned at
the potential damage of litigation to industrial relations.
Chamberlain, who had had responsibility for the Liberals´ 1880

Act, was in charge of the passage of the 1897 Bill, this time as a Unionist. He acknowledged that his main object was to avoid litigation, and he attacked the 1893 Bill which would have prevented contracting out instead.(35)

Sir John Brunner supported the 1897 Bill because it imitated his company's policy. Brunner, Mond paid compensation without assessing who was at fault, and so avoided the possibility of litigation.(36) The Mining Association of Great Britain agreed with the Bill for the same reasons.(37) Moreover, limitations on the compensation to be paid meant that employers could insure their risks. Contracting out agreements had similarly enabled employers to estimate the extent of their liability, and the very fact that compensation was automatically available under the 1897 Bill according to set limits was further to discourage private schemes. Nevertheless, the Registrar of Friendly Societies would certify mutual insurance schemes if they were voluntary and could pay on a par with the legal scales. Some funds, therefore, had to change their rules in order to continue. The government agreed that the section on mutual societies was "controversial even if the others are not". Although no worker would be able to sign away his right to compensation, the government wanted to promote mutual provision. It desired "to give them room to provide further advantages of any kind it may be in their power to provide".(38) The Act was passed in 1897.

* * * * *

By the 1870s, Employers' Liability law was clearly in need of reform and had become a political issue. Gladstone, who undertook to change the law, proved willing to make concessions to employers. The 1880 Bill was a threat to the existence of companies' accident provident societies until employers gained the right to contract out. Businessmen, therefore, were uniformly opposed to the 1893 Bill which was defeated because, unlike its predecessor, it was a contentious measure. Chamberlain had the political acumen in 1897 to emphasise to all sides the advantages of his Workmen's Compensation Bill. It removed employers' concern about litigation and limitless accident claims in return for an automatic right to compensation which could not be ceded by mutual contract. Chamberlain, however, did not seek to outlaw contracting out, although the solvency and benefits of private schemes had to be certified. The 1897 Act was also restricted in its application, and left many sectors, including seamen, domestic servants, and agricultural workers, unaffected. The logic of including most workers was accepted by a succession of Acts in 1900, 1906, 1920, and 1923, and contracting out continued until the National Insurance (Industrial Accidents) Act 1946.

(iii) THE SHOP CLUBS ACT 1902, AND THE LIBERAL WELFARE REFORMS, 1908-11

It was impossible for the Liberal governments of the Edwardian period to assess the affects of their welfare legislation on employers' pension and sick schemes because of the absence of figures indicating the number of them in existence. A Home Office Report in 1899 had investigated self-interested complaints from friendly societies about workers being compelled to join shop clubs as a condition of employment. It concluded that, "During the last few years, many large firms and companies have established Provident Funds and Societies for providing sick pay, superannuation, and funeral allowances for their employees". These funds were generally founded and controlled by employers. Such shop societies were either the more common slate clubs, which varied contributions according to needs and usually divided the surplus every Christmas, or more permanent institutions. Only the second category could be allowed voluntarily to register under the Friendly Society Acts 1876 and 1896, yet few actually did so. Registered societies had to have set contributions and benefits, and membership could not be a condition of employment.(39)

In evidence to the Report's investigative committee, employers replied that compulsion was necessary for actuarial reasons. Moreover, it would be hard for an employer to ignore a request of financial help from workers who were non-participants, despite the fact that such aid would then create a justifiable grievance amongst contributors. Where a majority of workers were members of a shop club, it was argued, they preferred membership to be made compulsory. The committee sympathised with these points, but agreed to compulsory and contributory shop clubs only if they were registered under the Friendly Society Acts. It required rules which would provide for compensation when a worker changed employers, set contributions and benefits, written rules for the election of officers, and a guaranteed subvention from the employer. These recommendations were made law under the 1902 Shop Clubs Act. Railways and municipal concerns, whose funds were established under individual Acts of Parliament, were specifically omitted from its terms.(40) The Engineering Employers Federation's Parliamentary Committee was concerned about any "legislation prejudicial to voluntary Sick Clubs", and had tried to restrict the Act's provisions to registered societies only. It decided to "compromise" and advised its members to make their societies voluntary. They thereby avoided the necessity of complying with the legislation.(41)

The Old Age Pensions Act introduced by the Liberal government in 1908 was a measure enjoying wide support. In 1892, Charles Booth calculated that the old formed nearly a third of all paupers. The size of this figure supported the case that all elderly paupers were members of the "deserving poor". Old age poverty did not stem from a lack of thrift in earlier life but from the inability of most workers to finance their retirement. Statistical evidence was refuting the charge of personal moral failing. Edward Cadbury, the chocolate manufacturer, was a prominent member of Booth's non-contributory pensions campaign in 1899. This movement influenced the Local Government Board to agreeing, in the same year, to grant all elderly paupers "adequate" relief. Having assumed some responsibility for all aged poor, the state clearly needed to tackle and solve the "pensions question". Administrative as well as political pressures, therefore, bolstered arguments in favour of pensions legislation. In 1900, the Unionist government declared itself in favour of state allowances.(42) William Lever of Lever Brothers, in 1907, proposed to the Commons the introduction of a weekly 5s pension for those of 65 years or over. 232 voted for his motion and only 19 opposed.(43) Although the Liberal Party was uncommitted to state pensions, individual candidates had declared their support during the General Election in 1905. The Cabinet had accepted the need for a non-contributory fund by April 1907, and the Old Age Pensions Act was passed in the following year. It provided for a pension of 5s to all men and women of 70 years or over.(44)

Walter Long for the Conservatives supported the Bill in general but claimed it would damage employers' pension schemes.(45) Alfred Mond M.P. of Brunner, Mond, however, said that businessmen would appreciate the proposed measure. He claimed that all employers had to tackle the problem of retiring workers, but could not afford to give pensions to workers who had not undergone long-service with their company. Several elderly workers, consequently, were left with no income.(46) The 5s pension was a small weekly sum and was not intended to provide sustenance. It was meant to encourage self-help and private provision. Retired workers would receive the full state benefit unless they had an income above £21 a year, which was a comparatively large figure. Pensions were then adjusted along a sliding-scale to a minimum of 1s for all incomes above £21 but below £31 10s. Employers could conveniently change the level of company pensions to ensure workers received the full state benefit plus an additional retirement income, which together would amount to a sum they considered adequate. Most workers, in any case, had ceased work or died before they were 70, and pensions were required before such a late age. Scope, therefore, was left by the terms of the Act for the continuation of industrial welfare. The London and North Western Railway, for instance, believed that the Act had left their funds intact since most of their men retired at 63. Even after 70 years, their workers still required a company allowance. Men at Cadbury Brothers retired at 60, and women at 56.(47)

The National Insurance Bill of 1911, tackling ill-health and unemployment, was the second phase of the Liberal government's attempts at "social reform". Its origins are legion. Civil servants, administrative pressures, National Efficiency, and defence against Socialism, democratic politics, growing unemployment, revision of the concepts of poverty, and electoral calculation all had a role. The dynamism and ambitions of politicians like Lloyd George and Churchill were also crucial, and they respectively guided Part I of the Bill on health insurance and Part II on unemployment insurance through the Commons. Lloyd George's visit to Germany in 1908 when he investigated its system of health insurance was a turning-point, but the evolution of unemployment provision is less certain.(48) Yet, the principle of contributory insurance fitted into Liberal traditions and the precepts of personal providence and self-help. But the final form of the National Insurance Act resulted from a number of expedients and compromises designed to placate insurance companies and friendly societies, the medical profession,(49) and, not least, employers.

Lloyd George said the German employers supported health insurance because it increased workers' efficiency. The Imperial scheme merely supplemented the welfare provided at their works and at their own expense.(50) Sir George White M.P., "on behalf of a very considerable number of employers" who had not been "prominent in the debates", approved of Lloyd George's Bill.(51) Sir Alfred Mond, however, explained why the German system would be unacceptable in Britain. The Imperial scheme had a central fund from which all benefits were paid. Its advocacy demonstrated "a curious want of knowledge of what is actually going on in our great industrial centres. There is scarcely one large works which has not got a sick club, or where some system of insurance between employer and workmen does not exist". These had to be incorporated into the legislation and their existence assured. He defended the competence of the joint committees that administered company schemes, because at Brunner, Mond they had greatly contributed to cooperation between employer and employee.(52)

In opposing the passing of the National Insurance Bill, therefore, the hostile views of the cotton employer and founder of the Employers Parliamentary Association, Sir Charles Macara, were not necessarily representative of industry in general.(53) Even the E.P.A., however, did not condemn the measure in principle but wanted to delay its passing for further consultation. The point was that Macara disagreed with employers having to contribute to the scheme because it would particularly hurt competitive and labour-intensive industries like cotton and coalmining. Although employers were certainly concerned at increased costs, they could see the value of sick pay whether paid by the company or the state.(54) The E.P.A. failed, however, to

become the representative organisation of British industry.
The engineering employers refused to join the Association and
argued that, when employers shared mutual interests, "joint
action could no doubt be arranged".(55)

Indeed, employers' reactions to health insurance
demonstrated a general lack of co-ordination. The railway and
gas industries both lobbied ministers but do not seem to have
consulted one another on the issue. By May 1911, the Midland
Railway company had been the first to see Lloyd George, and
had asked him to exclude their industry from the operation of
the Act altogether. Railways already had contributory sick
societies, established by Parliament under various railway
Acts. The company felt that their suggestion "had not been
unfavourably received". The Railway Companies Association, on
behalf of the whole industry, made similar representations to
the Chancellor, and appointed a special committee to watch the
course of the Bill. Despite earlier impressions, Lloyd George
refused to exclude railwaymen from the legislation, but agreed
to suggestions "which may enable railway societies to
undertake the administration of the benefits under the
Act".(56) The Association felt by late July that Lloyd George
had met all their fears by agreeing to contracting-out, and
convinced the industry that the government would allow company
friendly societies, in receipt of government donations, to
operate almost autonomously. Employees would be allowed to
join the National Health Insurance scheme by signing on with
an Approved Society. The idea of "transfer values", enabling
men to leave their employment with compensation for their
contributions, was also acceptable to the Association. The
R.C.A. was certain that contracting out "would be a very
valuable option".(57)

With the support of their employers, gas workers
campaigned for total exclusion from Health Insurance on the
grounds they already paid smaller contributions for better
sick benefits.(58) Woodal of the Gas Light and Coke Company
wrote to Lloyd George pointing out the existence of the
company's provident societies.(59) When the Chancellor refused
in early July 1911 to consider exclusion from the terms of the
Act, Carpenter of the South Metropolitan argued that, instead,
Parliament should allow gas companies to contract out.(60) To
obtain concessions, "activity behind the scenes" was initiated
with the S.M.G.C. encouraging its employees to lobby
ministers.(61) Lloyd George met South Metropolitan
representatives on the 14th August 1911 and said that the idea
of contracting-out was "favourably entertained" by the
Government.(62) The S.M.G.C. in total canvassed 107 M.P.s
about the Bill and felt, by the time of its passing, they had
left their mark upon it. Although preferring exemption from
its terms, the company was content with being able to form an
Approved Society.(63) Indeed, the S.M.G.C. was instrumental in
founding and promoting the National Federation of Employees

Approved Societies, whose president Henry Lesser worked for the South Metropolitan.(64)

Lloyd George finally introduced a clause into the National Insurance Bill in October 1911 which enabled employers' sick clubs to become approved societies.(65) Employers had been successful in ensuring that the amendment guaranteed the autonomy of approved societies and the control they could exercise over them.(66) They were allowed representation in the management of an approved society if they were responsible for its solvency or agreeable to making substantial contributions. They could then appoint one quarter of the committee. For small societies, the employers' donation was the factor which made it actuarially viable. An employer was also responsible for underwriting the level of benefits payable, the prime provision which in law enabled an approved society to avoid grouping within the General Fund. Part I of the Act also provided the opportunity for the setting up of supplementary funds to pay additional benefits. Alternatively, approved societies could be divided into two parts, the first to provide the basic benefits regulated by the terms of the Act, the second supplementary allowances.(67)

Masterman, Financial Secretary of the Treasury, admitted that he did not know how many unregistered company benefit societies were dissolved because of the Act, rather than continuing or becoming approved societies.(68) But it made no difference to the trades unionist and Labour M.P., G.N.Barnes, who spoke in opposition to the approved societies. Indeed, he was wary of the Act in general because "deductions (from wages) have been associated with truck or with the grandmotherly, or shall I say grandfatherly, schemes of employers who very often organise superannuation funds and schemes connected with shop clubs, not altogether for the benefit of the workmen, but incidentally having the effect, if not the intention, of splitting the workmen up into sections all over the country, and it is very largely because of that the workmen have been so bitter against any deductions from their wages".(69) Such shop clubs were depicted as anti-union tools, and contributory schemes placed the employer's proper burden upon his workers. Barnes acknowledged that ballots would ascertain the support of workers for a proposed approved society, and that any individual could join the General Fund. But "....those who have had experience of workshops know that such provisions on paper are absolutely no good when face to face with the facts". Barnes opposed the existence of shop clubs and, therefore, state assistance for the formation of approved societies. Government, as well as employers and employees, contributed to National Insurance. The experience of supposedly democratic shop clubs made him suspicious of the control workers, through their elected committees of management, would have over their own approved societies. Barnes accused Stewart and Lloyds of illegally pressuring workers not to join a union Approved Society.(70)

Part II of the Act introduced state Unemployment Insurance for the building, construction, shipbuilding, mechanical engineering, ironfounding, and vehicle construction industries. In 1909, a joint deputation from the Engineering Employers Federation and the Shipbuilding Employers Federation discussed its proposals with Churchill. As highly competitive industries, they wanted to avoid the cost of the employers´ contribution, and believed that Workmen´s Compensation should be solely financed by workers´ contributions. Churchill gave an assurance that any further developments in old age pensions provision would require workers´ donations. He drew their attention, however, to the apparent advantages given by his Bill to the shipbuilding and engineering industries. On the Clyde and North East coast, "employers there have paid out of their own pocket in charitable subscriptions and so forth, in keeping people going, far beyond anything which a really scientifically organised insurance scheme over a term of years would ever come to". These company out-of-work payments during periodic lay-offs helped retain the skills and loyalty of workers. Unemployment insurance would, by tiding workers over difficult periods, also create "a steadier class of men" and give employers "a hold over the men that you will have not have had before".(71) By 1911, Lloyd George was able to tell the S.E.F. that it was the only employers´ association still objecting to the National Insurance Bill. The shipbuilding industry was noticeably prone to foreign competition and increased costs. Buxton, Churchill´s successor at the Board of Trade, noted that employers in general had associated themselves with the National Insurance Act.(72)

* * * * *

The Liberal social reforms of 1908-1911 were primarily political initiatives which met a mixed response from employers. Objections were raised largely on grounds of cost, and because of their association with socialism. The latter objection seems to have been strongly voiced by Lancashire employers.(73) This attitude may have been a reflection of the nature of Liberal politics there. The Party was attempting to establish a solid working-class constituency there during this period.(74) The Old Age Pensions Act 1908 was least opposed because it did not interfere to any great extent with company provision. The railway and gas industries, which were experienced in the lobbying of M.P.s and ministers, were instrumental in convincing the government that, if it legislated for health insurance, company societies should be integrated into rather than absorbed by the state system. Unemployment insurance which employers did not finance privately in any case was less contentious. Companies had little interest in providing for workers they had discharged.

(iv) WHITLEY COUNCILS, HOUSING AND THE NATIONAL INDUSTRIAL ALLIANCE

During the First World War, the government faced a severe manpower shortage and a consequent increase in trade union strength. The labour disputes on Clydeside in May 1915 induced the government to consider reconstruction plans after the War. By 1916, a committee under the chairmanship of the Commons Speaker, John Whitley, was appointed to suggest improvements in the machinery of collective bargaining. Its reports, printed in 1917 and 1918, noted three problems confronting British industrial relations. There was a demand from workers for higher wages, and many were arguing for workers' control. In addition, the existing bargaining system and disputes procedures were seen as deficient. Whitley proposed a hierarchy of joint industrial councils on a national, district and factory level.(75) A sub-committee issued a report on works committees in 1918. It stated that better relations between employers and workers could "best be arrived at by granting to the latter a greater share in consideration of matters with which they are concerned". While rates of wages and hours of work concerned national or district committees, "there are also many questions closely affecting daily life and comfort in, and the success of, the business, and affecting in no small degree efficiency of working, which are peculiar to individual workshop matters". It was recognised that works councils had a long history, and that they had often been used to oppose trades unionism. Nevertheless, rather than government controlling the circumstances under which works committees would be set up, the report recommended that employers and employees be left to make independent arrangements.(76)

The trade unionist Robert Toothill M.P. in 1918 recalled the fact that works committees had existed before the Whitley Report. There was a "system of direct cooperation between the employers, the managers, the foremen, and other subordinate officials in the workshops". It relied, however, principally upon "the most trusted and capable and skilful men in the workshops" who could explain the difficulties of running a business to their workmates. Mutual confidence encouraged industrial peace.(77) Another commentator noted that "They dealt chiefly with complaints, welfare work, and conditions of employment, and they were generally consultative and advisory in their functions, the management reserving the power of making the final decision". These works committees were usually found in large factories where the size of the labour force was a managerial problem. Where labour turnover was low, they could build upon the workers' loyalty to their firm. Works councils were, therefore, rarely founded in industries where the size of the labour force was continually adjusted to meet short-term changes in demand. Moreover, established works committees seldom joined the Whitley Councils which were set up from 1918 onwards.(78)

Indeed, the Whitley scheme was designed to develop and not replace the existing organisation of industrial relations.(79) The Coalition government accepted that Whitley Councils were in general superfluous to the iron and steel industry, which had a comprehensive collective bargaining machinery.(80) An F.B.I. memorandum in 1917 favoured Whitley, but saw district and works committees as potentially dangerous to the authority of management. It opposed the concept of joint committees, and suggested instead a representative body of workers whose advice was not in any way binding on employers. The F.B.I. was willing to consider "consulting" their workers, and presented this concession as a "democratic" alternative to public ownership. The demand for nationalisation from power and transport workers was especially strong, as was the case for government control of natural monopolies. The memorandum was equally anxious to counter the propaganda of guild socialists and calls for direct workers' ownership. The Federation's response was to try and conciliate workers who might resent having no power of decision over their working lives. They were not offered participation in production and investment matters, however, but consultation over "working conditions".(81)

It was an attitude reflected in the policy of the Coalition government. Lloyd George upheld the principle of managerial prerogative. "Steps", he said, "ought to be taken to humanize industry, by the improvement of the conditions in the workshops", to give workmen "an interest in the industry", but "not management, because you cannot manage a business by committee".(82) The Ministry of Labour believed that works committees encouraged workers to have greater interest in and responsibilty for their work. Companies needed a "recognised means of consultation between management and workpeople". Sub-committees were necessary in large works, or when there was a need to promote separate but complementary activities like industrial safety or welfare.(83)

Interest in Joint Industrial Councils similarly waned with the Post-War Slump. By 1921, there were 74 national councils, and, by 1923, 62. The Whitley scheme originally affected some two million workers, and the numbers declined as the Inter-War years progressed.(84) Rather than becoming the recognised means for joint negotiation, many Whitley Councils gradually took up the administration of industrial welfare. In 1919, the Industrial Council for the Building Industry proposed that, when all capital claims on profits had been met, the surplus could be used to encourage education and research and to finance a superannuation scheme for all registered workers. The Labour Copartnership Association viewed the scheme as profitsharing. The problems of labour management, it asserted, would be eased by interesting workers in the quality of their work, which was usually low because of their "non-participation in control".(85) In 1920, the J.I.C.'s Education Committee established an apprenticeship training scheme. It saw no dividing line between education and welfare because both sought to develop a worker as a citizen and man.(86) Ben Turner, President of the cotton weavers union, concluded that "The promotion of works committees - which are separate organisations from trades unions shops committees - has brought along with it welfare work, and in many textile mills they have improved certain barborous conditions of things out of existence". Such work was to be developed, not out of patronage, "but on the lines of mutual respect and copartnership in friendship". Industrial welfare paid for itself through increased efficiency, and Turner urged trades unions to welcome the new trends in management.(87) Out of the four times a year that the Welsh Plate and Sheet Trade J.I.C. met, three meetings were devoted to discussion "partaking of the character of welfare work". They considered the different virtues of industrial or state insurance for sickness and old age.(88) The National Council of the Pottery Industry sought to improve welfare standards throughout the whole industry,(89) as well as concerning itself with research, industrial administration, apprenticeships, and works committ- ees.(90)

The establishment of Whitley Councils was promoted by the Industrial League and Council founded in 1919. It sought the voluntary cooperation of employers and employed for the drawing up of joint programmes. The League and Council was an amalgamation. One of its predecessors, the Industrial League was a result of discussions during the Great War between Labour M.P.s and M.P.s with business contacts. "So useful were these meetings, being composed of equal numbers of representatives of Labour and Commerce, and so quickly did they grow in size," argued its magazine Current Opinion, "that it became necessary to create a proper organisation". The League was formally founded in 1918 when it could count G.N.Barnes of the War Cabinet, the Food Controller J.R.Clynes, the Minister of Pensions John Hodge, and the Minister of Labour G.H.Roberts amongst its members. The one-time railway employer and President of the Board of Trade, Albert Stanley, had also joined, as had the engineering employer Colonel Armstrong, the shipbuilder Sir A.Denny, Hugo Hirst of G.E.C., and Huth Jackson of the F.B.I. Branches of the League were established throughout the country.(91)

Current Opinion held that "The employer is much to blame for the unrest that exists". It had seen "paternal associations" lapse into antiquity without being replaced by more up-to-date methods. Workers had, therefore, become "disinterested" in their work. They were driven to advocating legislation like the Truck Acts, the Employers' Liabilty Act, and National Insurance, "which should have been harmoniously considered and ungrudgingly given by the employers". The League argued that "Welfare Work should be actively pressed forward, as, after all, the solution of the industrial problem lies in closer relationships......" Industrial peace and faithful service could be promoted through "amenities and perquisites", and joint Whitley Councils provided the avenues by which industry could be humanised. The League sought to take advantage of the "Reconstruction period.....to change the whole face of future industry".(92)

In 1919, the League joined forces with the Industrial Reconstruction Council which John Whitley had himself helped to found to promote his report. The Council had argued that the War had brought the "era of unlimited competition" to an end. Trade parliaments and inter-company cooperation allowed the pooling of ideas and resources. So, "employers will certainly acquire more inside knowledge of the conditions and mentality of the workers than by the present spasmodic attempts at welfare work......", while unions might even believe employers to be "human beings". Whitley Councils were an alternative to state economic intervention.(93) When the new Industrial League and Council was founded in 1919, Whitley became its president. The new organisation made early contacts with the Industrial Welfare Society, because they both argued for more efficient and humane management as an alternative to the control of workers over the production process itself.(94) Indeed, the League and Council gave lectures in Scientific Management and tried to demonstrate it meant more than just "aggressive American hustling". It was contended that Scientific Management required the workers´ cooperation. Industrial councils would be the forum for finally deciding upon what "is really the proper unit of time" of work and the length of rest-periods, once experiments had been carried out "in a scientific way". The League and Council appointed a Scientific Management Committee in 1921.(95)

In 1925, it joined with the National Association of Employers and Employed to form the National Industrial Alliance.(96) The N.A.E.E. had been established in December 1916, and held that the experience of the Great War had demonstrated that industrial friction could be ended through better hours, wages, housing, education, and health provision.(97) The N.A.E.E. wanted to draw up joint employer and employee proposals for the greater regulation of employment after the War. The employers´ side was largely composed of F.B.I. members, and, at its first meeting, Huth Jackson made it clear that the Association had the Federation´s full support. In January 1917, the F.B.I. President, Dudley Docker, was asked to do everything possible "to emphasise (to his members) the fact that the body came into being under the wing of the Federation, and that on the employers´ side (of the N.A.E.E.) it is the Federation". The F.B.I. also provided the National Association with most of its

funds.(98) While attempting to establish connections with the
T.U.C. through the N.A.E.E., the Federation considered
establishing direct contact, so long as such talks were kept
secret and did not prejudice the N.A.E.E. negotiations. "If
this is done, we can still go ahead with the Alliance (sic),
keeping a second string to our bow....." It was felt that
whenever an agreement for cooperation could be reached with
labour leaders, public opinion in 1917 would ensure its
success.(99)

From 1918-1921, the N.A.E.E. lobbied the government over
questions of Reconstruction housing, unemployment insurance,
and Whitley Councils. The Association worked fully with the
F.B.I. in establishing industrial public utility societies
under the 1919 Housing Act as avenues for industrial
cooperation.(100) During the Great War, the Ministry of
Munitions had directed the transfer of workers to controlled
factories. It was soon clear, however, that private builders
could not construct enough houses to accommodate the influx of
workers. The housing shortage was an important contributory
factor to the labour strife in Glasgow in 1915.(101) The
Ministry undertook the financing of homes, particularly in
Glasgow, Coventry, and Barrow where the problem was most
acute.(102) The Salisbury Committee, which included Seebohm
Rowntree, the chocolate manufacturer, estimated that 300,000
houses would be needed after the War, and for many decent
housing was uniquely associated with Post-War Reconstruction
plans.(103) The resulting Housing Bill was intended to
stimulate the construction of 176,000 houses. Walter Runciman
for the government "hoped that a certain number of big
employing concerns may in the industrial areas put up a large
number of houses for their own people". He saw this as a sound
business proposition to attract labour, and, therefore,
opposed their subsidisation.(104) In response, the F.B.I. and
the N.A.E.E. formed a Joint Housing Committee to try and win
government aid for industrial housing projects. They
considered state support as essential to the financial success
of employers´ Public Utility Societies. They were trusts for
the construction of employees´ homes and were non-profitmaking
bodies registered under the Friendly Societies Acts.(105) The
F.B.I. emphasised the possibilities of Public Utility
Societies during the "reconstruction period", particularly as
their prospects were best in the industrial areas where
housing was most needed. All occupants would be members of
such societies. They would elect their own trustees, and own
the property and finances. As their homes would not be tied
dwellings, it was hoped that workmen would take an interest in
their upkeep and that members would help obtain rent arrears
from fellow workers. "Moreover the scheme.......forms an
admirable medium for establishing better relations between the
Employer and his workpeople." The F.B.I. argued that company
housing projects were more economical than local authority

buildings. Yet, their prospects were constrained by the high
costs of building.(106) The government finally agreed to
incorporate the subsidising of public utility societies into
its 1919 Housing Act.(107) The Ministry of Health would
provide 75% of a society's capital if employers guaranteed the
other quarter.(108) The N.A.E.E. argued that workers who
became tenant-shareholders with the assistance of their
employers had been shown a demonstrable proof of mutual
interests. Poor housing and slums were recognised as
contributors to social and industrial unrest. It was hoped
that workers who had a happy home life would be more reasonable to deal with.(109) The National Confederation of
Employers Organisations, however, noted that employers would
only bear the burden of house-building under the Act if they
faced acute labour supply problems. Industrial housing was
uncommon in the engineering industry because of a highly
mobile workforce. But there were numerous instances in the
papermaking industry, sometimes with the "object of increasing
the firm's hold on the workpeople". Gas and railway employers,
like municipalities, had permission to build homes under their
private Parliamentary charters.(110)

The N.A.E.E. and the F.B.I. favoured the idea of the
National Industrial Conference in 1919 and criticised the
government's "hand-to-mouth policy" on questions of wages and
hours.(111) But the Conference's failure was further proof
that a programme of industrial cooperation and reconstruction
had little relevance with the governmental decontrol of
industry from 1921 onwards. Like the League and Council, the
N.A.E.E. by 1921 had few means with which to promote its ideas
of industrial cooperation. The Whitley scheme and Reconstruction in general had proven a disappointment. Moreover, the
N.A.E.E.'s search for "consensus" could not cover over the
differences between its employer and worker representatives.
Arthur Henderson's hope that the N.A.E.E. would secure the
"democratic control of industry through Whitley Councils"
contrasted with the employers' aims.(112)

After the National Industrial Alliance was formed in
1925, it stated its support for the continuation of the
approved society system in health insurance, which was under
investigation from a Royal Commission. The Alliance believed
industrial welfare committees provided an opportunity for
joint cooperation,(113) and their attitude contrasted with
that of the Labour Party and the trades unions. The N.I.A.,
which could no longer just advocate the promotion of Whitley
Councils as its main objective, supported any form of welfare
provision in the factories which might encourage good
industrial relations.(114) A Ministry of Labour inquiry into
works committees in 1927 similarly focused not, as it had done
in 1918, on the rules and procedures for a formal system of
joint negotiation, but on any cooperative measure in industry
which work committees could effect. But the Ministry admitted

that "we really know very little as to the number of Works
Committees in existence, their success, the reasons for their
failure, or their scope".(115) The Alliance's interest in
industrial welfare led it to appoint in 1931 a Pensions
Sub-Committee. Because of the poor levels of state provision,
it finally reported in favour of adequate pensions for all
through company funds. It noted that industrial pensions for
workers had existed in the 1850s but that an increasing demand
had led to the replacement of ex gratia payments with
contributory schemes. It was a trend which gave workers rights
in the organisation and conditions of pensions. Set rules
freed workers from the arbitrary wishes of supervisors or
employers, and transfer values ensured the mobility of
labour.(116)

* * * * *

The Whitley Council scheme had no lasting influence on
British industry, and only gained permanency in civil service
or local government negotiations. Unable to establish
themselves as the trade parliaments for each industry, many
Joint Industrial Councils began to involve themselves in
company welfare schemes. Consequently, the Industrial League
and Council, the National Association of Employers and
Employed, and their successor the National Industrial Alliance
were organisations whose roles had lost much of their
relevance. The Industrial League and Council is interesting in
revealing the willingness of Labour politicians and
businessmen to establish a consensus workable enough to
operate a degree of economic planning. The N.A.E.E. was
supported by the F.B.I. as a means of gaining the cooperation
of trades unions at a time of labour shortage and the
involvement of the state in industry. The return to laissez-
faire in the 1920s left the National Industrial Alliance only
with the possibility of supporting voluntary company
initiatives.

(v) THE UNEMPLOYMENT INSURANCE ACT 1920, AND THE PENSIONS ACT
1925

The London and North Western Railway, the Gas Light and
Coke Company, the South Metropolitan, Cadburys, and Rowntrees
all gave evidence to the Departmental Committee on Old Age
Pensions in 1919. They agreed that the pension age of 70 years
was too high, and that retirement at 65 would more closely
accord with industrial experience. They also saw the amount of
the allowance as too small. Cadburys and the S.M.G.C. pressed
for the removal of the 1908 means test. It acted as a
disincentive to private providence, and inflation, in any
case, had made its level unrealistic. Large employers of
labour, they argued, tended to promise their workers a
substantial pension in order to make it worth their "while to

stay and work properly". But the Committee in its final report believed that the removal of the means test would prove too costly. It recommended, however, a 10s weekly pension, and an increased income limit of £63. The Committee called for further investigation into lowering the age for eligibility, and urged that all public assistance should be placed on an insurance basis. From listening to witnesses, the Committee was impressed with the notion "that it is desirable in the future for industry to be so organised as to provide adequate pensions for all employees on their retirement", and "that any system which tends to discourage the initiation of such schemes is detrimental to the community".(117)

The case for state contributory pensions was strengthened by the growing number of old people as a proportion of the population. Yet, despite the financial pressures, change was slow. By 1922, government pensions were costing £25.3 million and constituted the highest item of social security. 93% of pensioners were receiving the maximum state pension, and 70% of this group were women. Moreover, some 142,015 children of widows were in receipt of Poor Relief, although their poverty was clearly the result of tragic misfortune rather than an unwillingness to work. By 1923, all three major parties supported the principle of contributory pensions to finance the growing cost of provision for old age and widowhood.(118) Neville Chamberlain finally introduced his Widows, Orphans, and Old Age Contributory Pensions Act in 1925. The legislation adopted many of the 1919 Report's recommendations, which had received the support of those employers who had given evidence. Contributions would be collected from all those paying health insurance, their employers, and the state. 10s pensions would be paid at 65 years, and the contributory principle made the means test unnecessary. Uninsured workers would still receive the state grant of 5s at 70 under the 1908 Act. Furthermore, widows and orphans were covered by the legislation.(119)

The N.C.E.O. did not object to the notion of contributory state pensions, but opposed an overall increase in burdens upon industry at a time of economic depression. The Confederation, therefore, argued that the funding of widows and orphans' pensions should be met out of existing national insurance funds.(120) Like the N.C.E.O., the National Federation of Iron and Steel Manufacturers had no objection in principle to state schemes and wanted to meet the anxieties of workers about old age. The Federation sought, however, a concomitant reduction in the employers' health contributions if its members were to finance pensions.(121) Sir Alfred Mond, no enemy of state or industrial welfare, also felt that the projected extra costs of £22.5m to £54m on employers were too great.(122) The F.B.I. pressed for the postponement of the Bill to allow time for a review of social services. It hoped that, through the better coordination of government provision, savings could be made.(123) Employers, however, were compelled by Chamberlain's Act to make contributions. The N.C.E.O. had to acknowledge that the views of industry had been ignored by the government.(124)

Yet employers and their associations were satisfied by the inclusion of approved societies in the legislation. The Railway Companies Association had been involved in the drawing up of the Act at its committee stage. In consultation with the R.C.A.'s solicitors, Sir Robert Horne moved that, when employers' contributions to pensions were assessed, grants paid by them to company benefit funds should be taken into account. Employers could not be expected to pay for state and private pensions.(125) Although Horne's suggestion was defeated, the government responded by enabling company funds to become a part of the state system. Indeed, the government felt that "One of the most satisfactory things in connection with the scheme has been the demand for voluntary insurance......"(126) The N.C.E.O. advised their members of the advantages of "contracting out".(127) By 1927, the Federation of Master Printers negotiated with the Life Assurance Society to provide pensions additional to state allowances. For, the Federation believed that "There seems to be a feeling amongst employers that one of the solutions of the present state of unrest amongst employees is the introduction of some form of pension scheme for their workers......."(128)

The Coalition government's review of state benefits after the Great War included a reassessment of unemployment insurance as well as pensions. Unemployment pay, however, was of greater urgency because of the dislocation peace might bring to the labour market, and the government was largely unprepared when the armistice was signed. Fear of revolution amongst unemployed workers and ex-servicemen was a major consideration for the government. The setting up of an approved society system within the unemployment insurance scheme was considered as a means of defraying the state's extra costs. A Ministry of Labour memorandum in 1918 looked at the prospects of allowing employers and workers to contract out. Beveridge, then at the Ministry of Labour, favoured the idea, which also won the support of B.S.Rowntree. Unemployment insurance approved societies were to be organised on an industry-wide basis, since no single company had a direct interest in aiding a worker it had made redundant. The difficulties of drawing demarcation barriers between industries, however, were recognised. Moreover, the mobility of labour between industries would be hindered by insuring workers within their own trade. The financing of unemployment approved societies would also create insuperable problems for industries with high incidences of unemployment. Where the incidence was low and industry-based insurance consequently feasible, it would have served little purpose. Furthermore, the employers' ability to sack workers would be constrained if it led to an increase in insurance premiums.(129) Nevertheless, "Unemployment Insurance by Industry" achieved some credibility after the Great War because it could be organised through the proposed industry-wide Joint Industrial Councils.

The Unemployment Insurance Bill 1920 extended the 1911 scheme to all workers, improved benefits, and introduced the non-contributory out-of-work dole.(130) Section 18 allowed a J.I.C., with the sanction of the Minister of Labour, to create its own insurance scheme. It would receive a 30% subsidy from the Treasury. Proposals had to be submitted to the Ministry by July 1921. Supplementary schemes, under Section 20 and which improved the basic benefits under the Act, would also be allowed. It was thought possible that three and three-quarter million of the 12 million insured might contract out.(131) An N.A.E.E. deputation was interviewed by the Prime Minister and the Minister of Labour about the Bill. The Association's F.B.I. representatives argued that the proposed 15s insurance benefit was insufficient, and urged that the emergency of demobilisation and rising unemployment necessitated the payment of dole. They argued for public works and a fairer division of work.(132) As unemployment soared, it became unrealistic to expect industries voluntarily to undertake the cost and administration of unemployment insurance. Severe structural unemployment made the transfer of labour between industries imperative, and confirmed unemployment as a national and governmental problem. Although both the F.B.I. and the N.C.E.O. supported insurance by industry in 1920, the Act proved workable in banking and insurance only. In 1922, the Minister of Labour decided to suspend consideration of insurance by industry schemes. The views of employers were, therefore, canvassed, and the N.C.E.O. asked for the re-activation of Section 18. Both the Confederation and the F.B.I. seriously investigated insurance by industry as late as 1922,(133) because state schemes failed to encourage a "spirit of cooperation between employers and employed". Businessmen who accepted direct responsibility for out-of-work payments could win the attachment of workers.(134) Industrial Peace acknowledged that unemployment was the workers' greatest fear during these years. The workers' status had to be improved, and, it argued, "industries must themselves carry the work of insurance farther than the State could, and on better principles" by transferring the responsibility of unemployment insurance to those whose provision it directly affected.(135) The N.C.E.O. recognised the practical and administrative difficulties of insurance by industry, but placed greater hopes upon supplementary schemes within firms, especially as companies were increasing in size. The Confederation argued that all companies rather than employment exchanges should issue benefits, a right given only to those who operated supplementary schemes. The state was seen as having a duty to promote voluntary initiatives.(136) The National Federation of Employees Approved Societies contended that contracting out allowed a worker to sympathise with the circumstances of an employer who "helps them to tide over the period of depression by contributing jointly with them to their own unemployment fund".(137)

The National Federation of Iron and Steel Makers in 1920 talked to the Ministry of Labour, and a "Special Scheme" was drawn up requiring union agreement to joint contributions for an industry-wide approved society.(138) The Woollen Textile, Hosiery, Boot and Shoe, Printing, Wire-making, and Match-making J.I.C.s all drew up contracting out schemes in 1921.(139) The Council for the Hosiery industry and the N.C.E.O., in 1922, blamed the failure of such schemes on the government's lack of cooperation.(140) The Chemical Industries Federation had appointed an actuary to investigate the idea, but he had reported unfavourably. The Federation was still willing, however, to reconsider the proposal in 1922. Sir Charles Macara for the cotton spinning industry and the Association of British Chambers of Commerce favoured contracting out. The Food Manufacturers Federation and the National Employers of Vehicle Builders hoped to implement their schemes in more favourable circumstances. The Bradford Dyers Association argued for the more flexible administration of unemployment insurance. It envisaged a mixture of national, industrial, and company schemes, with each worker having the right to join or re-join the general fund if he left his employment. But the National Federation of Building Trades Employers and the Mining Association of Great Britain pointed out the parlous and unpredictable economic situation they faced and simply opposed contracting out.(141) Natural monopolies which enjoyed little unemployment, generally showed small interest in contracting out, although supplementary schemes were considered because of the low level of expected claims.(142)

* * * * *

The government's consideration of pensions policy after the Great War had to take account of the view of employers and the role of industrial pensions, and a general consensus seems to have existed. Those who gave evidence to the Departmental Committee in 1919 favoured state provision as supportive of their own company welfare policies. The state for its part was keen to encourage voluntary initiative. The Industrial Welfare Society in 1949 argued that when the state had first guaranteed a 10s pension, "many employers asked how this position was likely to affect the firm's pension schemes. Experience has furnished the answer to this question. Pensions and superannuation schemes grew at a far more rapid rate after 1926 than before", because "the very provision of government

pension directs the worker's attention to the need to provide
for his old age".(143) Contracting out in the 1925 Act was in
line with the precedents set in 1880 and 1911 and was passed
without controversy. State pensions after 1918 were generally
accepted without the type of anti-statist arguments deployed
against the Pre-War Liberal social reforms. Although the
F.B.I. and N.C.E.O. naturally sought some means of defraying
any extra costs industry might bear, their campaign to limit
increases in government expenditure was in effect ignored by
the government. Section 18 of the Unemployment Insurance Act
1920 proved a failure. While employers could administer health
insurance approved societies on a company-basis, obtaining the
necessary intra-industry cooperation for the contracting out
of unemployment insurance proved prohibitive. The Post-War
Slump, in any case, ended any prospect of insurance by
industry. But the interest of employers in the proposal as
late as 1922 illustrates their continued support for
contracting out, and the way during this period that state and
industrial welfare were considered as feasible alternatives
even in the area of unemployment insurance. As in the case of
pensions, the N.C.E.O. and the F.B.I. during the Inter-War
period attempted to reduce the cost of unemployment insurance
on industry, without directly attacking the principle of state
provision. Their efforts were, likewise, rebuffed by the
government.(144)

(vi) CONCLUSION

The state welfare system which had developed before 1939
was altered by the consequences of the Second World War. It
was remembered that promises of Reconstruction during the
1914-18 conflict had answered questions about the value of
fighting on, but had been broken on the actuality of
unemployment and poverty during the 1920s and 1930s. As during
the Great War, government were certain to consider matters of
state and industrial welfare as the shortage of labour
increased and its value grew.(145) The promotion of welfare
schemes through the joint production committees set up in 1940
by Ernest Bevin, Minister of Labour, was indicative of a
renewed interest in the health and efficiency of the civilian
worker.(146) The necessity of state control was more quickly
accepted during the Second World War than in the conflict with
Germany 25 years earlier, when the lessons of government
planning for a total, industrial war had still to be learnt.
Bevin in 1941 emphasised that the morale of the armed forces
and the home front depended upon state guarantees of social
security and full employment. The need for common sacrifices
during the War supported the case of those who argued for the
creation of a fairer society offering freedom from destitution
"from the cradle to the grave".

The Beveridge Committee was appointed in May 1941 to investigate the social services, and its proposals were published seventeen months later. The Beveridge Report argued for the replacement of the separate health, unemployment, and pensions schemes by a single, unitary and universal system of national insurance. Seeking merely to rationalise the payment of state benefits, it was not an innovative measure. Indeed, two of the Report's underlying assumptions, a National Health Service and full employment, were more revolutionary in concept than its proposals for action. The streamlining of the state's benefits system had been a familiar demand of the Federation of British Industries, the British Employers Confederation, and many businessmen in the Inter-War years.(147) Their support for contracting out, however, could not easily be matched with their wish to see centralisation and rationalisation. The payment of larger basic allowances by certain Approved Socities was attacked as unfair by the T.U.C. Beveridge also wanted equal, basic benefits, and popular support for the principles underlying his Report ensured its acceptance by the government in 1943.(148)

J.Harris has pointed out that the attitude of employers towards the Beveridge Committee and its Report was mixed. They agreed with the Report's aims, but opposed any increase in industrial costs.(149) Their opposition, therefore, was an exact reflection of the position they had taken towards the 1925 Pensions Act. The response of Lords Melchett and McGowan of I.C.I. was more positive. The paper they presented to the Beveridge Committee, "A National Policy for Industry", sought a partnership between corporate paternalism and state welfare. Industrialists would be responsible for the proper housing of employees, and would undertake to supplement state pensions and unemployment pay. Government, on the other hand, would provide the basic social benefits and family allowances, and raise the school leaving age to 16.(150) Melchett and McGowan's Paper had 120 signatories from industry, and, according to a survey, 73% of employers favoured the Beveridge Report. The opposition of the textile industry was, however, notably strong, because it was labour intensive and susceptible to competitive pressures.(151)

The Wool and Allied Textiles Employers Council, for example, wanted to end "the duplication of administrative machinery" which was employed in the processing of three separate insurance schemes, but sought guarantees of government economy and upper limits to the overall levels of social expenditure. The Railway Companies Association also saw the advantages of coordinating the state insurance schemes, but the cost to employers and the state was "the more important point". Due to the permanence of railway employment and the industry's high expenditure on company welfare, the R.C.A. wanted complete exemption from unemployment insurance and partial exemption from health insurance.(152) When Sir

William Jowitt's Advisory Panel on Home Affairs was established in 1942 to canvass expert opinion on the Beveridge Report, it interviewed employers like B.S.Rowntree, Samuel Courtauld, Sir Samuel Beale and representatives of Guiness, Marks and Spencer, British Copper, Austin and Morris, and various heavy engineering firms. None of them raised objections to the principles of a universal and contributory insurance scheme, and opposition proved greater amongst ministers and civil servants.(153)

Harris correctly points out the need for greater research into employers' responses to proposals during the Second World War for greater economic and social planning by the state.(154) Employers' attitudes in 1942, however, must have been influenced by their involvement in industrial welfare schemes and Approved Societies. Their usefulness to good industrial relations would have made them more sympathetic to Beveridge's proposals, and the creation of large corporate companies during the Inter-War period increased the need for welfare provision and the ability of industry to pay for it. Government, industry, and unions were impressed by the necessity of placing Britain on a war footing. Moreover, the failure of Lloyd George's Coalition to implement its Reconstruction proposals and memories of mass unemployment between the Wars were powerful influences on public opinion after 1939. Political realities made employers campaign for a close scrutiny of government expenditure while offering a cautious welcome to Beveridge's proposals. It was a tactic born of weakness, and, as during the Great War, it was the state which determined the nature of social and economic planning. State welfare, in any case, had often promoted the opportunities for industrial welfare. But, in accepting Beveridge's proposals, employers effectively abandoned contracting out. The rationalisation of state welfare, which had grown haphazardly, of course had its own logic. Yet, the success of Beveridge's campaign in support of an all-embracing state benefits system in 1943 was undeniable, and the election of a Labour government by a large majority in 1945 was further evidence of support for social and economic reform. The National Insurance Act and the National Insurance (Industrial Injuries) Act passed in 1946, to be implemented by 1948, wound up the Approved Societies.

Although the involvement of company provident societies in the administration of basic benefits had been terminated, supplementary private schemes expanded after 1945. In 1949, the Industrial Welfare Society stated that National Insurance allowances had helped bridge the gap between a worker's earnings and his needs, "but it was never pretended that they eliminated the need for private thrift schemes and assisted saving". Company welfare was in the employer's interest. Pensions, in particular, encouraged loyalty, and the Post-War National Insurance legislation provided a basis for industrial welfare. "It is not intended that this new national standard should in any way adversely affect those covered by existing provident schemes......." Supplementary sick schemes would still be attractive to married men earning above the basic state benefits of 46s or 26s for single men. The same was true of accident compensation for workers earning respectively above 45s or 35s. Such schemes could still be made compulsory if they were registered under the Shop Clubs Act 1902. A company donation which was deductable from tax, however, usually made the terms they offered attractive enough.(155)

* * * * *

Detailed research on the role of employers after 1939 still needs to be undertaken. The creation of the Welfare State, however, undoubtedly undermined the necessity of direct employer involvement in the provision of sick pay and pensions. The Approved Societies were ended, and state allowances were finally set at levels of sustenance. But the establishment of universally-available state benefits was not the only solution to the problems of income-maintenance. The wide-spread existence of industrial welfare before 1939 was an argument in favour of the continuation of a "Welfare Society" in which government would coordinate services and interfere directly only where private provision proved inadequate. There was no inevitable trend towards the "Welfare State". Indeed, systemised company benefits survived and flourished after 1948. The movement during the 20th Century in favour of welfare of whatever kind, therefore, is linked to proposals about better industrial relations and the labour requirements of the firm.

NOTES

1. Cf. B.B.Gilbert The Evolution of National Insurance: Origins of the Welfare State (1966), & British Social Policy, 1919-1939 (1970); J.F.Harris Unemployment and Politics: a Study in English Social Policy, 1886-1914 (1972); J.R.Hay The Development of the British Welfare State, 1880-1975 (1978), & The Origins of the Liberal Welfare Reforms, 1906-1914 (1975); A.Marwick "The Labour Party and the Welfare State in Britain, 1900-1939", Am.H.R., vol.73(I) (1967), pp.380-403; P.Thane Foundations of the Welfare State (1982), & The Origins of British Social Policy (1978).

2. K.Middlemas Politics in Industrial Society (1979).

3. G.Alderman The Railway Interest (1979), pp.222-8.

4. J.Turner "The British Commonwealth Union and the General Election of 1918", E.H.R. (1978), pp.528-551.

5. Cf. National Federation of Associated Employers of Labour (1873); Employers' Parliamentary Council (1898); Manufacturers' Association of Great Britain (1905); Employers Parliamentary Association (1911).

6. Cf. Turner (ed.) Businessmen and Politics (1984), p.42: "Report of the Labour Sub-Committee on Industrial and Commercial Efficiency", FBI Circular, 6 Dec 1917, EEF Archives. The report was drawn up by a sub-committee chaired by W.P.Rylands, a paternalistic producer of steel wire: cf. Ch.4, s.(iv).

7. Cf. W.P.Grant & P.C.Marsh The Confederation of British Industry (1977), chs.1,2; J.Turner "The Politics of Business" & "The Politics of 'Organised Business' in the First World War" in Turner (ed.) (1984), pp.1-19,33-49; S.Blank Industry and Government in Britain: the Federation of British Industries (1973), pp.4-40.

8. Cf. R.Miliband The State in Capitalist Society (1973).

9. Cf. J.R.Hay The Origins of the Liberal Welfare Reforms (1975), chs.1,2,3; J.F.Harris "Social Policy Making in Britain during the Second World War" in W.J.Mommsen The Emergence of the Welfare State in Britain and Germany (1981).

10. Gilbert (1966), pp.340-1,373-4,378-9,383,387, 428-9.

11. Railway News, 27 March 1880, pp.428-9.

12. Alderman (1973), p.63.

13. Bagwell (1963), pp.117-8.

14. Cf. P.S.Bagwell "The Railway Interest: its Organisation and its Influence", Jl. of Transport History (1965), pp.65-86.

15. Railway News, 11 Dec 1880, pp.781-2.

16. Iron and Coal Trades Review, 13 Feb 1880, p.180; Hansard, 28 May 1880, 3rd ser., vol.252, cols.638-9; Alderman (1973), pp.781-2.

17. Ibid.

18. Hansard, 3 June 1880, 3rd ser., vol.252, cols.1094-1102.

19. Iron and Coal Trades Review, 25 June 1880, p.719.

20. Railway News, 5 June 1880, pp.751-3.

21. Iron and Coal Trades Review, 30 July 1880, p.123.

22. Hansard, 4th ser., vol.48, cols.1437ff.

23. Cf. Sir H.P. Robinson The Employers' Liability Assurance Corporation Limited, 1880-1930 (1930).

24. Hansard, 20 Feb 1893, 4th ser., vol.10, cols.1943-55; E.L.Wigham The Power to Manage (1973), p.20; Liberty Review, 9 Dec 1893, pp.24-5; Rail 1098/51, RCA Minutes, 20 Feb 1893, no.2026.

25. P.S.Bagwell Industrial Relations (1974), pp.70-9; Liberty Review, 2 Dec 1893, p.1 & 17 Feb 1894, p.176; Railway News, 6 Oct 1894, p.485.

26. Liberty Review, 6 Jan 1894, p.82; 13 Jan 1894, p.98.

27. Hansard, 25 April 1893, 4th ser., vol.11, cols.1211-1212; 8 Nov 1893, vol.13, cols.483-494; 23 Nov 1893, vol.13, col.1648.

28. Ibid, 24 March 1893, vol.10, cols.684-9.

29. Ibid, 12 Dec 1893, vol.10, col.1167.

30. Hansard, 24 March 1893, vol.10, cols.1056,1581-88.
31. Ibid, 25 April 1893, vol.11, cols.1211-1212; 8 Nov 1893, vol.13, cols.483-494; 23 Nov 1893, vol.13, col.1648.
32. Ibid, 10 Nov 1893, vol.11, cols.684-9.
33. Rail 1098/51, RCA, 8 Nov 1893, no.2051; Railway News, 9 Dec 1893, p.907; Liberty Review, 16 Dec 1893, pp.40-41.
34. Iron and Coal Trades Review, 28 May 1897, p.803.
35. Hansard, 3 May 1897, vol.48, cols. 1424-37.
36. Ibid, 18 May 1897, vol.49, cols.763ff.
37. Ibid, 20 July 1897, vol.51, cols.529.
38. Ibid, 3 May 1897, vol.48, cols.1424-37.
39. PP 1899 (C.9203) xxxiii 871. Home Department Report on Shops Clubs.
40. Ibid.
41. EEF Minutes, Parliamentary Committees, 26 March 1902; 25 Feb 1903.
42. Gilbert (1966), pp.161-232.
43. Hansard, 10 May 1907, 5th ser., vol.174, cols.470-5.
44. P.Thane "Non-Contributory versus National Insurance Pensions, 1878-1908" in P.Thane (1978), pp.84-106; Hay (1975), pp.54-7.
45. Hansard, 16 June 1908, 5th ser., vol.190, cols.736-740.
46. Ibid, 15 June 1908, vol.190, cols.643-7.
47. PP 1919 (C.410) xxvii 299. Report of Departmental Committee on Old Age Pensions, Qs.3730-3810,3913.
48. Hay (1975), pp.25-42; W.Beveridge Power and Influence (1953), p.82.
49. Gilbert (1966), pp.319-20.
50. Hansard, 4 May 1911, vol.25, cols.618-9.
51. Ibid, 29 May 1911, vol.26, cols.818-828.
52. Ibid, 29 May 1911, cols.440-63.
53. For alternative views in the cotton industry in particular, cf. Ch.7, s.(ii).
54. Macara (1922), pp.166,217-225. Cf. also the Birmingham Chamber of Commerce's objection to employers' contributions in J.R.Hay "Employers and Social Policy in Britain: the Evolution of Welfare Legislation, 1905-1914", Soc.Hist. (1977), pp.435-456.
55. EEF Minutes, MSS 237, 26 April 1912. The E.P.A. was finally absorbed by the Federation of British Industries.
56. Rail 1098/53, RCA, NI Committee, 16 May 1911; 24 May 1911; 10 July 1911.
57. Rail 1098/53, RCA, Council Meeting, 25 July 1911.
58. The Anti-Socialist, 6 Sept 1911, p.247. Cf. also Journal of Gas Lighting, 16 May 1911, p.431; 11 July 1911, p.91; also Industrial Welfare, March 1927, pp.75-8.
59. G.L.R.O., B/GLCC/44/1.
60. Journal of Gas Lighting, 11 July 1911, pp.91-2.
61. Ibid, 1 Aug 1911, p.281; 8 Aug 1911, p.344.
62. Ibid, 28 Nov 1911, p.586.

63. Ibid, 20 Feb 1912, p.519.
64. PP 1919 (C.411) xxvii, Qs.3772,3879,4179-80,4332.
65. Hansard, 27 Oct 1911, vol.30, cols.440-463. Cf. also J.R.Hay "Employers' Attitudes to Social Policy and the Concept of Social Control, 1900-1920" in Thane (1978), pp.120-1.
66. Ibid, 27 Oct 1911, vol.30, cols.440-63.
67. PRO PIN4/7, Ministry of Health, Memo. on Employers' Funds. 1912-13; PRO MH/81/55/MS5004/1; Rail 226/530, GCR, Circular on NH Insurance, 1911, Feb 1912.
68. Hansard, 21 March 1912, vol.35, col.2209.
69. Re. working-class attitudes to social legislation, cf. H.M.Pelling Popular Politics and Society in Late Victorian Britain (1969), ch.1.
70. Hansard, 24 & 29 May 1911, 5th ser., vol.30, cols.308,440-63; 27 Oct 1911, cols.440-63.
71. LAB2/1483/LE(1)1750/1911; EEF Minutes, 16 June 1910, Parliamentary Committee, MSS 237.
72. LAB2/1483/LE(1)1750/1911, Deputation from S.E.F. to S.C.Buxton, 14 June 1911.
73. Cf. Macara above, and P.F.Clarke "The End of Laissez-faire and the Politics of Cotton", H.J. (1972), pp.493-512.
74. Cf. P.F.Clarke Lancashire and the New Liberalism (1971).
75. Charles (1973), pp.94-121.
76. PP 1918 (C.9001) xv 951. Ministry of Reconstruction Committee Report on Relations between Employers and Employees: Report on Works Committees.
77. Hansard, 6 March 1918, 5th ser., vol.104, cols.2084-2087.
78. J.B.Seymour The Whitley Council Scheme (1932), pp.81-2,84,86.
79. International Labour Review, Dec 1921, pp.563-78.
80. Cf. Ch.4, s.(iv).
81. FBI Archive, MSS/200/F/1/2/2, "The Control of Industry", Memo. to members of Nationalisation Committee.
82. Hansard, 18 Aug 1919, 5th ser., vol.119, cols.1996-2003.
83. LAB2/716/186/15/1920, Works Committees J.I.C.s.
84. Charles (1973), pp.130-60,215-26,299-306.
85. Labour Copartnership, Sept 1919, p.69; May 1920, pp.59-60.
86. Industrial Welfare, July 1920, p.216; Aug 1920, pp.260-1.
87. Unity, May 1920, p.7.
88. Labour Copartnership, May 1920, pp.294-6.
89. Industrial Welfare, Oct 1923, pp.321-2.
90. Current Opinion, Dec 1920, pp.477-8.
91. Ibid, Sept 1918, pp.1-3.
92. Ibid, Dec 1918, pp.19-23; March 1919, p.36.
93. Industrial Reconstruction Council Reconstruction

Handbook (1918).
94. Current Opinion, Dec 1919, pp.136-7; Sept 1920, pp.372-6; Industrial League The Industrial League (3) (1921); Industrial League and Council Whitley Councils: What they are and what they are doing (1920) by J.H.Whitley M.P.
95. Current Opinion, Feb 1920, pp.166-171; March 1920, p.207; April 1920, pp.210-11; Jan 1921, p.23.
96. Unity, June 1925, p.1.
97. Ibid, Feb 1919, p.3.
98. FBI Archive, MSS/200/F/3/D1/3/11, Memo. from FBI, 11 Dec 1916; Letter to Dudley Docker from FBI, 1 Jan 1917. Cf. R.P.T.Davenport-Hines Dudley Docker: the Life and Times of a Trade Warrior (1984).
99. Ibid, Letter to Docker from FBI, 6 March 1917.
100. Ibid, Letter to H.E.Morgan from FBI Director, 15 March 1917; Industrial Peace, Nov 1917, pp.24-6; Unity, Nov 1919, pp.8-9.
101. Cf. J.Melling(ed.) Housing, Social Policy, and the State (1980).
102. Ministry of Munitions (1919), Vol.V., pp.44-5,55-6.
103. Cf. M.Swenarton Homes Fit for Heroes: the Politics and Architecture of Early State Housing in Britain (1981). The 1919 Act was considered a failure, mostly because it fell victim, like the Education Act, to the Geddes Committee.
104. Hansard, 28 Oct 1918, vol.110, cols.1166-7.
105. MSS/200/F/3/D1/4/1, Meeting of Joint Housing Committee of FBI and NAEE, 17 Dec 1918.
106. Ibid, FBI Housing Committee Draft Report on Public Utility Societies, 5 April 1918.
107. Ibid, Minutes of Interview with Mr Tennyson of FBI, re. employers' capital investment in P.U.S.s after the War.
108. Industrial Welfare, May 1920, p.160. Cf. the housing trust founded by Dunlop Rubber Company (Unity, Feb 1928, pp.136-8, & B.S.C. 003/2/1); and passim in previous chapters.
109. Unity, Jan 1920, p.3; Industrial Welfare, April 1923, pp.91-6; Aug 1920, pp.254-6; Works Management, Nov 1919, pp.38-44.
110. Modern Records Centre, NCEO Archive, MSS/200/B/3/2/C591, Memo.on Housing Conditions.
111. Unity, June 1919, p.3.
112. Ibid, Feb 1919, pp.3-9, & passim; Industrial Peace, Jan 1918, p.12.
113. Unity, Nov 1926, p.99.
114. Ibid, 1928-1931, passim.
115. LAB2/1295/IR545/27, Works Committees, 14 April 1927.
116. Unity, Feb 1933, pp.179-182.
117. PP 1919 (C.410) xxvii 299, Qs.3730-3810,3913-4032, 1563-4120,4336-4454. Also, Recommendations, pp.6-11.
118. J.L.Cohen Social Insurance Unified (1924), pp.102-7.
119. PP 1924-25 (C.2405) xxiii 667. Memo., Explanatory to the Bill, pp.2,3,6.

120. NCEO Archive, MSS/200/B/3/2/C645, Pt.1, 15 May 1925.
121. BSC 802/6/35, CCWA, Minute Book, 10 July 1925, 11 Sept 1925; Iron and Coal Trades Review, 10 July 1925, p.876.
122. Ibid, Extract from Hansard, 20th May 1925.
123. NCEO Archive, MSS/200/B/3/2/C645 Pt.1, Draft of Statement by FBI on Old Ages Pension Bill.
124. Ibid, 21 May 1925.
125. Rail 1098/53, Meeting of RCA, 14 July 1925, minute 4259.
126. Hansard, 13 July 1926, 5th ser., vol.198, cols.369ff.
127. NCEO Archive, MSS/200/B/3/2/C645 Pt.2, Correspondence with solicitor, 4 & 6 July 1925.
128. Ibid, MSS/200/B/3/2/C595, 9 Feb 1927.
129. PRO PIN3/8. Cf. J.Harris Unemployment and Politics: A Study in English Social Policy, 1886-1914 (1972), pp.303-4,334.
130. Although the 1911 Act had already been expanded to include munitions workers in 1916.
131. J.L.Cohen Insurance by Industry Examined (1923), pp.26-32,51-2.
132. LAB2/1210/17624/1920, Pt.1, 9 Nov 1920.
133. NCEO Archive, MSS/200/B/1/2/1, General Purposes Committee, 3 May 1922.
134. Ibid, MSS/200/3/2/C4, Pt.1, Meeting of GPC, 23 Nov 1922.
135. Industrial Peace, Jan 1921, pp.165-7.
136. MSS/200/3/2/C4, Meeting of GPC, 23 Nov 1922; FBI, MSS/200/F/1/2/17, 1st Draft Report of the Unemployment Insurance Committee, 28 June 1922.
137. Unity, April 1925, pp.4-5.
138. BSC 802/6/5, Parliamentary Committee, 8 April 1920; 20 Oct 1920; 17 Nov 1920.
139. PP 1922 (C.1613-II) ii 1123; NCEO Archive, MSS/200/B/3/2/C240.
140. Current Opinion, Dec 1920, p.477; May 1922, p.7.
141. PIN7/61, Summary of Replies to Minister's circular, 22 Feb to 17 June 1922.
142. Cf. Rail 1115/4, GNR Sick and Funeral Allowance Fund, Report of Committee of Management, 31 May 1920.
143. IWS Employee Benefit Schemes (1949), p.7.
144. In 1927, the N.C.E.O. took up the recommendations of the Blanesburgh Committee on Unemployment Insurance. The Economy Act of 1926 had set payments at 8d an employer, 7d a worker, and 6d from the state. But the Committee had suggested parity of payments between all three contributors, and the setting of benefits at what the "nation could afford". The Confederation led a delegation to 10 Downing Street on the 7th November. Baldwin said that the balancing of economy with the cost of unemployment insurance was a problem but not the "deciding factor". He told the N.C.E.O. that there were factors which "perhaps we are better acquainted with than you,

and that is political pressure which it would have been almost impossible to avoid". The request for a cut in the employer's contribution was refused. Cf. PRO PIN3/117, 17 Nov 1927.

145. IWS Elements of Industrial Welfare and Personnel Management (1940).

146. A.Bullock The Life and Times of Ernest Bevin, vol.II: the Minister of Labour (1967), pp.94-5. Cf. H.M.Vernon The Health and Efficiency of Munition Workers (1940).

147. Cf. especially s.(v). The National Confederation of Employers Organisations was renamed the British Employers Confederation in 1932.

148. P.Addison The Road to 1945 (1977), pp.168-9. Cf. K.Jeffrys "British Politics and Social Policy during the Second World War", H.J. (1987), vol.xxx, pp.123-144, which challenges the notion of war-time consensus over reconstruction proposals.

149. J.Harris "Some Aspects of Social Policy in Britain during the 2nd World War" in W.J.Mommsen The Emergence of the Welfare State in Britain and Germany (1981), pp.249-50.

150. Addison (1977), pp.214-15.

151. Middlemas (1979), pp.286-8,292,294,314. The poll was carried out by the British Institute of Public Opinion (Gallup).

152. PRO 1098/9, Meeting of RCA, 6 Aug 1942; MSS200/B/3/2/C216 Pt.3., Observation from RCA to NCEO, 24 Feb 1942; Wool and Allied Textile Employers Council; Post-War Social Services, 14/4/42; Meeting of BEC Council, 15 Jan 1943.

153. Harris in Mommsen (1981), pp.253-5.

154. Ibid, p.260.

155. IWS Employee Benefit Schemes (1949), pp.5,7-9, 14,17,27,30-33,36,42-45.

EPILOGUE

The evidence of company records challenges the views of
commentators who hold that, while examples of industrial
welfare can be found in British industry, they were uncommon.
The prevalence of company benefits demonstrates that many
employers realised the impracticability of simply relying on
market forces to maintain a workforce suited to the needs of
production. In practice, firms depended on the often
"firm-specific" and even "machine-specific" skills of their
workers, and labour turnover could be an expensive problem.
Employers, therefore, created internal labour markets within
their firms, which were protected from external market forces
not only through improved security of employment but by the
provision of welfare benefits. Few works have yet assessed the
role of dual labour markets in British industry.

Company provision in British labour management from
approximately 1846 to 1939 had antecedents in small-firm
paternalism. The growth of larger companies, however, induced
crucial changes in the nature of management. Personal and ex
gratia paternalism became gradually less appropriate to many
industries. Changes in the administration of commercial
management often accompanied alterations in the administration
and scale of industrial welfare.

Each change has to be understood in the context of each
industry's market and structure. Just as markets determined
industrial structure, structure moulded the context of labour
relations. The nature of employment on the railways required a
systemised and comprehensive scheme of welfare benefits. In
the gas industry, the need for regularity and security of
supply proved more influential than the factor of seasonal
employment in the determination of welfare policies.

Yet, the natural monopolies contrasted strongly with
competitive industries. Changes in the welfare organisation of
the steel and chemical trades awaited the restructuring of
capital and management. Where industries continued to be
unrationalised, as in the cases of engineering and
shipbuilding, welfare remained less developed.

247

Epilogue

Those, like the dockers, who were engaged in casual
trades generally suffered from job-insecurity, low wages, and
a lack of welfare provision. The rationalisation of industries
and the establishment of more capital-intensive processes
increased the necessity for internal labour markets and
industrial welfare strategies. But the main aim of these was to
reduce the natural friction between employer and worker, and
the wage-relationship alone could not   remove the fear of
penury due to misfortune, illness or old age.

Social legislation before the Welfare State proved an aid
to company provision rather than a challenge. Governments did
not attempt to create a universal social safety-net, but
sought through state welfare to encourage private thrift.
Moreover, employers were able to exert influence on the final
form of social legislation. They ensured that, through a
system of "contracting-out" or Approved Societies within state
schemes, company provision could continue and even expand. A
significant reason for the growing support for provident
welfare in this period, therefore, can be attributed to
changes in the structure of companies and the economy. As for
the role of industrial welfare since 1945, its history still
needs to be undertaken.(1)

NOTE

1.   The Department of Employment's New Earnings Survey in
1970 showed that 62.9% of male manual workers and 91.6% of
salaried staff had occupational sick schemes; the figure was
48.8% and 82.3% respectively for female employees. 12 million
were   estimated as participating in occupational pension
schemes; 45.3% of male manual workers, 73.2% of male staff,
11.9% of female manual workers, and 38.6% of female staff were
believed to enjoy such benefits. A third of the companies
involved in the Survey were estimated as owning housing. Cf.
J.Moonman The Effectiveness of Fringe Benefits in Industry
(1973), pp.26-7,29-30,90-1.

PRIMARY SOURCES

Chapter 2
Public Record Office:
    Barry Docks Railway Company
    Great Central Railway
    Great Eastern Railway
    Great Northern Railway
    Great Western Railway
    Lancashire and Yorkshire Railway
    London and Birmingham Railway
    London and North Eastern Railway
    London and North Western Railway
    London, Midland and Scottish Railway
    London, Brighton and South Coast Railway
    Manchester, Sheffield and Lincolnshire Railway
    Metropolitan Railway
    North Eastern Railway
    South Eastern Railway
    Southern Railway
    Taff Vale Railway

    Railway Companies Association

Hansard

Report of the Home Department on Shop Clubs, PP 1899
(C.9203) xxxiii 871
Report of Board of Trade on Railway Superannuation
Funds, PP 1910 (C.5349) lvii 35
Minutes of Evidence for Report of Board of Trade on Railway
Superannuation Funds, PP 1911 (C.5484) xxix-I 687

Great Central Railway Journal
Great Eastern Railway Magazine
Great Western Railway Magazine
Herapath's Railway Journal
L.M.S. Railway Magazine
Railway News
The Railway Review
The Railway Vigilant

Chapter 3
Greater London Record Office:
    Central Gas Company
    Commercial Gas Company
    Gas Light and Coke Company
    Imperial Gas Company

Independent Gas Company
Phoenix Gas Company
South Metropolitan Gas Company

Metropolitan Board of Works

Public Record Office:
Board of Trade, BT1
Joint Industrial Council for the Gas
Industry, LAB2

Hansard

Report of Select Committee on the Metropolis Gas Industry, PP 1859 (C.225-I) i 507
Minutes and Report of Select Committee on Gas (Metropolis) Bill, PP 1860 (C.493) xxi 29; PP 1860 (C.417) xxi 37
Minutes and Report of Select Committee on the Sale of Gas (Amendment) Bills, PP 1860 (C.462) xxi 429; PP 1860 (C.78) iii 485
Report and Minutes from Select Committee on London (City) Corporation Gas, &c. Bills, 1866 (C.270) xii 63
Special Report from the Select Committee on the Metropolis Gas Bill, PP 1867 (C.520) xii 1
Correspondence of City of London, Metropolitan Board of Works, London Vestries, and gas companies re. supply of gas in Metropolis, PP 1867 (C.118-I,118-II) lviii 497,557,565
Report from Select Committee on Metropolitan Gas Companies Bill, PP 1875 (C.281) xii 1
Reports to Board of Trade on Profitsharing, PP 1890-91 (C.6267) lxxviii 15; 1894 (C.7458) lxxx 575
Royal Commission on Labour, PP 1892 (C.26) iv 308
Report to Board of Trade on Profitsharing, PP 1895 (C.7848) lxxx 103
Report from the Select Committee appointed to Inquiry into the Powers of Charge conferred by Parliament on the Metropolitan Gas Companies, PP 1899 (C.294) x 19
Report of Departmental Committee on Gas Testing in the Metropolis, PP 1904 (C.2118) xxiv 667; 1904 (C.2203) xxiv 577
Report on Profitsharing and Labour Copartnership, PP 1912 (C.6496) xliii 853
Report of the Joint Select Committee of the House of Lords on Gas Authorities (Residual Products, PP 1912-13 (C.392) vii 253
Report from the Select Committee on Gas Undertakings (Statutory Prices), PP 1918 (C.74) iii 589
Report from Fuel Research Board on Gas Standards, PP 1919 (C.108) xxii 569
Report and Proceedings on Gas Regulation Bill, PP 1920 (C.127) vi 1071
Report and Proceedings on Public Utility Companies Bill, PP 1920 (C.47) viii 413

Report on Profitsharing and Labour Copartnership, PP 1920
(C.544) xxiii 157

Copartnership Herald, Journal of the Commercial Gas Company
Copartners' Magazine, Journal of the Gas Light and Coke
Company
Gas Trade Circular and Review
Journal of Gas Lighting
Liberty Review

Chapter 4
British Steel Corporation:
    Abercarn Tinplate Company
    Bolckow-Vaughn
    Cargo Fleet Company
    Consett Iron Company
    Dorman-Long
    Stanton and Stavely Iron Company
    Stewart and Lloyds
    Richard Thomas and Company
    United Steel Companies

    British Iron and Steel Federation
    National Federation of Iron and Steel Makers

Gwent Record Office:
    Blaenavon Coal and Iron Company
    Guest, Keen & Nettlefords
    Tredegar Coal and Iron Company
    Iron and Steel Wires Manufacturers Association

Public Record Office:
    Iron and Steel Wires Manufacturers
    Association, LAB2

Royal Commission on Trades Unions, PP 1867 (C.3980-I) xxxix 1
Report of the Departmental Committee on Iron and Steel Trades
after the War, PP 1918 (C.9071) xiii 423
Imports Duties Advisory Committee, PP 1937 (C.5507) xii 393

Colvilles Magazine
Edgar Allen Magazine
Iron and Coal Trades Review
Marshall News
WISC Group News

Chapter 5
Unilver PLC

Imperial Chemicals Industries

Chemical Trade Review
I.C.I. Magazine
Port Sunlight Monthly
Progress

Chapter 6
The Brewers Society:
    Brewers Society
    Country Brewers Trade Association
    London Brewers Company
    National Trade Defence Association

Westminister City Library Archives Department:
    Watneys & Sons

Brewers Journal
Brewing Trade Review
House of Whitbread

Chapter 7
Public Record Office:
    Miners Welfare Fund, POWE1 & 10

Gwent Record Office:
    The Tredegar Iron and Coal Company

Royal Commission on Trades Unions, PP 1867 (C.3980-I) xxxix 1
Report on Profitsharing, PP 1892 (C.6708-VI) xxxiv 1
Report on Profitsharing and Copartnership, PP 1894 (C.7458)
lxxx 575
Royal Commission on Labour, PP 1892 (C.6078) xxiv 1
Report on Profitsharing and Copartnership, PP 1920 (C.544)
xxiii 765

Hansard

W.H.Allen & Sons
Beardmore News
The Colliery Guardian
Electric Railway and Tramway Journal
The Engineer
Iron and Coal Trades Review
Liberty Review
Magazine of the Boot Manufacturers Association
Master Builders Association Journal
Osram G.E.C. Bulletin
Palmer Record

Shoe and Leather News
Shoe Manufacturers Monthly
Shipbuilding and Shipping Record
Smith's Docks Monthly
Team Spirit
Textile Manufacturer
Thames Ironworks Gazette
Vickers News
Woollen Gazette

Chapter 8
The Industrial Society:
    Industrial Welfare Society, Minutes & Reports

The Industrial Participation Society:
    Labour (later Industrial) Copartnership Association,
Minutes and Reports

Public Record Office:
    Ministry of Labour: LAB2

Report of the Board of Trade on Profitsharing, PP 1890-91
(C.6267) lxxviii 15
Report on Profitsharing and Copartnership PP 1894 (C.7458)
lxxx 575
Report on Profitsharing and Copartnership, PP 1912 (C.6496)
xxxiii 853
Report on Profitsharing and Copartnership, PP 1920 (C.544)
xxiii 765

Beardmore News (formerly Forge News)
Industrial Peace
Industrial Welfare
Labour Copartnership
Liberty Review
Ministry of Labour Gazette

Chapter 9
Modern Records Centre, University of Warwick Library:
    Engineering Employers Federation
    Federation of British Industries
    National Confederation of Employers Organisations

Public Record Office:
    Railway Companies Association

    Joint Industrial Councils: LAB2

    Ministry of Health: PIN3, PIN4, PIN7, MH81

Ministry of Labour: LAB2
Ministry of Reconstruction: RECO1

Hansard

Old Age Pensions: Tables & Memoranda, PP 1907 (C.3618) lxvii 1
Consultative Committee on Education, PP 1909 (C.4757) 6
Ministry of Reconstruction Report on Relations between
Employers and Employed, PP 1918 (C.9001) xv 951
Report of Departmental Committee on Old Age Pensions, PP 1919
(C.410) xxvii 299
Memorandum explanatory of the Old Age, Widows, and Orphans
Contributory Pensions Bill, PP 1924-25 (C.2405) xxiii 667
Report of Royal Commission on National Health Insurance, PP
1926 (C.2596) xiv 311
Report of Departmental Committee on Effect of the Rule of Law
against Perpetuities in its Application to certain
Superannuation Funds and Funds with Analogous Purposes, PP
2918 (C.2918) xi 9

The Anti-Socialist
Current Opinion
Industrial Peace
International Labour Review
Iron and Coal Trades Review
Journal of Gas Lighting
Liberty Review
Railway News
Unity
Works Management

SELECT BIBLIOGRAPHY

N.Abercombie & S.Hill "Paternalism and patronage", Brit. Jl.
of Sociology (1977), vol.27, no.4, pp.413-429
P.Abrams "The Failure of Social Reform, 1918-20", Past and
Present, no.24, (1963), pp.43-64
G.Alderman "The National Free Labour Association: a Case Study
of Organised Strike-Breaking in the Late 19th Century and the
Early 20th Century", I.R.S.H. (1976), vol.xxi, pp.309-336
Pressure Groups and Government in Great Britain (1983)
"The Railway Companies and the Growth of Trades Unionism in
the Late Nineteenth and Early Twentieth Century", H.J. (1971),
vol.14, pp.129-152
The Railway Interest (1973)
S.Armitage The Politics of Decontrol (1968)
B.W.E.Alford W.D. & H.O.Wills and the Development of the U.K.
Tobacco Industry, 1786-1965 (1973)
P.W.S.Andrews & E.Brunner The Life of Lord Nuffield: A Study
in Enterprise and Benevolence (1955)
P.W.S.Andrews & E.Brunner Capital Development in Steel: A
Study of United Steels Companies (1951)
W.H.G.Armytage Heavens Below (1961)
P.S.Bagwell Industrial Relations (1974)
"The Railway Interest: its Organisation and its Influence",
Jl. of T.H. (1965), no.2, pp.65-86
The Railwaymen: a history of the N.U.R. (1963)
T.C.Barker The Glassmakers: the rise of an international
company, 1826-1976 (1977)
T.C.Barker & R.M.Robbins A History of London Transport:
Passenger travel and the development of the metropolis, Vols.I
& II (1963 & 1974)
A.Barnard The Noted Breweries of Great Britain and Ireland,
Vols.I-IV (1889-91)
J.Baxter "The Organisation of the Brewing Industry" (London
Ph.D., 1945)
J.Benson British Coalminers in the 19th Century: A Social
History (1980)
J.Benson & R.G.Neville Studies in the Yorkshire Coal Industry
(1976)
A.F.Bentley The Process of Government (1908)
W.Beveridge Power and Influence (1953)
S.Blank Industry and Government in Britain: the Federation of
British Industries in Politics, 1945-1965 (1973)
H.Bolitho Alfred Mond, First Lord Melchett (1933)
M.R.Bonavia The Four Great Railways (1980)
The Organisation of British Railways (1971)
Railway Policy between the Wars (1981)
J.S.Boswell Business Policies in the Making: Three Steel

Select Bibliography

Companies Compared (1983)
E.W.Brabrook Provident Societies and Industrial Welfare (1898)
I.C.Bradley Enlightened Entrepreneurs (1987)
R.A.Brady Business as a System of Power (1943)
H.Braverman Labor and Monopoly Capitalism (1974)
A.Briggs Social Thought and Social Action: a study of the work of Seebohm Rowntree, 1871-1954 (1961)
E.Bristow "The Liberty and Property Defence League and Individualism", H.J., vol.xviii, (1975), pp.761-789
F.H.C.Brook Personnel Management and Welfare (1952)
F.H.C.Brook & G.Poulton Personnel Management (1943)
K.D.Brown Essays in Anti-Labour History (1974)
K.Burgess The Origins of British Industrial Relations: the 19th Century Experience (1975)
T.H.Burnham & G.O.Hoskins Iron and Steel in Britain, 1870-1930 (1943)
D.Burns The Economic History of Steel Making, 1867-1939 (1940)
N.K.Buxton The Economic Development of the British Coal Industry (1979)
"Efficiency and Organisation in Scotland's Iron and Steel Industry during the Interwar Period", Econ.H.R. (1976), vol.29, pp.107-124
"The Scottish Shipbuilding Industry between the Wars: a Comparative Study", Bus.Hist. (1968), vol.10, pp.101-120
P.J.Cain "Railway Combination and Government", Econ.H.R., vol.xxv (1972), pp.623-41
"Traders versus Railways: the Genesis of the Railway and Canal Traffic Act of 1894", Jl. of T.H., 2nd ser., no.2 (1973), pp.65-84
C.Carpenter Industrial Copartnership (1927)
L.P.Carpenter "Corporatism in Britain, 1930-45", Jl. of Contemporary Hy, vol.xi, (1976), pp.3-25
J.C.Carr & W.Taplin History of the British Steel Industry (1962)
A.D.Chandler Management Thought in Britain (1979)
"The Railroads: Pioneers in Modern Corporate Management", Bus.H.R. (1965), vol.30, pp.16-40
Strategy and Structure: Chapters in the History of Industrial Enterprise (1973)
The Visible Hand: the Managerial Revolution in American Business (1977)
A.D.Chandler & H.Daems Managerial Hierarchies (1980)
D.Chandler The Gas Industry: from Light to Heat (1946)
Outline of the History of Lighting by Gas (1936)
D.Chandler & A.Lacey The Rise of the Gas Industry in Britain (1949)
D.F.Channon Strategy and Structure in British Enterprise (1973)
S.D.Chapman The Cotton Industry in the Industrial Revolution (1971)
The Early Factory Masters (1984)
256

Select Bibliography

<u>Jesse Boot of Boots the Chemists: a Study in Business History</u>
(1974), esp. ch.8
D.A.Chatterton "State Control of the Public Utilities in the
Nineteenth Century: the London Gas Industry", <u>Bus.Hist.</u>,
vol.xiv (1972), pp.166-178
J.Child <u>British Management Thought: A Critical Analysis</u> (1969)
"Quaker Employers and Industrial Relations", <u>Sociological
Review</u>, 12,3,Nov., pp.293-315
R.Church <u>Herbert Austin: the British Motor Car Industry</u> (1979)
<u>Kenricks in Hardware, A Family Business, 1791-1966</u> (1969)
"Innovation, Monopoly and the Supply of Vehicle Components in
Britain, 1880-1930 : the Growth of Joseph Lucas Ltd",
<u>Bus.Hist.</u>, vol.20 (1978), pp.246-49
"Labour Supply and Innovation, 1800-1860: the Boot and Shoe
Industry", <u>Bus.Hist.</u>, vol.xii (1970), pp.25-45
"Messrs Gotch & Sons and the Rise of the Kettering Footwear
Industry", <u>Bus.Hist.</u>, vol.viii (1966), pp.140-9
"Profit-Sharing and Labour Relations in the Nineteenth
Century", <u>I.R.S.H.</u>, vol.xvi (1971), pp.2-16
P.F.Clarke "The end of laissez-faire and the politics of
cotton", <u>H.J.</u>, vol.xv, (1972), pp.493-512
<u>Lancashire and the New Liberalism</u> (1971)
H.A.Clegg <u>General Union: a Study of the National Union of
General and Municipal Workers</u> (1954)
<u>Labour Relations in London Transport</u> (1950)
J.L.Cohen <u>Insurance by Industry Examined</u> (1923)
J.M.Cohen <u>The Life of Ludwig Mond</u> (1956)
P.L.Cook <u>Effects of Mergers: Six Studies</u> (1958)
T.A.B.Corley <u>Quaker Enterprise in Biscuits: Huntley and
Palmers of Reading, 1822-1972</u> (1966)
H.S.Corran <u>A History of Brewing</u> (n.d.)
S.Courtauld <u>Ideals and Industry</u> (1949)
Croydon Gas Company <u>A Hundred Years of Public Service,
1847-1947</u> (1947)
M.J.Daunton "The Dowlais Iron Company in the Iron Industry,
1800-1850", <u>Welsh H.R.</u>, vol.vi (1972), pp.16-48
"Miners´ Houses: South Wales and the Great Northern Coalfield,
1880-1914", <u>I.R.S.H.</u>, vol.xxv (1980), pp.143-175
"Down the Pit: Work in the Great Northern and South Wales
Coalfields, 1870-1914", <u>Econ.H.R.</u> (1981), 2nd ser, vol.35,
pp.578-597
R.P.T.Davenport-Hines <u>Dudley Docker: the Life and Times of a
Trade Warrior</u> (1986)
A.Deacon "Concession and Coercion: the Politics of Unemployment
Insurance in the 1920s" in A.Briggs & J.Saville <u>Essays in
Labour History</u>, Vol.III (1977), pp.9-35
R.Douglas "The National Democratic Party and the British
Workers League", <u>H.J.</u>, vol.xv, (1972), pp.533-552
H.I.Dutton & J.E.King "The Limits of Paternalism: the Cotton
Tyrants of North Lancashire, 1836-54", <u>Soc.Hist.</u> (1982),
vol.7, no.1, pp.59-74

Select Bibliography

C.Erickson Steel and Hosiery, 1850-1950 (1959)
S.Everard A History of the Gas Light and Coke Company (1949)
M.Falkus "The British Gas Industry before 1850", Econ.H.R.
(1967), 2nd ser., vol.20, pp.494-518
"The Development of Municipal Trading in the Nineteenth
Century", Bus.Hist., vol.xix, (1977), pp.134-161
"The Early Development of the British Gas Industry,
1790-1815", Econ.H.R. (1982), 2nd ser., vol.35, pp.217-234
S.E.Finer Private Industry and Political Power (1958)
R.Floud The British Machine Tool Industry (1976)
F.E.Gannett & B.F.Catherwood Industrial and Labour Relations
in Great Britain (New York, 1939)
Gas Light and Coke Company The History of the G.L.C.C.,
1812-1912 (1912)
W.L.George Labour and Housing at Port Sunlight (1911)
B.B.Gilbert The Evolution of National Insurance: Origins of
the Welfare State (1966)
British Social Policy, 1919-1939 (1970)
H.Gintz "Effects of Technological Change on Labour in Sections
of the Iron and Steel Industries of Great Britain, the United
States, and Germany, 1900-1939" (London Ph.D. 1954)
H.F.Gospel & C.R.Littler Managerial Strategies and Industrial
Relations (1983)
T.R.Gourvish "Captain Mark Huish: A Pioneer in the Development
of Railway Management", Bus.Hist. (1970), vol.12, pp.46-84.
Mark Huish and the L.N.W.R.: a Study of Management (1972).
"A British Business Elite: the Chief Executives of the Railway
Industry, 1850-1922", Bus.H.R., vol.lxvi (1973), pp.289-316
"The Performance of British Railway Management after 1860: the
Railways of Watkins and Forbes", Bus.Hist., vol.xx, (1978),
pp.186-200
Railways and the British Economy, 1830-1914 (1980)
A.Grant Steel and Ships: the History of John Browns (1950)
W.P.Grant & P.C.Marsh The Confederation of British Industry
(1977)
P.S.Gupta "Railway Trades Unionism in Great Britain,
c.1880-1900", Econ.H.R. (1966), 2nd ser., vol.19, pp.124-153
W.L.Guttsman The British Political Elite (1963)
L.Hannah Electricity before Nationalisation (1979)
Inventing Retirement: the Development of Occupational Pensions
in Britain (1986)
The Rise of the Corporate Economy (1979)
Management Strategy and Business Development: An Historical
and Comparative Study (1976)
"Managerial Innovation and the Rise of the Large-scale Company
in Inter-War Britain", Econ.H.R. (1974), 2nd ser., vol.27,
pp.267-9
C.G.Hanson "Craft Unions, Welfare Benefits, and the Case for
Trade Union Law Reform, 1867-75", Econ.H.R. (1975), vol.28,
pp.243-259
"Craft Unions, Welfare Benefits, and the Case for Trade Union

Select Bibliography

Law Reform, 1867-75: A Reply", Econ.H.R. (1976), vol.29,
pp.631-5
J.Harris Unemployment and Politics: a Study in English Social
Policy, 1886-1914 (1972)
William Beveridge: a Biography (1977)
N.G.Harte & K.G.Ponting Textile History and Economic History
(Manchester, 1973)
K.H.Hawkins & C.L.Pass The Brewing Industry (1979)
J.R.Hay The Development of the British Welfare State,
1880-1975 (1978), esp. pp.32-52
The Origins of the Liberal Welfare Reforms, 1906-1914 (1975)
"Employers and Social Policy in Britain: the Evolution of
Welfare Legislation, 1905-14", Soc.Hist. (1977), vol.2,
pp.435-455
A.J.Heeson "The Northern Coal-Owners and the Opposition to the
Coal Mines Act of 1842", I.R.S.H., vol.xxv (1980), pp.236-271
E.Hobsbawm Labouring Men (1976)
G.J.Holyoake The History of Cooperation (1906)
A.Howe The Cotton Masters, 1830-1860 (1984), esp.
pp.178-192,273-309
J.R.Hume & M.S.Moss Beardmore: the History of the Scottish
Giant (1979)
Workshop of the British Empire: Engineering and Shipbuilding
in the West of Scotland (1977)
C.Hunt History of the Introduction of Gas Lighting (1907)
A.R. & F.B.Ilersic Parliament of Commerce: the Story of the
Association of British Chambers of Commerce, c.1860-1960
(1960)
R.J.Irving The North Eastern Railway Company, 1870-1914: an
Economic History (1976)
"The Profitability and Performance of British Railways,
1870-1914", Econ.H.R. (1978), vol.31, pp.46-66
J.B.Jeffrys "Trends in Business Organisation in Great Britain
since 1856" (London Ph.D., 1938)
D.Jeremy Dictionary of Business Biography (4 volumes,
1984-1986)
W.P.Jolly Lord Leverhulme (1976)
G.Jones The State and the Emergence of the British Oil
Industry (1981)
H.Jones "Employers' Welfare Schemes and Industrial Relations
in Inter-War Britain", Bus.Hist. (1983), vol.xxv, pp.61-75
R.Jones & O.Marriot Anatomy of a Merger: A History of G.E.C.,
A.E.I., and English Electric (1970)
P.Joyce "The Factory Politics of Lancashire in the late 19th
Century", H.J., vol.xviii (1975), pp.525-53
Work, Society, and Politics (1980)
B.S.Keeling & A.E.G.Wright The Development of the Modern
British Steel Industry (1964)
R.Kimber & J.J.Richardson Pressure-Groups in Britain: a Reader
(1974)
P.W.Kingsford "Labour Relations on the Railways, 1835-1875",
Jl.of T.H., vol.1, (1953-54), pp.65-81

Select Bibliography

Victorian Railwaymen: the Emergence and Growth of Railway
Labour, 1830-1870 (1970)
M.W.Kirby The British Coal Industry, 1870-1946: a Political
and Economic History (1977)
"The Control of Competition in the British Coalmining Industry
in the Thirties", Econ.H.R., 2nd ser., xxvi, (1973),
pp.273-284
"Government Intervention in Industrial Organisation: Coal
Mining in the 1930s", Bus.Hist., vol.15 (1973), pp.160-173
"The Lancashire Cotton Industry in the Inter-War Years: a
Study in Organisational Change", Bus.Hist., vol.16 (1974),
pp.145-159
S.Koss Sir John Brunner: Radical Plutocrat, 1842-1919 (1970)
D.Knox "The Development of the London Brewing Industry"
(Oxford B.Litt., 1956)
W.T.Layton The Early Years of the South Metropolitan Gas
Company, 1833-1871 (1920)
C.H.Lee A Cotton Enterprise, 1795-1840: a History of McConnel
and Kennedy, Fine Cotton Spinners (1972)
C.E.Lindblom Politics and Markets (New York, 1977)
R.Lowe "The Failure of Consensus in Britain: the National
Industrial Conference, 1919-1921", H.J., vol.21, (1978),
pp.649-675
C.R.Littler The Development of the Labour Process in
Capitalist Societies (1982)
A.F.Lucas Industrial Reconstruction and the Control of
Competition (1937)
P.Lynch & J.E.Vaizey Guinesses´ Brewery in the Irish Economy,
1759-1876 (1960)
H.W.Macrosty The Trust Movement in British Industry: a Study
in Business Organisation (1907)
P.Mathias The Brewing Industry in England, 1700-1830 (1958)
N.McKendrick "Joseph Wedgwood and Factory Discipline", H.J.,
vol.iv (1961), pp.30-45
B.Meakin Model Factories and Villages: Ideal Conditions of
Labour and Housing (1905)
G.Mee Aristocratic Enterprise: the FitzWilliam Industrial
Undertakings, 1795-1857 (1975)
J.Melling "British Employers and the Development of Industrial
Welfare, c.1880-1920: an Industrial and Regional Comparison"
(Glasgow Ph.D., 1980)
"Employers, Industrial Housing, and the Evolution of Company
Welfare Policies in Britain´s Heavy Industry: West Scotland,
1870-1920", I.R.S.H., vol.xxvi (1981), pp.255-301
(ed.) Housing, Social Policy, and the State (1980)
"Industrial Strife and Business Welfare Philosophy: the Case
of the South Metropolitan Gas Company from the 1880s to the
War", Bus.Hist., vol.xxi (1979), pp.163-179
"Non-Commissioned Officers: British Employers and their
Supervisory Workers, 1880-1920", Soc.Hist., vol.v, no.2
(1980), pp.183-221

Select Bibliography

K.Middlemas Politics in Industrial Society (1979)
R.Milliband The State in Capitalist Society (1983)
W.E.Minchinton The British Tinplate Industry (1957)
W.J.Mommsen The Emergence of the Welfare State in Great
Britain and Germany (1981)
A.D.Murray (ed.) John Ludlow: the Autobiography of a Christian
Socialist (1981)
A.E.Musson "Craft Unions, Welfare Benefits, and the Case for
Trade Union Law Reform, 1867-75: A Comment", Econ.H.R.(1976),
vol.29, pp.626-630
Enterprise in Soap and Chemicals: Joseph Crosfields and Sons
Ltd, 1815-1965 (Manchester, 1965)
D.Nelson & S.Campbell "Taylorism versus Welfare Work in
American Industry", Bus.H.R. (1972), vol.46, no.1 (1972),
pp.1-16
M.N.Niven Personnel Management: The Growth of Personnel
Management and the Development of the Institute (1961)
H.Nockolds Lucas: the First One Hundred Years, Vols.I & II
(1976)
C.H.Northcott (ed.)Factory Organisation (1928)
M.Olsen The Logic of Collective Action (1968)
D.Owen English Philanthropy, 1660-1960 (1965)
P.Pagnamenta & R.Overy All Our Working Lives (1984)
J.R.Parkinson The Economics of Shipbuilding in the United
Kingdom (1960)
H.Parris Government and the Railways in 19th Century Britain
(1965)
P.L.Payne Colvilles and the Scottish Steel Industry (1979)
"The Emergence of the Large-scale Company in Great Britain,
1870-1914", Econ.H.R. (1967), 2nd ser., vol.20, pp.519-542
Essays in Scottish Business History (1967)
H.M.Pelling Popular Politics and Society in Late Victorian
Britain (1968)
E.T.Penrose The Theory of the Firm (1972)
R.B.Perks "Real Profitsharing: William Thomson & Sons of
Huddersfield, 1886-1925", Bus.Hist., vol.xxiv (1982),
pp.156-174
M.J.Piore & P.Doeringer Internal Labour Markets and Manpower
Analysis (1971)
S.Pollard "The Decline of Shipbuilding on the Thames",
Econ.H.R., 2nd ser., vol.iii, (1950-51), pp.72-89
"The Economic History of British Shipbuilding, 1870-1914"
(London Ph.D., 1951)
The Genesis of Modern Management (1965)
Three Centuries of Sheffield Steel: the Story of a Family
Business (a history of Marsh Brothers) (1954)
S.Pollard & R.Turner "Profitsharing and Autocracy: the Case of
J. T. & J.Taylor of Batley, Woollen Manufacturers, 1892-1966",
Bus.Hist. (1976), vol.18, pp.4-34
N.Poulantzas "The Problem of the Capitalist State", New Left
Review (1969), no.58, pp.67-78

Select Bibliography

R.Price Masters, Unions, and Men (1980)
G.F.Rainnie The Woollen and Worsted Industry: An Economic Analysis (1965)
W.J.Reader Birds Eye: the Early Years (1963)
Bowater (1982)
I.C.I.: A History, Vols.I & II (1970)
Fifty Years of Unilever, 1930-1980 (1980)
Metalbox (1976)
SPD: a Story of Distribution (1969)
G.Rees St Michael: a History of Marks and Spencer (1969), esp. chs. 9 & 16
G.L.Reid & D.J.Robertson Fringe Benefits, Labour Costs, and Social Security (1965)
D.Roberts Paternalism in Early Victorian Britain (1979)
P.L.Robertson "Shipping and Shipbuilding: the Case of William Denny and Brothers", Bus.Hist., vol.xvi (1974), pp.36-47
M.Rose Industrial Behaviour: Theoretical Development since Taylor (1982)
B.S.Rowntree Industrial Unrest: A Way Out (1922)
D.F.Schloss Methods of Industrial Renumeration (1898)
J.D.Scott Siemens Brothers, 1858-1958: An Essay in the History of an Industry (1958)
Vickers: A History (1962)
G.R.Searle The Quest for National Efficiency (Oxford, 1971)
"The Edwardian Liberal Party and Business", E.H.R., vol.98, (1983), pp.28-60
B.Semmel Imperialism and Social Reform (1960)
O.Sheldon The Philosophy of Management (1965, 1st edn. 1923)
E.Sidney The Industrial Society, 1918-1968 (1968)
A.Slaven The Development of the West of Scotland, 1750-1960 (1975)
"A Shipyard in Depression: John Brown of Clydebank, 1919-38", Bus.Hist., vol.xix, (1977), pp.192-217
A.Slaven & D.H.Aldcroft Business, Banking, and Urban History (1982)
South Metropolitan Gas Company A Century of Gas in South London (1924)
G.Stoddart-Kennedy Dog-Collar Democracy: the Industrial Christian Fellowship, 1919-39 (1982)
P.D.Stubley "The Churches in the Iron and Steel Industry in Middlesborough, 1890-1914" (Durham M.A., 1979)
G.B.Sutton "Shoemakers of Somerset: A History of C. & J. Clark, 1833-1903" (Nottingham Ph.D., 1959)
M.Swenarton "An 'Insurance against Revolution': Ideological Objectives of the Provision and Design of Public Housing in Britain after the First World World War", B.I.H.R., vol.liv (1981), pp.86-134
Homes Fit for Heroes: the Politics and Architecture of Early State Housing in Britain (1981)
R.H.Tawney "The Abolition of Economic Controls, 1918-21",

Select Bibliography

Econ.H.R., 2nd ser., vol.xiii (1943), pp.1-30
F.W.Taylor The Principles of Scientific Management (1913)
Shop Management (1911)
P.Thane Foundations of the Welfare State (1982)
The Origins of British Social Policy (1978)
E.P.Thompson The Making of the English Working Class (1968)
"Time, Work-Discipline and Industrial Capitalism", Past &
Present, vol.38 (1967), pp.56-97
S.Tolliday "Industry, Finance, and the State: an Analysis of
the British Steel Industry in the Inter-War years" (Camb.
Ph.D., 1979)
J.H.Treble "The Attitudes of Friendly Societies towards the
Movement in Great Britain for State Pensions, 1878-1908",
I.R.S.H., vol.xv (1970), pp.266-299
B.H.Tripp Renold Chains: A History of the Company and the Rise
of the Precision Chain Industry, 1879-1955 (1956)
J.A.Turner "The British Commonwealth Union and the General
Election of 1918, E.H.R. (1978), pp.528-551
Businessmen and Politics (1986)
"Man and Braverman", History (1985), vol.70, pp.236-242
L.F.Urwick Personnel Management in Relation to Factory
Organisation (1943)
J.Vaizey The Brewing Industry, 1886-1952 (1960)
R.Waller The Dukeries Transformed, the Social and Political
Development of a 20th Century Coalfield (1985)
C.H.Ward-Jackson A History of Courtaulds (1941)
F.A.Wells Hollins and Viyella: A Study in Business History
(1968)
N.Whiteside "Industrial Welfare and Labour Regulation in
Britain at the Time of the First World War", I.R.S.H., vol.xxv
(1980), pp.307-331
"Private Agencies for Public Purposes: Some New Perspectives
on Policy Making in Health Insurance between the Wars", Jl. of
Social Policy (1983), pp.165-194
"Welfare Insurance and Casual Labour: a Study of
Administrative Intervention in Industrial Employment,
1906-26", Econ.H.R., (1979), vol.32, pp.507-532
R.C.Whiting "The Working Class in the ´New Industry´ Towns
between the Wars: the Case of Oxford" (Oxford D.Phil., 1977)
T.I.Williams A History of the British Gas Industry (1981)
O.E.Williamson Markets and Hierarchies (1980)
C.Wilson The History of Unilever, Vols.I & II (1954)
W.Woodruff The Rise of the British Rubber Industry during the
19th Century (1972)
A.H.Yarmie "Employers´ Organisations in Mid-Victorian
England", I.R.S.H., vol.xxv, (1980), pp.209-235

INDEX

Index

Steel, Peech & Tozer 97-8
Stephen & Sons, A. 165,168
Stewart & Lloyds 79,88-91,
93,96,105-7,224
Stockton & Darlington Railway
34
shops, company 85,107,126
strikes 13,19,38-41,46,54,58-
60,62-4,66-7,72,81,96,127,131,
142-4,161-2,165-6,171,178,181,
197-8,201-2,205,208,212,226
Strutt & Co., Jedediah 153
sub-contracting 2,4,165-6
suggestion schemes 69,98,126,
144,174,199
swimming baths 35
systematic welfare 11-12,15-
16,19-20,25-6,31,33,35,38,
42,48,54,58,64,66-7,71-2,78,
83,88-9,98-100,107-8,115-6,
120-125,129-131,146,149,158,
168,174,179,181-2,184-6,206,
220,225,232,247-8

Taff Vale Railway 34
Tangye Bros 170,172,199,219
tariffs 78,91,93,107,213
Taylor & Co. 156
Territorial Army 42,67
Thames Ironworks Company 165-6
Thomas & Co., Richard 79,
87-90,93,96,102-5,107
Thomsons, George 156
tobacco 18,152,179,183-4,186
Tootal, Broadhurst & Lee 154-5
trades unions 1,3-7,9,13-14,
22,38-40,42-3,45,59-61,63,66-
8,72,81,84,91,95-6,101,104-7,
110,118,128,131,138,142,144,
150,156,158-161,164-5,170,197,
199-206,213-5,217-8,224-31,240
tramways 64,220,236
Trollopes, G.F. 150
troops (in strikes) 61
Truman, Hanbury & Buxton 140-1
Tullis & Co., R. 151

unemployment benefits 14,70,
94,124,128-130,135-6,150-1,
154,173,181,183,207,214,222,
225,230,232-40,245-6,248

Unemployment Insurance Act
1920 69-70,92,150,207,214-5,
232-7
Unilever 14,115-8,125-131
United Alkali Company 115
United Steels 93,96-100,107

Vauxhall Motors 178
Vickers 171,202

wages and hours 4-8,13,16,18,
36,39-40,42,44-6,58-62,64,66-
8,77,79,84,96,124,142-3,158,
165,170,178,181-4,194,198,202,
206,212,226,248
Walker & Sons 142
war benefit funds 42-3,67,
90-1,166,168
Watney, Coombe & Reid 141-6
Watson & Sons, Joseph 129
Wedgwoods, Josiah 151
Welfare Workers´ Institute
204-5,208
Western Electric Company 8-9
Wharncliffe Silkstone Colliery
159
Whiffen & Sons 132
Whitbreads 140,145-6
Whitehead Iron and Steel 94
widows & orphans´ funds 14,37,
46-7,59,66,70,85,103,106,126,
144,150,159-60,166,174,177,
179-81,183,202,208,216,232-7
Widows, Orphans, & Old Age
Pensions Act 1925 46-7,70,92,
101,124,155,202,232-4,236-8
Wills, W.D. & H.O. 183-4
Wolseley cars 177
wool & worsted 11,18,115,137,
152,156-7,186,236,238
work conditions 53-4,58-61,
66-7,156,167,170-3,176-8,
202,206-7,226-7
work-disaffection 13,15,17,19,
59-61,71,81,94,96,102,127,154,
167,197,199,203,208,212
work discipline 1-7,9,11-14,
26,32-33,42-3,53-4,58,60-1,63,
84-5,96,110,118-9,137,143,151-
3,157,165-6,167-8,171,174,181,
184-5,199-200,204-8,215,227

270

For Product Safety Concerns and Information please contact our
EU representative GPSR@taylorandfrancis.com Taylor & Francis
Verlag GmbH, Kaufingerstraße 24, 80331 München, Germany